1 pyramid of Sahure
2 pyramid of Neferirkare
3 pyramid of Raneferef
4 pyramid of Nyuserre
5 pyramid of Khentkaus II
6 pyramid Lepsius no. 24
7 mastaba of Nakhtsare
8 mastaba of Kakaibaef
9 mastaba of Khentkaus III
10 mastaba of Werkaure
11 mastaba of Hanebu
12 mastaba of Nebtyemneferes
13 mastaba of Ptahshepses
14 mastaba of Ptahshepses junior I
15 mastaba of Princesses
16 mastaba of Djadjamankh
17 anonymous mastaba
18 mastaba of Weserkafankh
19 mastaba of Khekeretnebty
20 mastaba of Hedjetnebu
21 mastaba of Neserkauhor

FACULTY OF ARTS
CHARLES UNIVERSITY
IN PRAGUE

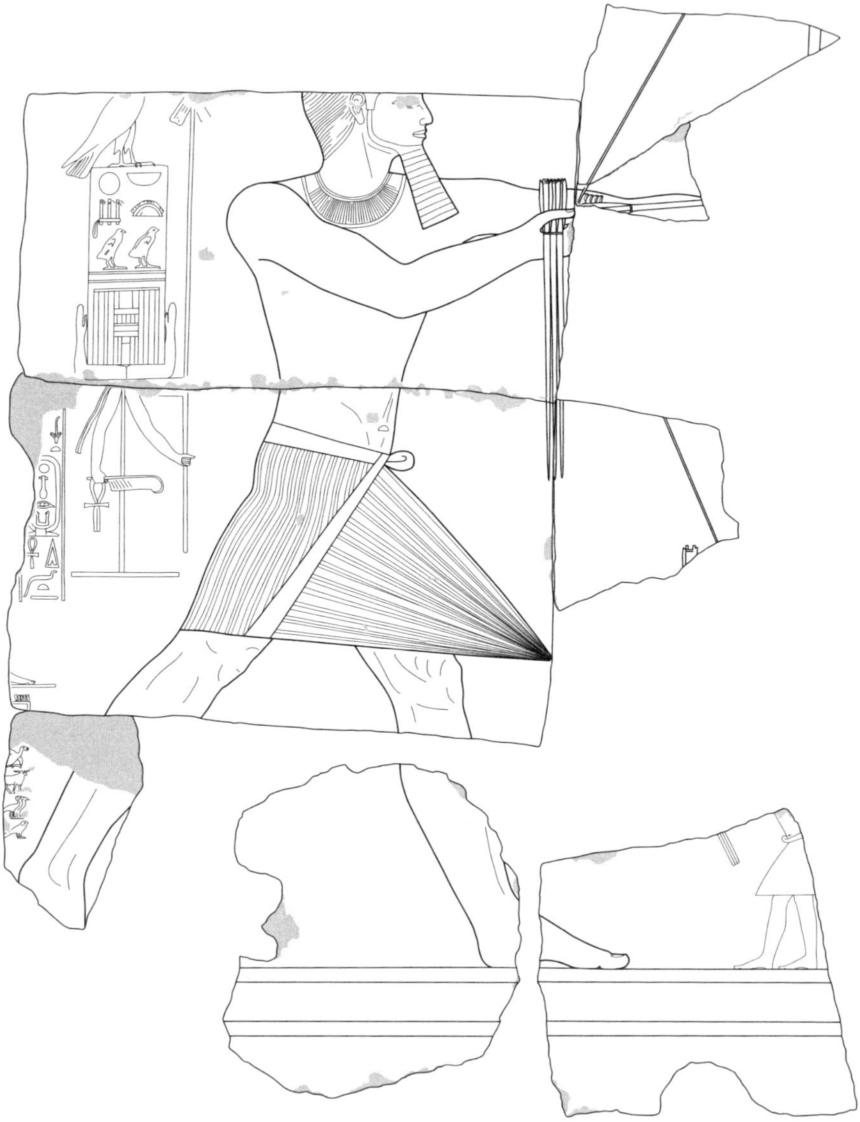

Sons of the Sun

RISE AND DECLINE OF THE FIFTH DYNASTY

MIROSLAV VERNER

Charles University in Prague
Faculty of Arts
Prague 2014

Reviewers
Vivienne G. Callender
Břetislav Vachala

The monograph was published within the Programme
for the Development of Fields of Study at Charles University,
No. P14, Archaeology of non-European regions

Frontispiece: Sahure hunting in the desert, see Borchardt, 1913, Blatt 17;
drawing Jolana Malátková

Photographs: Ahmed Amin Azmi, Jan Brodský, Marianne Franke, Sameh Abdel Mohsen, Sandro Vannini, Milan Zemina, Egyptian Museum in Cairo, Metropolitan Museum of Art in New York, State Collection of Egyptian Art in Munich and Archives of the Czech Institute of Egyptology

Illustrations: Jolana Malátková, Hana Vymazalová, Luděk Wellner
and Archives of the Czech Institute of Egyptology

ISBN 978-80-7308-541-4

CONTENTS

ACKNOWLEDGMENTS

The author would like to thank everyone who has assisted him in publishing this book, especially to Anna Bryson for translating it into English, Jolana Malátková for editing of the text, Miroslav Ottmar for scanning and editing the plans and photographs and Oleg Man for designing its lay-out.

The author would like to extend his thanks to Vivienne G. Callender for her stimulating comments on some topics discussed in this book. He also owes his thanks to Anthony Spalinger for suggestions concerning Ancient Egyptian feasts.

Special thanks are due to Dr. Zahi Hawass, former Minister of Antiquities in Egypt, for his kind permission to take photographs of the Fifth Dynasty royal statues in the Egyptian Museum in Cairo; the Department of Egyptian Art of the Metropolitan Museum of Art, New York, for permission to publish the photograph of the statue of Sahure (Rogers Fund 18.2.4); Staatliches Museum Ägyptischer Kunst, München, for permission to publish the photograph of the dyad of Nyuserre.

Concerning the photographic and design credits, see the respective illustrations in the text.

FOREWORD

"Djedi said: She is the wife of a wab*-priest of Re, Lord of Sakhbu, giving birth to three children of Re, Lord of Sakhbu, of whom it is said that they shall exercise this magisterial office in the entire land. The eldest of them will be the chief seer in Heliopolis.*
As for His Majesty, his heart became very sad at this, and Djedi said: What now is this mood, Sovereign, l. p. h., my lord? It is because of the three children? I say: First your son, then his son, then one of them."

(Simpson, Ritner, Tobin, Wente, Jr., 2005, 20f.)

There is no doubt that the 5th Dynasty was a very important epoch in the history of Ancient Egypt. It was not just that events at the end of the 4th and beginning of the 5th Dynasty left deep traces in the historical consciousness of generations to come, becoming the stuff of legend, but that the 5th Dynasty was altogether a time of major transition and sometimes dramatic change in political, economic and social conditions of the country. The economy of Egypt was faltering under the burden of the construction of huge, prestigious pyramid complexes, while the efficiency of state administration was compromised by increasing centralisation and the associated growth of the bureaucracy, which was gaining in wealth and influence at the expense of the previously absolute power of the monarch, conceived as a god on earth and guarantor of the order of the world. Certain principles of social order, for example the idea of the monarch as exclusive authority with sole responsibility for the welfare of 'his people', contributed to the growth of social tension, since the system of government from one power centre, the royal family, was no longer adequate to meet the demands on the government made by an increasingly complex society. There was a need to develop a new model of social organisation and government more appropriate to the new realities. As the problems of the old system multiplied and mounted, the catalyst for a change in direction seems to have been provided by chance events in the royal family at the end of the 4th Dynasty: Menkaure, the last of the powerful ruling line founded by Snofru, appears to have died without leaving a male heir able to ascend the throne as his legitimate successor.

Although this book does not avoid questions relating to overall social and socio-economic processes during the 5th Dynasty, it does not aim to offer a comprehensive analysis of change within Egypt during this epoch. Its focus is the complicated, legend-clouded history of the royal line of the 5th Dynasty, which ruled Egypt for roughly one and half centuries and played a significant role in the profound transformation of Egyptian society.

According to the Ptolemaic historian Manetho (Waddell, 2004, 51), the 5th Dynasty originated from Elephantine, but Manetho gave no reasons for this statement and modern scholarship has not supported it. One scholar to have examined the claim sympathetically is Bogdanov (Bogdanov, 2006 no. 1, 16f.), but unfortunately he relies on an inaccurate transcription of the relevant passage (*Urk* I, 241.3; 243.3; 245.3) in the royal annals from the time of Weserkaf and Sahure and mistakenly interprets the term *ẖryt-ʿ gm pr Ḥr Stẖ* 'list of the inventory of the House of Horus and Seth' (Gauthier, 1916, 175; Wilkinson, 2000, 220f.) as meaning 'discovery of the house (i.e. dynasty) in Elephantine'. Munro (Munro, 1993, 17) has argued that the belief that Elephantine (*ꜣbw*) was the cradle of the 5th Dynasty may have been the result of the later corruption of the toponym, Sakhebu (*Sꜣẖbw*), given in the Westcar Papyrus as the place of birth of the first three kings of the 5th Dynasty. The belief may also, however, have developed at a later period on the basis of the inscription of Wenis to be found on the island of Elephantine (*Urk* I, 69).

The earlier Egyptian tradition, as it is presented by one of the stories recorded on the Westcar Papyrus, derives the origin of the 5th Dynasty directly from the sun god. The story tells how the dynasty was established under very unusual circumstances: the first three kings were born as triplets from the union of the sun god with an earthly woman Rudjdjedet, wife of the priest of the temple of the god in Sakhebu named Raweser. Sakhebu, probably what is today Zat el-Kom, is an as yet archaeologically relatively little known locality, situated in the Western Delta roughly opposite Heliopolis on the eastern branch of the Nile (Sauneron, 1950, 63–72; *id.* 1955, 61–64; a summary of the discussion of Sakhebu up to his time is given by G. Goyon, 1979, 43–50). The Westcar Papyrus, today usually dated to the Second Intermediate Period, (i.e. a period almost a thousand years later than the events described in the stories it records), has been the subject of linguistic and literary research and debate ever since it was first published by Adolf Erman. Since his edition in 1890, the Westcar Papyrus has been studied by a whole series of scholars (see e.g. Lefebvre, 1949; Derchaine, 1969, 19–25; Hornung, 1973, 33–35; Goedicke, 1993, 23–36; Blackman, 1988; Jenni, 1998, 113–141; Bagnato, 2006; Spalinger, 2007, 174–184; Lepper, 2008). While Erman (Erman, 1890, 1) at first suggested that the papyrus could have come from the Old Kingdom, after full analysis of the text he later favoured dating it to the Hyksos Period (Erman, 1898, 10) and this is the prevailing view today.

A more precise dating of the papyrus and an explanation of its broader historical context has been proposed by Lepper (Lepper, 2008, 319f.), who argues that it reflects a direct link made between the birth of the first three kings of the 5th Dynasty and a similar situation that arose in the 3rd part of the 13th Dynasty, when three brothers ascended the throne in succession: Neferhotep I, Sahathor and Sobekhotep IV. In the turbulent times of the 13th Dynasty, beset with unrest, the roughly twenty-year reign of this family brought a certain stability and prosperity, and so was hopefully perceived as a parallel to the flowering of the country in the 12th Dynasty and the even earlier Old Kingdom. The story in the papyrus was therefore a prophecy of better times. According to Lepper the texts in the Westcar Papyrus were a response to events in the 13th Dynasty, although the final redaction of the text occurred under the 17th Dynasty.

The tale of the divine birth of the first three kings of the 5th Dynasty – Weserkaf, Sahure and Kakai (Neferirkare) – is primarily a literary not a historical work, but scholars have nonetheless considered the question of whether and to what extent it might contain some genuine historical elements. For example, present knowledge suggests there could be some historical basis to the prediction made by the narrator, Djedi, to King Khufu, at whose court the story takes place, that the three first rulers of the 5th Dynasty will come to power, i.e. replace the line of Khufu, only after the reign of Khufu's son (Khafre), and Khufu's son's son (Menkaure). On the other hand some other historical conclusions deduced from this text are mistaken. For example it was commonly assumed that at least two of the first three rulers of this dynasty, Sahure and Neferirkare, were brothers, and some secondary modifications of the relief decoration of Sahure's mortuary temple (see p. 48f.), as well as some passages from the papyri of Neferirkare's mortuary temple archive (see p. 52) have been adduced as evidence in support of this idea. Similarly, on the basis of the story it was considered that the first of these rulers, Weserkaf, was a high priest in the temple of the sun god in Heliopolis (see p. 30).

The possibility of a historical core to the story in the Westcar Papyrus was also taken seriously by Otto (Otto, 1966, 68f.), who argued that the Rudjdjedet of the story, the mother of the supposed royal triplets, was a pseudonym for the royal mother Khentkaus I, believed to be a key figure at the end of the 4th and beginning of the 5th Dynasty. Otto's view was accepted by Altenmüller (Altenmüller, 1970, 223–235), who came up with the additional theory that Khentkaus I was the daughter of Hardjedef, one of Khufu's sons. Khentkaus I had immediately become a focus of scholarly attention following the discovery and excavation of her tomb by Hassan (Hassan, 1943, 1–63) in the 1930s. Particular interest was aroused by the peculiar two-step shape of her large tomb and by her very unusual title 'Mother of the Two Kings of Upper and Lower Egypt', which could theoretically also be interpreted as 'King of Upper and Lower Egypt and Mother of the King of Upper and Lower Egypt'. A fragment of papyrus discovered at the end of the 19th century in the mortuary temple of Neferirkare, which mentioned the mortuary cult of the 'Royal Mother Khentkaus' in the context of this temple, then led to the conclusion that Khentkaus I was the mother of Neferirkare and Sahure and also the mother-founder of the 5th Dynasty.

This long accepted view of Khentkaus I and the beginning of the 5th Dynasty (and much else) has now been altered fundamentally by new discoveries made in the course of archaeological research of the pyramid field in Abusir since the end of the 1970s. Our knowledge of the royal line of the 5th Dynasty has also been significantly enlarged and enriched by archaeological excavations at other sites, especially in the cemeteries of Giza and Saqqara, and last but not least by a range of more specialised historical research studies. All of this provides the basis for the reconstruction of the history of the royal line of the 5th Dynasty presented in this book. However much I have tried to use the most recent findings, the book will definitely not be the last word on the subject. Current and future research and their results will undoubtedly supplement and correct this account in many respects.

THE END OF THE FOURTH DYNASTY: WHAT WENT WRONG?

The end of the celebrated 4th Dynasty, founded by Snofru, is surrounded by many questions and uncertainties concerning not just the ruling line but conditions in Egyptian society in general. Finding the answers is no easy task when there is so little direct evidence from the period itself and the indirect evidence is often ambiguous. The complexity of problems surrounding the end of the 4th Dynasty can be briefly exemplified on three key protagonists of this period of Egyptian history – Menkaure, Shepseskaf and Khentkaus I.

Menkaure, the last important ruler of the 4th Dynasty, is generally considered from indirect evidence to have been the son of Khamerernebty I and Khafre. One clue is a ritual knife, or *pesesh-kaf*, which was found in a crack in the floor of Menkaure's pyramid temple and bears the inscription, 'King's Mother Khamerernebty' (Reisner, 1931, 233 and pl. 19a). Menkaure and his mother Khamerernebty I (as human complement to Hathor) are depicted, in a role probably related to the *sed*-festival, in a dark grey greywacke dyad found in the king's pyramid complex (now in the Museum of Fine Arts, Boston, acc.no. 11.1738) (Friedman, 2008, 144). Other indirect indications, although they are rather debatable (Gundacker, 2010, 30–44), include scenes and inscriptions from the tomb of Nymaatre in Giza (Grdseloff, 1943, 52f.) or the fragment of the head of a greywacke statue of a queen (Uppsala Museum no. 31), who may be this supposed mother of Menkaure (Fay, 1999, 103f. and fig. 11 on p. 130). Uncertainty over the identity of Menkaure's father is exacerbated by the fact that in the Royal Canon of Turin (RCT) there is another king (col. III. 13), whose name has not survived, between the partly preserved name of Khafre in position col. III. 12 and the position attributed to Menkaure, although his name does not survive there either (Gardiner, 1959, pl. II column III).

Khamerernebty II, whose mother was Khamerernebty I and whose father was perhaps Khafre, is thought to have been Menkaure's wife. Although the title 'king's daughter' shows that Khamerernebty II had a royal father, we have no direct proof that he was Khafre (Callender, 2011-a, 129–133). If there are question-marks over the precise relationship between Menkaure and his mother and wife, identifying the king's children is even harder.

Khamerernebty II was probably not Menkaure's only wife, and the prevailing view is that Rekhetre was another (Callender, 2011-a, 135; Baud, 1999, 515 [149]). On the other hand, Rekhetre could theoretically have been the wife of an ephemeral king in the period between Khafre and the end of the 4th Dynasty. In Rekhetre's tomb in Giza her titulary indicates that she was the daughter of the king (Hassan, 1950, 1) who is identified as Khafre in an inscription in the tomb of Kaemnofret (Hassan, 1950, 22 and fig. 15). The queen's titulary also includes the title 'king's wife', but not the title 'king's mother'. If Rekhetre was Menkaure's wife, then, she was not the mother of his successor to the throne.

The 'Eldest Son of the King of His Body Khuenre', whose tomb lies in Giza (MQ 1, see Reisner, 1942, 219), in a cemetery founded in the time of Menkaure, may have been his son. In his tomb Khuenre is depicted as a child with his mother Khamerernebty II (Callender, 2011-a, Fig. 54 on p. 130; Baud, 1999, 536). He is believed to be the subject of an anepigraphic yellowish limestone statue of a young man sitting cross-legged (Museum of Fine Arts, Boston, no. 13.3140), which was found in the tomb (Do. Arnold, Grzymski, Ziegler, 1999, 233 no. 74). It is interesting that Khameretnebty II is not titled 'king's mother' in Khuenre's tomb, but does have the title 'controller of the Acacia House', which shows her important role in the burial rituals for the dead king. If the dead king were Menkaure (theoretically it could have been his predecessor, see the text above), then the decoration of Khuenre's tomb and Khuenre's actual burial would not have taken place until the reign of Menkaure's successor, who was not Khamerernebty II's son. If so, then Khuenre must have died after Menkaure. Khuenre could even have been born after the death of Menkaure.

We also encounter Khuenre in his mother's tomb, known as the *Galarza Tomb* in Giza, where he is depicted both with her and his grandmother Khamerernebty I (Daressy, 1910, 46; Kamal, 1910, 118f.). Found in this tomb, originally intended for Khamerernebty I but later taken over by her daughter Khamerernebty II, was the statue of yet another prince, 'Eldest King's Son Sekhemre' (Kamal, 10,1910, 118f.). He was long believed to have been the son of either Khafre or Menkaure (Baud, 1999, 574 [217]), but recently Callender (Callender, 2011-b, 44) has argued from some typological features that the statue is much later, from the reign of Pepi I or thereafter. Probably, Sekhemre could not therefore have been Menkaure's son.

Reisner considered the 'Eldest King's Son Kai', whose name appears on five alabaster models of bowls discovered under the floor of the temple of Pyramid G III a in Giza, to be the son of Menkaure (Reisner, 1931, 55, 199 (5) and fig. 52). This theory was shown to be mistaken by Hassan (Hassan, 1941, 31) after excavation of Kai's tomb in Giza, dated to the first half of the 5th Dynasty, and the finding that Kai's mother was princess Khen… Probably still alive in Menkaure's time were other princes, who were either sons of Khafre, e.g. Iunre (Baud, 1999, 408f. [14]), or for whose parentage we have no evidence, let alone that they were sons of Menkaure.

A difficult dynastic situation may, then, have arisen at the end of the reign of Menkaure. Prince Khuenre, who was quite possibly the son of Menkaure and

Khamerernebty II, was either born after the king's death or was still far too young to succeed to the throne. It seems that after Menkaure's death there was no available heir to succeed to the throne in line with Egyptian tradition and the state ideology of legitimacy.

All these considerations raise further questions about the length of Menkaure's reign, his family and last but not least his pyramid complex. We have two kinds of date relating to the reign of Menkaure: dates recorded at the time and dates attributed in much later sources on the basis of archive documents and tradition – RCT and the work of Manetho. In the fragmentary and incomplete part of the RCT dealing with the 4th Dynasty Menkaure is assigned position 14 in column III where there is a damaged number of years of reign which some scholars have reconstructed as 18 (Barta, 1981, 23), and others as 28 (Beckerath, 1997, 159). According to Manetho (Waddell, 2004, 47) Menkaure reigned for much longer – 63 years.

Contemporary dates are few. They include builders' inscriptions discovered in non-royal tombs in Giza and are sometimes difficult to interpret (Verner, 2001, 381–383). The highest of the dates associated with Menkaure's reign are the year of the 11th cattle-count (builders' inscription from tomb G VI S, see Junker, 1951, 75 fig. 35.10 and 77 no. 9) and the year after the 11th cattle-count (papyrus of Gebelein, scroll IV, see Posener-Kriéger, 1975, 215f.) but it is not absolutely certain that these dates relate to Menkaure. The first, a builder's inscription on a loose block, is attributed to his reign simply because the names of Menkaure's work crews appeared on other blocks nearby. There are also doubts about the interpretation of the second date, in a Gebelein Papyrus. It is also striking that the rest of the contemporary dates relating to Menkaure are much lower, mentioning just the 2nd or 3rd cattle-count. We cannot be sure that the two high dates relate to Menkaure's reign at all, and so whether the 18 or 28 years of rule attributed to him on the basis of the RCT are plausible. Menkaure may have reigned for a shorter period.

Indirectly relevant to the issue of the length of Menkaure's reign is different kind of evidence, which Helck (Helck, 1975, 48–50; *id.* 1957, 108) defines as the "economic power of the pyramid complex", i.e. the property, especially the field acreage and associated personnel, with which an owner had managed by the time of his death to endow his pyramid complex and future mortuary cult. Just a few references to mortuary estates bearing Menkaure's name are known only in the 5th Dynasty tombs of Kanefer and Rawer (Jacquet-Gordon, 1962, 242 and 267, and Index). On this basis Helck argues that Menkaure failed – perhaps because of premature death – to secure his mortuary cult adequately and so it was largely dependent on allocations established by decree of his successor Shepseskaf.

The actual building of his tomb as well as the endowment of his mortuary cult suggests lack of means or time or both. In comparison with the complexes of his predecessors Khufu and Khafre, Menkaure's pyramid complex in Giza was by far the smallest (the volume of Menkaure's pyramid represents about a tenth of the volume of Khufu's pyramid), but even so, Menkaure left it very incomplete. According to calculations by Krauss (Krauss, 1997, 11), construction work on Menkaure's pyramid alone may have been underway for about one year! Its casing in red granite may have been intended to compensate for the small dimensions of the pyramid, but this too remained unfinished.

In the mortuary temple, Reisner (Reisner, 1931, 29–33) dated only the unfinished mostly core stone masonry to the reign of Menkaure, and in the valley temple little more than the foundations of some walls. Reisner's chronology of the building has essentially been accepted by Maragioglio and Rinaldi (Maragioglio, Rinaldi, 1967/ VI, 50–62 and 66–70) and most recently also by Lehner (Lehner, Jones, Yeomans, Mahmoud, Olchowska, 2011, 143–191). It seems that all the rest was finished later by Shepseskaf and partially also by Nyuserre and Merenre.

The building history of Menkaure's pyramid, which involved alterations to the original plan (although opinions differ on their character, extent and dating), is much harder to reconstruct than the other components of the pyramid complex. According to Petrie (Petrie, 1990, 40) the pyramid was originally planned as even smaller. He based this view on the existence of an upper descending passage, later replaced by a lower access passage following the enlargement of the building. On the other hand Stadelmann (Stadelmann, 1990, 196) believes that the upper passage was just a ventilation and working passage and that the whole substructure was built on a unified plan in the reign of Menkaure. Stadelmann thus disagrees not only with Petrie but also Ricke (Ricke, 1950, 108 and 126), who thought that the lower part of the substructure including the burial chamber in red granite was not completed until the reign of Shepseskaf. Ricke (Ricke, 1950, 120) further believed that when Menkaure died the substructure of the pyramid was so incomplete that a temporary substitute burial place had to be hastily prepared for the king in the originally cult pyramid G III a. Also Maragioglio and Rinaldi (Maragioglio, Rinaldi, 1967/ VI, 106f. obs. 16) argue that the substructure was built in two phases.

A detailed building analysis of Menkaure's pyramid complex would be out of place in this book, but it is hard to credit that a change in the plan of the pyramid substructure as radical as the deeper sinking into the ground of a red granite burial chamber, which was moreover orientated north-south in a complete break with tradition, would have been made in haste after Menkaure's death. The same applies to another important innovation: the addition to the plan of the substructure of the six (2 + 4) deep niches that we also encounter in the more or less contemporary tombs of Shepseskaf and Khentkaus I (see further text).

Until recently, discussion of Menkaure's pyramid has entirely overlooked one feature, which is that unlike the pyramids of his predecessors Khufu and Khafre its south-eastern corner does not touch the line leading to the centre of the solar cult in Heliopolis, but overshoots it by several metres (Verner, Brůna 2011, 289 Fig. 3). Was this the result of a change to the original plan of the pyramid, or of a deliberate decision to ignore the symbolic 'solar' line linking the Giza pyramids with Heliopolis?

Whatever the significance of these innovations and alterations, the very incomplete state of Menkaure's pyramid at his death is at odds with the high dates attributed to his reign. The contradiction is all the more striking considering what was achieved in a comparable time in the building of pyramid complexes by Menkaure's predecessors Snofru (RCT 24 years) and Khufu (RCT 24 years), and even by Radjedef in a much shorter time (RCT 8 years).

The questions surrounding the length of Menkaure's reign and his unfinished pyramid complex are further complicated by problems with the interpretation of the three small pyramids G III a–c, built along the south side of the king's pyramid. Judging by the small mortuary temples in front of their east sides and unmistakable traces of a mortuary cult, including the granite sarcophagi found in G III a and G III b, Reisner (Reisner, 1931, 55–65) thought that queens had been buried in all three. At the time of Menkaure's death G III a and G III b were incomplete. G III a was originally planned as a cult pyramid, but at some time not precisely established it was modified for a real burial. G III b was from the outset intended as a real tomb, but it is unclear whether together with G III c it was part of the original plan of Menkaure's complex (Maragioglio, Rinaldi, 1967/VI, 128 obs. no. 40; Jánosi, 1996, 22–26). There is no direct evidence of the identities of the persons buried in the three small pyramids, but only guesses and speculations (for instance, Reisner, *loc. cit.*; Ricke, 1950, 126 and 245 n. 280; Baud, 1999, 618f.; Jánosi, 1996, 25). If still unidentified queens were indeed buried in them (Menkaure's mother? Two or even three of his wives?) the absence of a son and heir to Menkaure becomes all the more of a mystery.

Menkaure's successor Shepseskaf is the last 4th Dynasty ruler for whom we have contemporary written and archaeological records. In the RCT he is believed to be the king in position 15 in column III, with an attributed 4 year reign. Manetho calls Shepseskaf Sebercherés and credits him with a reign of 7 years. Shepseskaf may be the king Sasychis of later tradition, who according to Herodotus (Herodotus II, 136) reigned after Mycerinus and had a portico built in the temple of Ptah despite having to face an economic crisis. According to Diodorus (Diodorus I, 94,3) Sasychis was an important legislator and a man of exceptional intelligence.

The Palermo Stone provides data on the beginning of Shepseskaf's reign (Wilkinson, 2000, Figs. 2 and 3). He probably came to the throne (the 'year of the unification of the Two Lands') on the 11th day of the 7th month of the calendar year, as Strudwick (Strudwick, 2005, 68) believes. Other contemporary dates relating to Shepseskaf are from tombs in Giza, all referring to the year of the 1st cattle-count (Verner, 2001, 383f.). Yet another date, the 'year after the 1st cattle-count', appears in his decree on a stela found in Menkaure's pyramid complex (Reisner, 1931, 278 no. 1). The contemporary dates therefore suggest that Shepseskaf's reign was short, probably no longer than the 4 years attributed to him by the RCT, and archaeological evidence (large parts of his tomb complex were hastily completed in mudbrick) seems to support this assumption.

Contemporary written sources provide no direct evidence of Shepseskaf's parentage. Reisner (*loc. cit.*) took the statement, "he made it as his monument for his father, the King of Upper and Lower Egypt, [Menkauwra]" in a text from the decree on the stela to be proof that Shepseskaf was Menkaure's son. Goedicke (Goedicke, 1967, 16f., fig. 1; also Jánosi, 1994, 49–54) correctly pointed out that this was a misunderstanding, since the inscription commemorates not the completion of Menkaure's pyramid complex but an endowment of reversionary offerings for Menkaure's pyramid, in which the priests of the king's cult were to enjoy a share. Nor is the reference to "his father" in the text a concrete proof, since it is not immediately followed by a cartouche with Menkaure's name and so could be just a general term for a royal ancestor as is the case in similar inscriptions.

There remain just a few hints that Shepseskaf was connected with the royal line of the 4th Dynasty through his mother, who may have been Khentkaus I (see the text below). A queen Bunefer, whose tomb adjoins that of Khentkaus I (Hassan, 1941, 176–199) is sometimes indirectly linked with her. From Bunefer's titulary we know that she was 'king's daughter of his body' and 'king's wife', but unfortunately we do not know which kings. The most likely candidate for her father is Menkaure, but there is no safe evidence for this. The fact that she was a *ḥmt-nṯr*-priestess of Shepseskaf, makes her more likely to have been his wife than his daughter. Callender (Callender, 2011-a, 157) has highlighted some similarities between the tombs of Khentkaus I and Bunefer and believes that they might have been closely related. This would make it all the more surprising that Bunefer's son, with whom she is depicted in her tomb, does not have the title of prince but only the relatively low title 'juridicial inspector of scribes'. Hassan concludes that Bunefer's son was the child of her second marriage, after Shepseskaf's premature death.

Only some clues suggest that Shepseskaf may not have been of the 'full blood royal'. For example, as with that of his successor, Weserkaf, his name signally lacks direct reference to the god Re, which since the time of Radjedef had been an integral part of rulers' throne name. Together with the fact that the king's tomb is not a pyramid but resembles a sarcophagus, this has sometimes been interpreted as evidence of Shepsheskaf's opposition to the solar religion (Jéquier, 1928, 36f.). But it is more likely that Shepseskaf hesitated to identify himself directly with Re in his name because his parentage did not give him an entirely legitimate claim to the throne. Shepseskaf's name may in fact include a merely implicit, hidden reference to Re: 'His (i.e. Re's ?) *ka* Is Noble' (Ricke, 1950, 64f.).

The location and form of Shepseskaf's tomb, today known as the Mastabat Faraun, is indeed suggestive. Shepseskaf must have had very compelling reason to abandon the royal cemetery in Giza, given that it was in Giza that the main building capacities of the time were concentrated, and it was there that he had had to complete Menkaure's pyramid complex in the interests of his own legitimation. Lack of an appropriate site may have been the reason, but consciousness of the shakiness of his legitimacy could have been a factor too. At any rate, he selected a site in South Saqqara, then a relatively empty part of the Memphite necropolis. Not that the chosen site was not without its own symbolism, however, since it lay nearly half way between the pyramids of the founder of the 3rd Dynasty, Djoser, and the founder of the 4th Dynasty, Snofru.

It is undoubtedly significant that Shepseskaf's tomb is in the shape of a sarcophagus (Müller, 1985, 21f.) and not a pyramid, as Lepsius (1897, 199–201) originally noted. The pyramid was regarded at the time as the supreme symbol of royalty, and so the unusual shape of the tomb may have reflected Shepseskaf's not wholly legitimate origins. Economic can hardly be ruled out, however, for the tomb was from the start planned as a relatively very small building. Nevertheless the plan of its substructure is fully compatible with the substructure of a pyramid and just as in the pyramids of Menkaure and Khentkaus I it includes 6 deep niches (4 + 1 + 1). In layout the mortuary temple of the Mastabat Faraun resembles the temple of G III a (Maragioglio, Rinaldi, 1967/VI, 166), likewise built in the reign of Shepseskaf, but it has some new features: it has no shrines for statues, the offering hall takes a form that later became standard, the open court is adorned with niches, etc. (Ricke, 1950, 62–64).

All these facts indirectly suggest that Shepseskaf probably did not enjoy full royal authority. His royal titulary (at least in all surviving instances) is incomplete (Golden Falcon? Two Ladies?). We do not even have a likeness of Shepseskaf that might help to identify him. The limestone head in the Royal Museum in Brussels, once considered to be Shepseskaf, is a fake (Capart, 1927, 7f. and pl. 5; Tefnin, 1988, 20). The theory (Dobrev, 1999, 27 fig. 19) that the calcite head (Museum of Fine Arts, Boston 09.203) found in Menkaure's valley temple (Reisner, 1931, pl. 52) represents the young Shepseskaf, has not been generally accepted.

In contemporary written sources we find relatively few mentions of events relating to the time of the reign of Shepseskaf. Apart from the stela (already mentioned) found in Menkaure's pyramid complex, the Palermo Stone gives information on the year after his accession to the throne, relating that in this year he chose a site for his tomb, conducted the 'feast of the diadem', visited important shrines of the land and had two standarts made for Wepwawet. The few written records relating directly to government include a sealing found in the temple of Khontamenty-Osiris in Abydos, which bears Shepseskaf's Horus and throne name and thc title of the seal-bearer, the '(overseer) of the royal (store of) spelt in Abydos' (Petrie, 1901, 27f. pl. 55.1; Kaplony, 1981, II, 134 no. 1).

According to Manetho Shepseskaf's death was followed by the short (2-year) reign of Thamphthis, but there is not the slightest trace of evidence for the existence of this supposed ruler in contemporary sources. On the contrary, the inscriptions containing sequences of names of kings in the tombs of dignitaries of the time, such as Nesupunetjer, Sekhemkare and Ptahshepses, list no ruler between Shepseskaf and Weserkaf (see e.g. Roccati, 1982, 70f.).

The parentage and position of the royal mother Khentkaus I, the third prominent figure of the end of the 4th dynasty, have been the subject of controversy (see e.g. Verner, 1995, 168–170 and most recently Callender, 2011-a, 149–153) ever since the discovery and excavation of her tomb by Hassan (Hassan, 1943, 1–62). There is nonetheless much to suggest that Khentkaus I and her eventual high status, reflected in her unusual tomb and exceptional titulary, is probably one of the main keys to the understanding of the complex situation at end of the 4th and beginning of the 5th Dynasty.

Some scholars, such as previously cited Otto (Otto, 1966, 68f.) and Altenmüller (Altenmüller, 1970, 223–235), have identified Khentkaus I with the heroine of the much later recorded tale of Rudjdjedet (see p. 11). Altenmüller argued that she was the daughter of Hardjedef, another of Khufu's sons, thus building on the ideas of Goedicke (Goedicke, 1958, 35–55) on the peculiar fate of this prince, whose tomb was deliberately damaged before it was completed but who became an honoured local saint in Giza as early as the end of the Old Kingdom. According to Goedicke the first three kings of the 5th Dynasty were Khufu's grandsons and legitimate rulers, although their father was not himself a king. While interesting, these theories cannot be proved one way or the other.

The basic source of information on Khentkaus I remains the contemporary archaeological and written records that Hassan discovered in his excavations of her tomb complex in Giza. Unfortunately little further relevant evidence has come to light since then, but it is hoped that current new archaeological research on the tomb and its surroundings (see e.g. Lehner, Jones, Yeomans, Mahmoud, Olchowska, 2011, 143–191) will yield important new findings in this context. Earlier designated the 'Fourth Pyramid' in Giza, the tomb is very unusual, and indeed unique. Since its excavation by Hassan, the theme of its building history has attracted a whole series of Egyptologists, among whom we should particularly mention Müller (Müller, 1985, 23), Maragioglio and Rinaldi (Maragioglio, Rinaldi, 1967/ VI, 168–195 and pls. 18–21), Jánosi (Jánosi, 2005, 401–406), and most recently Lehner (Lehner, in press).

Khentkaus I's tomb would be remarkable for its location alone. It lies on a prominent site in the royal cemetery in Giza in close proximity to Menkaure's valley temple on one side and the quarry of Khufu and Khafre on the other, and was built into a rocky outcrop deliberately left standing in the quarry. Later rock tombs and mastabas adjoin it to the north. Khentkaus I's tomb, built probably in at least two phases –

judging by the unfinished decoration of its bedrock pedestal – was subsequently covered with a fine limestone casing. The precise dating of the monument has not yet been established. Originally it may have been constructed as a rock mastaba in the form of a truncated pyramid, a smaller superstructure in the form of a sarcophagus may have been added later (Maragioglio, Rinaldi, 1967/ VI, 186 obs. no. 2). Lehner (Lehner, in press) assumes that the monument was built under Menkaure, in the time when the major red granite construction work on the king's pyramid complex had not yet been stopped. However, he sees the bedrock pedestal and the mastaba on its top, including the casing, as one, unified project. This conclusion would mean that Menkaure preferred the building of a tomb for Khentkaus I to the completion of his own pyramid complex, even to the extent of denying work on his own pyramid, a circumstance which does not seem to be plausible.

More probably, the work in granite, though scaled down, continued in Giza still under Menkaure's successor Shepseskaf. An indirect proof of this assumption seems to be offered by Shepseskaf's tomb itself. In spite of its substructure in red granite, the king's monument in South Saqqara, the Mastabat Faraun, was from its very beginning planned as a small, low-cost building – a fact which certainly did not anticipate the king's short reign. Obviously, Shepseskaf's building activities in Giza may have not been confined to the completion of Menkaure's pyramid complex in mudbrick only.

The plan of the above-ground and the substructure of the tomb of Khentkaus I has features of a king's tomb. The two-step tomb, influenced by the older Memphite – Lower Egyptian tradition of tomb architecture, thus acquired the shape of a huge stylised sarcophagus resting on a rock pedestal (Müller, 1985, 23). It is not impossible that in the enlargement of Khentkaus's tomb the builders were inspired by Shepseskaf's 'Mastabat Faraun' which might have been built at approximately the same time.

Apart from the main eastern façade, it is interesting that only the south wall of the tomb, i.e. the side visible from Menkaure's valley temple, is adorned with alternating niches: three simple and one double; in the subsequent building phase of the monument, this decoration was covered with a fine limestone casing. A surviving fragment of red granite entrance gate in the south-eastern part of the rock mastaba bears hieroglyphic inscriptions with the name of the tomb's owner and a part of her titulary reading 'Mother of Two (Both ?) Kings of Upper and Lower Egypt, Daughter of the God, Every Good Thing She Orders Is Done for Her, Khentkaus' (Hassan, 1943, 16, Fig. 2 a pl. IV). Obviously, this inscription must date from the time when her second son ascended to the throne. In the south-eastern part of the tomb there were three cult rooms, their walls originally adorned with polychrome scenes and inscriptions in low relief, mere fragments of which have survived. Inset in the western wall of the northernmost cult room was a double false door which originally bore a scene of the mortuary banquet and the titulary and name of the royal mother, although no more than remnants of the decoration remained.

In the west wall of the quite extensive underground burial chamber there is a deep niche with a rounded ceiling (originally the niche contained a cabinet with arched ceiling built of granite ashlars) recalling the stylised form of the archaic Upper Egyptian shrine *pr-wr*. False doors without further decoration were carved in the rock on both sides of the niche. An alabaster sarcophagus was originally set in a hollow in the paving, but only fragments of it have survived, and no human remains of the tomb owner were found. In the east wall of the chamber there are four and in the south wall two deep niches like the niches that we encounter in the tombs of Menkaure and Shepseskaf. The arched lid of the case for the sarcophagus and decorative element of niches also link the tomb of Khentkaus I with these two tombs.

The tomb also had some important exterior elements. One was the narrow, east-west orientated trench for the funerary boat, lying by the south-west corner of the tomb. Carved into the rock east of the north-eastern corner of the tomb is a relatively large right-angled basin for rain water, which may have served for ritual purposes. During the second building phase an approximately 3 m wide enclosure wall was built in mudbricks around the tomb. At the same time as the wall, or shortly afterwards, a dwelling complex for the priests of Khentkaus I's mortuary cult was built on a unified plan to the east of the tomb (F. Arnold, 1998, 2–18). Its plan is in the shape of a reversed L, and the shorter side is turned towards Menkaure's valley temple although the complex is separated from the valley temple by a lower placed causeway. The dwelling complex seems to have been built in mudbrick of the same type as that in Menkaure's valley temple (Lehner, in press) and very probably dates from the time of Shepseskaf.

Khenkaus I's exceptional status is also evident from the fact that her tomb became the centre of a small cemetery which grew up in its immediate vicinity. Among those buried there were the priests who served in the royal mother's mortuary cult, such as Akhtyshepses, 'inspector of the *ḥm-nṯr*-priests of the king's mother' and Renpetnefer, '*ḥm-nṯr*-priest of the king's mother'. Although she is not explicitly named in their titulary, it follows from the archaeological context that the reference is to Khentkaus I. At the time it was the privilege of a king alone to have a priest of the rank of *ḥm-nṯr* 'god's servant' in his cult, because the god in the title meant the king himself. Priests of lesser rank ('funerary priests') also served in the mortuary cult of Khentkaus I (Baud, 1999 t. 2, 402).

What has survived of Khentkaus I's titutlary does not include the title 'king's daughter', or 'king's wife', but on the other hand features the not entirely usual title 'daughter of the god' (Callender, 1991, 89–111). Her main title (and at the time of its discovery unique) can be translated as either 'king of Upper and Lower Egypt and mother of the king of Upper and Lower Egypt', or as 'mother of two (both?) kings of Upper and Lower Egypt'. According to Junker the translation 'both kings' is more precise than 'two kings' in terms of sense and grammar (Junker, 1932, 131).

Each of the two possible translations entails a quite different interpretation of the status of Khentkaus I, with different consequences for the reconstruction of events at the end of the 4th and beginning of the 5th Dynasty. The first raises the possibility that Khentkaus actually ruled, most probably as royal mother – regent. While her name is not presented in cartouche and does not appear in the lists of kings, some alterations (?) to a depiction of Khentkaus I on the entrance gate (a king's beard on the chin or flail on the breast?) might be considered evidence for her status as ruler. On the other hand, it is unclear whether these are really secondary additions or just illusions created by the damaged structure of the stone. Today prevailing scholarly opinion favours the second interpretation of Khentkaus I's unusual title, i.e. 'mother of two (both?) kings of Upper and Lower Egypt'. Yet there are problems even with this interpretation: she was not the only woman in the history of Egypt to give the country more than one king (see e.g. p. 10) but the title does not appear in the titularies of the others. It seems that an explanation should be sought elsewhere.

New clues to the mystery of Khentkaus I have emerged from two unexpected archaeological finds. One was the discovery of the small pyramid complex of Neferekirkare's wife (see text on p. 168f.) in Abusir in the later 1970s. This queen was three generations younger than Khentkaus I, but the same unusual title 'mother of two (both?) kings of Upper and Lower Egypt' appeared in her titulary (Verner, 1995; *id.* 1997, 109–117; *id.* 1999, 215–218). More new information was provided by blocks with scenes and inscriptions found during reconstruction of the causeway of Sahure's pyramid complex (Awady, 2006, 191–218; *id.* 2009, 166–174 and Fig. 83 on p. 171). According to Awady it is clear from the scenes and inscriptions that the king's two eldest sons were twins (for more detail see p. 39).

The unusual title shared by the two royal mothers seems to suggest that both Khentkaus I and Khentkaus II might have given birth to two sons who then ruled successively. In both cases these sons may even have been twins, who in the case of Khentkaus I would most probably be Shepseskaf and Weserkaf, and in the case of Khentkaus II Raneferef and Nyuserre (Verner, 2011, 778–784). If this theory is correct, then at the transition from the 4th to the 5th Dynasty twins were born three times over four generations in the royal family: to Khentkaus I, Sahure's wife Meretnebty (although only one of her twins became king) and Khentkaus II. Whether or not the two sons were twins in the cases of Khentkaus I and Khentkaus II, both these royal mothers seem to have played an important role in securing the legitimacy of succession to the throne, for their second sons would not have been succeeding to the throne in line with tradition and royal ideology, i.e. not as a son after a father, but as a brother after a brother.

If we provisionally accept the theory that Khentkaus I's sons were Shepseskaf and Weserkaf, then her original tomb was probably built under Shepseskaf and was then in some parts completed under Weserkaf. These two kings are connected by certain indications that their legitimacy was not entirely unchallengeable (for more detail see p. 19 and 30). The identity of their father, Khentkaus I's husband, is not quite clear. An assumption that Khentkaus I's husband was the high priest of Heliopolis (see p. 30) is just speculation that cannot be proved one way or the other. All the same, whether Khentkaus I's husband was a high-ranking official of non-royal origin or one of the secondary royal sons, Khentkaus I herself was the higher ranking partner by birth.

To sum it up, all this evidence concerning the titulary of Khentkaus I and the form and location of her tomb in the royal cemetery in Giza clearly suggests that she not only belonged to the royal line buried there, but that at the end of the 4th Dynasty she was a key figure in dynastic politics. We have no direct evidence of her precise relationship to the line. Theoretically, Khentkaus I may have been either Menkaure's daughter, or his sister. In weighing up these possibilities we need to take into account of the following indirect evidence:

- the fragment of a mace bearing the name of Khafre, found in the tomb of Khentkaus I (Hassan, 1943, pl. 7 E)
- the base of a diorite statue of Khafre (Hassan, 1943, pl. 25 A), found in the immediate vicinity of the tomb of Khentkaus I in front of Menkaure's valley temple in a building mistakenly identified by Hassan as the 'valley temple of Khentkaus'
- Hassan also identifies as Khafre an anepigraphic schist seated figure likewise found in the 'valley temple of Khentkaus' (Hassan, 1943, pl. 25 B)
- the fragment of a limestone panel found in the 'valley temple of Khentkaus' and bearing remnants of an inscription (Hassan, 1943, 58 and pl. 27 C), in which some scholars discern part of the title and name of Khentkaus I (Callender, 2011-a, 144); if Hassan's partial reconstruction of this inscription is correct, Khentkaus I was 'king's daughter, beloved one of her father'.

These pieces of indirect evidence suggest that Khentkaus was probably the daughter of Khafre rather than of Menkaure. She might then have been Menkaure's sister.

The discontinuity in the royal family, after Menkaure died without leaving a legitimate male heir to the throne, was an important but not the only cause of the decline of the 4th Dynasty.

The available sources seem to indicate that it was probably a combination of several difficult circumstances that led to the end of the celebrated royal line founded by Snofru and the change of dynasty. Although contemporary written sources do not mention it, one of these circumstances was very probably a deteriorating economic situation in the country. This is indirectly suggested by the difficulties with the building of Menkaure's pyramid complex even though the pyramid itself had been planned on a much reduced scale. The same applies to Shepseskaf's tomb, designed from the outset as a very small, relatively cheap building. The construction and operation of gigantic

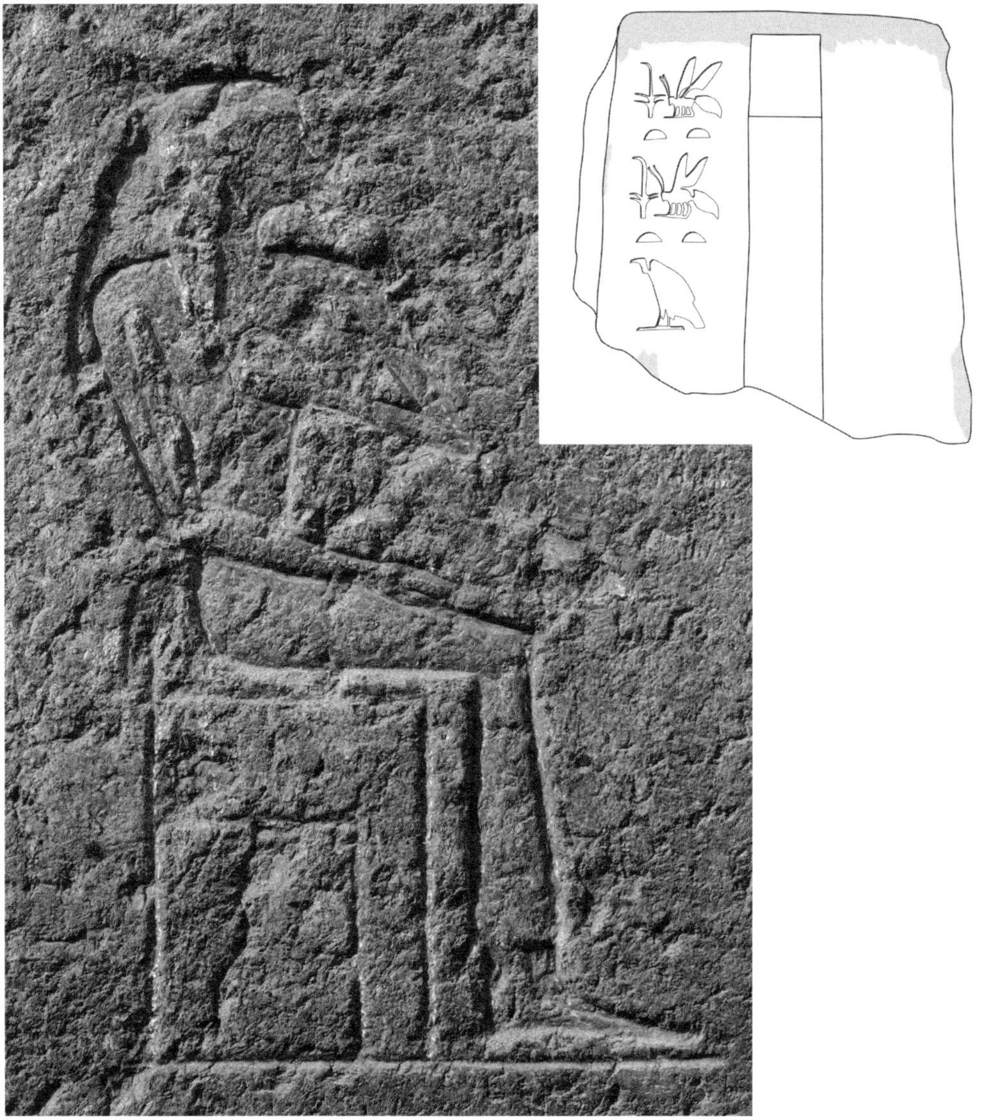

Fig. 1 The remains of the inscription on the gate in the tomb complex of Khentkaus I in Giza:
– detail of the figure of the seated Khentkaus I at the end of her titulary (CUP FA CEI, photo Milan Zemina)
– Khentkaus I's title '[Mother] of Two (Both?) Kings of Upper and Lower Egypt'

pyramid complexes must have been a huge economic burden on the country even though it undoubtedly contributed to the development of crafts, labour organisation and state government. Given the nature of the economy of the time, which depended on extensive agricultural production, immense resources would inevitably have been diverted into this economically unproductive 'dead end'.

The existing structures of government and administration (see e.g. Helck, 1975-a, 134–136; Andrassy, 2008, 130–135), although their development, including redistribution system, must initially have been positively stimulated by these organisationally demanding building projects, were probably also hitting the limits of their capacity: at the end of the 4th Dynasty it was no longer possible to govern the country just from the narrow circle of the power centre of the royal family. The principles – the power centralized in the hands of the autocratic ruler, the god living on earth and guarantor of the world order, the redistribution system, etc. – which hitherto helped develop the Egyptian society were progressively becoming counter-productive.

As shown by recent research, serious climatic changes in the course of the 4th Dynasty and early 5th Dynasty may also have contributed to the deterioration of the economy. For example, paleoclimatic data from the Western Desert seem to indicate rainy pulsation around 4500–4200 BP (Schild, Wendorf, 2013, 129). Also new geoarchaeological and geological data collected within the 'Nile Delta Climate Change Project' show that in spite of the aridification trend in north-eastern Africa in the 3rd Millenium BC, relatively wet intervals occurred especially in northern Egypt between 4600 and 4200 BP (Welc, 2014, 108).

According to the geo-archaeological and palaeo-environmental research, which was conducted on the site of Menkaure's pyramid complex and the so-called 'Lost City of the Pyramids in Giza', this period coincided with a "coeval high-amplitude precipitation anomaly of perhaps 120 years, during which mudbrick meltdown, catastrophic flash floods, and mass-movements destroyed the royal complex of mudbrick galleries, workshops and bread-making kilns once every 4 years or so" (K. W. Butzer, E. Butzer, S. Love, 2013, 3340). According to this study "some 10 flood surges ravaged the Lost City from the end of Khafre's reign to the beginning of Userkaf's" (*o. c.* 3362). However, Lehner, director of the research on the aforesaid site, expressed in a personal communication (August 8, 2014) doubts about some conclusions of this study. In Lehner's opinion, this study "ignores massive transformation of the wadi (i.e. the desert valley to the west of the aforesaid site – MV) by quarrying, topographic and architectural evidence that the wadi could not flowed with water in the time of Menkaure" and, finally, disregards "evidence from excavations over the last decade across the exact path of the projected wadi channels". Nevertheless, Lehner himself is "open" to the idea that there was "more rain in the 4th Dynasty, and to the episodic hard rain and wadi flooding". Be that as it may, the climatic events must have very probably affected the whole country and economy, and not just the cemetery in Giza.

The discontinuity in the royal family following Menkaure's death caused by the absence of a legitimate male heir to the throne thus might have only become a catalyst in the accumulating political, economic and social problems of the country at the end of the 4th Dynasty. Although after Menkaure's death other sons of Khafre may well have still been alive at the time (for example Iunmin, Iunre, Nykaure, Nebemakhet), in the new situation in the royal family the person who came to the fore seems to have been the highest ranking woman, unchallengeably directly related to the royal line: Khentkaus I. To her, rather than to one of the royal male representatives, fell the task of securing the continuity of the monarchy.

I. LIVING KINGS

I.1 WESERKAF

Ỉr-m3ˁt ‘He Who Has Established (lit. made) Order’
Bik-nbw-nfr ‘Perfect Golden Falcon’
Wśr-k3.f ‘His (i.e. Re’s ?) *ka* Is Powerful’

His Horus name, ‘He who has established (lit. made) order’ expresses Weserkaf’s determination to bring permanent stability to the country and legitimise the new ruling dynasty. It is clearly no accident that the name recalls the Horus name of the founder of the 4th Dynasty, Snofru, *Nb-m3ˁt* ‘Lord of Order’. Weserkaf’s Two Ladies name was the same as his Horus name. Another of his names, ‘Perfect Golden Falcon’, reflected his position as the founder of a new dynasty. (On the political connotations of the name Golden Falcon see e.g. Berlev, 1979, 41–59; Dobrev, 1993, 179, and recently also Spalinger, in press.) His throne name Weserkaf strikingly resembles the name of his predecessor Shepseskaf.

Kammerzell (Kammerzell, 2001, 161) has suggested that the king’s name be phonetizied as Wasilkaarif.

Sources of the time offer only a few dates from Weserkaf’s reign. In the annals on the Palermo Stone (Wilkinson 2000, 152 and Figs. 3 a 6) we find references to events of Weserkaf’s reign in the year after the 1st cattle-count, the year of the 3rd cattle-count and the year after the 3rd cattle-count. A date on a builder’s inscription found in Weserkaf’s sun temple ‘(year of the 3rd occasion (of the cattle-count), 3rd month of the season of winter, … day)’ very probably refers to the reign of Weserkaf (Haeny, 1969, 41f. no. 6). According to the RCT, where Weserkaf is considered to be the king in the 17th position in the 3rd column (only part of a cartouche with *k3* as the final sign has survived, while the omission of the sign *f* which comes last in Weserkaf’s name was probably due to carelessness), Weserkaf reigned for 7 years. The 28 years long reign is attributed to Weserkaf (Usercheres) by Manetho (Waddell, 2004, 51). According to modern scholars, Weserkaf reigned for 8 years (Barta, 1981, 23; Beckerath, 1997, 159).

Surviving written sources throw no light on Weserkaf’s parentage. Some scholars assume, for example Moursi (Moursi, 2005, 22f.), that Weserkaf was originally a high

< Fig. 2 Fragment of the dark greywacke statue of Weserkaf wearing Lower Egyptian crown found in the valley temple of the king’s sun temple complex in Abusir, now in the Egyptian Museum, Cairo, JE 90220. (Courtesy Egyptian Museum Cairo, photo Sandro Vannini)

priest of the sun god in Heliopolis. For this assumption, obviously based on a passage from the Papyrus Westcar ("... *The eldest of them will be chief seer in Heliopolis* ...", see e.g. Simpson, Ritner, Tobin, Wente Jr., 2005, 20), there is no support in contemporaneous historical sources.

Altenmüller (Altenmüller, 2010, 272) believes that Weserkaf was the son of Menkaure and Khentkaus I, but this is mere supposition with no support from any direct evidence of the period. Reconstruction of the chronology at the transition from the 4th to the 5th Dynasty, and above all the title of Khentkaus I, 'mother of two (both?) kings of Upper and Lower Egypt', allows us only to consider it likely that Weserkaf was, like Shepseskaf, her son. As previously mentioned, it is even possible that Khentkaus I gave birth to twins, Shepseskaf and Weserkaf, who each later became king in turn. The similarity of the throne names of the two kings is striking, as is the fact that neither name, unlike those of their three royal predecessors, is theophoric, i.e. the name of the god Re is absent for both kings (being possibly only indirectly represented simply by the suffix *f*). This could be an indirect clue that the father of Shepseskaf and Weserkaf was not a king. It is also notable that *k3/k3w* figure prominently in the names of the four main royal protagonists at the transition from the 4th to the 5th Dynasties (Menkaure, Khentkaus I, Shepseskaf and Weserkaf), and this may reflect a changing status in the circles of the ruling elite, or a changing religious allegiance.

It is puzzling that no written record of members of the royal family has been found anywhere in Weserkaf's pyramid complex. This absence is not to be explained just by the extensive damage to the complex caused by the later construction of shaft tombs. A single fragment bearing the remnant of a cartouche and the last letter *w*, believed to be part of Sahure's name, hardly counts as clear evidence (see the text below).

For some time now researchers have believed that Neferehetepes was Weserkaf's wife and Sahure's mother on the basis of indirect evidence, particularly an inscription from the tomb of Persen (Mariette, 1882, 300) in Saqqara. According to this inscription, dated to the reign of Sahure, Persen obtained a share in a reversionary offering provided to the Royal Mother Neferhetepes from the temple of Ptah in Memphis (Strudwick, 2005, 412). A queen-mother's mortuary domain is also mentioned in the tomb of Persen (Jacquet-Gordon, 1962, 21f., 335/1). An inscription found inside a queen's pyramid complex which mentions another two of her funerary domains supports the theory that Neferhetepes was the owner of the pyramid complex, which closely adjoins Weserkaf's, and his wife (Labrousse, Lauer, 2000/I, 158 and 2, Fig. 365 a,b). It is likewise supported by recently published relief scenes and inscriptions on blocks from the causeway of Sahure's pyramid complex, which confirm that Neferhetepes was Sahure's mother (Awady, 2009, 169). What is our most complete titulary for Neferhetepes appears here in a scene of the return of the Egyptian expedition from Punt, where she is styled 'Mother of the King of Upper and Lower Egypt, Daughter of the God, Controller of the Butchers of the Acacia House, Priestess of Bapef and

Priestess of Tjasepef' (Awady, 2009, 162). Callender (Callender, 2011-a, 165) finds no direct evidence but concedes that she might have been Weserkaf's wife. Overall, written and archaeological records suggest that it is more than likely.

Neferhetepes's parentage remains unclear. Today the earlier view of Grdseloff (Grdseloff, 1943, 65–66) that she was Radjedef's daughter is not accepted, partly because there was a gap of several decades between the reigns of Radjedef and Weserkaf. All the same, she was probably a daughter of the royal line of the 4th Dynasty, for among the titles of the mortuary domains that maintained her cult and were recorded in her mortuary temple we find a domain bearing Khufu's name (Labrousse, Leclant, 2000/I, 158). In theory Neferhetepes could have been Menkaure's daughter, but there are other possibilities. If the theory that both Khentkaus I and Meretnebty, wife of Sahure and possibly a daughter of Neferhetepes (see below), gave birth to twins is correct, then the heritability of the tendency to conceive fraternal twins might suggest a direct blood tie between the three women. In that case Neferhetepes could have been the daughter of Khentkaus I. Neferhetepes seems to have survived her husband Weserkaf, to judge by her title 'controller of the butchers of the Acacia House'. She may even have survived her son Sahure, since we still meet her in a scene from the latest phase of decoration of Sahure's pyramid complex (Awady, 2009, 243).

In the titulary of Neferhetepes, unfortunately preserved only in a very incomplete form, the titles to the fore are 'mother of the king of Upper and Lower Egypt' and 'daughter of the god', which emphasise her importance at the start of the new dynasty (Callender, 2011-a,161f.; *id.* 1991, 89–110). The absence of the title 'daughter of the king', and 'wife of the king' in her titulary so far known is striking. The sheer scantiness of the record may account for the absence of the title 'wife of the king', while the absence of the title 'daughter of the king' would not of course be surprising if Neferhetepes were the daughter of Khentkaus I and sister of Shepseskaf and Weserkaf.

The already cited fragment of a relief (Labrousse, Lauer, 2000, Doc. 176, Fig. 248) from Weserkaf's mortuary temple shows part of the back of a falcon and behind it a name in cartouche – in which only the last letter *w* survives. Labrousse and Lauer have reconstructed this name as Sahure. If the king, the falcon Horus, had been followed by his first-born son, then the cartouche might have been attached to his figure secondarily after that son became king himself and adopted the throne name Sahure. There may be an indirect connection between this and another fragment of relief (Labrousse, Lauer, 2000, Doc. 177, Fig. 249a-b), on which a male figure, part of whose head and trunk survives, had been secondarily altered by the addition of a ritual beard and perhaps also a head covering (Labrousse, Lauer, 2000/I, 116 and 2, Fig. 248). On the basis of these two fragments we can theorise that Weserkaf's first-born son was Sahure, who after succeeding to the throne completed the building of the pyramid complexes of his parents, Weserkaf and Neferhetepes, and when doing so had some of the depictions of himself changed from prince to king. This theory is supported by the already cited scene from the decoration of Sahure's causeway in which Neferhetepes is depicted as Sahure's mother. The scene certainly casts doubt on Callenders's idea (Callender, 2011, 151), that Sahure was Weserkaf's grandson or nephew rather than his son.

Neferhetepes may have been the mother of the only wife of Sahure so far known – Meretnebty (interestingly, she lacks the title 'king's daughter' in her titulary). On the blocks from Sahure's causeway Meretnebty appears twice in the company of Neferhetepes. In a scene of a banquet in the garden of a royal palace (Awady, 2009, 171, Fig. 83, and p. 241 Fig. 105) there is a figure seated immediately behind Neferhetepes. Although in this place the relief is damaged and the queen's name is missing, from the context we can justifiably identify the figure as Meretnebty. In the second scene Meretnebty is accompanying Neferhetepes on a viewing of an exotic incense tree from Punt (Awady, 2009, 241, Fig. 105 a *id.* 2006, 195, Fig. 2). The two women are walking after the king and are hand in hand, which eloquently suggests a close relationship, most probably mother and daughter. (Queen Meresankh III is depicted in a similar way in her tomb – standing in a little boat by her mother Hetepheres II and holding her around the waist, see Dunham, Simpson, 1974, Fig. 4.) It is therefore likely that Sahure and Meretnebty were siblings, with the same mother and possibly also father.

As Dorman has shown (Dorman, 2002, 95–110), Khamaat, who married Ptahshepses, the High Priest of Ptah, was another daughter of Weserkaf. Earlier, on

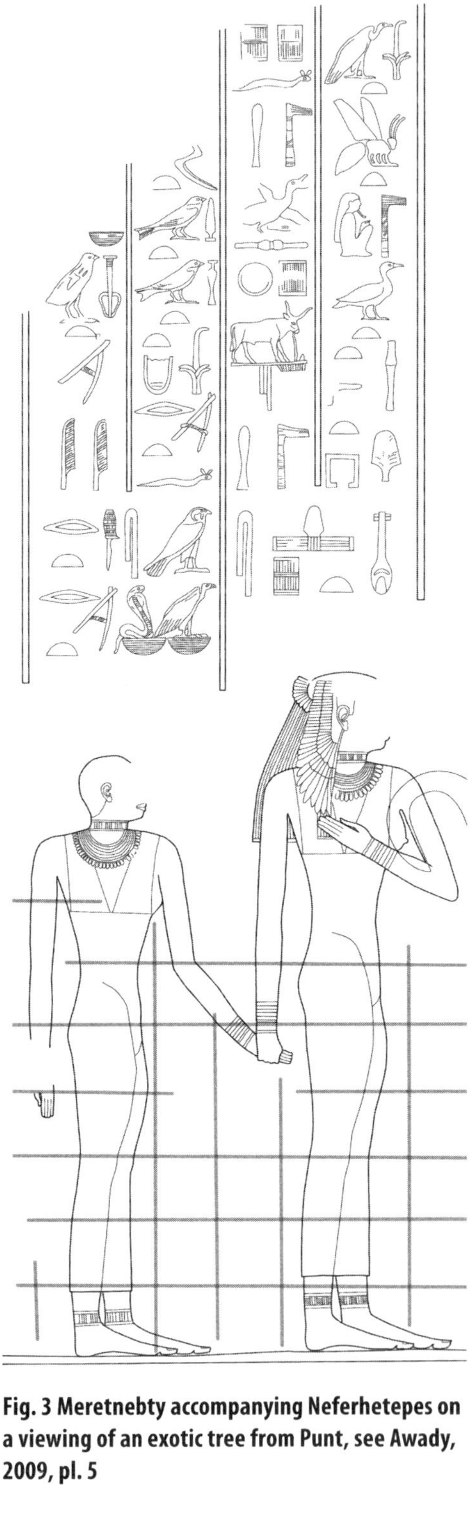

Fig. 3 Meretnebty accompanying Neferhetepes on a viewing of an exotic tree from Punt, see Awady, 2009, pl. 5

the basis of Sethe's (*Urk* I, 52.3) inaccurate transcription of a text from Ptahshepses's tomb in Saqqara, Khamaat was believed to be a daughter of Shepseskaf. We have no evidence as to whether Khamaat was also Neferhetepes' daughter.

Nothing in the surviving written sources, e.g. inscriptions in tombs of magnates of the same period, suggests a break between the reigns of Shepseskaf and Weserkaf. Continuity of government is confirmed for example by the sequence of kings in the inscriptions in the tombs of the already mentioned High Priest of Ptah, Ptahshepses, in Saqqara (Mariette, 1882, 464), the vizier, Sekhemkare, in Giza (Hassan, 1943, 103–120) and Nesutpunetjer, in Giza (Gautier, 1925, 180). Nor do any later records indicate any disruption in state government. Cylindrical sealing sticks bearing Weserkaf's cartouche have been found in Saqqara and on Elephantine (Kaplony, 1981/II, 145 no. 1 and 2; 165 no. 32). Finds of clay sealings with Weserkaf's name (although they sometimes do not relate directly to the period of his reign) are documented from Giza, Abusir, Abydos and faraway Buhen (Kaplony, 1981/II, 146–163, nos. 5, 8, 14, 29–31; Verner, 1995, 97, no. 143/A/78-a; Verner *et al.*, 2006, 215 no. 24 a 228 no. 81).

Although we have no detailed records of Weserkaf's ascent to the throne and the first and most of the second year of his reign, we can assume that one of his first decisions concerned the founding of his own tomb, the pyramid complex 'Purified Are the (Cult) Places of Weserkaf' (see p. 154). On the Palermo Stone this pyramid is mentioned as early as the end of the year after the 1st cattle-count in Weserkaf's reign in connection with the arrival of pardoned exiles, who brought with them 70 inhabitants of desert countries (Vachala, 1991, 93–101; Altenmüller, 1995, 37–48).

It was evidently only after the founding of the pyramid complex in Saqqara that work also commenced on the building of Weserkaf's sun temple, 'Re's Nekhen (see p. 199) in Abusir, which is first mentioned in the cited annals in the context of the year of the 3rd cattle-count (Wilkinson, 2000, 153). In the surviving first part of the text of the annals relating to the year of the second cattle-count there is no reference to the sun temple. For there to have been a reference to it in the missing final part of the text on this year would have been unusual, because a sun temple would have been mentioned in the first part of the text immediately after donations to the gods in Heliopolis, as is the case in the section concerned with the 3rd cattle-count.

In the year of the 2nd cattle-count (Wilkinson, 2000, 218 and Fig. 6; Roccati, 1982, 44; Strudwick, 2005, 69) on the occasion of the (new year) feast, the king donated a considerable quantity of offerings (bread and cakes, beer, cattle and poultry) to the *b3w* (powers, deities) of Heliopolis (for a more detailed discussion of this term see Goedicke, 1979, 124ff.), land parcels to the cult of Re and other land parcels to the cult of Hathor in front of Weserkaf's pyramid complex.

In the year after the 2nd cattle-count the 'third listing of the inventory of the house of Horus and Seth' (Wilkinson 2000, 152) took place (for more on this act see p. 40).

In the year of the 3rd cattle-count (Wilkinson, 2000, 153–154) Weserkaf again, on the occasion of feasts, provided offerings for the *b3w* of Heliopolis and donated land parcels in the regions of Lower Egypt and offerings of bread, cake and beer to the gods of the sun temple, Re and Hathor. The king also had temples built and established a series of new foundations (*Urk* I 241f., 1–25) comprising lands for the gods of the temple in Buto and daily offerings of bread, beer and cakes for Nekhbet of the Divine Palace of Upper Egypt, Wadjet of the Lower Egyptian Shrine and the gods of the Divine Palace of Upper Egypt.

Weserkaf also devoted attention to the cult of the gods in other parts of the country, as is attested by a fragment of a red granite pillar bearing his name found in the temple of Montu in Tod (Bisson de la Roque, 1937, 61f. and fig. 15; Desroches Noblecourt, Leblanc, 1984, 83f.). Although Uphill (Uphill, 1984, 232) assumes that the fragment might have been brought to Tod from a damaged building of Weserkaf in the surroundings of Memphis, the dimensions of the fragment seem to exclude it (Bussmann, 2010, 63). From an inscription in the tomb of Nykaankh in Tehna (Goedicke, 1970, 131–148; Edel, 1981, 38–64) it appears that Weserkaf probably fully endowed the local cult of Hathor here, 'the Lady of the Mouth of the Valley', which although founded earlier under Menkaure had lacked its own economic base in the form of land and depended simply on allocations (Goedicke, 1979, 122f.).

Hathor was also worshipped in a still not entirely clarified type of shrine called a *mrt*, which Weserkaf had rebuilt after a long interval of time after Snofru's reign (see text on p. 227).

Momentous changes affecting not only the power centre but society as well, were reflected in the administrative organisation of the country, headed by the official known as the vizier. Earlier, this office had been held by members of the royal family, but now influential men of non-royal origins were increasingly appointed to it (Schmitz, 1976, 166f.; Strudwick, 1985, 312f.; Dulíková, 2008, 47f.). In the reign of Weserkaf, several important men became vizier, but the relative chronology of their tenure of the office is hard to establish. Some were of royal origin and others commoners. In that time, at the end of the 4th and beginning of the 5th Dynasty, two viziers were very probably in office, one from the royal family and one commoner; the executive vizier seems to have been the latter one (Strudwick, 1985, 337f.). This situation may have been reflected by several viziers to whose title of vizier was added a phallus. (So far, the sign was read as *t̠3y* and interpreted as 'son' and considered as evidence of a blood relation of its holder with the king, see e.g. Dulíková, 2011, 327–336. The term, however, can also be read as *mty* 'true, right'. If this reading is correct, such an appendix could have distinguished the executive vizier from the honorary one.)

One vizier of the time was Ankhmare, who is thought to have been a son of Khafre (Strudwick, 1985, 74 no. 29; Baud, 1999, 423 [33]). Sekhemkare (Strudwick, 1985, 136f. no. 125), another son of Khafre (and Hekenuhedjet), whose career ended in

Sahure's time, may already have been vizier under Weserkaf (Baud, 1999, 575 [218]). Babaf, who seems to have occupied important posts under Weserkaf, also appears in the position of vizier at the beginning of the 5th Dynasty, but according to Strudwick (Strudwick, 1985, 1985, 82 no. 42), he was a commoner and it was only when appointed vizier that he obtained the rank 'king's son of his body, sole companion of his father'. There is a statue of Babaf in the Museum of Fine Arts, Boston (no. 34.1461). Sometimes Seshathotep Heti has been considered a vizier of this period. Baud (Baud, 1999/2, 576f.) assumed that his career was earlier, perhaps under Radjedef, but Jánosi (Jánosi, 2006, 178) considers Baud's argument for circular and confirms the dating of Seshathotep Heti's to the end of the 4th and beginning of the 5th Dynasty.

The Ptahshepses mentioned above, high priest of Ptah and husband of Weserkaf's daughter Khamaat, started to build his career under Menkaure and according to an inscription in his tomb climbed higher under several successive kings. Menkaure, Shepseskaf, Weserkaf and Sahure are mentioned by name in the inscription, and Neferirkare appears indirectly in the title of his sun temple, of which Ptahshepses was also priest. Although Raneferef and Shepseskare are not mentioned even indirectly, in the names of buildings, Dorman accords them the second and third column of the inscription on the right side of Ptahshepses' false door. On this basis he infers that it was not Neferirkare but Shepseskare who allowed Ptahshepses to kiss his foot (Dorman, 2002, 108). These and other theories advanced by Dorman are very dubious, however, for on the one hand is impossible to determine precisely to which king the text in the second and third column relates, and on the other Shepseskare's reign was so brief (if he reigned at all), that he left no monuments and is not even mentioned (except for few fragments of sealings) in inscriptions in the tombs of his presumed contemporaries. Dorman's estimate of Ptahshepses' age as 69 + x years is wholly unfounded, since it is based on the very problematic premise that, for example, according to the RCT Raneferef reigned for 11 years (in fact it could only have been 2 incomplete years at most, see text on p. 58) and the ephemeral Shepseskare for 7 years (see text on p. 55).

The extent of the destruction of Weserkaf's mortuary temple leaves us with no direct records of members of the royal court. All the same, Weserkaf's courtiers most probably included Kaaper, who was administrator of pastures and cattle and held a series of high offices including administrator of the border territories, as suggested by his titles 'scribe of the king's army in Wenet, Serer, Tepa, Ida, the Turquoise Terraces and in the western and eastern foreign lands'. His tomb lies in south Abusir (Fischer, 1959, 233–272; Bárta, 2001, 143–191). According to Fischer's (Fischer, 1959, 254f.) hypothetical genealogical reconstruction, Kaaper might have come from a family of expedition leaders. His father might have been 'expedition leader' Iy buried in Saqqara (tomb C 26) and Kaaper's son may have been 'expedition leader' named also Kaaper and buried in Giza (Hassan, 1939, 155–158).

Several archaeological finds providing evidence of economic life and perhaps also trading contacts date from the reign of Weserkaf. They include a set of three copper tools now in the British museum, two pointed chisels and one adze bearing Weserkaf's throne name, the provenience of which is unknown (James, 1961, 36–43 and pl. 12 and 13; Odler, in press). Weserkaf's name also appears on a jasper weight (Metropolitan Museum of Art in New York 35.9.5) corresponding to 5 debens – also of unknown provenience (Cour-Marty, 1997, 133 no. 3). A small calcite vessel found in Kythera (National Archaeological Museum of Athens, no. 4578), bearing the name of Weserkaf's sun temple, evidently comes from the original equipment of this temple (Sethe, 1917, 55–58; Helck, 1979, 15). It is unsafe to deduce trading contacts between Egypt and the Eastern Mediterranean in the reign of Weserkaf from this one isolated find, however, since the separation of the vessel from the temple inventory seems to have happened at a later date.

Fragments of two statues of Weserkaf are today kept in the Egyptian Museum in Cairo. One is a head with a *nemes* headcover (JE 52501) from a colossal, seated statue of the king in red granite, originally approx. 4.2 metres in height, which was probably placed on the south side of the pillared courtyard of the king's mortuary temple (see p. 157). A head with Lower Egyptian crown in dark greywacke is all that remains of the second statue (JE 90220), see p. 28. Originally considered to represent the goddess Neith, the head was found in the valley temple of Weserkaf's sun temple in Abusir (Ricke, 1969, 142–148 and pls. 1 and 4). Also believed to be of Weserkaf is the fragment of a statue – a limestone polychrome head with Upper Egyptian crown and ritual beard, now in the Cleveland Museum of Art (L. C. Hanna, Jr. Fund no. 1979.2), (Kozloff, 1982, 210–233; Berman *et al.*, 1999, 124f. no. 69), which may have been part of a pair-statue (Malek, Magee, Milles, 1999, 9, no. 800-297-000S). Callender (Callender, 2011-a, 164), however, doubts that the Cleveland head represents Weserkaf.

The remnant of an inscription on a fragment of the false door from a tomb by the entrance to Djoser's complex, which reads 'Flutist of the Great House, Revered with Weserkaf, Temi' (Labrousse, Lauer, 2000/II, Fig. 26a) is considered evidence of Weserkaf's cult.

I.2 SAHURE

Nb-ḫꜥw 'Lord of Appearances in Glory'
Nb-ḫꜥw-Nbty 'Lord of the Two Ladies' Appearances in Glory'
Bikwy-nbw 'Two Golden Falcons'
Ś3ḥw-Rꜥ 'Re Reached Me' ('One Reaching Re'?)

Sahure's Golden Falcon name, 'Two Golden Falcons' is similar to Khufu's and was presumably intended to express continuity of government and the king's direct blood tie with his predecessor – the founder of the new dynasty (Kitchen, 1987, 131–141). The king's throne name can be read in two different ways (Höveler-Müller, 2010, 62).

If we consider the later sources, the RCT col. III, 18 (?) attributes a reign of 12 years to Sahure, and Manetho (Waddell, 2004, 51), who calls the king Sephrés, gives a comparable 13 years for his reign. Contemporary dates relating to Sahure are provided by the Cairo Fragment (Gauthier, 1915, 47 ; Daressy, 1916, 172) and the Palermo Stone (Wilkinson 2000, 160–171 and 220f.). Particularly important, but alas damaged, is a record of the last year of Sahure's reign, which Schäfer (Schäfer, 1902, 28) reads as the year after the 7th cattle-count. Strudwick (Strudwick, 2005, 72) concurs with this interpretation while Wilkinson (Wilkinson, 2000, 171) reads it as the year after the 6th (?) cattle-count. If the cattle-counts in the reign of Sahure were held on a regular biennial basis, then according to Schäfer and Strudwick he would have reigned for around 15 years.

Contemporary dates have also been found in builders' inscriptions discovered in Sahure's mortuary temple: one from the year of the 2nd cattle-count (Borchardt, 1910, 88 M 26) and the other from the year of the 4th cattle-count (Borchardt, 1910, 89 M 29). Probably also from the reign of Sahure are dates on limestone tablets discovered in Weserkaf's sun temple (Verner, 2001, 387–389), referring to the year of the 5th cattle-count and the year after the 5th cattle-count (Edel, 1969, 1–22).

There is no direct evidence of the identity of Sahure's father in the sources of the time, but we know that his mother was Neferhetepes (Awady, 2009, 240–244), who is regarded on the basis of indirect evidence as the wife of Weserkaf. A smooth succession between Weserkaf and Sahure, and probably their direct blood relationship, is suggested by their similar Golden Falcon name, which in Weserkaf's case reads 'Perfect Golden Falcon' and in the case of Sahure 'Two Golden Falcons' (Dobrev, 1993, 190 and n. 41). Several secondary changes in the relief decoration of Weserkaf's mortuary temple may also suggest that Sahure was Weserkaf's son (see p. 158).

The previously mentioned scene from the causeway of Sahure's pyramid complex showing Sahure's mother Neferhetepes leading his wife Meretnebty by the hand (Awady, 2009, 244f. and pl. 5), can be indirect evidence that Meretnebty was the daughter of Neferhetepes. Meretnebty is depicted on a rather smaller scale than Neferhetepes, reflecting her younger age and lower rank. Meretnebty is the only wife of Sahure mentioned in any source so far known although the king may well have had other wives (Callender, 2011-a, 167–170). She was the mother of Sahure's two eldest sons, probably twins (Awady, 2009, 250).

The name of Sahure's wife Meretnebty was earlier mistakenly reconstructed from an incomplete record as Neferhanebty (Borchardt, 1913, 116). Her complete name appears several times on recently discovered blocks from Sahure's causeway.

Fig. 4 A gneiss statue of an enthroned Sahure accompanied by a god of the Coptos nome, New York, The Metropolitan Museum of art, Rodgers Fund 18.2.4. (Photo courtesy the Department of Egyptian Art of the Metropolitan Museum of Art, New York)

Meretnebty's father was most probably Weserkaf, given that except for Neferhetepes we know of no other wife of Weserkaf from available sources. If so, Meretnebty was Sahure's full sister and their sibling marriage entirely in harmony with Ancient Egyptian royal dogma. Meretnebty's titulary has survived on a fragment of relief from Sahure's mortuary temple: 'she who sees Horus and Seth, great of praise, she who sits with Horus, king's wife, beloved of him' (Borchardt, 1913, Blatt 48). In the scene from the causeway showing Meretnebty watching the planting of the frankincense tree from Punt in the royal garden with Sahure, her titulary also includes 'great one of the *ḥṯś*-sceptre, great of praise, she who joins him (i.e. the king) who is beloved of the Two Ladies, companion of Horus' (Awady, 2009, 162f.).

Several of the king's sons were already known from the relief decoration of Sahure's mortuary temple (Borchardt, 1913, Blatt 32; 33; 48 and 49) and scenes from the newly discovered blocks from the causeway have provided us with more information about them. For example, in the scene of the king and his family admiring the frankincense tree from Punt (Awady, 2009, pl. 6), there are six of them, depicted in an order expressing not just order of age but social ranking:

1. Hereditary Prince, Eldest King's Son of His Body, Chief Lector-priest Ranefer
2. Eldest King's Son of His Body Netjeryrenre
3. King's Son Khakare
4. [King's Son Nebankhre]
5. King's Son Raemsaf
6. King's Son Haremsaf

The fourth Sahure's son, Nebankhre, from which only knees survived at the edge of the scene, is known from two other fragments of reliefs (Borchardt, 1913, Blatt 33 and 49) from the king's mortuary temple. The first two of Sahure's sons, Ranefer and Netjeryrenre, both have the title 'eldest king's son'. Ranefer was probably the first to be born. According to Awady (Awady, 2009, 250) this gave him precedence over his brother and so it was he who succeeded Sahure to the throne under the name Neferirkare, and was eventually succeeded not by his twin, Netjeryrenre, but by his own son, who was called Ranefer just like his father before his ascent to the throne. Awady's theory is interesting and plausible in the wider historical context of the transition from the 4th to 5th Dynasty. This is not the only instance in the Old Kingdom where it is considered likely that the two oldest sons of the same mother were twins (Allam, 2007, 29–34; see also Kanawati, 1976, 235–251; McCorquodale, 2012, 71–88).

Interestingly, no daughters of Sahure appear in known relief decoration of the king's mortuary temple or in other contemporary written sources.

Sahure's sister was probably Weserkaf's daughter Khamaat (Dorman, 2002, 95–110), the wife of Ptahshepses, the high priest of Ptah.

Archaeologists have not yet found the tombs of the members of Sahure's immediate family, although these can be assumed to lie in the still unexplored vicinity of Sahure's

Fig. 5 King Sahure and his family admiring the frankincense tree from Punt, see Awady, 2009, pl. 6

pyramid. In view of the fact that Queen Meretnebty gave birth to Sahure's heir, her tomb might well have been in pyramid form (though not necessarily) and located by the southern side of Sahure's pyramid. The tombs of the remaining members of Sahure's family probably lie in the areas south and west of his pyramid. These will include the tomb of prince Netjeryrenre, whose name (in a builder's inscription) has been found on a block used in the construction of the earliest phase of the mastaba of Ptahshepses.

According to Gauthier (Gauthier, 1916, 175), the fragments of the later annals just quoted show that at the very beginning of Sahure's reign an inventory of the House of Horus and Seth, i.e. the royal property, was drawn up. Gauthier also argued that two parallel dating systems existed at the time, i.e. not just the cattle-count system but the 'list of the inventory of the House of Horus and Seth'. According to Gauthier, the 1st listing of the inventory of the House of Horus and Seth took place in the 2nd year of the king's reign. Wilkinson has adopted this theory (Wilkinson, 2000, 220), but it is more logical to suppose that the 1st inventory took place immediately after Sahure's accession and probably referred only to the royal property. In the same year six striding statues of Sahure were made and 'brought to life'.

According to the annals cited, in the year after the 2nd cattle-count Sahure gave gifts to the gods throughout Egypt. In first place he endowed Heliopolis, to which the mention of 200 *wꜥb*-priests and perhaps also a divine barque probably refer. Nekhbet in the Upper Egyptian shrine *pr-wr* was endowed with daily allocations of 'divine offerings' of beer, bread and cakes, while Wadjet in the *pr-nsr*-shrine received particularly generous allocations of the same offerings and Re smaller rations in a number of his cult places: in the *śnwt*-shrine, in the shrine of Upper Egypt and on the roof terrace (of a temple?). Daily allocations of 'divine offerings' were also given to Hathor in Sahure's sun temple *Śḫt-Rꜥ*. The king donated considerable lands in various regions of Lower Egypt to other gods: to Re of Sahure's sun temple, Harpooner (One of Mesen) and Sem, Ptah-Khentyiautef , Hathor in Sahure's *r3-š* and Hathor in Sahure's pyramid complex and to the White Bull. In the immediately following year (the 3rd cattle-count; only the beginning of the entry has survived in the annals), Sahure gave gifts to the Ennead in the *śnwt*-shrine.

On the Palermo Stone only the final part of one entry relating to the closing period of Sahure's reign – the year after the 7th (?) cattle-count, has survived. In this year a particularly large quantity of copper was transported to Egypt from the Turquoise Terraces, mines in the Sinai. The last important recorded event of Sahure's reign falls into the same period; it was the return of an expedition into Punt, where the Egyptians managed to obtain a large amount of myrrh, malachite, turquoise and fine gold. These were not the only rare commodities brought back from Punt, as we know from recently discovered reliefs on Sahure's causeway. The royal court was evidently fascinated by the frankincense trees (there may have been 20) transported from Punt, which were then ceremonially planted in the garden of the royal palace 'Extolled is Sahure's Beauty' in the presence of the whole royal family (Awady, 2006, 43f.; *id.* 2009, pls. 5 and 6).

Although it is not mentioned in the annals referring to the beginning of Sahure's reign, one of his first decisions must have been to embark on the building of his pyramid complex, called 'Sahure's *b3* Appears in Glory' (*b3*, often translated as 'soul', is the creative force of an individual), in the new burial ground at Abusir (see p. 158). The site of Abusir had already been chosen by Sahure's predecessor Weserkaf, who built a sun temple there. At the latest in the year of the 2nd cattle-count, Sahure's own sun temple 'Re's Field (of Offerings)' (see p. 207) was already standing although not complete, as we know from the annals. The king's cult buildings were supplemented by a *mrt*-sanctuary (see p. 227), but neither Sahure's sun temple nor his *mrt*-sanctuary have yet been located.

In addition to buildings for his own cult, Sahure devoted attention to the cults of the gods and constructed or enlarged their temples all over the country. A gneiss statue of an enthroned Sahure accompanied by a god of the Coptos nome (New York, The Metropolitan Museum of Art, Rogers Fund 18.2.4, see p. 38) may originally have been a gift from the king to the temple of Min in Coptos and could even be indirect evidence that the king carried out major building works in this temple (Sourouzian,

2010, 78). On the other hand, the statue may come from Sahure's pyramid complex in Abusir (Hill, 1999, 328–330) in which fragments of several statues of the king were found (Borchardt, 1910, 51, 58 and 111).

Sahure's activities in Karnak are a matter of some dispute. An inscription on the base of a red granite statue of an enthroned Sahure that Senwosret I donated to the temple of Amon in Karnak states that Senwosret I had it made as a memorial for his father (i.e. ancestor) Sahure, so that he might live eternally. Wildung therefore regards the statue as evidence of the development of the cult of ancestors from as early as the Middle Kingdom (Wildung, 2010, 276 and fig. 225). Wildung's dating preference is shared by Gabold (Gabold, 2008, 176f.) who also regards the statue of Sahure as Senwosret I's gift to the temple of Amun in Karnak. A different explanation, however, was suggested by Bothmer's research on the statue of another 5th Dynasty king, Nyuserre (Bothmer, 1974, 167ff.). Examining the torso of a red granite statue of Nyuserre in Rochester's Memorial Art Gallery (acc. no. 42.54; the torso fits with another fragment now in the Egyptian Museum, CG 42003), Bothner concluded that it had been in Karnak since the Old Kingdom, probably in the earliest, as yet unexcavated part of the temple of Amon. This conclusion was in line with Daumas's opinion (Daumas, 1967, 201–214) that the cult of Amon in Karnak was much older than generally believed. It can be objected that while the god is already spoken of in the Pyramid Texts (1540b) as 'the heir of Geb on the throne of Amon', it is not clear whether the passage is referring to god Amon or to a taboo, i.e. the designation of the 'Hidden' god, and that the oldest unambiguous record of the cult of Amon dates from significantly later time, the 11th Dynasty (Morenz, 2003, 110, n. 2). All the same, it cannot be excluded that the statue of Sahure donated to the temple of Amon by Senwosret I might have commemorated Sahure's part in the development of this temple. Perhaps only unearthing of the earliest building phase of the temple may help resolve this question.

According to late inscriptions in the temple in Esna (Sauneron, 1959/I, 28f.), there originally existed a *Pr-Ś3ḥw-Rˁ* 'House (Temple) of Sahure' in a site which is today considered to lie somewhere north of the village of Esna. Abd el-Rahman (Abd el-Rahman, 2009, 1f.) believes that the temple was founded by Sahure and served as a stop on the route of the procession that set out in the 1st month of the inundation from the northern temple of Khnum. He bases this theory on the fact that in another text (Sauneron, 1959/II, no. 77,14) the aforesaid temple name is replaced by the name *W3ḥ-Ś3ḥw-Rˁ*, 'Sahure Is Resting'.

Sahure's building projects were not limited to cult buildings, and we have evidence that he built at least two palaces. In the biographical inscription from the tomb of the king's physician Nyankhsakhmet in Saqqara (*Urk* I, 38.7–40.3; Kloth, 2002, 21 Kat. no. 40) there is a mention of the king's palace *Ḫˁ-Wrrt-Ś3ḥw-Rˁ* 'Sahure's *Wrrt*(-crown) Appears in Glory' (*Urk* I, 38). Archaeological excavation of Raneferef's pyramid complex in Abusir turned up evidence of another of Sahure's palaces, called

Wṯś-nfrw-S3ḥw-Rʿ, 'Extolled is Sahure's Beauty'. This palace, with its slaughterhouses supplying some meat products to Raneferef's mortuary temple, must have been located not far from the pyramid cemetery in Abusir (see p. 113).

All these building activities are indirect testimony to Egypt's economic stability or even advance in the time of Sahure. Prosperity is also suggested by the hundreds of estates that Sahure founded in selected parts of the country, as we know from recently discovered blocks from his pyramid complex. Although these were mortuary estates, they contributed to the overall expansion of cultivated land and the development of agricultural and craft production. The management of the country was in the hands of an ever larger administrative apparatus, as can be seen from the growth in numbers of the titles of officials and also numerous sealings and cylinder seals found in various parts of Egypt (Kaplony, 1981, 167–200; Verner *et al.*, a-2006, 222–263; Emery, 1963, 119 Fig. 2 C4-1).

The top administrative position in the country in the early reign of Sahure held the vizier Werbauba. We meet him in a hunting scene (Borchardt, 1913, 89 and Blatt 17) originally located at the eastern end of the south circular corridor of Sahure's mortuary temple, where he is depicted in first place between two courtiers following the king. The scene is the only record of this vizier. Werbauba no longer figures in the inscriptions on blocks from the causeway dating from the final period of Sahure's reign. The latter show another vizier, Seshemnefer (Awady, 2009, 164, 173, 226), who probably replaced Werbauba on his death. This means that Werbauba could not still have been vizier under Neferirkare, as Strudwick (Strudwick, N., 1985, 301) believes. Werbauba's tomb has not yet been found. Seshemnefer was probably still vizier at the beginning of Neferirkare's reign. His tomb has not yet been found either. It is possible that the tombs of both viziers lie in the still unexplored part of the Abusir cemetery between the pyramids of Sahure and Neferirkare.

Sahure's royal court included a number of other important people, some of whom figure in the decoration of the king's pyramid complex (Borchardt, 1913, *passim*; Awadi, 2009, *passim*). One is the already mentioned high priest of Ptah, Ptahshepses, who held important posts directly associated with the king including 'overseer of the king's domain' and '*ḥm-nṯr*-priest of Sahure in all his (cult) places'. The already mentioned royal military scribe Kaaper may also have continued to hold many offices at this time. Whether Ptahshepses, later vizier and owner of the large mastaba in the immediate vicinity of Sahure's pyramid, was already a young courtier under Sahure is a matter of debate (see p. 66).

As vigorously as domestic policy seems to have been pursued, so too was the foreign policy in the reign of Sahure. Foreign ventures were not confined only to the expedition to Punt but were also directed to the north-east, to the Sinai and into Syro-Palestine. The main Egyptian trading goal in this area had for some time been Byblos on the shore of what is today Lebanon, and the high-quality timber from its cedar forests. These trading relations are documented both by the find of a fragment of a stone vessel bearing Sahure's name in Byblos (Dunand, 1939, 272 no. 3920 and pl. 125; Jidejian, 1977, 18), and relief decorations on the walls of his mortuary temple in Abusir showing the return of ships (Borchardt, 1913, Bl. 12 and 13) from Syro-Palestine with Asians, including women and children, on their decks. Borchardt and a number of others believed that these were Asian slaves brought back from a campaign of conquest, while Montet (Montet, 1939, 191–195) even speculated that they were the retinue of a Syrian princess – a bride of Sahure. Bietak (Bietak, 1988, 35–40) has shown persuasively that they are Asian sailors with their families in Egyptian service. The qualities of cedar wood had made it a very desirable and necessary commodity in Egypt from the times of the builders of the oldest pyramids, both on building sites and in the construction of boats. It is no accident that a certain type of boat intended for long-distance voyages was called *knbt*, 'Byblosian'. It is possible that the Egyptians themselves felled the cedar wood, or at least organised the felling on the spot, as indirectly suggested by the find of an Egyptian bronze axe in the mouth of the Syrian river Nahr Ibrahim (Rowe, 1936, 283–289 and pl. 36). On the axe is the semi-cursive inscription "work team 'The Two Golden Falcons Are Reconciled', phyle *t3-wr*, group *śnṯ*", the reference being to the Golden Falcon name of an Egyptian king. The axe is most often dated to the time of Sahure, but Khufu had the same 'Golden Falcon' name, and so this dating is not quite certain.

Byblos may not have been the only Egyptian trading destination in the area. New excavation in Ebla suggests that this town too may have been trading with Egypt as early as the reign of Khafre (Matthiae, 1977, 415f.). Nor can we entirely exclude the possibility of trading relations with distant Anatolia, where the so-called Treasure of Dorak, allegedly including a wooden, gold-covered throne with a cartouche of Sahure, was found under strange circumstances, and never properly catalogued and publicised (Leclant, 1969–1968, 298f.; *id.* 1969–1970, 261). It is certainly very hard to imagine circumstances in which a royal throne would become an item of long-distance trade. Unless the whole Treasure of Dorak is a fake, it could be just a luxury piece of furniture bearing Sahure's name.

To judge by archaeological finds, trading relations between Egypt and Syro-Palestine were very extensive in Sahure's time and included the exchange of goods from copper to vessels in rare kinds of stone and wine (Sowada, 2009, 8–15; 251–252; 183–205; Wright, 1988, 143–162). Among curious articles of this trade were the bears depicted in Sahure's mortuary temple (Borchardt, 1913, Blatt 3), which probably came from Syria or Anatolia unless they were merely representations of exotic animals.

Copper was a commodity in which Egyptians had a particularly strong interest. They obtained it mainly from sources in the Sinai, as we know (apart from the already mentioned record on the Palermo Stone) principally from inscriptions found in Wadi

Maghara (Gardiner, Peet, Černý, 1957, I, pl. V.8 and II, 59, no. 8; *o. c.* I, pl. VII.9 and II, 59 no. 9). They also obtained copper from more distant mines in Wadi Feinan on what is now the Israel-Jordanian border (Sowada, 2009, 185; Espinel, 2012, 364). Another trading article is indicated by a rock inscription, evidently of the same apotropaic character as the inscriptions from Wadi Maghara, found in Wadi Kharig (Giveon, 1977, 61–63 a *id.* 1978, 76; see also Edel, 1978, 77) and mentioning not only Sahure's Horus and throne name but also Thoth as 'Lord of Terror, Subduer of Setjet'. The latter name referred to a territory comprising the Sinai and Negev. The metal known as *śṯty* 'setjetian', recorded in the Abusir papyri as used to make some rare ritual vessels, was probably called after this territory (Posener-Kriéger, 1969, 419–426). It may have been an alloy of copper and tin, i.e. the oldest bronze imported into Egypt (Sowada, 2009, 187).

Mutual relations between Egypt and Syro-Palestine seem to have had a broader cultural as well as commercial dimension. According to Espinel (Espinel, 2002, 105f.), the plan of the temple of Ba'alat Gebal 'Lady of Byblos' may even have been influenced by the plan of the valley temple of Sahure's pyramid complex in Abusir, and it is not impossible that Egyptian artists were present in Byblos.

At the beginning of the 5th Dynasty Egyptian attention was also directed to the areas to the east and west of the Nile valley and of course Nubia to the south. Kasudja, 'overseer of commissions' (probably the owner of tomb G 5340 in Giza, see Awadi, 2009, 183 and n. 1093), very probably commanded not only the expedition to Punt but other expeditions, for example in search of rare types of stone in the Eastern Desert. In Wadi Gudami in the Eastern Desert, about forty kilometres south of Wadi Hammamat, a group of inscriptions has been found bearing personal names and titles dated to the reign of Sahure (Green, 1909, 320 and pl. 52). From the titles it is evident that the inscriptions were left here by an expedition sent into the Eastern Desert probably for rare kinds of stone. One of the tasks of the expedition may have been to obtain stone for the pyramidion of Sahure's pyramid, transport of which is depicted on one of the recently discovered blocks from the king's causeway (Awady, 2009, pl. 9). Some inscriptions found in Wadi Hammamat were most likely left there by expeditions sent by Sahure to find rare kinds of stone (Eichler, 1993, 47–81).

In the same period similar expeditions were sent into the Western Desert, as is evident from an inscription with Sahure's cartouche found on a stela in the diorite quarries in Gebel el-Asr (Toshka area, see Rowe, 1938, 391–396, pl. 55, No. 2). The (wishful ?) inscription is also interesting for the date, which mentions Sahure's '1st (occasion) of the true (?) *sed*-festival'. The previsously cited statue of the enthroned Sahure accompanied by the god of the Coptos nome is made of diorite coming precisely from these quarries (Nicholson, Shaw, 2000, 33). The evidence of the scene of Libyan captives and booty from Sahure's mortuary temple is not entirely unambiguous (Borchardt, 1913, 73f. and Blatt 1). Sometimes the scene has been considered purely symbolic, but the fact that the ruler of Libya and his wife and two sons are identified by their names tends to support the idea that there was a real military campaign against the Libyans in the reign of Sahure.

The apparently uninterrupted development of Egyptian activities in Nubia at the time is attested by sealings from Buhen bearing Sahure's name (Kaplony, 1981, 200 nos. 36–48). Sahure's cartouche also appears in the inscription of Khnumhotep in Tomas in Nubia (Weigall, 1907, 108, pl. 57 and pl. 58 no. 27).

Among artifacts referring to Sahure are two stone weights of unknown provenance. One of them is a weight of greywacke, now in the British Museum in London (no. 65836), bearing the hieroglyphic inscription 'Sahure (is) one beloved of gods: 35 (debens)'. Another weight, now in Berlin (former Staatliche Museen Preussischer Kulturbesitz, West Berlin, no. 22635), also bears the hieroglyphic inscription reading 'Sahure, may he live eternally: 10 (debens)' (Cour-Marty, 1997, 133 and 145 no. 5).

We do not know the circumstances of the end of the reign of Sahure. He may have suffered a disease of the upper respiratory tract, as Reeves (Reeves, 1992, 23) has speculated on the basis of a mention of Sahure's 'healthy (healed?) nose' in the biographical inscription of the physician Nyankhsakhmet (Strudwick, 2005, 303). Another possibly veiled reference to such health problems is the otherwise common mention of the 'king's nose blessed by life' in an inscription accompanying a scene from the causeway showing Sahure stretching out nets while hunting fish and birds. On the other hand, for Awady (Awady, 2013, 63) is just this text evidence of Sahure's supernatural power and health. On the basis of the Palermo Stone (although the text is damaged precisely in this place), Schäfer (Schäfer, 1902, 38f.) dated Sahure's death to the 6th day of the 9th month of the year of the 6th (?) (occasion of the cattle-)count his reign. Strudwick (Strudwick, 2005, 72), however, revised the date suggested by Schäfer to the 23rd day of the 9th month of the 7th year so that it would correspond better to the date of Neferirkare's ascent to the throne in the following section of the annals.

The cult of Sahure lasted in his pyramid complex to the end of the 6th Dynasty and was briefly revived at the beginning of the Middle Kingdom. From the 18th Dynasty it was supplanted in the king's mortuary temple by the cult of Sakhmet, or more precisely 'Sahure's Sakhmet' (Borchardt, 1910, 112–129; Horváth, 2003, 63–70). This cult may have been inspired by a relief depiction of Sakhmet sticking up from the then already half-ruined temple, and also perhaps by the pieces of lion statues (offering table decorated with lion figures) also to be found here. It is possible, however, that the cult of Sakhmet here had already been developing from the Middle Kingdom, as is suggested by the restoration inscription of Senwosret I found in the temple, which is strikingly similar to the inscription on the statue mentioned above, which Senwosret I donated to the temple of Amon in Karnak (Bareš, 1985, 92).

I.3 NEFERIRKARE

Wśr-ḫˁw 'Powerful (One) of Appearances in Glory'
Wśr-ḫˁw-Nbty/Ḫˁ-m-Nbty 'Powerful (One) of Appearances in the Two Ladies' Glory'/
'One Who Appears in Glory of the Two Ladies'
Śḫmw-nbw 'Golden Mighty Ones'
Nfr-ir-k3-Rˁ 'Perfectly Is Made the *ka* of Re'
birth name *K3-k3.i*

The king's Horus name may suggest circumstances of ascent to the throne requiring decisiveness and effort (see text below), as may one of the variants of his Two Ladies name. It is not without significance that Neferirkare's Horus name is identical with Radjedef's, and also that his Golden Falcon name with three *śḫm* signs copies the model of this name of Radjedef. The three *śḫm*-signs of the kings' Golden Falcon name (Dobrev, 1993, 189f.) would testify that he is the grandson of Weserkaf which would give support to the presumption that he was the son of Sahure. Neferirkare was probably trying to emphasise dynastic continuity and blood links with his predecessors. He quite frequently recorded his birth name, Kakai, which may be derived from his throne name (Schneider, 1996, 266).

Kammerzell (Kammerzell, 2001, 161) has suggested that the king's throne name be phonetizied as *Nafiljalkarliiduw*.

In the RCT, Neferirkare is considered to belong in position col. III. 19, where both the name and length of reign of the king are missing. Manetho (Waddell, 2004, 51) calls the king Nefercherés and accords him a 20-year reign, and some modern scholars accept this information (Beckerath, 1977, 155). Neferirkare's name is recorded in both the Abydos king list and the Saqqara king list; in the former after Sahure and before Raneferef, and in the latter after Sahure and before Shepseskare and Raneferef. It is presumed that the note *ir.n.f m nśyt* 'he reigned for a period of' in the RCT in the position attributed to Neferirkare is a relic of the original document with list of kings, in which a new column always began with this formula; a new column of names had started in the original document with Neferirkare's name and the formula had not been removed during transcription (Helck, 1956, 83f.; Malek, 1982, 94).

The Palermo Stone offers incomplete dates from the 1st and 5th year and the year after the 5th cattle-count. Unfortunately, the text with a date relating to the end of Sahure's and beginning of Neferirkare's reign is damaged and cannot be reconstructed with certainty. If the previously cited Strudwick's (Strudwick, 2005, 72) reconstruction of the damaged date is correct, then Sahure died on the 23rd day of the 9th month of the year after the 7th cattle-count and Neferirkare reigned for 2 months and 7 days of that same year. This would be evidence of an immediate transition of power.

We have other recorded contemporary dates. A date mentioning the year of the 5th cattle-count was uncovered by Perring on a masonry block near the burial apartment in Neferirkare's pyramid (Perring, 1839, pl. 6 inscr. I) and this was later confirmed by Borchardt (Borchardt, 1909, 46). This date, which undoubtedly related to Neferirkare, is unfortunately ambiguous but probably reads, 'year of the 5th cattle-count, 4th month…'. A builders' inscription found in the pyramid of Neferirkare's wife, Khentkaus II, comes from the same year (Verner, 1995, 43 no. 2).

Direct records of Neferirkare's origin are not available, and so we have only indirect evidence that is not of a kind to support a firm conclusion. On the basis of the Westcar Papyrus, and especially Borchardt's opinion (Borchardt, 1938, 197–208), it was long believed that Sahure and Neferirkare were sons of the royal mother Khentkaus mentioned in papyri from the archive of Neferirkare. This theory relied on Sethe's older interpretation (Sethe, 1913, 90) of secondarily modified reliefs in Sahure's mortuary temple, where the figure depicted immediately after Sahure had in all places been changed to Neferirkare and supplemented with a name in cartouche and symbols of royal power. According to Sethe, who also argued from the tale of the divine birth of the kings of the 5th Dynasty in the Westcar Papyrus, Neferirkare was Sahure's brother. Neferirkare's ascent to the throne was thus not in harmony with the Osirian myth and so not entirely legitimate, so the king considered it essential to strengthen his legitimacy by making the alterations on the reliefs.

The discovery of the tomb of Neferirkare's wife Khentkaus II and the find of new blocks with reliefs from the causeway to Sahure's pyramid, however, provided the basis

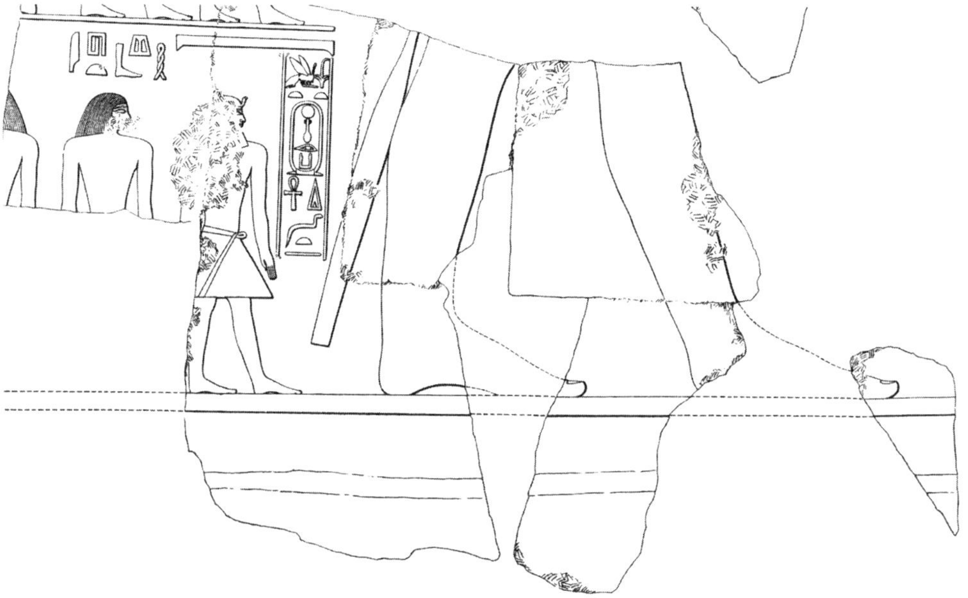

Fig. 6 The figure of the eldest Sahure's son Ranefer has been altered into 'King of Upper and Lower Egypt Neferirkare, granted life forever', see Borchardt, 1913, Blatt 33

for an alternative to Sethe's interpretation of the changed relief scenes and a different reconstruction of Sahure's family (see text above). According to the previously cited Awady's theory (Awady, 2009, 250f. and pl. 6), Ranefer and Netjeryrenre, the two eldest sons of Sahure and Meretnebty, were twins, and because Ranefer came into the world first, his position was higher than Netjeryrenre's. If this theory is correct, then the person whose figure was secondarily altered would be none other than Prince Ranefer, whose picture and name is also strikingly absent in the whole of Sahure's pyramid complex with the exception of the family scene from the causeway (see Fig. 5). The reason why his figure was not changed and supplemented by the title 'King of Upper and Lower Egypt' in this scene too can be explained by the nature of the scene: in its narrow register with seated figures a striding figure of King Neferirkare would have been in undesirably very small scale, and also Neferirkare would not be following Sahure, but striding towards him – a representation that would have been acceptable to neither of them. Very probably, it was Neferirkare who ordered the changes to the reliefs after his accession to emphasise the legitimacy of his succession, which his twin brother, Netjeryrenre, might theoretically have challenged. It is not impossible that Netjeryrenre tried to stake his claim later, after either the death of Neferirkare or Raneferef. According to a very few contemporary records it was at some stage in this period that the rather mysterious King Shepseskare appears, and he might theoretically have been Netjeryrenre (Verner, 2000, 581–602).

The only wife of Neferirkare attested in known contemporary sources is Khentkaus II: this evidence includes for example an inscription on a block from the king's mortuary temple found in the village of Abusir (Posener-Kriéger, 1976, 531) and the indirect evidence of a builders' inscription found by the king's pyramid (Perring, 1839, pl. 6 L). Archaeologically there is the further indirect evidence of the position of the queen's pyramid complex in close proximity to the king's pyramid, as well as papyri from the archive of Neferirkare's mortuary temple showing the integration of the cults of Khentkaus II and the king and other written records found in the king's pyramid complex (Borchardt, 1909, 68 Fig. 73). We do not know the queen's parentage but, to judge from her name, she may have come from the royal family founded by Khentkaus I. Her connection with the royal family of the 4th Dynasty is also suggested by the fact that one of the domains contributing to her mortuary cult bears the name of Khufu (Verner, 1995, 88 no. 62/A/78). She perhaps was a member of Weserkaf's or Sahure's extended family; on the reliefs in her mortuary temple she is depicted as an older woman (Sweeney, 2004, 67–84). It is notable that like Khentkaus I, Khentkaus II had the unusual title 'mother of two (both?) kings of Upper and Lower Egypt'.

From the evidence of all the sources available today, it is clear that the Royal Mother Khentkaus mentioned in Neferirkare's papyrus archive was definitely Khentkaus II and not Khentkaus I as Borchardt believed, and as Posener-Kriéger also supposed (Posener-Kriéger, 1976, 527–533) before changing her mind after the discovery of the tomb of Khentkaus II (Posener-Kriéger, 1997, 17–23). On the (already mentioned) block from Neferirkare's mortuary temple there is a fragment of a scene of the king followed by his wife Khentkaus II and their eldest son Ranefer (see Fig. 8). As builders' inscriptions and other written records found in the pyramid complex of Khentkaus II show, the queen's prestige rose considerably during her lifetime. Builders' inscriptions from the earlier phase of the complex refer to her as the 'king's wife', but in the later

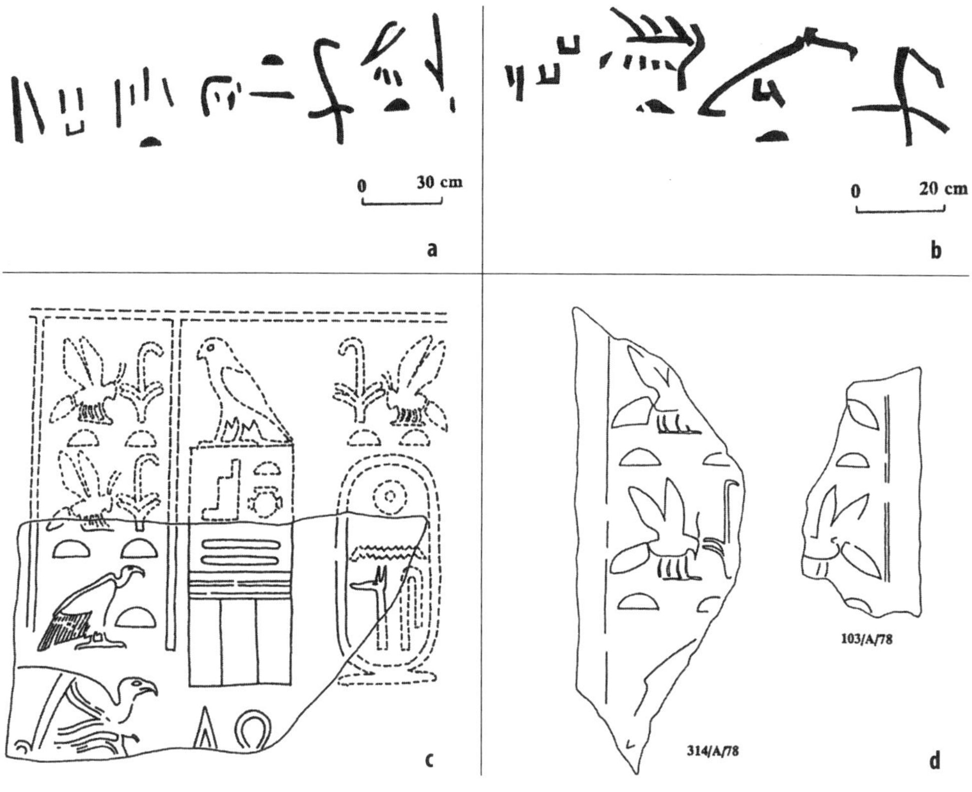

Fig. 7 Gradual development of the principal title of Khentkaus II, see Verner, 1995, 43 no. 1; 47 no. 13; 60 no. 314/A/78; 84 no. 200/A/78

a) original builder's inscription (no. 13) *ḥmt-nśwt* **'king's wife' on the corner block of the foundation platform for the queen's pyramid was additionally, when her son (Raneferef) resumed the work on it after Neferirkare's death, corrected by adding the title** *mwt-nśwt* **'king's mother'**

b) builder's inscription (no. 1) *mwt-nśwt* **'king's mother' on the casing block of the pyramid**

c) fragment of relief (no. 200/A/78) from the mortuary temple showing King Nyuserre standing in front of Khentkaus II bearing the title *mwt nśwt bity nśwt bity* **'mother of two (both ?) kings of Upper and Lower Egypt'**

d) Two fragments of the false door of Khentkaus II bearing her title *mwt nśwt bity nśwt bity* **'mother of two (both ?) kings of Upper and Lower Egypt'**

Fig. 8 Limestone block bearing the remains of a scene with Neferirkare followed by his wife Khentkaus II and his eldest son Ranefer, see Verner *et al.*, 2006, xxiii, Fig. 0.5

phase as the 'king's mother'. Finally, in the relief decoration of the mortuary temple and some objects relating to her cult, she has the title 'mother of two (both?) kings of Upper and Lower Egypt' (Verner, 1999, 215–218). This makes it clear that the building of Khentkaus II's pyramid complex was started by her husband Neferirkare and then continued by her sons, probably first by Raneferef and after his premature death by Nyuserre. Her mortuary temple was enlarged under Nyuserre and gained the status of a *ḥwt nṯr* – a 'god's abode (divine temple)' – which, together with the title 'mother of two (both?) kings of Upper and Lower Egypt', only underlines the exceptional social position that Khentkaus II achieved at this time.

Neferirkare's eldest son Ranefer (he had the same name as his father before the latter became king), possibly changed his name to Raneferef when he ascended the throne. The interpretation of this name is ambigous because it was written in different ways (see p. 58). Nyuserre was probably, like Raneferef, the son of Neferirkare and Khentkaus II. This is indirectly supported by a fragment of relief from the original decoration of the mortuary temple of Khentkaus II, in which Nyuserre's *serekh* and cartouche stand in front of the queen (or her statue) who is entitled 'mother of two (both?) kings [of Upper and Lower Egypt]' (Verner, 1995, 84 no. 200/A/78). This royal mother is clearly a representation of the owner of the tomb, Khentkaus II, who, as her title indicates, may have played an important role in the ascent of Nyuserre to the throne. This title, held by only two women – Khentkaus I and Khentkaus II, in the entire history of Egypt, may denote the mother of twin sons both of whom became kings (Verner, 2010, 778–784). If so, then Nyuserre would be the second of the twins born to Neferirkare and Khentkaus II.

In contemporary sources there are mentions of a few other royal sons and daughters apart from Raneferef and Nyuserre, but their relationship to Neferirkare and Khentkaus II is not quite certain. A fragment of papyrus, 46 A 1 from the archive of Neferirkare's mortuary temple, mentions supplies of offerings from the property of the 'Royal Mother Khentkaus' (undoubtedly Khentkaus II) and from the property of the 'Royal Son Irenre' (Posener-Kriéger, 1976, 306). The interlinkage of the property of these two people and their shared connection with the cult of Neferirkare has led Posener-Kriéger to consider Irenre to be the son of Khentkaus and Neferirkare (Posener-Kriéger, 1976, 531). The theory is further supported by a scene of the mortuary banquet of Khentkaus II on a fragment of relief from the decoration of her temple where Irenre, this time with the title 'hereditary prince' appears as lector-priest performing the relevant rites (Verner, 1965, 70 block 90/A/78).

In builders' inscriptions from Neferirkare's pyramid two other princes are mentioned: 'King's Chamberlain (?), King's Son Neferseshem...' and 'King's Chamberlain, King's Son Rahotep' (the latter is probably a shortened version of the name Rahotepudja, also found preceded by the same title) (Borchardt, 1909, 47). In both cases the relationship of these princes to Neferirkare is unclear; they could be his sons, but could be dignitaries raised by him to the rank of prince.

If the horizontal stratigraphy of the buildings in the pyramid field in Abusir has some bearing on questions relating to Neferirkare's family, the anonymous queen from the pyramid Lepsius no. 24 may have been Neferirkare's daughter (see text on p. 65).

Nebuibnebty, the 'king's daughter of his body' and spouse of Sankhuiptah, might have been either Neferirkare's or Nyuserre's daughter (Baud, 1999, 483).

According to the annals on the Palermo Stone, after his accession to the throne Neferirkare embarked on extensive endowment activities, at first, in honour of the gods worshipped in Heliopolis (Wilkinson, 2000, 172f.). He provided smaller parcels of land in the 1st Lower Egyptian nome to all these gods and the *śnwt*-shrine. Goedicke has argued that the reference to these divine beneficiaries as gods "in the house of divine writing (in the god's registry)" was a way of specifying the administrative form and status of the donated land (Goedicke, 1979, 113–133). Neferirkare gave further, this time quite extensive lands (352 aruras) to the '*b3w* (i.e. powers, deities) of Heliopolis' and gods of the 'Battlefield', a shrine near Memphis with cult links to Heliopolis. It is interesting that two Heliopolitan high priests gained control of these lands, which must have immensely increased the economic resources of the Heliopolitan cult. Numerous offerings were also sent to the altars of Re and Hathor in a building that is rather hard to identify and which Strudwick (Strudwick, 2005, 72) suggested interpreting as 'wall of the fortress of the sovereign'. One important event in the year of Neferirkare's accession was the making of a statue of Ihy out of fine gold for 'Hathor in Snofru's *mrt*-sanctuary' (see p. 227).

One of the first steps taken by Neferirkare after his succession must have been to start work on his pyramid complex named 'Neferirkare is *b3*' in Abusir (see text on p. 165). Neferirkare's pyramid occupied a dominant position in the cemetery. Thanks to remnants of the papyrus archive found in his mortuary temple, today Neferirkare's pyramid complex and its original operation is – together with Raneferef's – the best documented royal mortuary cult from the entire Old Kingdom.

We do not know when work commenced on Neferirkare's sun temple *Śt-ib-Rˁ* 'Place of Re's Pleasure' (see text on p. 209) but the text on the Palermo stone gives us good grounds for thinking that in the year of the 5th cattle-count the temple was already functioning, that it was equipped with an obelisk and that the barque of *m3ˁt* was placed by its southern side. In this and the following year a copper statue of Neferirkare was created, a canal was built around a further unspecified building and the king donated cult objects made of fine gold 'to the *b3w* of Heliopolis' and a land parcel to the temple of Ptah South of His Wall.

Probably towards the end of Neferirkare's reign work started close to his own pyramid on the building of the small pyramid complex of his wife Khentkaus II. Like Neferirkare's own pyramid it was completed after his death by his sons Raneferef and especially Nyuserre.

Neferirkare also supported other temples even in more remote areas, as is shown by a decree of protection that he issued for the temple of Khontamenty-Osiris in Abydos (Goedicke, 1967, 22–36). The oldest known example of its kind, this decree gives us important information on the temple economy and social conditions of the time. It explicitly forbids, 'on pain of heavy punishments' the drafting of priests for work other than their religious duties, and the recruitment of corvée people (*mrt*) allocated to the temple fields (divine land) for other work. It thus separated the interests of the state and religious cult and secured the economic and social position of priests of the category *ḥm-nṯr* 'god's servant' (tenured priests). The legal basis for the privileged position and independence of these priests became not their service to the god but the holding of land donated to the god and exempt from tax burdens. Papazian believes that Neferirkare pursued this policy for reasons of both personal piety and political advantage (Papazian, 2012, 128).

According to Baer (Baer, 1960, 300), Neferirkare's reign saw the introduction of a standardised system of ranking the titles of officials; previously the system had not been completely chaotic but fluctuations had been common. The move was probably associated with the rise of a new official stratum, which was separate from the royal family even at the highest levels and was gradually to gain ever more independence. In the field of state administration there were probably other reforms intended to increase efficiency, for example the creation of the posts of 'overseer of the Six Great Houses' and 'overseer of the scribes of the king's documents', which were taken up by the vizier (Strudwick, 1985, 238). The continuity and stability of the government of the country is indirectly shown by the seal cylinders and sealings bearing Neferirkare's name found in various parts of Egypt, including Lower Nubia (Kaplony, 1981, 207–227; Pätznick, 2005, 217; Emery, 1963, 119 Fig. 2 C4-1).

At the beginning of Neferirkare's reign the vizier was probably still Seshemnefer, who had been appointed to this function by Sahure (Strudwick, 1985, 138f. no. 129). His successor was Washptah, who like Seshemnefer was the holder of a range of other important administrative and religious functions. From Washptah's biographical inscription (Grdseloff, 1951, 129–140 and pl. I on p. 141; Kloth, 2002, 14 Kat. no. 26; Strudwick, 2005, 318–321), which unfortunately has not survived in its complete form, we learn that during a visit by Neferirkare, probably to his sun temple, Washptah collapsed into unconsciousness in the king's presence. The reason for his collapse may have been an infectious disease (Picardo, 1991, vol. 2, 93–104). Washptah's tomb has not yet been found. It is sometimes hypothetically located north-east of Tjy's mastaba in Saqqara (Spencer, 1974, pl. I). In fact, from Washptah's biographic inscription it seems that his tomb might be closer to Abusir. According to the respective passage of this inscription (Grdseloff, 1951, 141 pl. I; Strudwick, 2005, 320; Kloth, 2002, 14 Kat. no. 26) it was "... [the tomb built of?] limestone on the funerary compound (*š ḏt*) of 'Sahure's Soul Appears in Glory' (i.e. Sahure's pyramid complex)". If the missing part of the inscription indeed refers to Washptah's tomb, does it mean that the area north of the present northern Saqqara was in Washptah's time taken for a part of the Abusir cemetery generally determined by Sahure's pyramid complex?

The biographical inscription (Egyptian Museum, Cairo, no. JE 66682) of another of Neferirkare's high officials, Rawer (Hassan, *Giza* I, 1–61; Kloth, 2002, 23f. Kat. no. 47), director of the palace, the king's secretary and bearer of many other titles, records another interesting episode. It happened during the ceremony 'Taking the Prow-rope of the God's Bark', either at Sahure's burial or the coronation of Neferirkare (Allen, 1992, 14–20). Probably by accident Rawer disrupted the ceremony by stumbling on the king's stick, but he was pardoned, not punished.

The high priest of Ptah, Ptahshepses, continued in his office throughout Neferirkare's reign and even enjoyed the king's special favour as 'the master of secrets of any project that his majesty would desire to accomplish' (Dorman, 2002, 102). His namesake and the future vizier Ptahshepses may have been just starting out on his career at the royal court at this time. Also on the rise was Tjy, who eventually became the overseer of two pyramid complexes, those of Neferirkare and Nyuserre, and four sun temples – Sahure's, Neferirkare's, Raneferef's and Nyuserre's.

As can be deduced from both written (Posener-Kriéger, 1975, 491) and archaeological (Borchardt, 1909, 58) sources, the cult of Neferirkarc in his mortuary temple flickered out in the second half of the 6th Dynasty. It is therefore surprising that his cult was revived at the beginning of the Middle Kingdom, to which date two statues of the priest Sakhmethotep – one found in Abusir (Bareš, 1985, 87–94) and the other in Giza (Hassan, 1953, 60 and fig. 51). The inscription on the statue from Giza mentions the (mortuary?) temple of Neferirkare.

I.4 SHEPSESKARE

Śḫm-ḫꜥw 'Mighty (One) of Appearances in Glory'
Špśś-kꜣ-Rꜥ 'Noble Is the *ka* of Re'

Only the king's Horus name has been preserved in sources of the time. His throne name is recorded merely in much later sources, from the New Kingdom.

Shepseskare is generally accorded the 20th position in column III of the RCT and the 7 years of rule pertaining to it. Beckerath (1997, 155) and Barta (1981, 23) even proposes 7 full and 2 incomplete years, but these estimates are at odds with written and archaeological sources of the time. The name Shepseskare does not appear at all in the sequences of kings that we find in several contemporary tombs, and is also absent in later lists of kings with the exception of the Saqqara king list dating from the New Kingdom (Malek, 1982-a, 21–28; Malek-b, 1982, 94), in which it appears between the names of Neferirkare and Raneferef.

Shepseskare's parentage is entirely obscure, and we can do no more than speculate about it in the context of indirect evidence from the first half of the 5th Dynasty (Verner, 2000, 582–585). Earlier in this section (sub Sahure) we mentioned the problems that may have been caused in the succession by the birth of Sahure's twins, Ranefer and Netjeryrenre, if indeed they were twins. Theoretically, both could have had a claim to the throne – in line with the Osirian myth – which eventually went to the one born first, Ranefer (future Neferirkare). It is therefore possible that Netjeryrenre, if he outlived his brother, could have made a claim to the throne, and from the point of view of legitimacy Netjeryrenre, if he survived even longer, would have had an even better opportunity to assert his claim after the premature death of Neferirkare's son Raneferef. Whether Netjeryrenre or someone else (see the discussion on p. 58f.) is hidden behind the name Shepseskare, it was very likely someone from the narrow circle of members of the ruling royal family.

In view of the find of a few fragments of sealings bearing the Horus name *Śḫm-ḫꜥw* it is likewise theoretically possible that this was a king (Raneferef?, Nyuserre?), who changed his name right at the beginning of his reign. Such a change would have been very unusual, but not absolutely exceptional (e.g. Pepi I changed his Horus name from Nefersahor to Meryre).

So far, no one has managed to find Shepseskare's tomb (see p. 169) or any other building associated with him. The only contemporary written sources relating to

Shepseskare are two cylinder seals, one found in Mit Rahina and the second from the collection of Michailidis, and a few sealings found in Abusir during earlier German and especially later Czech excavations. None of these finds, however, enable us to place Shepseskare more precisely in the chronology of the first half of the 5th Dynasty.

Taking all these direct and indirect pieces of evidence on Shepseskare together, it would seem that he was probably an ephemeral king who reigned too briefly to leave any deeper traces in the sources of the time. The theory (Callender, 2011-a, 181f.), that Shepseskare's wife might be the Nimaathap II buried in tomb G 4712 in the western cemetery of Khufu in Giza, is therefore purely speculative.

I.5 RANEFEREF

Nfr-ḫꜥw 'Beautiful (One) of Appearances in Glory'
Nfr-m-Nbty 'Beautiful (One) in Two Ladies'
Bik-nbw-nfr 'Beautiful Golden Falcon'
Rꜥ-nfr.f 'Re Is Beautiful' (lit. Re, he is Beautiful)
birth name *Ꞽsi*

The king's throne name seems to have undergone certain changes at the start of his reign before it acquired a stable graphic (and semantic?) form. The written versions of the king's throne name appear in cartouches on sealings from his mortuary temple and it is not impossible that all recorded variants of the writing of his name should be read as Ranefer. If so, then the king would rather unusually have left his existing name unchanged after his accession to the throne. (For more detail see Verner *et al.*, 2006, xx–xxiv.) Concerning the alternating reading of the king's name in egyptological books as Neferefre/Raneferef, see Valloggia's (Valloggia, 2011, 3f.) thorough discussion on the reading of Radjedef's name. Vallogia's arguments for the reading Radjedef rather than Djedefre seem to support the reading Raneferef preferred also by Posener-Kriéger.

In the RCT, unfortunately damaged in this section, the 21st position in column III, belonging in order to the fourth king of the 5th Dynasty, is thought to have been Raneferef. The name itself has not survived here, however, but only a fragment of the data on the length of the reign – i.e. the upper edge of one counting stroke. Manetho (Waddell, 2004, 51) identifies Raneferef with Cherés (this may be a corruption of the king's Horus name Neferkhau) and accords him a reign of 20 years. When combined with Manetho's evidence, the remnant of the figure 1 on the RCT has led some scholars to suppose that Raneferef reigned for 10 or 11 years (Barta, 1981, 23; Beckerath, 1997, 155). Yet this high figure is at odds with the sources of Raneferef's own time.

> **Fig. 9 Seated statue of Raneferef protected by a falcon god, Egyptian Museum Cairo, JE 98171. (CUP FA CEI, photo Jan Brodský)**

Fig. 10 Recorded variants of the writing of Raneferef's throne name, see Verner et al., 2006, xx

In Raneferef's unfinished pyramid a builder's inscription has been found with the date 'year of the first occasion (of the cattle-count), 4th month of inundation' (Verner *et al.*, 2006, 190 no. 8). The inscription therefore comes from the 2nd year of Ranefer's reign (the first after the year of his accession), and the king probably died at the end of this year (Verner, 2006-a, 399–401). Anthropological analysis of the remains of the king's mummy found in the burial chamber of his pyramid has shown that he died at the age of 20–23 (Strouhal, Němečková, 2006, 517f.). The cause of his premature death is unclear, but histological examination of the remains of Raneferef's mummy suggests an excess of fat tissue.

The inscriptions on an already mentioned block from Neferirkare's mortuary temple (see p. 49) is direct evidence that Raneferef was the son of Neferirkare and Khentkaus II. This matches the situation in the cemetery in Abusir, where Raneferef 's pyramid follows immediately after Neferirkare's. The pyramid of Khentkaus II lies in close proximity to both.

Recently, a largely devastated tomb (AC 30) was unearthed in the row of four small mastabas lying south of the mortuary temple of Raneferef. Judging by their position, direct members of Raneferef's family were very probably buried in these tombs. The first tomb (Q) from the north (and closest to Raneferef's temple) belonged to the King's Son Nakhtsare (see p. 58) and the second one (AC 29) to Kakaibaef (Krejčí, 2013, 26–37). The third tomb (AC 30) in the row belonged, according to the revealed builders' inscriptions, to Khentkaus who bore the titles 'King's wife' and 'King's mother' (courtesy Jaromír Krejčí). The horizontal stratigraphy may indicate that the tomb owners were probably buried in the chronological sequence respecting the date of their death: first Nakhtsare, then Kakaibaef (Raneferef's eldest son ?) and after the latter Khentkaus III. Considering the broader historical context of the find, the queen, Khentkaus III, was very probably the spouse of Raneferef and the daughter of Neferirkare and Khentkaus II.

This discovery has highlighted once again how complicated the situation in the royal family could become after the unexpectedly early death of a king, this time, Raneferef. If Khentkaus III had indeed been his wife, and if, indeed, she had had sons to Raneferef, their son may have been a very young child (about 5 to 8 years old), for the king himself was quite young when he died. There is thus a hypothetical possibility that the child might have been the ephemeral ruler, Shepseskare (see p. 55). Whether Shepseskare briefly ruled or not, Raneferef was succeeded by his brother Nyuserre. However, there are also other options for these events which might have followed Raneferef's death. For example, Nyuserre could then have married Raneferef's widow, Khentkaus III.

After Nyuserre's death the situation may have become even more complicated by the early death of presumably Nyuserre's eldest son, Werkaure, who probably predeceased his father (see p. 65). If Khentkaus III was *not* the mother of Shepseskare, and if she survived Nyuserre, was she the mother of Nyuserre's successor Menkauhor who may have been her and Raneferef's son? Do the diorite plates bearing Menkauhor's name, found in the mortuary temple of Raneferef (Vlčková, 2006, 84f.), have a deeper meaning in this context?

No less intricate problem concerns Menkauhor's successor, Djedkare. Was he Menkauhor's or Nyuserre's son? Some clues may support the second option. Djedkare (see p. 85) not only paid attention to the restoration of the funerary monuments of his ancestors buried in Abusir, but part of his family was buried there, in the area east of the anonymous queen's pyramid, Lepsius no. 24. Was this anonymous queen Djedkare's mother? Let's hope that future research on the as yet unearthed part of the Abusir royal cemetery will answer some of these questions.

Nyuserre, likewise the son of Khentkaus II, was probably Raneferef's full brother. If we are right in thinking that the unusual title 'mother of two (both?) kings of Upper and Lower Egypt' refers to the birth of twins, then Nyuserre was Raneferef's twin brother. Raneferef may have had other siblings in Neferirkare's family (see the text above).

After Raneferef's premature death his successor Nyuserre had his incomplete pyramid hastily finished as a quasi-mastaba. He also had Raneferef's mortuary temple completed and progressively expanded; it was made mainly of mudbrick and wood. By Djedkare's time, however, the temple was already very dilapidated and mortuary priests had built dwellings in it (Verner, 2012, 407–410 and pl. 38).

Probably immediately after his accession Raneferef also started work on the building of his sun temple known as *Ḥtp-Rꜥ* 'Re's Offering Table', the only written record of which has been found in Tjy's mastaba. The building (which did not get past the initial stage, or even just preparation of the site) has not been archaeologically identified (for more detail see p. 211).

Only a very few records relating to the government of the country have survived from Raneferef's short reign. They include a royal decree found on the façade of the tomb of Iaib in Bersha (Meyer, 2011, 57–72). The decree promoted Iaib, 'local prince' and 'controller of the Two Thrones', to the rank of the 'local prince, the seal bearer of the king of Lower Egypt' and some other important social positions, but the reasons for Iaib's advancement remain unclear.

We do not know who held the post of vizier in Raneferef's reign. It could have been Minnefer, who probably held the position in the first half of Nyuserre's reign. The magnate Tjy, who in addition to several important offices was also 'overseer of Neferirkare's pyramid complex' and 'overseer of the sun temples of Sahure, Neferirkare and Raneferef' lived in the time of Raneferef (Wild, 1966, pl. 182; Verner, 1987, 293–297). The king's *ḥm-nṯr*-priest was Nykaure (Mariette, 1882, 314; Baer, 1960, 82 (242)).

During Raneferef's reign the office of High Priest of Ptah was occupied by Ptahshepses, but it is not quite clear whether the episode in which the king allowed him to kiss the royal foot and not the ground in front of it concerns king Raneferef. Dorman (Dorman, 2002, 108) believes that this happened under Shepseskare, but Raneferef is a more likely candidate, for if Dorman were right then Ptahshepses's biographical inscription would be the only historical record of the ephemeral king Shepseskare in the written sources of the time, which is not very credible.

By a combination of lucky circumstances (including the fact that the temple was made of brick and relatively soon fell into ruins), a set of statues of Raneferef survived and was found in the mortuary temple. They are now in the Egyptian Museum in Cairo (Benešovská, 2006, 360–437). Apart from a few fragments the set principally consists of:

- Striding statue of the ruler with the crown of Upper Egypt. Basalt. JE 98181
- Head and body of a statue of the seated ruler. Basalt. JE 98177
- Torso of a seated ruler. Diorite
- Head of statue of the king with the false beard. Diorite
- Head of statue of the king. Diorite
- Statue of the seated ruler, gripping the *hedj*-sceptre on his chest. The king is protected by a falcon god. The base of the throne bears the hieroglyphic inscription 'King of Upper nad Lower Egypt Raneferef, may he live eternally'. Pink limestone. JE 98171
- Head of the ruler protected by the falcon god Horus. Yellowish limestone
- Fragment of a head (lower part of the crown). Quartzite.

Several other statues have been identified as Raneferef, in most cases erroneously. These include a limestone head with circular wig, belt and ureus (Berlin, Ägyptisches Museum 14369) (Finneiser, 1998, 53–70). The head almost certainly belongs to a different king (perhaps Khafre or Radjedef). Müller identified as either Raneferef or Neferirkare the remains (from the waist down) of a calcite statue of a kneeling and offering king with a *nemes* and two uraei (the statue is in private ownership but earlier belonged to the American Collection, New York, NY), and the remnant of the inscription *Rˁ-nfr*… on its back pillar. Pamminger (Pamminger, 2000, 153–173), however, argues persuasively that it is an archaising statue from the 25th Dynasty. Also considered to be Raneferef is a small head in limestone with remains of paint found by Petrie under the paving of a temple of the 12th dynasty in Coptos. The statue is now in the Petrie Museum of Egyptian Archaeology, University College London, UC

14282 (Roehrig, 1999, 316; Do. Arnold, Grzymski, Ziegler, 1999, 316 no. 101). This identification is highly improbable. Tefnin (Tefnin, 1988, 20f. No. E.7117) considers a head in the the Royal Museums of Fine Arts in Brussels to be of Raneferef. Also this sculpture probably does not represent Raneferef.

I.6 NYUSERRE

Śt-ib-tȝwy 'Delight of the Two Lands'
Ny-wśr-Rʿ 'Re Belongs to the Power'
Śt-ib-Nbty 'Delight of the Two Ladies'
Bik-nbw-nṯry 'Divine Golden Falcon'
birth name *Ini*

The king's Horus and throne names create the impression of continuity and stability assured by his succession to the throne.

Kammerzell (Kammerzell, 2001, 161) has suggested that the king's throne name be phonetizied as Niwasilliiduw.

Nyuserre's name has not been preserved in the RCT but he is generally thought to be the king in position 22 in column III (before Menkauhor, who is safely identified), where he is recorded as having reigned for 10 + *x* years. Manetho (Waddell, 2004, 51) calls him Rathurés and claims that he ruled for 44 years. Egyptological estimates of Nyuserre's reign have been anything from 11 years (Gardiner, 1961, 435) to 31 (Beckerath, 1997, 155) or as much as 33 years (Barta, 1981, 23).

When he succeeded to the throne, Nyuserre was probably not much younger than Raneferef (if not his twin, i.e. about 20–23 years old). The date 'year after the 2nd occasion (of the cattle-count), 3rd month of inundation, 24th day' found on the masonry of the southern 'Eckbau' of Nyuserre's mortuary temple (Borchardt, 1907, 145) may show (if indeed referring to Nyuserre which is not quite ceratin) that at that time work on the king's pyramid complex was already advanced. From the year of the 2nd cattle-count also dates an inscription found in Gallery 5 in Ayun Sokhna and containing probably Nyuserre's cartouche (Tallet, 2012, 215–217; Doc. 245). A builders' inscription with the date 'year of the 5th (?) occasion (of the cattle-count), 3rd month of winter, 1st day' found on masonry from the oldest building phase of the mastaba of Ptahshepses (Verner, 1992, 110 no. 194) is very probably from the reign of Nyuserre. So far the latest contemporary date likely to relate to Nyuserre, 'year of the 7th occasion (of the cattle-count), 3rd month of inundation, 1st (or 7th ?) day', is in an inscription on a vessel for grease found in Raneferef's mortuary temple (Verner, 2006a, 276 no. 16).

One argument sometimes used to support the view that Nyuserre's reign was long refers to the scenes of the *sed*-festival in his sun temple in Abu Ghurab (Kees, 1928). In fact, in the Old Kingdom, similar scenes were already standard parts of the decorative programme of important royal buildings such as pyramid complexes (Hornung, Staehelin, 1974, 66f.; Hornung, 1991, 169–171), and so are hardly conclusive proof that the respective king actually reigned for the thirty years needed for the holding of a real *sed*-festival. On the other hand, we cannot be sure that in Nyuserre's case these scenes were not historically authentic.

One indirect indication that Nyuserre's reign was relatively long is the basiliform name of Raneferefankh which appears on blocks of the core of the south wall of the courtyard dating from the final phase of building of the king's pyramid (Borchardt, 1909, 54). Judging by the name, its bearer was very probably born in the reign of Raneferef, while, at the time when the wall was built, Raneferefankh was already the holder of the not insignificant title 'district administrator', and so must have been around twenty years old. (Another ?) Raneferefankh we encounter as 'inspector of the Great House' in builders' inscriptions from the final building phase of the mastaba of the vizier Ptahshepses (Verner, 1992, Catalogue nos. 55, 64 and 392). With a variant writing of his name as Isiankh, he also appears among dignitaries depicted in Nyuserre's mortuary temple (Borchardt, 1907, 72). On the basis of the indirect evidence and other indications (for instance, a number of buildings completed during his reign) mentioned below, Nyuserre would seem to have reigned for at least twenty years, and probably as long as thirty.

We have only indirect evidence on Nyuserre's parentage. This includes the previously mentioned remnant of a scene from the relief decoration of the mortuary temple of Khentkaus II in Abusir. Interpretation of the scene, from which several more small fragments have survived, is difficult; it may show a meeting of Khentkaus II with Nyuserre and his family or the veneration of a statue of this royal mother (Verner, 1999, 219–224). All the same, this fragment strongly suggests that Khentkaus II was Nyuserre's mother, and his father would then have been Neferirkare. Khentkaus II seems to have played an important role in legitimising the succession of Nyuserre, who was not Raneferef's son but, very probably, his twin brother.

Although likewise indirect, the archaeological evidence also strongly suggests a close family link of Nyuserre with Khentkaus II, Neferirkare and Raneferef. Nyuserre completed the building of their pyramid complexes (Verner, 1995, 36–41; *id et al.* 2006, 100–106). He also sited his own pyramid complex close by the north side of Neferirkare's mortuary temple, in the cemetery. By all these actions Nyuserre seems to have been demonstratively including himself in the Abusir cemetery in the family of Neferirkare and so further strengthening the legitimacy of his claim to the throne.

One unusual written record suggests that Nyuserre may well have had certain

> Fig. 11 Seated statue of Nyuserre wearing the nemes headcover and uraeus, Egyptian Museum Cairo, JE28466. (Courtesy Egyptian Museum Cairo, photo Ahmed Amin Azmi)

Fig. 12 Text on a limestone cylindrical seal from the collection of the Brooklyn Museum, New York (no. 44.123.30), see Kaplony, 1981/IIB, pl. 70 no. 1

problems establishing his claim to the throne: this is a limestone cylindrical seal from the collection of the Brooklyn Museum, New York (no. 44.123.30) (James, 1974, 12f. no. 35 and pl. 19). Neferirkare's and Nyuserre's Horus names appear beside each other in the text, but although Kaplony (Kaplony, 1981/IIA, 235f.) considers this evidence of the co-regency of the two kings, Neferirkare was dead by the time of Nyuserre's succession, Raneferef having reigned briefly between the two. The text is therefore further indirect evidence (besides the support of Khentkaus II) of Nyuserre's anxiety to consolidate the legitimacy of his claim by referring also to his father's authority (Verner, M., 2011, 333f.). Nyuserre's efforts concerning his legitimacy may also be behind his building activities in the memorial monuments of his great ancestors, the valley temple of Menkaure and the tomb complex of Khentkaus I in Giza (Lehner, in press).

A small fragment of a statue bearing part of an inscription, 'King's Wife Reputnebu' was found in Nyuserre's valley temple (Borchardt, 1907, 25). Fragments of several statues, including the right half of the face of an alabaster statue of a woman (now housed in the Egyptian Museum Berlin, no. 17438) were found by the north 'Eckbau' of the king's mortuary temple; they may also be parts of representations of this queen (Borchardt, 1907, 99). The remains of an inscription on a fragment of relief from the mortuary temple of Khentkaus II, dated to the reign of Nyuserre, which mentions 'King's Wife, [His] Beloved One, Reput[nebu?]' very probably refers to the queen Reputnebu (Verner, 1995, 85 s. no. 10). Fragments of an alabaster statue (or two statues?) have been found very close to Nyuserre's mortuary temple, in the mastaba of the vizier Ptahshepses, the king's son-in-law: they are part of a base with a left foot and the central part of a back pillar, with the remnant of an inscription including the titulary of a queen. Vachala (Vachala, 1979, 176) identified this queen as Reputnebu even though her name does not appear in the inscription. The theory has some plausibility, because Ptahshepses' wife was the princess Khamerernebty, Nyuserre's daughter. Khamerenebty might well have placed a statue (statues?) of her mother Reputnebu in the tomb where she was probably eventually buried together with Ptahshepses. On the other hand, we cannot exclude the possibility that these are fragments from Nyuserre's mortuary temple, intruded into the tomb after that temple was destroyed.

We do not know the parentage of Reputnebu (Callender, 2011-a, 182–184), who is so far Nyuserre's only known wife. We can only suppose that she came from the immediate royal family even though the title 'king's daughter' does not appear in the very limited surviving record of her titulary. Her tomb has not been located anywhere near Nyuserre's pyramid, where, it seems, there is no room for it. It is therefore possible that Reputnebu was buried in the as yet anonymous pyramid, Lepsius no. 24. The mummy of a woman of about 25 years old was found in the burial chamber of this pyramid, but provisional anthropological analysis concluded that she had probably never given birth (Krejčí, Callender, Verner, 2008, 146f.). This analysis will have to be carefully checked, for it is very improbable that a pyramid complex would have been built for such a woman, especially the first queen's complex to include a cult pyramid. Earlier in the 5th Dynasty only the royal mothers Neferhetepes and Khentkaus II (the tomb of Sahure's wife Meretnebty has not yet been found) had tombs in the form of a pyramid, and we would expect the owner of pyramid Lepsius no. 24 to have enjoyed a similarly high social standing. It is probably significant that two lines, one extrapolated from the east side of Neferirkare's pyramid and the other from the south side of Raneferef's pyramid, intersect in the centre of pyramid Lepsius no. 24 (Vymazalová, 2010, 62 Fig. 6). If these imaginary lines indicate her close relationship to these two kings, then the anonymous queen could be Neferirkare's daughter and Raneferef's sister.

We have no direct evidence concerning other close relatives of Nyuserre either. In inscriptions from the king's mortuary temple (Borchardt, 1907, 71–74) we find a partially preserved title and the name, 'hereditary prince, king's son ...' and '... Werkau[re ?]'. The first of these titles appears in connection with the previously discussed Irenre in Document 46 A of Neferirkare's papyrus archive. Irenre was probably the brother of Nyuserre and Raneferef. Werkau[re?], whose name is mentioned in Nyuserre's temple may be the same person as the 'king's eldest son Werkaure' (Krejčí, 2009-b, 30–37), whose tomb lies by the south-east corner of the mortuary temple of Khentkaus II. From the position of his tomb (its south side is aligned with the northern side of Raneferef's pyramid and its west side with the east side of the pyramid Lepsius no. 24), Vymazalová (Vymazalová, 2010, 62) believes that Werkaure might have in this way symbolically indicated his close relationship to Raneferef and the anonymous owner of pyramid Lepsius no. 24. However, some recently discovered builders' inscription in Werkaure's tomb seem to indicate that Werkaure was probably the eldest son of

Nyuserre who predeceased his father and was replaced in the succession to the throne by Menkauhor (Vymazalová, in press).

In the previously cited builders' inscription in the tomb of Werkaure (see p. 76) we encounter not only the name Menkauhor (Vymazalová, Coppens, 2008, 37f.), unaccompanied by any title and the date '2nd month of inundation, 3rd day', but also an inscription according to which Menkauhor appears as a man who was in charge of the construction of Werkaure's tomb: under his command were "the four (building) gangs of the king" (Vymazalová, Coppens, 2013-b, 126 and Fig. 2).

Among the members of Nyuserre's royal court there were at least three more princes: 'the eldest [king's son] Ra...', 'the eldest [king's son] Min...' and especially an 'hereditary prince, king's son ... lector-priest' whose name is missing (Borchardt, 1907, 74). To judge by the titles, the last named (if the inscription does not refer to Irenre, who had the same titles), may have been Nyuserre's eldest son and heir to the throne.

Khamerernebty, the wife of the vizier Ptahshepses, is believed to have been Nyuserre's daughter, although the evidence is indirect. A tomb was originally prepared for her in the so-called Mastaba of the Princesses, which lies on the eastern side of Nyuserre's mortuary temple, but the princess was never actually buried there. Although again there is no direct evidence, she is considered to have been interred in the smaller red granite sarcophagus secondarily placed in the burial chamber of the mastaba of Ptahshepses, which lies close to the Mastaba of the Princesses; no skeletal remains of a woman, but those of two men, were found in Ptahshepses' burial chamber (Krejčí, 2009-a, 65–78). A builders' inscription mentioning 'local prince Ptahshepses' (Borchardt, 1907, 144) was found in the Mastaba of the Princesses, while three builders' inscriptions 'King's Daughter Khamerernebty' have more recently been found in the oldest building phase of Ptahshepses' mastaba (in this phase of the tomb Ptahshepses only has the title 'sole companion' on builders' inscriptions) (Verner, 1992, nos. 3, 7 and 136). Whether this indicates mutual gifts of building material or an accidental confusion of stones on the building site because the two tombs were so close, it is clear that the two tombs were built at roughly the same time, i.e. Ptahshepses' around the year of the 5th (?) cattle-count in the reign of Nyuserre (see text above) and Khamerernebty's perhaps shortly after that. The princess later abandoned her own tomb plans and was buried in the tomb of her husband Ptahshepses.

With appeal to various circumstances, and especially Khamerernebty's titles, Callender (Callender, 2011-b, 101–120) has expressed doubts as to whether she was Nyuserre's daughter. According to Callender it is not certain that the vizier Ptahshepses was a younger contemporary of Nyuserre, and Khamerernebty is more likely to have been Nyuserre's sister (or at least his contemporary), rather than his daughter. This challenge to received opinion rests, however, on a misunderstanding for the lesser title 'king's acquaintance' (*rḫt-nśwt*) was included in the princess's titulary (Callender, 2011-b, 118); this title refers not to Khamerernebty but to her and Ptahshepses's

Fig. 13 Princess Khamerernebty kneeling at the feet of her husband, vizier Ptahshepses, see Verner, 1977, pl. 16

daughter Meretites (Verner, 1977, 93 no. 120). Moreover, the titularies in the Mastaba of the Princesses and in the mastaba of Ptashepses not only clearly state that Khamerernebty is 'his (i.e. the king's) own beloved daughter', but also indicate that her mortuary cult was secured by her (royal) father: 'king's daughter of his body, provided by [her] father' (*s3t nśwt nt ḫt.f im3ḫt ḥr it*[*.ś*]) (Borchardt, 1907, 127; Verner, 1977, 42 no. 43).

The relative chronology of Nyuserre, Khamerenebty and Ptahshepses, who crowned his career by marriage to Khamerenebty and elevation to the rank of 'king's son', may have been clarified by two further pieces of evidence. The first is a scene in the mastaba of Ptahshepses (on the south wall between the rooms 3 and 4), in which his sons are depicted in two registers (Verner, 1977, 44f. a pl. 24). The first male figure in the upper register was secondarily carved off, including the inscription (name and titles) which could have been reconstructed as 'His Eldest Son, Sole Friend, Lector-priest Khafini'. The name includes Nyuserre's birth name Ini in cartouche. Surprisingly, the title 'his eldest son' has also the first son in the bottom register, who was called Ptahshepses. Since Khamerernebty (very probably the daughter of Reputnebu) was the only spouse of the vizier Ptahshepses documented in his mastaba, Khafini and Ptahshepses Junior I, two eldest sons of the vizier, might have been twins. If so, it would be another piece of evidence supporting the theory that twins were inherent in the early 5th Dynasty royal family. The same secondary alterations had been repeated in a similar scene in room no. 10 (Verner, 1977, 100–103, pl. 51). It is clear that Ptahshepses's first-born son Khafini was born when Nyuserre was already on the throne, and that his father was very probably the king's contemporary. The precise dating of the alteration and changing of the sequence of Ptahshepses' sons remains unknown. Theoretically, it may have been done either by the tomb owner, the vizier Ptahshepses, himself or by Ptahshepses Junior II, whose tomb lies in the immediate vicinity of the vizier's mastaba. However, the reasons for the damnation of Khafini's memory remain unclear.

The owner of the tomb Lepsius no. 25 'king's daughter Hanebu' may have been another daughter of Nyuserre (Krejčí, Callender, Verner *et al.*, 2008, 229–232). Her mastaba lies south of the pyramid complex Lepsius no. 24, at the south-eastern edge of the pyramid field in Abusir.

Nebtyemneferes, whose mastaba lies in front of the east side of the pyramid complex Lepsius no. 24 may also have been a daughter of Nyuserre (Krejčí, Callender, Verner *et al.*, 2008, 22–34). Both the horizontal stratigraphy and the typological plan of the mastaba suggest a close personal link between the owners (mother-daughter?) of the two buildings and the plans of the tombs of other members of Nyuserre's family.

Sheretnebty, whose tomb has been recently found in South Abusir, might have been according to Vymazalová and Dulíková (Vymazalová, Dulíková, 2012, 339–356) yet another daughter of Nyuserre. Sheretnebty has what at the time was the so far earliest known title of its kind namely, 'king's daughter of his body [belonging] to the (pyramid complex) Stable Are the (Cult) Places of Nyuserre'. The title probably referred to the conferring of reversion offerings from the pyramid concerned to the funerary establishment of the princess. In her surroundings are tombs of officials from Djedkare's reign, such as Iti, whose names are already known from Neferirkare's papyrus archive (Posener-Kriéger, 1976, 317).

Fragments of relief decoration from the mortuary temple of Khentkaus II provide possible evidence of other members of Nyuserre's evidently large family (more indirect proof of the considerable length of his reign?). They probably feature in parts of a scene of the royal family venerating the royal mother, an important ancestor. In this scene we encounter the King's Daughter Reputnebty (daughter of queen Reputnebu?) and

[King's Son] Khentykauhor. The king's entourage also includes the 'Hereditary Prince Irenre', probably the son of Neferirkare and Khentkaus II, and 'His Son Irenre Junior' (Verner, 1995, 83 no. 186/A/78; 84 nos. 201 and 230; 86 no. 90/A/78).

On his accession to the throne Nyuserre must have been faced with a number of immediate major tasks. First and foremost he had to consolidate the legitimacy of his rule – and this included rapid completion of the pyramid complexes of the closest members of his family: his brother Raneferef (for whom he also had hastily to organize funeral rites) and his father Neferirkare. His mother Khentkaus II was very probably still alive, but it was important for him to ensure the completion and enlargement of her tomb complex. It was also in his interests to start on the building of his own pyramid complex 'Stable Are the (Cult) Places of Nyuserre' (see p. 173) as soon as possible. To do so he pragmatically exploited the site originally planned for Neferirkare's valley temple and causeway. But, at the same time, by the very choice of site for his pyramid, Nyuserre was visibly demonstrating his identification with the family of Neferirkare.

We cannot determine exactly when Nyuserre started work on the building of his own sun temple *Šsp-ib-Rꜥ*, 'Re's Delight' but can reasonably suppose that he did so quite soon and we can not exclude that he may have exploited his predecessor's sun temple, still only in the initial stage of construction (see p. 212). It was later in his reign that the pyramid Lepsius no. 24 was built; we have an idea of the dating from builders' inscriptions there that mention Ptahshepses, but with titles that do not yet include the title vizier. It is unlikely that they refer to vizier Ptahshepses' son Ptahshepses Junior I of the same name (Bárta, 2000, 45–66), and likewise the holder of some of the titles appearing in these builders' inscriptions ('sole companion', 'prince'). Ptahshepses Junior I was a contemporary of Menkauhor and Djedkare.

During Nyuserre's probably long reign several important reforms were introduced as the monarchy tried to respond to increasing problems in control of the country and the growing power of an ever larger class of officials. It was at this period that the results of certain long-term trends with their roots in social changes at the end of the 4th and the beginning of the 5th Dynasty seem to have become fully apparent. The officials no longer depended solely on the king for their power, but increasingly based it on their own property, particularly ownership of land (Helck, 1994, 12). This new growing power and wealth found expression in efforts that they made to ensure their own eternal life: they started to build big tombs, often with features originally reserved for royal architecture, with lavish decoration and many storage chambers indicating sumptuous funerary equipment and the number of offerings (Bárta, 2005, 105–125). By contrast, the tombs of members of the royal family in the period were already much more modest than before.

Either at the end of the reign of Nyuserre, or a little later, the office of 'overseer of Upper Egypt' was created. Among its first holders ranked, besides Kai, also the aforecited Ptahshepses Junior I. Basing this office in Abydos, the archaic government centre of Upper Egypt, may have been an attempt to counter the weakening of the central political power and to increase its influence in the south of the country, or the measure may have been intended as no more than a new instrument for a more efficient collection of taxes and the concentration of labour forces in Upper Egypt for the needs of central government (Martin-Pardey, 1976, 155f.; Brovarski, 2013, 98).

Under Nyuserre or shortly afterwards, archaic-sounding titles started to be adopted among officials, and the use of these older and magically so much more potent titles may have been an attempt to express individual independence (Helck, 1991, 167). There was also a change in priestly titles in the royal burial complexes, with the name of the king's pyramid being added to the earlier formula of '*ḥm-nṯr*-priest of King X'.

It was probably during Nyuserre's reign that long-term changes produced a fundamental shift in beliefs about life after death and the mortuary cult reflecting those beliefs as proves the rapidly growing strength of the cult of Osiris (see the discussion on p. 225f.) as a ruler of the dead (Mathieu, 2010, 77–107). The so far earliest evidence of the name of Osiris comes from the Saqqara tomb (from the funerary formula on a lintel now in the British Museum in London no. 682) of the high priest of Ptah, Ptahshepses whose wife was Weserkaf's daughter Khamaat. Ptahshepses died in Nyuserre's reign (Dorman, 2002, 95–110). As funerary offering formulae show, the key role as giver of gifts, and guarantor of the eternal life, had until this time been played by the king. Now that role was either taken over by Osiris or shared between the king and Osiris which may yet be another indication of some weakness perceived by the king.

It is in the context of these social developments that we need to understand the changing position of the royal tomb and cult. The economic and political significance of the pyramid complexes had been increasing since the beginning of the 5th Dynasty, and this trend found its full expression in the time of Neferirkare and Nyuserre (Helck, 1957, 94). Part of the process was the rise of the institution known as *ḫnty-š*, usually translated as 'land tenant', which we encounter at the time in connection with both the royal court (*pr-ꜥꜣ*), and the pyramid complexes. In the case of the royal court the beneficiaries were members of the royal entourage, while in the case of the pyramid complexes they were staff of the mortuary temples – often highly placed officials with access to material resources (Roth, 1995, 40–43; Baud, 1996, 13–49; Fettel, 2010, 281f.).

Continuity in the government of the country is evident from sealings of the period found in various places, from the cemeteries at the pyramids (Kaplony, 1981/IIA, 237–266) to a town by the fortress of Buhen (Emery, 1963, 119 Fig. 2 C 4-1).

In the early years of Nyuserre's reign the position of vizier was held by Minnefer, who is known only from written sources. His tomb has not yet been found, although the discovery of Minnefer's sarcophagus (Donadoni Roveri, 1969, 129 and pl. 34), now in the Rijksmuseum in Leiden (AMT 106), indicates that it was robbed at one point. Minnefer evidently directed the building of the king's pyramid complex since his name appears among the builders' inscriptions on the core of the southern enclosure wall of Nyuserre's pyramid (Borchardt, 1909, 53). Minnefer is one of the high officials mentioned in Nyuserre's mortuary temple, where, in addition to the title of vizier, he is accorded the titles of 'lector-priest' and 'overseer of all works of the king' (Borchardt, 1907, 76c and 77a). That he was an important person in his time is indicated by his relatively long-lasting mortuary cult and by the fact that the priestly phyle entrusted with his mortuary cult also took part in Neferirkare's mortuary cult by the bringing of offerings (Posener-Kriéger, 1976, 590).

Minnefer was probably succeeded in the office of vizier by Ptahshepses. We already encounter a 'sole companion Ptahshepses' in inscriptions in Sahure's mortuary temple (Borchardt, 1913, Blatt 50 and 54), but this is probably a different person. The vizier Ptahshepses was probably a (younger?) contemporary of Nyuserre and held this office after Minnefer in the second half of the reign of Nyuserre. This dating agrees with that of Strudwick (Strudwick, 1985, 89f.).

It is believed that the office of vizier was also held by Pehenukai and Sekhemankhptah in Nyuserre's reign. References to domains of Sahure and Neferirkare in the tomb of Pehenukai (Jacquet-Gordon, 1962, 366–369) may have influenced Cherpion (Cherpion, 1989, 66 n. 96 and 228) when she dated Pehenukai's tomb to the reign of Neferirkare. Strudwick (Strudwick, 1985, 84f.), by contrast, dates Pehenukai to the late years of the reign of Nyuserre, partly on the basis of the horizontal-stratigraphic context of his tomb (D 70) in the cemetery in northern Saqqara. Harpur (Harpur, 1987, 191, 212) is in partial agreement, dating Pehenukai's tomb to the period of late Nyuserre to mid Isesi on the basis of its decoration.

The type of the false door in the tomb of Sekhemankhptah led Strudwick (Strudwick, 1985, 134f.) to date his vizierate to the middle period of Nyuserre's reign. Harpur (Harpur, 1987, 167 and 214) favours a later dating – sometime from mid Djedkare to Wenis, on the basis of analysis of the decoration of Sekhemankhptah's tomb in Giza (Giza G 7152) (Badawy, 1976, 15–24). The dating of Sekhemankhptah's vizierate is therefore uncertain.

Strudwick (Strudwick, 1985, 142–144) argues from the position of the tomb of Kai (D 19) in the cemetery in north Saqqara, and from the typological features of his false door, that this official lived early in the reign of Nyuserre and may have been one of the first of the king's viziers. Harpur believes that Kai's tomb was built in the reign of Djedkare (Harpur, 1987, 40) and her view is supported by the siting of Kai's tomb north of the Step Pyramid, where there are tombs from the reign of Djedkare. However, during recent excavation of the Headless Pyramid in Saqqara, a complex mostly attributed to Menkauhor, a pit was revealed east of the antechamber which the excavator of the pyramid, Hawass, interprets as the remains of a serdab. If so, it would be the earliest piece of evidence of a serdab – the meaning of which has been linked to the cult of Osiris (Mathieu, 1997, 289–302). Is it therefore possible that Kai began his career as a vizier only in the late reign of Nyuserre or in the time of Menkauhor and continued in this office to the early years of the reign of Djedkare?

Kai has been considered probably the first to hold the office of 'overseer of Upper Egypt' and the newly defined supreme judicial office of 'overseer of Six Great Mansions'. According to Martinet (Martinet, 2011, 175), the office of 'overseer of Upper Egypt' was introduced in order to improve the administration of the southern part of the country which, compared to the Delta, was somewhat neglected by the kings of the 4th Dynasty. Brovarski (Brovarski, 2013, 98) inferred from the inscription of Weni that the main task of 'overseer of Upper Egypt' was "tax collection and financial management".

Both written and material evidence from the reign of Nyuserre testify to an active foreign policy in all areas of interest to Egypt. A rock stela in the name of Nyuserre (Gardiner, Peet, Černý, 1957/II, 59f. no. 10, I pl. VI.10), today in the Egyptian Museum in Cairo (JE 38570), was found in Wadi Maghara in the Sinai. The inscription gives the king's name and titulary and an apotropaic formula concerning the destruction of Asian nomads. In front of this inscription, and probably rather later, a large libation vessel was carved with Nyuserre's throne name on it and above it the words "Thoth, lord of foreign countries, may he give cool draughts". This may have been a reference to the discovery of a new spring or the digging of a new well, although no well has been found in the vicinity (Eichler, 1993, p. 31, No. 10). Postel (Postel, 2004, 69) dates this secondary inscription to the 6th Dynasty. Yet another rock inscription with the Horus name of Nyuserre was also found in Wadi Maghara, originally by the Lepsius expedition (Gardiner, Peet, Černý, 1957/II, 60 no. 11, I pl. IV).

Not surprisingly, Nyuserre's name was also found in the galleries in Ayun Sokhna, a harbour from which set the expeditions to Sinai. An inscription with Nyuserre's cartouche from the year of the 2nd cattle-count was found in the gallery G 5 (Tallet, 2012-a, 215–217 Doc. 245). In the galleries were also found sealings bearing the king's name (Tallet, 2012-b, 110).

A red granite bust of the king discovered in Byblos is probably evidence of lively trading contacts with this area and the worship of Nyuserre in the temple of the local goddess Ba'alat Gabal (Bothmer, 1973, 11–16.). On the other hand, the fact that the statue was found on the surface and not in a stratigraphically clear context has led Espinel (Espinel, 2002, 113) to speculate that the statue did not reach Byblos in the reign of Nyuserre but only a long time after. Another piece of evidence from Byblos is a fragment of a stone vessel with part of Nyuserre's cartouche (Sowada, 2009, Fig. 25, no. 152).

It is starting from the time of Nyuserre that references appear in inscriptions to the people known as *fnḫw*, who are considered to have been 'woodworkers' from Lebanon, with the term then extended to the whole of population of Lebanon (Sethe, 1916, 20 ff.).

A rock inscription with Nyuserre's name was found in Bir Menih, in the Eastern Desert not far from el-Kab (Green, 1909, pl. 34 No. 19). This may be the record of an expedition sent to obtain the rare kinds of stone there. Nyuserre's Horus and throne name also appear on a fragment of a stela in the diorite quarries in Gebel el-Asr in the Nubian part of the Western Desert (Shaw, Bloxam, 1999, 3). It was from these quarries that the material for the king's statues came. Nyuserre's activities in Nubia are also evident from sealings with his name found near the 2nd Cataract in Buhen (Kaplony, 1981/ II, 251f. no. 15 and 272ff. nos. 45–49).

Fragments of scenes of triumph over Libyans and other hostile foreign nations from Nyuserre's mortuary temple (Borchardt, 1907, 47 and Blatt. 8–12) have led some scholars to believe that the king launched military campaigns into Libya and other lands. Although these and similar scenes are regarded as standard features of the decorative programme of royal buildings rather than as actual historical events, we cannot rule out that there was a military expedition against the Libyans during Nyuserre's relatively long reign.

Luckily there are several surviving statues of Nyuserre, two of which are now in the Egyptian Museum in Cairo. One is a 65 cm high seated statue of the king in reddish granite wearing the *nemes*-headcover and uraeus (JdE 28466, Cairo 38). He is identified by the inscription 'King of Upper and Lower Egypt Nyuserre' on the base by the foot. The statue was allegedly found in Saqqara in 1888, but Barsanti believes it was discovered in Mit Rahina deep under the floor of the temple of Ramesses II. Together with another four statues – Cairo no. 39 (anonymous), no. 40 (Menkauhor), no. 41 (Khafre) and no. 42 (Menkaure), it was reported by E. Brugsch to have been purchased for the museum from a dealer (Borchardt, 1911, 36f. pl. 10 no. 38).

The lower half of a striding statue of Nyuserre, now in the Egyptian Museum in Cairo (CG 42003), came from a cache discovered in Karnak in 1904. Bothmer managed to find the upper half of the statue in the collection of the Memorial Art Gallery of the University of Rochester, Rochester, NY (R. T. Miller-Fund no. 42.54) (Bothmer, 1974, 165–170). The statue shows the striding king in a short kilt and with the *nemes*-headcover and uraeus, which is now missing. The right hand holds the *hedj*-sceptre across the breast, while the left arm hangs loosely by the body but with fist clenched. The statue is in red granite and 82.5 cm high. Wildung (Wildung, 1969, 212–222) considers it be a votive statue, like the statue of Sahure already mentioned, and dates it to the beginning of the 12th Dynasty, regarding it as part of the cult of kings-ancestors. Wildung's opinion is shared by Gabold who also takes the statue to have been a gift of Senwosret I to the temple of Amon in Karnak (Gabold, 2008, 176f.). In contrast, Bothmer believes that the statue was not made in Karnak and was already there in the Old Kingdom (see p. 42).

Yet another statue of the king in red granite, this time seated, was dedicated to Nyuserre by Senwosret I. Nyuserre's cartouches appear on the statue. Only its lower part has survived. It was originally in the collection of Baron C. K. J. von Bunsen, and is now in the British Museum (EA 870) (Malek, Megee, Miles, 1999, 4 no. 800-246-900).

We have already mentioned the red granite statue of Nyuserre found in Byblos. Only a part of it – the bust – has survived, and it is today in the National Museum in Beirut (no. B. 7395). The king wears the *nemes*-headcover. The surface of the statue is seriously eroded and the left and lower part of the face is missing (Bothmer, 1973, 11–16).

There is also a very remarkable dyad of Nyuserre now in the State Collection of Egyptian Art in Munich (Wildung, 1984, figs. 3–6 and figs. on the cover; Schoske, 1995, 44 and fig. 44). Its provenance is unclear: according to one version it was found in the Abu Ghurab – Abusir area, and according to another in the Delta. The dyad shows two royal figures standing beside each other with their arms hanging loosely and their hands grasping an enigmatic scroll. Both figures wear the *nemes*-headcover, both are dressed in the *shendjet*-kilt and each is identified as Nyuserre by his Horus and throne name. The one important difference is that the left figure represents a younger and the

Fig. 14 Dyad of Nyuserre in the State Collection of Egyptian Art in Munich (AS 6794). Limestone. (Courtesy © State Museum of Egyptian Art, photo Marianne Franke)

right an older man. Wildung interpreted the left, younger figure as Nyuserre – the sun god. No doubt, like his predecessors since Radjedef, Nyuserre considered himself to be the son of the sun god, whom he also worshipped in his own sun temple. In this era, an Old Kingdom representation of a king as a sun god – as Wildung assumes the dyad to be – would be unique. Moreover, such a representation would surely be somewhat suprising in Nyuserre's reign, since it was precisely during this time that the cult of Osiris was setting in. There is an alternative interpretation of the dyad, which is to set it in the context of the *sed*-festival, which is the main theme of the king's sun temple in Abu Ghurab. In this context the older figure may represent Nyuserre before the holding of the *sed*-festival, and the younger figure may show him after his symbolic rejuvenation by the festival. If this theory is correct, the statue could well come from the king's sun temple at Abu Ghurab (Verner, 2002, 1195–1204).

Nyuserre's relatively long reign, his administrative measures, his architectural monuments in Abusir and Abu Ghurab and last but not least perhaps also the name of his pyramid complex, 'Stable Are the (Cult) Places of Nyuserre', all combined to ensure that he enjoyed lasting official and popular honour and his cult was maintained in Abusir long after his death (Morales, 2006, 311–341). It is therefore not surprising that, during the brief revival of the royal cults in Abusir at the beginning of the Middle Kingdom, their centre was, besides convenient topographical conditions, in Nyuserre's mortuary temple and its immediate surroundings (Schäfer, 1908, 15–110).

I.7 MENKAUHOR

Mn-ḫʿw '[One] Stable of Appearances in Glory'
Bik-nbw-ḥḏ 'Shining Golden Falcon'
Mn-k3w-Ḥr 'Stable Are the *k3w* of Horus'
birth name *Ỉ-k3w-Ḥr*/*Ỉ-k3w*

By omitting the name of Re from his throne name Menkauhor broke with the tradition of all the 5th Dynasty kings except for Weserkaf and Wenis. We can only speculate whether this omission had some deep significance and reflected, for instance, a shift in Menkauhor's religious preferences (see the text below). In his choice of throne name, Menkauhor seems to have been ostentatiously copying Menkaure. His Two Ladies name is as yet unknown.

There is no date in contemporary records that can safely be linked to the reign of Menkauhor, but, unlike the situation regarding Shepseskare, there is enough written evidence referring to the king to reliably date his rule to the time between Nyuserre and Djedkare. The RCT, col. III.23, credits Menkauhor with a reign of 8 years, and Manetho (Waddell, 2004, 51) 9 years (Mencherés). The general view is that Menkauhor reigned for nine years (Barta, 1981, 23; Beckerath, 1997, 155). A statue of the king in the ceremonial robe of the *sed*-festival (see text below) has been discovered, but this obviously refers simply to a symbolic rather than real celebration of thirty years of his rule.

We have no direct record of Menkauhor's parentage, but indirect evidence suggests that he was probably related to the royal family buried in Abusir (see p. 59). Nevertheless, his name is missing Re which may reflect the fact that his succession to the throne was not fully in accordance with the traditional standards (father – son). The previously mentioned builders' inscription, '2nd month of inundation, 3rd day, Menkauhor' (Krejčí, 2009-b, 35), found in the tomb of the 'Eldest King's Son Werkaure' (probably the eldest son of Nyuserre), may suggest it (Krejčí, 2008, 124). Vymazalová and Coppens argue that the inscription refers to the Menkauhor who subsequently became king and consider him to be the son of Nyuserre (Vymazalová, Coppens, 2008, 38). Another prince with a name similar to Menkauhor's, Khentykauhor, appears in Nyuserre's family (Verner, 1995, 66: 230/A/78). A similar name, Prince Neserkauhor, also appears in Djedkare's family (Verner, Callender, 2002, 55–61).

We lack direct evidence not only of Menkauhor's parentage but of his immediate family. As far as Menkauhor's wife is concerned, Callender (Callender, 2011, 186) has suggested that she may have been the Nebunebty buried in Saqqara (D 18), north of the western end of the road to the Serapeum. Menkauhor's children have likewise not been precisely identified, and neither has the precise relationship between Menkauhor and his successor Djedkare; they could have been father and son, brothers or even had other blood ties. It is interesting that unlike Menkauhor, his successor, Djedkare, not only again included Re, but even emphasised him in his throne name.

We have enough evidence to be certain that Menkauhor finished his pyramid complex 'Divine Are the (Cult) Places of Menkauhor' (see p. 176) and that his funerary cult lasted a relatively long time (Berlandini, 1987, 24–34). The prevailing opinion is that the so-called Headless Pyramid in North Saqqara is Menkauhor's pyramid complex, and this theory seems to be supported by recent archaeological exploration of the monument. A pit revealed east of the antechamber in the substructure of the Headless Pyramid in Saqqara was interpreted by the excavator, Hawass, as the remains of a serdab, the meaning of which is linked with the cult of Osiris (Mathieu, 1997, 297f.). If so, it is an indirect piece of evidence of the impact of the Osiris religion on the royal mortuary cult.

Although not himself buried there, Menkauhor devoted considerable attention to the mortuary cults of his predecessors who had their pyramid complexes and tombs in Abusir. The evidence for this attention includes the relatively large number of sealings from the reign of Menkauhor that have been found in the Abusir monuments

> Fig. 15 Seated alabaster statue of Menkauhor wearing the cloak of the sed-festival and the Upper Egyptian crown, Egyptian Museum Cairo, JE 28579. (Courtesy Egyptian Museum Cairo, photo Ahmed Amin Azmi)

(Borchardt, 1907, 132; Verner, 1995, 99 and 114; Verner *et al.*, 2006, 215–330; Verner, Callender 2002, 94). Diorite bowls with the king's Horus name *Mn-ḫꜥw* carved in it (Vlčková, 2006, 84f.), which were found in the 'House of the Knife' of Raneferef's pyramid complex, may have been Menkauhor's personal gift to the mortuary cult of his ancestor.

Menkauhor was the last 5th Dynasty king to build a sun temple in the Memphite necropolis, but archaeologists have not yet identified its location. The temple was called *ꜣḫt-Rꜥ* 'Re's Horizon'.

From two sealings, one from the reign of Djedkare and the other from the reign of Wenis, we know that Menkauhor also built a *mrt*-shrine (Kaplony, 1981, 342).

Sealings from the reign of Menkauhor have been found not only in Abusir but, for example, in Abu Ghurab and Giza (Kaplony, 1981, 300–306). Other finds include several cylinder seals with his name, including the wooden cylinder seal of an 'adoratrix of Hathor' from Gebelein with a remnant of the string on which it was originally hung (Brunton, 1940, 522 no. 2 and pl. 51 no. 17). Another cylindrical seal of Menkauhor, found in Abydos, is now in the British Museum in London (no. 48989).

At the beginning of Menkauhor's reign, Pehenukai may have continued in the office of vizier. Another vizier could have been Ptahhotep Desher, whose tomb in Saqqara (C 6) Strudwick (Strudwick, 1985, 85f. no. 47) typologically dated to Menkauhor's reign or the earlier years of Djedkare's rule. Baer (Baer, 1960, 74) also dates Ptahhotep Desher to the middle- to late-5th Dynasty. We cannot rule out the possibility that the Kai cited above (see p. 71) was also briefly vizier under Menkauhor.

Several other important figures, such as Ankhmare and Neferiretptah, both of whom held the positions of 'the supervisor of the pyramids of Menkauhor' and 'the *ḥm-nṯr*-priest of Re in the sun temple of Menkauhor', lived in the reign of Menkauhor or shortly thereafter .

An expedition to the Sinai in Menkauhor's time is recorded by a rock stela now in the Egyptian Museum in Cairo (JE 38566). The inscription reads: "Horus Menkhau, King of Upper and Lower Egypt Menkauhor, granted life and stability … Mission performed by …" (Gardiner, Peet, Černý, 1957/II, 60 no. 12, I pl. VII.12; see also Eichler, 1993, 31, No. 12).

A find in Byblos – a fragment of an alabaster vessel bearing the remains of the name *Mn-kꜣ*… in a cartouche (Montet, 1928, 86), is ambiguous, since it could refer either to Menkaure or to Menkauhor. Nevertheless, Albright (Albright, 1926, 63) was in favour of Menkauhor, and even believed that one of the king's predecessors, Sahure or Nyuserre, founded a temple in Byblos.

Allegedly from a tomb of a princess in north-west Anatolia, in the area near Dorak, comes a gold-plated cylinder seal bearing the throne name of Djedkare (today in the Museum of Fine Arts Boston no. 68.115) (Helck, 1975, 79; Kaplony, 1981/II, 339 no. 38). The text on the cylinder seal mentions the pyramid complex of Menkauhor (see p. 44). The cylinder seal was either a gift to the princess concerned, or else it was evidence of Egyptian commercial contacts with this country.

According to Barsanti, the alabaster seated statue of Menkauhor now in the Egyptian Museum in Cairo (JE 28579) was found in 1888(?) in a cache under the floor of the temple of Ptah in Mit Rahina (Borchardt, 1911, 36–37, pl. 10 no. 39). On the upper side of the base, to the right of the foot, is the inscription 'king of Upper and Lower Egypt Menkauhor, may he live eternally'. Dressed in the cloak of the *sed*-festival, the king wears the Upper Egyptian crown and holds the *hedj*-sceptre in the right hand laid on his chest.

Either to Menkauhor or Teti is attributed a limestone head wearing the Upper Egyptian crown now in the Louvre (N 450; AF 2573) (Ziegler, 1997-b, 69–71). The head, 9,6 cm high, was found by Mariette in the Serapeum. Berlandini (Berlandini, 1979, 27) is inclined to see features similar to Menkauhor's *sed*-festival statue (Egyptian Museum in Cairo JE 28579) also on the face of the anonymous red granite statue found in a tomb east of the pyramid of Teti and kept in the same museum (JE 39103).

The New Kingdom saw a revival of the cult of some kings of the Old Kingdom, including the divinised Menkauhor, as is attested by some inscriptions revealed in Saqqara (Berlandini, 1976, 18–22). Among them is, for instance, a fragment of relief from the 18th Dynasty tomb of Tjutju, now in Louvre (B 48), with the representation of Menkauhor (Berlandini-Grenier 1976, 303–316 and pl. 53). Moreover, Menkauhor's name also occurs in the king list from the 19th Dynasty Saqqara tomb of Tjunuroy (Malek, 1982, 22 Fig. 1). All these inscriptions indirectly provide the evidence for the location of Menkauhor's pyramid complex in Saqqara.

I.8 DJEDKARE

Ḏd-ḫʿw '[One] Enduring of Appearances in Glory'
Ḏd-ḫʿw-Nbty '[One] Enduring of Appearances in Glory of the Two Ladies'
Bik-nbw-ḏd 'The Golden Falcon Endures'
Ḏd-k3-Rʿ 'Re's Spirit Endures'
birth name *Ỉssi*

Djedkare's choice of throne name, 'Re's spirit endures', may have been a reaction to his predecessor Menkauhor's break with the tradition, whereby Re was always an integral part of a king's throne name (the practice had started under Radjedef and the only other exceptions until that time were Shepseskaf and Weserkaf in what were very unusual circumstances). The use of Djedkare's birth name, Isesi, is reminiscent of Raneferef's name of Isi: it is quite a frequent occurrence in the records.

Kammerzell (Kammerzell, 2001, 161) has suggested that the king's throne name may have been phoneticised as *C'it'karliiduw* and his birth name as *Jasasaj*.

Fig. 16 Lower part of the seated statue of Djedkare, Egyptian Museum Cairo, no. SR 2/15691/Temp. 4.4.17.1. On the upper surface of the pedestal, at the feet of the king, are inscribed the Horus and throne names of the king. (Courtesy Egyptian Museum Cairo, photo Ahmed Amin Azmi)

RCT col. III.24 ascribes a reign of 28 years to Djedkare, while Manetho (Waddell, 2004, 51), who calls him Tancherés, states that he reigned for 44 years. The views of modern researchers on the length of Djedkare's reign diverge markedly: for example Barta (Barta, 1981, 23) estimates it at 29 years, while Beckerath (Beckerath, 1997, 155) suggests 38 years.

So far, the highest known contemporary date relating to Djedkare's reign – the year of the 22nd cattle-count – appears on a fragment of papyrus from the archive of Neferirkare's mortuary temple (Posener-Kriéger, Cenival, 1968. pls. 41, 41 A). Posener-Kriéger (Posener-Kriéger, 1976, 490) transcribed this as the year 21, but a closer examination of the figure reveals the visible remnant of yet another calculation line, and so the figure is probably actually 22. It is possible that in the reign of Djedkare the cattle-counts did not take place in a regular two-year rhythm (Verner, 2001-b, 408), so an automatic doubling of the cattle-counts for him is not absolutely certain (though precisely matching Manetho's date). Even so, Djedkare's reign was clearly relatively long. This is also indirectly confirmed by the results of the anthropological study of the king's physical remains. The original estimate, that he had lived to 50 years of age (Batrawi, 1947, 100) has been adjusted to 50–60 years (Strouhal, Vyhnánek, Gaballah, Saunders, Woelfli, Němečková, 2001, 15–23). Consequently, Djedkare may well have ascended the throne at a relatively young age.

The length of Djedkare's reign is attested by the evidently real *sed*-festival mentioned in the inscription "1st occasion of the *sed*-festival of the King of Upper and

Lower Egypt Djedkare, beloved by the *b3w* of Iunu, granted with life, endurance and power forever" on a small alabaster vase (now in the Louvre no. E 5323) (Ziegler, 1997, 464 and Fig. 1). The same formula 'may he celebrate (lit. make) million of *sed*-festivals' appears on a fragment of papyrus from Neferirkare's archive that very probably dates from the reign of Djedkare (Posener-Kriéger, 1976, 5). The incomplete text on this fragment, "palace of the *sed*-festival...", may well relate to Djedkare rather than Neferirkare, since the building of a palace on the occasion of Djedkare's *sed*-festival is explicitly mentioned in an inscription in the tomb of Djedkare's vizier Senedjemib Inti, who was entrusted with the project (Brovarski, 2001, 97).

We do not as yet know Djedkare's parentage. Theoretically he could have been Menkauhor's son, brother, cousin or uncle, but we can be fairly safe in assuming that he came from the royal family buried in Abusir (see p. 59). To judge by the available written sources, his accession caused no break in the continuity of government of the country, and family continuity is indirectly indicated by Djedkare's care for the pyramid complexes of the royal ancestors in Abusir, which he had repaired, (Borchardt, 1905, 72f.; Borchardt, 1907, 157f.; Kammerzell, 2001, 153–164) even though he did not build his own tomb there. The small cemetery of some members of his family there also suggests that he was far from indifferent to Abusir and royal ancestors buried here (Verner, Callender, 2002, *passim*).

Djedkare's relatively long life and perhaps as many as four decades of rule could suggest that he had several wives and a many-branched family, within which relations may have been complicated. Although there is no direct proof, some scholars, for example Reisner (Reisner, 1942, p. 407f.), assume that Isesiankh, Raemka and Kaemtjenenet, whose tombs (D 8, D 3 and D 7) lie between the north enclosure wall of Djoser's complex and the northern wing of the Dry Moat, were the sons of Meresankh IV and Djedkare. Meresankh IV was buried in Saqqara (D 5) north of the Step Pyramid. However, two of the princes, Isesiankh and Kaemtjenenet, were only titular princes (Schmitz, 1976, 88). Callender, nevertheless, points out that there is no evidence which would confirm such a link (Callender, 2011, 193). Kuchman Sabbahy (Kuchman Sabbahy, 1982, 87f.) and Baud (Baud, 1999, t. 2, p. 463) believe that Meresankh IV antedated Djedkare. However, buried beside the previously cited persons are some high-ranking officials from the time of Djedkare, such as the vizier Rashepses and his son Perneb, and Ptahmaakheru, *ḥm-nṯr*-priest of Re and Hathor in Neferirkare's sun temple *Śt-ib-Rꜥ* and *ḥm-nṯr*-priest of Re in Nyuserre's sun temple *Šsp-ib-Rꜥ*. This generational cluster, including Meresankh, may suggest that the queen also belongs to Djedkare's time.

An anonymous queen, whose still only partially excavated large tomb complex lies on the northern side of Djedkare's mortuary temple in south Saqqara (see text on p. 84), seems to have played an important role in Djedkare's life. The complex consists of a pyramid of unusual size for a queen and a mortuary temple of unique plan, more reminiscent of a king's than a queen's temple. Baer (Baer, 1960, 299) put forward the theory that this queen might have ruled herself after Djedkare's death and that the king's successor Wenis was not related to her. However, the very opposite set of circumstances may be true since the queen's pyramid complex, as its current archaeological investigation shows, seems to have not been finished posterior to Djedkare's pyramid complex (personal communication of Mohammed Megahed).

Although it has been said (Kanawati, 2003, 3) that Djedkare's successor, Wenis, may have been his son, an idea supported by contemporary written and archaeological sources indicating no discontinuity between their reigns, Helck (Helck, 1991, 168) has argued that Wenis was a newcomer – a representative of the powerful families from the Delta that had been acquiring ever more influence in the capital since the mid 5th Dynasty. With Wenis, these 'new families' would have finally come to power (see text on p. 90).

While not positive proof of Helck's theory, there are signs that the transition of rule from Djedkare to Wenis might not have been as smooth as Kanawati supposes. For instance, a clay sealing, now in the Egyptian Museum in Berlin no. 20386 (Kaplony, 1981/IIA, 327f.), may indicate either a corregency of the two kings or, more probably, Wenis's weak position at the beginning of his reign (see below the text).

Djedkare had two daughters, Khekeretnebty and Hedjetnebu and a son Neserkauhor, all of whom were buried in Abusir (Verner, Callender, 2006, 13, 55 and 85). We can only speculate who the mother of these children might have been, but she may have come from Nyuserre's family, which might then explain the founding of a cemetery for her children with Djedkare close to Nyuserre's causeway. Should that have been the case, then this queen herself may have been buried in Abusir, but if so, her tomb and her identity have not yet been ascertained.

We know of several viziers in the reign of Djedkare, but we cannot always establish precisely when they held their offices or which of them held the office in parallel with any one of the others. One of these men was Rashepses, but his title of vizier appears only in a letter in which the king praised his services, which the official had then recorded with pride in his tomb in Saqqara (L 16). The letter was recorded in the tomb in its very last building phase, and so Rashepses probably only gained the title in the last years of his life. Harpur (Harpur, 1987, 191 and 212) dates the tomb of Rashepses to some time between the last years of Nyuserre's reign and the middle of Djedkare's reign, and Rashepses is also dated to the middle of Djedkare's reign by Strudwick (Strudwick, 1985, 116f.; see also El-Tayeb, 2014-a, 8–9). In the recent excavation of the tomb two builders' inscriptions with dates were revealed, one referring to the year of the 3rd occasion (of the cattle-count), 1st month of inundation, 22nd day, and the second to the 10th occasion (of the cattle-count), 1st month of summer, 20th day. According to the excavator the first date refers to the beginning and the second to the end of the construction of the tomb (Tayeb, 2014-b, 171). In one final record, the vizier Rashepses is mentioned in the biographical inscription of Kaemtjenenet, whose false door Rashepses obtained in the quarries of Tura on Djedkare's instructions (E. Schott, 1977, 450).

Another vizier might have been Ptahhotep Desher, whose tomb Strudwick (Strudwick, 1985, 86) typologically dated to Menkauhor's reign or the earlier years of Djedkare's rule. Baer (Baer, 1960, 74) also dates him to the middle- to late-5th Dynasty.

The chronological position of the vizier Ptahhotep I has been debated. According to both Strudwick (Strudwick, 1985, 87f.) and Baer (Baer, 1960, 74 [160]), the vizierate of Ptahhotep I falls into the last years of Djedkare. Strudwick bases his dating on the generally accepted view that Ptahhotep I was the father of Akhtyhotep and the grandfather of Ptahhotep Tjefi (Davies, 1900), and the fact that Djedkare is the earliest of the royal names that appears in their shared tomb complex in Saqqara. Harpur (Harpur, 1987, 191 and 212), however, prefers to date Ptahhotep I to the period from the last years of Nyuserre's reign to the middle years of Djedkare's. On balance, it might seem that Ptahhotep I flourished as vizier during the middle reign of Djedkare because we cannot exclude that his son, Akhtyhotep, had already become vizier (he might have either succeeded the vizier Senedjemib Inti, or overlapped with him in the position) under Djedkare (Munro, 1993, 11 and 141). The prevailing opinion is that Ptahhotep I was the author of the famous literary work *Admonitions of Ptahhotep* preserved on the Prisse Papyrus from the 12th Dynasty.

In the middle to later years of Djedkare's reign the office of vizier was held by Senedjemib Inti, whose tomb lies in the cemetery in Giza (Reisner, Giza 2370). From the king he received three letters of praise which he had recorded in his tomb. The date on one of the letters might have allowed us to identify the period of his vizierate, but it is damaged and so we are uncertain whether it should read the year of the 16th or the year of the 26th cattle-count (Brovarski, 2001, 23). The second of these dates seems too high, since it does not match the anthropological findings on Djedkare's physical remains. If the date were the year of the 16th cattle-count, which is the reading favoured by Brovarski, then Senedjemib Inti was probably not the last of Djedkare's viziers, as Strudwick believes (Strudwick, 1985, 117). Our last recorded date in Djedkare's reign is probably the year of the 22nd cattle-count, but Brovarski (Brovarski, 2001, 23) appeals to additional indirect evidence that Senedjemib Inti predeceased Djedkare: the sarcophagus requested from the king by the vizier's son Senedjemib Mehi for his father was transported by a boat bearing Djedkare's name. Later, in the reign of Wenis, Senedjemib Mehi himself became vizier, as did another of Inti's sons, Khnumenty, who was an important architect and director of all the royal building works.

The vizierate of Seshemnefer III may have fallen into Djedkare's late reign: Strudwick (Strudwick, 1985, 139f. no. 131) argues that archaeological context places it between the early reign of Menkauhor and early to middle reign of Djedkare. However, Altenmüller's examination of the Seshemnefer-family tree seems to indicate that

Seshemnefer III should be dated towards the end of Djedkare's reign (Altenmüller, 2008, 160).

A number of other important figures lived in the reign of Djedkare. His reign saw the start of the careers of officials such as Hesi, Kagemni and Nykauisesi, whose rise continued under Wenis and culminated under Teti (Kanawati, Abder-Raziq, 2000, 21; Kanawati, Abder-Raziq, 2001, 15f.). The vizier Isi of Edfu states in his biography that he was 'governor of the nome' in the reigns of Djedkare, Wenis and Teti (Alliot, 1937, 94).

The reasons why Djedkare did not build his pyramid complex in Abusir were probably due to the same reasons as Menkauhor's – the absence of a suitable building site. The site he chose was in south Saqqara, and roughly halfway between the pyramid of Djoser and the tomb of Shepseskaf. The pyramid complex of Djedkare's anonymous queen (already mentioned) was built on the north side of the king's mortuary temple, and it was according to Megahed (personal communication) completed at the same time as the king's temple, certainly not after the latter temple. It would seem, however, that in their own choices of tomb sites Djedkare's courtiers and officials were not so keen to follow their king to southern Saqqara in any numbers. This is sometimes considered evidence of a decline in the king's authority and the rise of the independence among the high officials and propertied elite – a feature that is also reflected in their biographical inscriptions and their great and richly adorned tombs in the cemeteries of central Saqqara and Giza. On the other hand, members of some patrician families, such as the vizier Senedjemib Inti, may have had to build their tombs in Giza because their cult was already materially linked to the old foundations established by the kings buried there (Brovarski, 2001, 23). At all events, evidence for the pyramid town associated with the king's complex (Davies, 1901, pl. 29) comes only from the reign of Djedkare himself. This factor led Helck (Helck, 1957, 110; *id.* 1991, 167) to conclude that this town and, consequently, Djedkare's cult did not last long. Is this fact indirect evidence that there was some post-mortem opprobrium associated with Djedkare?

We can presuppose that Djedkare paid during his long reign due attention also to local divine cults and temples all over Egypt. Unfortunately, not many pieces of evidence support this assumption. One of them is a fragment of stone from Hierakonpolis with the cartouche bearing the name of Djedkahor, possibly a graphic variant of Djedkare (Bussmann, 2010, 51). Beckerath (Beckerath, 1999, 60 n. 2) contemplates that Djedkahor could have been one of the 8th Dynasty kings but eventually prefers the attribution of the cartouche to Djedkare. Another one is a fragment of relief with the king's cartouche, and a torso of the king's statue found in the temple of Khontamenty-Osiris in Abydos (Simpson, 1995, 7: OK 2; Bussmann, 2010, 176). According to Arnold (Di. Arnold, 1996, 50), columns have been found in the Delta bearing the name of Djedkare; these possibly came from a hypostyle hall of a so far unknown sanctuary located in the area of Tanis – Qantara – Tell el-Dab'a. Arnold's calculations exclude the king's pyramid complex as the provenance of the columns.

Like Nyuserre before him, Djedkare reigned for quite a long time, giving him a chance to react to changing social conditions which had many causes: apart from the rise in the economic and political influence of the ever larger class of highly placed government officials, religious beliefs were also changing, perhaps as another consequence of the same social trend. Concerning the religious beliefs, it was primarily the rapid spread of the cult of Osiris (see p. 226) considered sometimes as an important feature of the 'democratisation of the afterlife' (as for this questionable theory, see e.g. Hays, 2011, 115–130).

The ranking system of the bureaucracy was reformed for the first time since its introduction, and the title 'king's son' appeared again in the titulary of administrative officials; in addition, old and obscure religious titles returned into use. The title *iry-pꜥt* 'hereditary prince' again became the usual ranking title of a vizier, but without it having the same prestige as in the 4th Dynasty. Helck (Helck, 1954, 133) saw all this as an expression of the aspiration of officials to achieve personal independence, which eventually led to the disintegration of the government of the country. This interpretation and the associated theory of the emergence of powerful families of nomarchs striving for independence is not, however, supported by recent research (Andrassy, 2008, 133). All the same, the king sometimes appears to have made personal efforts, for example with letters, to cement the loyalty of such high and wealthy officials as Rashepses or Senedjemib Inti. It is also significant that especially in the tombs of middling and lower officials particularly we increasingly see depictions of fictive 'processions of estates' with titles combining the name of the owner of the tomb and the product expected (Andrassy, 2008, 134).

Djedkare devoted considerable attention to the reorganisation of the royal mortuary cults in the pyramid complexes, which by this time had already become very important economic and political as well as religious institutions. This is evident in the Abusir papyri, most of which date from his reign. The documents in these papyri include a whole series of royal decrees by which Djedkare regulated the access of different categories of temple staff, including priests and land tenants, to the offerings, i.e. to a share of the supplies for the royal mortuary cult (Posener-Kriéger, Verner, Vymazalová, 2006, 234ff.). It is not impossible that Djedkare's reorganisation related only to the royal cults in Abusir in association with his decision to abandon this cemetery and build his own pyramid complex in south Saqqara, but is likelier to have been a more universal royal policy intended to reorganise and economically secure the cults in the context of changing religious beliefs and the ending of the construction of sun temples. Given the important position of the sun temple in the royal mortuary cult up to that time, it was a major economic as well as religio-political decision.

It may be that by taking all these steps Djedkare was trying, as Baer theorises (Baer, 1960, 298–302), to consolidate or restore a weakened central power. This was also the line taken by Ricke (Ricke, 1950, 83ff.) on the basis of a number of modifications in the king's mortuary temple and an evident attempt to reintroduce several earlier elements abandoned at the beginning of the 5th Dynasty when the solar cult was adopted.

Despite all these new measures and changes, the activity of the central administration is evidenced by the seals and clay sealings bearing Djedkare's name that have been found in different parts of Egypt (Kaplony, 1981/II^A, 309–339; Pätznick, 2005, 217; Verner, 1995, 97–132; *id.* 2006, 205–270).

Under Djedkare the political and trading interests of Egypt continued to be orientated in the traditional directions: north-east to Sinai and on into Syro-Palestine, and south into Nubia. The goal of expeditions in the Sinai was 'the Turquoise Terraces' – local sources of copper ores and turquoise. One of these expeditions is attested by rock inscription no. 13 in Wadi Maghara (Gardiner,.Peet, Černý, 1957/I, pl. 7 no. 13), which has recently been re-interpreted by Baines and Parkinson (Baines, Parkinson, 1997, 9–27) on the basis of a collation of 19th century prints in the British Museum. The inscription, which dates from the year after the 4th cattle-count, is considered one of the oldest known examples of divine consultation and guidance, i.e. an oracle. This inscription has been most recently re-translated by Kammerzell who deduced from the text that in the 8th or 9th year of his reign, Djedkare ordered the demolition of the old, perhaps already damaged brick altar in Weserkaf's sun temple and its replacement by a more solid stone altar. The expedition was therefore connected with Djedkare's efforts to reconstruct the dilapidated monuments of his predecessors in Abusir.

Expeditions to the Sinai in the year after the 3rd cattle-count (if the reading of the date is correct) are documented by rock inscription no. 14 (Gardiner, Peet, Černý, *o. c.* I pl. VIII.14 and II, 61f. no. 14) and an inscription on which the date has not been survived (Gardiner, Peet, Černý, 1957/I pl. IV.15 and II, 62 no. 15). Both inscriptions were found in Wadi Maghara. Also relating to expeditions to the Sinai is an inscription from the year after the 7th cattle-count, probably also dating from the reign of Djedkare, which was recently discovered in a rock gallery G 1 in Ayun Sokhna (Tallet, P., 2010, 18–22; *id.* 2012-b, 29 Doc. 8 and 226–229 Doc. 250). The inscription records an expedition to the Turquoise Terraces under the leadership of Sedhetep. Another inscription from Djedkare's time was found in gallery G 6. In addition to these inscriptions, a sealing bearing Djedkare's name was also found in Ayun Sokhna (Tallet, 2012-a, 110). Other finds in the galleries at the foot of a mountain included remnants of carbonised cedar timbers (C^{14} dates the wood to the end of the Middle Kingdom or to the Second Intermediate Period), which were taken apart and stored here. The find suggests that it was from this place in Ayun Sokhna that boats set out for the Sinai.

On a fragment of a relief from Djedkare's mortuary temple there is a mention of cedar (?) trees *mrw* from a place called *Wn*(*t ?*) (Megahed, in press). If reconstruction of the damaged toponym is correct, this would be a reference to a territory (stronghold?) situated in Syro-Palestine. An alabaster vessel bearing Djedkare's name, believed to be the king's gift to the local temple, testifies to continuing contacts with this area via the harbour in Byblos (Nelson, 1934, 20: 1, pl. 3; Helck, 1954, 26 n. 64).

Catalogued as coming from north-west Anatolia, but without precise specification of the place of the find, are previously mentioned objects (see p. 44) from the robbed tomb of a princess that include a gold-plated cylinder seal bearing the throne name of Djedkare (today in the Museum of Fine Arts Boston no. 68.115) (Helck, 1975, 79; Kaplony, 1981/II^{A}, 339 no. 38). Its holder was the '*ḥm-nṯr*-priest of (the pyramid complex) Djedkare is Perfect' and 'inspector of land-tenants of (the pyramid complex) Divine Are the (cult) Places of Menkauhor'. According to Helck (Helck, 1979, 16f.), this was either a gift to the princess concerned, who wore the sealing stick like an amulet, or else it belonged to an Egyptian merchant sent to trade with this country. The find may be considered evidence of traditional links between Egypt and Anatolia in the time of Troy II. Egyptian interest in this region, famous for metallurgy and the production of silver, is clear, but at the end of the 5th Dynasty Egyptian contacts with the region lapsed, perhaps because it suffered extensive devastation.

In much the same way as to the north-east, Djedkare seems to have pursued an active trading policy to the east and south. He sent expeditions into the Eastern Desert (*ḫ3śt*), to the plateaux (*t3w*) and Nubia (*t3 nbw ḏ*ᶜ*m*) to obtain various commodities. Records mention three African toponyms in the Nubian-Sudan region, *B3ṯ*/*Bṯ*, *Śnsḫ* and *Ḥst* – places where gold was to be found (Grimm, 1985, 34–40 and pl. 1). According to Grimm, during the expedition the Egyptians obtained 30 trees *mnḳ* in the Eastern Desert and collected up 'all the lizards' for medicinal or cult (?) purposes. However, Redford (Redford, 1986, 137f.) translates this passage differently: "Prostrating all the multitudes, overthrowing the foreign land [...]; ...," suggesting more bellicose activities. Fragments of names of foreign countries have also been found in the king's mortuary temple (Megahed, in press).

Attested are also Djedkare's activities directed to the south. A faience plate bearing Djedkare's Horus name has been found in the temple of Satet on the island of Elephantine, on the borders between Egypt and Nubia (Dreyer, 1986, pl. 56 no. 444). Moreover, the mining of diorite in the quarries in Toshka in the Western Desert at this time is documented by the find of Djedkare's name there (Rowe, 1938, 687).

In Djedkare's reign an expedition was sent under the leadership of Baurdjed to Punt, from which a dwarf was brought back to Egypt. This expedition is mentioned in an inscription citing a letter from Pepi II in the tomb of Harkhuf (*Urk* I, 128.17 – 129.1, 131.2; Breasted, 1906, § 351). Djedkare's cartouche also appears in Khnumhotep's inscription in Tomas in Nubia (Weigall, 1907, 108, pl. 57 no. 2 and pl. 58 no. 22). These records therefore reveal an active interest in regions beyond Egypt's borders.

The lower half (from the waist down) of a seated limestone statue of Djedkare, found by Petrie (Petrie, 1902, pl. 55.2) in the temple of Khontamenty-Osiris in Abydos and now deposited in the Egyptian Museum in Cairo (SR 2/15691/Temp. 4.4.17.1), shows not only the king's interest in the temple in Abydos, but his desire to link his own cult with that of the god who was worshipped there. Bussmann (Bussmann, 2010, 473) assumes that the statue might have been placed in the temple at the occasion of the king's *sed*-festival. The upper half of the statue was originally attached to the lower half by pins. Djedkare's Horus name is carved on the upper surface of the base, by the left sole of his foot, and his throne name lies by the right sole. It is quite unusual for a king's statue to be made in two parts and so it seems likely that in the finishing stages its upper part was damaged and had to be replaced with a new part.

It is possible that an anonymous statue found with statues of Nyuserre and Menkauhor in Mit Rahina is also of Djedkare. If so, the statue might have originally been placed in one of the Memphite temples, perhaps that of Ptah. The fragments of statues of the king found in his pyramid complex in South Saqqara are still waiting to be studied (Megahed, in press).

Among artifacts which may have originally belonged to Djedkare's funerary equipment is the so-called razor of fine chert, bearing on the underside the hieroglyphic inscription 'King of Upper and Lower Egypt Djedkare, may he live eternally' (Petrie, 1927, 63 pl. 56.9). The artifact is now in The Petrie Museum of Egyptian Archaeology, University College, London (UC 11771). One curious small object dating from the reign of Djedkare is a little conical alabaster vase of unknown provenance (now in the British Museum, no. 57322) bearing two hieroglyphic inscriptions: one with the titles and epithets of Djedkare, and the second specifying the contents of the vase – fragrant oil for the king's adornment (Goedicke, 1957, 61–71).

Even though the short-lived existence of Djedkare's pyramid town indicates that his cult did not last long, there is attested from the Middle Kingdom a priest of the king's cult (Wildung, 1969, 217 n. 6).

I.9 WENIS

W3ḏ-t3wy 'Two Lands Flourish'
W3ḏ-m-Nbty 'Flourishing (one) in the Two Ladies'
Bik-nbw-w3ḏ 'Flourishing Golden Falcon'
Wniś 'Wenis' (both his throne and Son of Re name)

Wenis's Horus name 'Two Lands Flourish' evokes tranquil and prosperous conditions, but may just have been wishful thinking (see text below). On his accession to the throne Wenis did not adopt a new throne name but kept his personal name formed from the verb root *wn* and the hypocoristic ending *iś* (Scheele-Schweitzer, 2001, 153–164).

Kammerzell (Kammerzell, 2001, 161) has suggested that the king's throne name be phonetizied as *Wanjash*.

It is surprising that so few recorded dates can be ascribed to the reign of Wenis (two of them are alleged to belong to either Wenis or Djedkare), given that he is a king credited by the RCT (col. III.25) with a 30-year reign and by Manetho (Waddell, 2004, 51) with a 33-year reign (Onnus). Moreover, what is puzzling is not only the shortage of documents with dates referring to his reign but the absence of any higher dates. The year of the 8th cattle-count from the papyrus archive of Neferirkare is so far the highest date that can be attributed to Wenis (Posener-Kriéger, 1976, 491; Verner, 2001, 410–412). There are no dates among the few builder's inscriptions found in the pyramid complex of Wenis and recorded by Petrie in Sayce MSS (personal communication by Jaromír Málek).

On the basis of examination of both the available written evidence and the stratigraphy in the North-West cemetery at the pyramid of Wenis, Munro (Munro, 1993, 8ff.) eventually accepted the length of the reign attributed to the king by the later tradition, i.e. 30 (RCT) up to 33 (Manetho) years. Referring to Franke's (Franke, 1988, 129ff.) and Munro's (Munro, 1993, 11) work on Middle Kingdom chronology, he proposed for Wenis an absolute dating of 2348/78–2318/48 (±1–3 years) BC. Altenmüller also considered Wenis's reign to have been long, and regarded the later deification of Wenis as yet more support for this theory (Altenmüller, 1974, 1–18).

On the other hand, written and anthropological evidence found in the Saqqara tomb of Nykauisesi has cast further doubt on the idea that Wenis's reign was long. According to Kanawati, Nykauisesi started his career under Isesi and died (at the age of 40–45 years as indicated by anthropological examination of his skeletal remains) in the "11th count, 1st month of inundation, day 20" of Teti. Kanawati concluded that the 30-year reign with which Wenis is credited on the basis of the RCT is at odds with the results of the anthropological examination of Nykauisesi's skeletal remains and such biographical information as we have about him. In Kanawati's view, Wenis cannot have reigned for more than 15 years (Kanawati, 2001, 1f.; Kanawati, Abder-Raziq, 2000, 22). Though the mostly biennial cattle-count seems to have prevailed during the reign of Teti, the chronological interpretation of this date raises some questions which were discussed in more detail by Baud (Baud, 2006, 154f.).

More light on the question of Wenis's age and the possible length of his reign may be shed by the study of four fragments of the king's mummy (TR 2.12.25.1), which were found in his pyramid and together with fragments of the king's sarcophagus (JE 25029) are now in the keeping of the Egyptian Museum in Cairo.

The parentage of Wenis continues to be shrouded in mystery. In the preceding text we mentioned that Wenis might have been the son of Djedkare, but it is not quite clear whether he was also the son of the anonymous queen buried close to Djedkare's pyramid complex. Callender argues that Wenis could indeed have been the son of this anonymous queen (Callender, 2011-a, 191). There are, however, other theories. For example, Schneider (Schneider, 1996, 475) assumes that the king's simple name and commoner wife suggest Wenis may not have been a member of the royal line. However, the commoner wife is not a determining factor since most of the kings married also commoners. One highly original and somewhat daring theory (already mentioned) has been proposed by Helck (Helck, 1991, 163–168, and *id.* 1994, 103–106). He believes that Wenis was a representative of the rich and powerful 'new families', who came from the Delta and in the preceding period had been moving to the capital and taking important positions there. Altenmüller (Altenmüller, 1974, 12f.) believes that Wenis may have ascended the throne against the will of the ruling 5th Dynasty family. Wenis's demolition of earlier, 2nd Dynasty royal tombs, plundered and burnt thoroughly at the end of the 2nd Dynasty, as well as a group of recent private tombs (is it suggestive of royal punishment?) in order to clear the site for the construction of his pyramid complex in central Saqqara, in the vicinity of the tomb of Djoser, might also be regarded as evidence of an effort to assert tradition as Weserkaf previously did.

From blocks bearing the name of Djedkare excavated in the pyramid complex of Wenis, Lauer concluded that Wenis's accession to the throne was preceded by a conflict with his predecessor (Lauer, 1939, 454). Lauer's view even became the basis for the later proposal (Baer, 1960, 297ff.) that Wenis rather than Teti was the founder of the 6th Dynasty.

These theories on Wenis's origin were reviewed and challenged by Munro (Munro, 1993, 8–20) who argued that the blocks used in the construction of Wenis's pyramid temple which bear Djedkare's name did not necessarily indicate a violent transition between the two reigns. Baud and Dobrev (Baud, Dobrev, 1995, 57f.) agreed that the blocks are not evidence of the demolition of a monument of Djedkare by Wenis. Stadelmann (Stadelmann, 1994, 329) concurred, and went on to suggest that the blocks might simply have been materials re-used by Khamwaset in his reconstruction of Wenis's pyramid temple. Munro's view is supported by a range of indirect evidence. For example in Wenis's complex we encounter basiloform names of officials containing the name of his precedessor Isesi with no signs of damage. Continuity is also suggested by cases of high officials such as Senedjemib Mehi, who started his career under Djedkare and became vizier under Wenis, and who calls himself the *im3ḫw* of both kings. Stable conditions and continuity may likewise by inferred from the building of the tomb complex of Ptahhotep I, his son Akhtyhotep and grandson Ptahhotep II, started under Djedkare and completed without problems under Wenis, and so forth.

On the other hand, the questions raised by material coming from an earlier demolished building and recycled in Wenis's pyramid complex have been reignited by a recent discovery made by Yousef (Yousef, 2011, 820–822 and pls. 43–45; 2014, 14–19) during photo-documentation of Wenis's burial chamber. Surprisingly, it turned out that two huge calcite blocks, on which there is a scene in low relief depicting a king standing in a boat and harpooning a hippopotamus (see p. 183) had been used secondarily in the north and south wall of the burial complex of Wenis. Discernible by the king's head there are remnants of Horus name, of which the first sign *mḏd* survived only partly but the last letter *w* can be identified with certainty. The most likely possibility is therefore Khufu's Horus name *Mḏdw*. The find prompts further questions about the unscrupulous exploitation of part of older (already damaged?) buildings, probably the declining economic situation of the country and also the circumstances in which Wenis came to the throne and embarked on the building of his own pyramid complex.

Another object that raises questions about the relationship between Wenis and his precedessor Djedkare is the previously mentioned clay sealing (now in the Egyptian Museum Berlin no. 20386) (Kaplony, 1981/II^{A}, 327f.) discovered by Ludwig Borchardt during excavations in Neferirkare's pyramid temple in Abusir. According to the text imprinted on the clay sealing, among the seal bearer's titles was that of a '*wꜥb*-priest of the pyramid complex Perfect Are The Cult Places of Wenis'. Surprisingly, the sealing bears the Horus name of Djedkare.

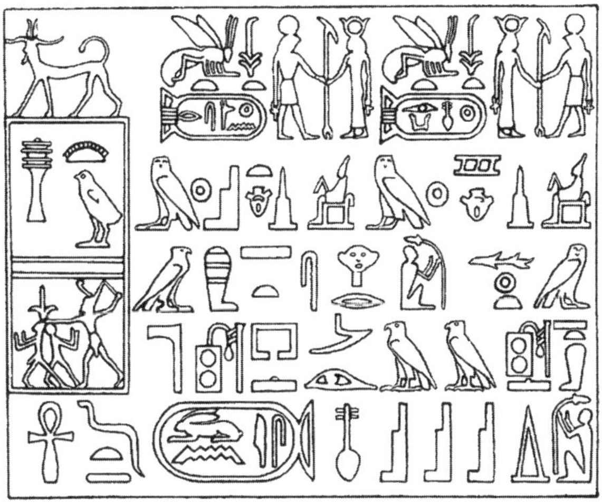

Fig. 17 Text on a sealing (Ägyptisches Museum Berlin no. 20386) bearing Djedkare's Horus name and the name of the pyramid complex of Wenis, see Kaplony, 1981/IIB, pl. 88 no. 23

There is a consensus among Egyptologists that the Horus name on seals and sealings, as well as in administrative papyri and other administrative documents, represents the reigning king under which the document was issued. As Goedicke (Goedicke, 1961, 70) pointed out some time ago, a sealing issued for an official and bearing a king's Horus name authorised that official to carry out his office in the king's name, i.e. the Horus name on the Old Kingdom seals was reserved for the ruling king. In the case of the sealing under discussion, however, the Horus name of Djedkare antedates the building of the funerary monument of his successor Wenis. Kaplony sees this as evidence of a co-regency between Djedkare and Wenis – which would probably imply the relationship of father and son. Yet in the case of a co-regency, we would expect the Horus names of the two co-ruling kings, Djedkare and Wenis. If there was no co-regency, might not the sealing be evidence that Wenis's dynastic legitimacy was weak in the early years of his reign and so he had to rely on the authority of his predecessor? Was Wenis not of full blood royal? Was there a dispute on the succession due to the several wives and children in Djedkare's family?

As the South Saqqara Annals have definitively confirmed, Seshseshet I was the mother of Wenis's successor Teti (Baud, Dobrev, 1995, 27f.). The relationship of Seshseshet I to Teti is quoted in the Ebers Papyrus, in connection with a recipe for long hair (Yoyotte, 1957, 91–98). A block with the title 'mother of the king of Upper and Lower Egypt' and the Horus name of Teti was found together with other broken blocks in the pyramid complex of Pepi I (see e.g. Leclant, 1971, 233 and pl. 31, fig. 23), in a state indicating deliberate damage to her tomb. Clearly the destruction of the building needs to be understood in the wider context of events that followed the (violent?) death of Teti and left their mark on the brief reign of Weserkare and the beginning of the reign of Pepi I. Jánosi (Jánosi, 1996, 37f.), for example, believes that Pepi I either destroyed the tomb of his grandmother or else her tomb had already been destroyed and the king simply re-used some blocks from it.

The origins of Seshseshet I has been the subject of debate for many years which has been reviewed by Callender (Callender, 2011-a, 206–214). Though the mother of a king (Teti), her spouse is not quite obvious. The problem arises from the absence in the known titulary of Seshseshet I of the title of 'king's daughter' and 'king's wife', raising doubts as to whether she was Wenis's wife. Stasser (Stasser, 2013, 66f.), following Kanawati (Kanawati, 2010, 119–120), assumes that Seshseshet I was not a spouse of Wenis but a relative (sister?, cousin?) of one of his queens, Nebet. This is, however, a rather doubtful conjecture. A mere conjecture is also the conclusion that the family of Seshseshet I came from Delta.

The problem of Seshseshet I is complicated by the fact that there may have been another queen of the same name, Seshseshet II, considered to have been the wife of Teti, who lived at roughly the same time (Callender, 2011-a, 228–230). One solution to the puzzle has been suggested by Altenmüller (Altenmüller, 1990, 7–20), who argues that Teti's father may not have been Wenis but the king's son Shepes(pu)ptah (see the text below). This theory, supported by Baud (Baud, 1999, 580), is considered doubtful by Callender (Callender, 2011-a, 213).

A pyramid in the cemetery, close to Teti's pyramid, which was discovered in 1995 and in 2009 excavated by Hawass, has been ascribed to Seshseshet II (Hawass, 2011, 175–189). Hawass admits that there is no direct proof that the pyramid belongs to Sheshseshet II, but bases the identification on the horizontal stratigraphy in Teti's cemetery and the fact that her pyramid has not yet been found elsewhere. On the other hand he does not exclude the possibility verbally suggested by Philippe

Collombert (based on the text on a fragment of papyrus found in 1939 by Lauer south of the pyramid of Wenis) that the pyramid might belong to Hetepheres or Tjetu, both previously unknown and possible wives of Teti. Callender (Callender, 2011-a, 209) doubts that this pyramid belongs to Seshseshet II, because her monument seems to have been built at South Saqqara, and it is improbable that a queen had two such monuments.

Apart from the blocks from the demolished building of Seshseshet I, a re-used block with the remnant of the name of another royal mother, whose name started with Khentet… was found in the masonry of Pepi I's mortuary temple. We can only speculate whether her husband was Wenis or Teti, and no records of her origins exist. According to Seipel (Seipel, 1980, 245ff.) Khentet… may have been the wife of Weserkare. Also speculative, but chronologically not impossible, is Callender's idea (Callender, 2011-a, 216), that Khentet… might have been Djedkare's wife and the owner of the still anonymous queen's pyramid complex beside Djedkare's pyramid.

Wenis's wives included Nebet and Khenut, whose twin-tomb, lying on the north side of the king's mortuary temple, was excavated by Saad (Saad, 1941, 683-5). Nebet's false door was the subject of a publication by Fischer (Fischer, 1974, 95 Fig. 1). The building was constructed in a single phase and the plans of its two parts are identical. From the architectural-historical point of view the twin-tomb combines building elements typical for the tomb of a queen and for private persons (Jánosi, 1996, 37). It is not impossible that the owners were sisters, or even twins. Both women have the standard titulary of queens, but without the title 'king's mother', and so neither of them gave birth to an heir to the throne (Callender, 2011-a, 200f. and 205f.). Even so, after their deaths they were to become the subjects (at least Khenut) of a special cult, which may have been related to the later deification of Wenis (Munro, 1993, 52). Both Nebet and Khenut were of non-royal origin which may be evidence of the Wenis's efforts to strengthen his weak political position by allying himself with families of influential commoners.

The origin of Wenis's successor Teti is not quite obvious either. As already noted, an opinion prevails that Teti might have been his son. Besides Teti and the previously mentioned Shepes(pu)ptah, Wenisankh is another whose father may have been Wenis. Significantly, neither Wenisankh nor Shepes(pu)ptah bears the title 'eldest king's son of his body'. Nevertheless, Wenisankh was according to Munro (Munro, 1993, 21) Wenis' son who predeceased the king and also Schmitz (Schmitz, 1976, 89f.) seems to prefer Wenisankh's filial relation to Wenis. Baud (Baud, 1999, 422) takes Wenisankh's royal parentage for unknown. An assumption (Onderka, 2009, 64) that Wenisankh was a commoner born in the first half of Djedkare's reign who changed his name to Wenisankh after Wenis's accession to the throne and died, before reaching full maturity, in about 10th regnal year of Wenis, is confused. To sum it up, Wenisankh's name and title 'king's son', and position of his tomb in the Saqqara cemetery, suggest a link with Wenis but there is no safe evidence for the relationship. If he were Wenis' son, he might well have predeceased his father.

Obscurities surround Prince Shepes(pu)ptah buried (re-buried?) on the terrace by the valley temple of Wenis (Drioton, 1944, 77–90; Brunton, 1947, 125–133). The problem is that Shepes(pu)ptah's sarcophagus, made of dark greywacke, is typologically older than the archaeological context of his burial, and its shape resembles that of Menkaure and Shepseskaf. According to Brunton, who examined and published the burial, Shepes(pu)ptah was the son of Wenis (Brunton, 1947, 125–33). Though not fully sure, also Baud (Baud, 1999, 580) sees Wenis as a probable father of Shepes(pu)ptah. Stasser (Stasser, 2013, 66f.) conjectures that both Wenisankh and Shepes(pu)ptah may have predeceased Wenis who eventually chose Teti, married him to his daughter Khuit II and raised him to the royal rank.

Wenis evidently had several daughters. Besides the already mentioned Khuit II and Iput I, another spouse of Teti and mother of Pepi I, Wenis's daughters seem to have been Khentkaus, Hemetre, Neferut and Neferkaus (Stasser, 2013, 96f.).

One of the first viziers of Wenis's reign was Akhtyhotep, who is generally considered to have been the son of Ptahhotep I. One question is whether this vizier directly succeeded his father in the post. Strudwick (Strudwick, 1985, 56) dates Akhtyhotep's vizierate to the early part of Wenis's reign, but it is possible that he had already become vizier under Djedkare (Munro, 1993, 11 and 141) and Akhtyhotep either succeeded the vizier Senedjemib Inti, or overlapped with him in the position. Under Djedkare it was usual for there to be two Memphite viziers (Strudwick, 1985, 328). This latter possibility would fit better with the dating of Akhtyhotep proposed by Harpur (Harpur, 1987, 1987, 195, 214) to the period mid-Isesi to Wenis, in line with the views of Baer (Baer, 1960, 53 [13]).

Under Wenis the office of vizier was also held for a time by Senedjemib Mehi, the eldest son of Senedjemib Inti. The tomb of Senedjemib Mehi lies in Giza and an inscription originally on its architrave gave the name and titulary of Senedjemib Mehi but without the title of vizier. Wenis's cartouche also appeared there (Brovarski, 2001, 133). Senedjemib Mehi must then have become vizier only later in the reign of Wenis, although his career had begun under Djedkare, as is evident for example from the inscription on his false door: 'one honoured by Isesi, whom the King of Upper and Lower Egypt Wenis remembered on account of this' (Brovarski, 2001, 30). There must then have been at least one other vizier (Akhtyhotep?) between Senedjemib Inti and Senedjemib Mehi.

Another vizier in Wenis's time was Akhtyhotep Hemi, whose tomb in Saqqara, located near the causeway of Wenis, was later usurped by the vizier Nebkauhor Idu (Hassan, 1975). We can accept Strudwick's (Strudwick, 1985, 57) dating of Akhtyhotep Hemi to the middle of the reign of Wenis.

In the last years of Wenis's reign there were some other viziers who may have held the office in parallel. They include Ihy (Strudwick, 1985, 63) whose tomb in Saqqara near the pyramid complex of Wenis was usurped by Princess Idut Seshseshet (Macramallah, 1935, 12), who may have been Teti's daughter (Kanawati, 2003, 47).

Another is Iynefret Shanef, buried in Wenis's cemetery in Saqqara, probably one of the last of Wenis's viziers. On the basis of a survey of Iynefret's tomb Strudwick (Strudwick, 1985, 58f.) dates him to the middle to late period of Wenis's reign. Hölscher and Munro, however, dated the tomb to an even later period – the very end of Wenis's reign and beginning of Teti's reign (Hölscher, Munro, 1975, 121).

The dating of the vizier Khnementy is uncertain. Strudwick (Strudwick, 1985, 128) dates him to the end of Wenis's and beginning of Teti's reign on the basis of genealogical connections and the presence of cartouches of Wenis and Teti in his tomb in the Western Cemetery in Giza. Baer, however, shifts him to the time of Teti (Baer, 1960, 118). This large number of viziers, even if in double office, might be symptomatic of an increasing power and influence of high officials in the reign of Wenis and, at the same time, weakening position of the king.

Apart from these viziers, several other figures held important offices in Wenis's reign. For example, on the king's instructions Khenu,'noble of the king of the Great House' went to Aswan to obtain granite columns, and transported them within a short time to the building site of the king's pyramid complex (Edel, 1981, 72–75). Other high officials of the time included Isesiankh, 'foreman of all the royal works', and Hesesi 'greatest of the directors of craftsmen' (high priest of Ptah).

Several unanswered questions still surrounding the great project initiated at the start of Wenis's reign – the building of his pyramid complex 'Beautiful Are the (Cult) Places of Wenis'– are discussed in more detail below in the text (see p. 181). Wenis's other building associated with his own cult was his *mrt*-sanctuary (see p. 229). This has not yet been archaeologically identified, but we know of priests and priestesses who served in the sanctuary. Wenis's building activities were not confined to his pyramid and *mrt*-sanctuary. A diorite vase that was allegedly found in Ehnasiya el-Medina and now in the Egyptian Museum in Cairo (JE 39409) dates from his reign. On the vase (75 cm high and 56 cm in diameter), which Wenis may have donated to the local temple of Heryshef (we currently have archaeological evidence for the status of Ehnasiya el-Medina as a cult place only from the Middle Kingdom, but there is written evidence from as far back as the Early Dynastic Period), is the partly damaged inscription 'King of Upper and Lower Egypt Wenis, may he live eternally … unified Two Lands' A similar but smaller and broken diorite vase (seven pieces survive) bearing the inscription 'King of Upper and Lower Egypt Wenis, may he live eternally' was found in the pyramid complex of Pepy II in Saqqara (it is now in the Egyptian Museum in Cairo TR 8.4.36.3). How the vase found its way from the equipment of the complex of Wenis to the vestibule in the underground part of the pyramid of Pepy II is unclear. It is probably mere chance

Fig. 18 Greenish diorite vase bearing the throne name of Wenis. Egyptian Museum Cairo, JE 39409. (Courtesy Egyptian Museum Cairo, photo Sameh Abdel Mohsen; drawing Jolana Malátková)

that more records of Wenis's building activities in other temples and religious temples of the country have not survived.

Apart from the sealing noted earlier, which bears Djedkare's Horus name and Wenis's pyramid complex, several other interesting cylinder seals and sealings date from the time of Wenis. A cylinder seal of the priestess of Neith and Hathor was found in Mendes (Kaplony, 1981/II, 356 no. 29) and another belonging to an 'overseer of linen', in Fayyum (Kaplony, 1981/II, 381 no. 19). The largest number of sealings bearing Wenis's name come from the sun temple in Abu Ghurab and pyramid complexes in Abusir (Kaplony, 1981/II^{A}, 344–350; Verner, 1995, 119 no. 104/A/80-a; *id. et al.* 2006, 209–263). These sealings, and also remnants of administrative papyri from the complexes of Neferirkare and Raneferef, show the unbroken continuity of the royal mortuary cults and, indirectly, the administration of the country in the reign of Wenis.

Among a number of artefacts relating to Wenis is a small round calcite vase engraved with a figure of Horus with outspread wings, holding an *ankh*-sign in his claws (Ziegler, 1997-a, 465 a figs. 2–4 on p. 471–2). Engraved between the spread wings is the text 'King of Upper and Lower Egypt Wenis'. The text and image together are Horus's promise of eternal life to Wenis.

According to Baer (Baer, 1960, 298–302), under Wenis there was a major change of the ranking system of the priests of the royal pyramid complexes, which may be connected with the introduction of the Pyramid Texts in his pyramid. Baer considers this a reason to associate Wenis more with the 6th than the 5th Dynasty. He sees the change as an attempt by the king to respond to the problem of the growing power and independence of the bureaucracy on a religious level.

The evidence for foreign activities in the reign of Wenis is rather meagre. A rock inscription on Elephantine (*Urk* I, p. 69) bearing Wenis's Horus and throne names and the epithets 'Lord of all foreign lands endowed with life and power forever' and 'beloved by Khnum and endowed with life and power forever', can be interpreted in more than one way. It may be evidence of the king's interest in the development of the local temple and cult of Khnum or just the work of a royal envoi travelling through this southern part of the country; but it also may be indirect evidence of instability on the southern border of Egypt – an expedition into Nubia during the king's reign (?), a meeting between Wenis and Nubian chieftains on Elephantine (?), etc. Last but not least, just this inscription might have led Manetho to seek the origin of the 5th Dynasty in Elephantine.

An alabaster vase from Byblos (Montet, 1998, 69f. and Fig. 21 and pl. 39) and the fragment of another alabaster vessel from the same area (Montet, 1928, 86) attest continuing commercial exchange between Egypt and Syro-Palestine (Wright, 1988, 148 no. 3; Redford, 1986, 138). Such contacts are also suggested by the depiction of an Asian crew on sea-going boats in Wenis's pyramid complex. An interesting albeit indirect and uncertain piece of evidence for these relations is a false door found in Giza, whose owner Kebenwentjet (PM III, Pt. 1, 48) lived at the end of the 5th Dynasty: the root of Kebenwentjet's name is the toponym Keben, 'Byblos', and so he may originally have come from Byblos.

Less peaceable relations between Egypt and its eastern neighbours are perhaps suggested by the fragment of another scene from Wenis's pyramid complex, which could be interpreted as a military clash with the Bedouin of the Shas (in the Sinai ?) (Labrousse, Lauer, Leclant, 1977, Doc. 65/66). We also learn of military confrontations from scenes from two private tombs of the time (Petrie, 1898, pl. IV and Quibell, Hayter, 1927, frontispiece; Kanawati, McFarlane, 1993, 24f., pls. 2, 26–27). To Egyptian activities in Sinai also refer sealings found in the galleries in Ayun Sokhna and bearing Wenis's name (Tallet, 2012, 110).

The Horus name of Wenis' successor Teti, 'One Who Reconciled the Two Lands', might indirectly suggest that at the end of Wenis's weakening reign there were destabilised political and social conditions in the country, including disputes within the multi-branched ruling family, which were probably further aggravated by military confrontations on Egypt's borders. Also a number of viziers may be indicative of the same. Such disputes may have continued into the reign of Teti, who according to later tradition died a violent death. Gradually, then, a picture is emerging of Wenis as a relatively weak monarch who may not have been of the full blood royal, and who sought to strengthen his legitimacy and consolidate his power by alliance with influential private persons and high-ranking officials, while at the same time trying to control them by administrative reforms.

Nevertheless, it seems that Wenis may have been deified as early as the end of the Old Kingdom and his cult still existed in the Middle Kingdom. Altenmüller (Altenmüller, 1974, 1–18) supports this theory by an appeal to an inscription on a stela of Wenisemsaf with an invocation to Ptah and Wenis justified. The name of the owner of the stela, like the names of a number of his relatives cited in the inscription, contains the name Wenis (Moussa, 1971, 81–84).

II. ETERNAL KINGS

II.1 THE INSTITUTIONS INVOLVED IN THE MAINTENANCE OF THE FUNERARY CULT OF THE FIFTH DYNASTY KINGS, AS APPARENT FROM THE ABUSIR PAPYRI

II.1.1 The Residence (*ẖnw*)

As Posener-Kriéger has demonstrated (Posener-Kriéger, 1976, 621f.) on the basis of evidence from Neferirkare's papyrus archive, the 'Residence' (*ẖnw*) played a key role in maintaining the royal funerary cults. The Residence centralised the supply of products from the royal funerary domains, distributed these products to individual pyramid complexes and so in times of economic difficulty could function as a regulator between the consumption of the cemeteries and the needs of the state treasury. Posener-Kriéger argues that this helps explain why officials who did not belong to the central administration, had no link with the cult of Neferirkare and were not even his contemporaries, could present the king's domains among the suppliers for their own cult in their tombs. The more recent discovery of Raneferef's papyrus archive has provided us with new evidence of the role of the Residence in the royal funerary cult and allowed us to examine all the available pieces of evidence from the two archives and see how far they match Posener-Kriéger's conclusions.

In Neferirkare's archive, the Residence is mentioned in several documents. In three documents – **5** c, **82** c, **93** A b3 – there is a record of delivery of the 'divine offering' followed by a list of offering bearers. According to some other documents, various different offerings were sent from the Residence to Neferirkare's mortuary temple: **42** a (*dś, sft, ḥṯ3, ḥṯ3t, 3pd*), **43** A 1b (*dś, sft, ḥṯ3, ḥṯ3t, 3pd*), **60** A (*ḥḏt, ḥḏrt* on the occasion of 'the night of Re'), **74** B (*ḥṯ3t*).

The monthly account **33–35** 1c (Posener-Kriéger, Cenival, 1968, pl. 33–35 1c) concerning the 'divine offering' supplied by several institutions for Neferirkare's cult is particularly significant. The 'divine offering' consisted of various items coming from *r3-š K3-k3.i* (*ḥṯt, ẖ3ḏw*), the Residence itself (*ḥṯ3, ḥṯ3t, ps, ḫt-nfrt*), sun temple (*p3t*) and Palace (*id3, p3ḏ, ḥṯ3, psn, ḥnḳt*). In addition, special supplies were sent from the Residence consisting of different items (*ḥṯ3, ps, bśt, ḏw nmśt, dḥḏ*) arriving on different days from *r3-š K3-k3.i, Ḏd-Śnfrw, Ἰw-Śdfw* and those of the sun temple. The heading of the document explicitly states that 'the divine offering is brought to *B3-K3-k3.i* (Neferirkare's pyramid complex) from *Śt-ib-Rʿ* (Neferirkare's sun temple)'.

The document thus indicates that the delivery of offerings did not come from the Residence directly but via the sun temple (Posener-Kriéger, 1976, 263). Meat was also supplied from the latter.

In document **50** 1a (Posener-Kriéger, Cenival, 1968, pl. 50 1a), we find that wheat *st* and grains *pẖ* coming for the king's cult from *Ḥr-Śt-ib-tȝwy* (concerning the meaning of this institution, see p. 129) and King's Domain (*pr-nśwt*) were sent via the administration office of the Residence to the sun temple *Śt-ib-Rˁ*. It seems that as a rule the regular deliveries of various kinds of breads and cakes and also beverages came from the Residence. Sometimes special offerings were sent for special occasions (Posener-Kriéger, Cenival, 1968, pl. 60 A). There are grounds for supposing that the raw materials for offerings were delivered from the magazine (*pr-šnˁ*) of the Residence (Posener-Kriéger, Cenival, pl. 45 F) to the sun temple where they would then be processed and finished in production facilities and only then sent on to the king's mortuary temple.

This evidence from Neferirkare's archive is supplemented by interesting information from Raneferef's archive. According to document **13** b (Posener-Kriéger, Verner, Vymazalová, 2006, 225 a pl. 13 A b), different kinds of cloth for dressing the statues in temple rituals were sent from the treasury (*pr-ḥḏ*) of the Residence to Raneferef's mortuary temple. Dated in the year of the 14th cattle-count (very probably referring to Djedkare's reign), account **66** B b (Posener-Kriéger, Verner, Vymazalová, 2006, 290 and pl. 66 B b) concerns the donation of 1 bull and 4 birds from the Residence to Raneferef's mortuary temple. Fragment **67** A b is particularly important; it is an account mentioning another donation from the Residence to Raneferef's pyramid complex, consisting specifically of two kinds of cloth from the robing room, ointment (?) from the king's private quarters together with the storeroom of ointments, sticks from the storeroom of leather and mats from the storeroom of products from the marshes (?). The items specified in the account evidently came from both the king's private quarters and the non-royal part of the Residence. (We would probably be not far from the truth in assuming that the main features of the organisation and infrastructure of the Residence in the Old Kingdom did not fundamentally differ from those described in the early New Kingdom duties of the vizier, see Boorn, 1988, 310–327.)

Document **67** A b is evidence of the very close physical proximity of the king's private quarters and the Residence as central administration institution of the country. The seeming lack of clear separation between the royal seat and various top administrative institutions obscures our understanding of *ẖnw* and other relevant terms such as *ˁḥ*, *pr-nśwt* and *wśẖt* as early as the Early Dynastic Period. According to Kaplony, the term *ẖnw* 'Residence' appears as early as on the sealing from the time of Den (Kaplony, 1963, 364 and Fig. 299). Old Kingdom written sources do not offer evidence permitting us to attach an unambiguous meaning to the Residence, and so different scholars interpret the term *ẖnw* in different ways. For instance, for Helck

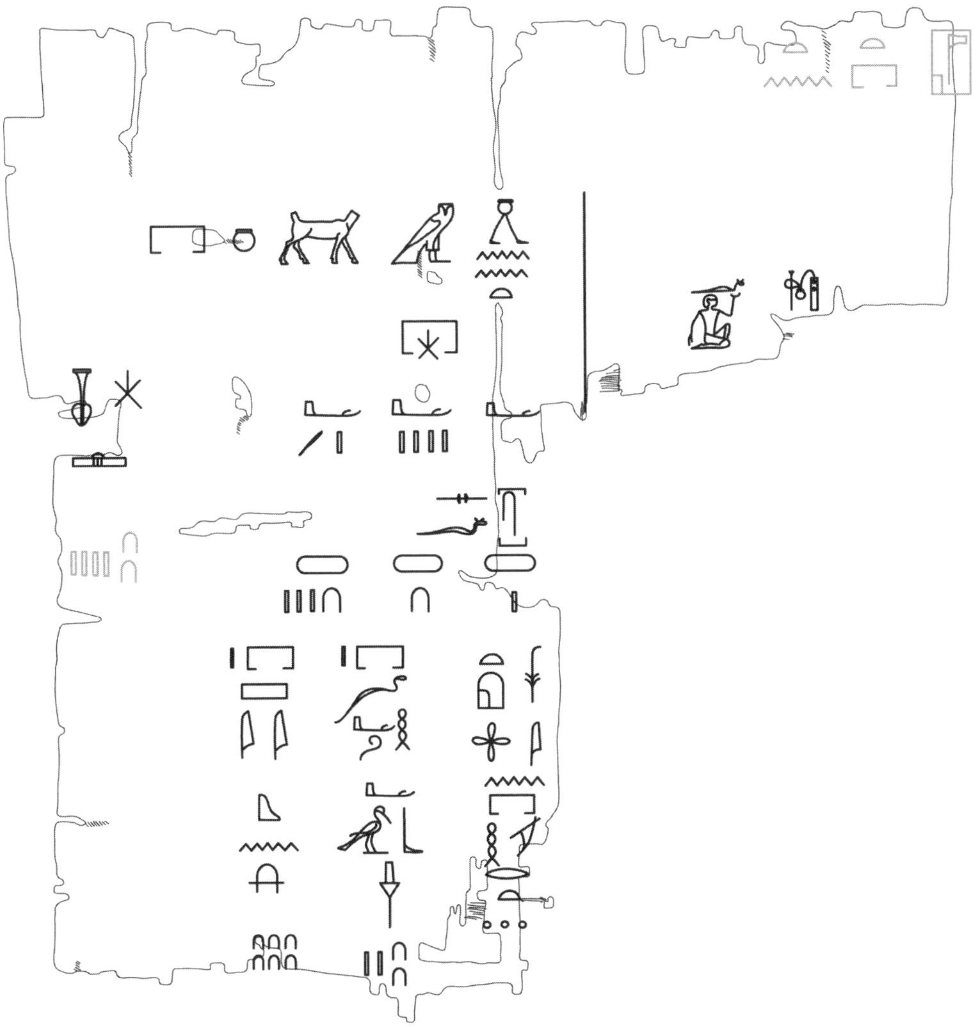

Fig. 19 Fragment of papyrus no. 67 A from the archive of Raneferef's mortuary temple referring to the Residence and its departments, see Posener-Kriéger, Verner, Vymazalová, 2006, 159, pl. 67A

(Helck, 1975, 96) the Residence was separate from the 'king's living palace' (*ꜥḥ*) and 'administration of the king's domain' (*pr-nśwt*), and according to Andrassy (Andrassy, 1993, 27), the term *ẖnw* 'Residence' refers only to the seat of the government of the country, as contrasted with the term *pr-nśwt* which refers to the king's personal property.

We owe what is so far the most exhaustive examination of the term *ẖnw* 'Residence' in Old Kingdom written documents to Goelet (Goelet, 1982, 3–182), and he too came to the conclusion that it is not always clear whether the term *ẖnw* refers to 'a building', 'a complex of buildings' or 'a whole city'. For instance, from the biography of Harkhuf (*Urk* I, 127.4-6) it would seem that the Residence meant not only the seat of government but the whole town. From the papyrus archive of Neferirkare's mortuary temple Goelet inferred that *ẖnw* was not a unity but "the name under which several institutions operated"; it also had a special administrative significance as seat of government and could function as a circumlocution for the ruler himself.

New light would be shed on the meaning of the Residence in the Old Kingdom society and economy if the physical remains of this institution could be examined, but despite all efforts its site has not so far been archaeologically identified. It can merely be inferred from the contemporary documents mentioned (and others) that it was a large institution with a royal palace and a number of departments, and components operating throughout the country. The question of the location of the Residence in the Old Kingdom has divided scholars for years and is a major archaeological challenge.

The discovery of a large settlement on the edge of the Nile valley around the entrance to Nyuserre's sun temple in Abu Ghurab led Borchardt (Borchardt, 1928, 7f.) to believe that this was the site of the Residence at the time. Subsequently other scholars tried to identify similar settlements called pyramid towns, established around valley temples and inhabited by people involved in the functioning of the respective pyramid complexes, as the Residence. Not surprisingly, they eventually concluded that in the Old Kingdom the Residence moved from one place to another and had no permanent location (Erman, Ranke, 1923, 74f.). The theory was challenged by Winter (Winter, 1957, 223) who assumed that for practical reasons settlements of workmen, craftsmen and priests could hardly have been the Residence, the place where the king actually resided. He argued for the existence of the permanent royal residence in a pyramid town. Of course, even if the Residence were elsewhere the king might have had a palace in the precinct of his pyramid complex, as is suggested e.g. by the title 'overseer of the palace of (the pyramid complex) Great is Khafre' (Junker, 1938, 175f.).

It has always been the prevailing view that initially, in the Early Dynastic Period, the Residence was an integral part of the newly founded capital, the White Wall, but that this situation may have changed when the Egyptian state and its administration started to expand rapidly and become ever more complex, especially from the 3rd Dynasty onwards. On the basis of circumstantial evidence, Stadelmann (Stadelmann, 1981-b, 76f.; *id.* 1984-a, 11) resuscitated Erman's theory and argued that in the Old Kingdom the Residence probably had no fixed location but moved in dependence of the newly founded pyramid cemeteries from Meidum to Dahshur, Giza, Abusir and Saqqara. If this were the case, then given the great administrative demands of the pyramid building projects, the Residence might indeed have been successively associated with pyramid towns on these sites.

The view that the Residence in the Old Kingdom was mobile is to some extent shared by Malek (Malek, 1997, 90–101) who considers that the Residence was originally located in the northern part of Memphis, opposite the escarpment in northern Saqqara with the tombs of the Early Dynastic elite, but that in the Sixth Dynasty it moved southwards in line with the development of the Memphite necropolis to the area to the east of South Saqqara, and eventually, in the First Intermediate Period, moved back to the north, to the area of Teti's valley temple (Helck, 1977, 63). The evidence on which Malek bases his case includes the RCT in which the kings of the Memphite dynasty are divided into two groups: Dynasty 1 to 5 and Dynasty 6 to 8. This division in Malek's view reflects the shift of the Residence within Memphis from the North to the South. What remained unexplained, however, is why Southern Memphis should have been abandoned at the end of the Old Kingdom and its centre with the presumed Residence moved back to northern Memphis (was it to do with the theorised location of the pyramid of Merykare and the re-use of Teti's valley temple?).

Recently, Goedicke (Goedicke, 2011, 132–134) has questioned the theory that in the Sixth Dynasty the area near or around the pyramid town of Pepy I in southern Saqqara became the centre of Memphis with a new royal residence. He points out that the term denoting a place named *Men-nefer* after Pepi I's pyramid complex only appears at the end of the Hyksos Period in the autobiography of Ahmose son of Ebana (Goedicke, 1974, 38), and argues that it was the role of Pepi I in the historical memory of the ancient Egyptians rather than the importance of the pyramid town around Pepi I's valley temple that was behind the use of *Men-nefer* as the name of the capital in the New Kingdom and later.

Until Memphis is archaeologically thoroughly explored, and the Old Kingdom Residence(s ?) discovered, the problem of its (their) location will probably remain unsolved, but this does not mean that new pieces of evidence cannot contribute to a better understanding of the problem. Among such new evidence is the previously discussed papyrus fragment **67** A b, which confirms that the Residence included the king's private quarters – as could already have been inferred indirectly from the title of Hemmin, a *ḥm-nṯr*-priest of Menkaure in the palace (*ꜥḥ*) of the Residence (Mariette, 1882, 199). The fragment of papyrus also shows what a complex institution the Residence must have been from both the building and administrative points of view (Boorn, 1988, 310–327). From written sources, last but not least the titles of officials of the Residence (Jones, 2000, *passim*), we know that in addition to executive offices the Residence had treasuries, granaries, storerooms (obviously, a large number if there existed special storerooms for sticks, leather and mats and other marshland products) and other secular buildings. It also employed specialised workmen such as weavers, carpenters, builders, stonemasons and even herdsmen (which indirectly shows that it had its own herds of cattle).

If we bear in mind the meaning of the Residence as the central government of the country, its complex building structure and also its function of a principal point of redistribution, it seems more than likely that it had a permanent location in Memphis during the Old Kingdom. As a place that centralised the products of the funerary domains and regulated their distribution (Posener-Kriéger, 1976, 621f.), the Residence must have had not only large storage and production facilities but also a direct connection with the Nile via a relatively large harbour. It would have been difficult and impractical to move so large a building complex, closely linked with a river harbour, from one place to another, regardless of the gradual expansion of urban settlement towards the south (Andrassy, 2008, 31). In the topography of Old Kingdom Memphis, the area delimited by the White Wall, the temple of Ptah and the Nile (which at the time took a course about four kilometres farther to the west than today, see Jeffreys, Tavares, 1994, 158), seems to be the most probable location of the Residence.

II.1.2 King's Domain (*pr-nśwt*)

The *pr-nśwt,* the existence of which is attested in the written documents as early as the Early Dynastic Period (see e.g. Kahl, Bretschneider, Kneissler, 2002, 149f.), was one of the most important institutions of the ancient Egyptian state. However, it is not the purpose of this book to examine thorougly all the aspects of the *pr-nśwt* and its evolution in the course of the Egyptian history. Rather, it seeks to point out the role of the *pr-nśwt* in the Abusir Papyri and its meaning for the economy of the royal funerary cult in the Old Kingdom. A seminal work on the subject we owe to Goelet (Goelet, 1982, 477–533). The discovery of Raneferef's papyrus archive brought new evidence of the *pr-nśwt* which enlarged the hitherto known evidence of Neferirkare's papyrus archive.

In Neferirkare's archive we meet the *pr-nśwt* three times, however, only once in a clear context: namely, in the daily account **50** 1 (Posener-Kriéger, 1976, 332f.) concerning the delivery of wheat *st* and grains *pḫ3*. Besides the *pr-nśwt*, another source for this delivery was the aforecited *Ḥr-Śt-ib-t3wy*. The delivery did not come from the cited institutions to Neferirkare's pyramid complex directly, but via the Residence. The second and third, less clear, documents **72** D^2 and **100** U (Posener-Kriéger, Cenival, 1968, pls. 72A D^2 and 100A U) from Neferirkare's archive are fragments of accounts possibly referring also to cereals. In the two last cited documents, Posener-Kriéger (Posener-Kriéger, 1976, 333) translated the term *pr-nśwt* as "la maison du roi".

Additional new evidence from Raneferef's archive involves also three pieces of papyri. An account no. **66** A (Posener-Kriéger, Verner, Vymazalová, 2006, 289f. and pl. 66 A b, c) consists of three sections separated by a vertical line. Section **66** A b, dating from the 23rd day of an unspecified year, refers to the delivery of wheat, Upper Egyptian barley and *pḫ3* grains from the *pr-nśwt* via (its ?) administratve office, *gś-pr*. These commodities are followed by a list of men and their rations in heqats. The account also includes the delivery of the cake known as *p3t*. Section **66** A c (without the date) refers to the delivery of wheat (in heqats) from the temple (*ḥwt*) and from the *pr-nśwt*. One part of the delivery was assigned for 'an offering in the open courtyard' (*imyt-wśḫt*), the second part was destined for the storeroom. Unfortunately, due to the missing initial part of the document, we do not know whether the delivery came directly from the *pr-nśwt* and the temple (and which temple is as yet unknown) or, via the Residence. The account no. **76** D (Posener-Kriéger, Verner, Vymazalová, 2006, 300 and pl. 76 D) dates from the 23rd day of the 1st month of inundation of the year after the 7th cattle-count and refers to the delivery of wheat and Upper Egyptian barley for the phyle *śṯ*. The delivery came from the *pr-nśwt* via its administration office *gś-pr*. The last document, **77** D (Posener-Kriéger, Verner, Vymazalová, 2006, 301 and pl. 66 A b, c), is a daily account referring to the delivery (probably of cereals) from the *pr-nśwt* via the administration office *gś-pr*. Also in these two last cases we do not know which way the delivery came, directly from the *pr-nśwt* or via the Residence.

The previously cited documents do not mean that in the Old Kingdom the *pr-nśwt* was a source of offerings exclusively for the royal funerary cults: the cults of private, though high-ranking persons could also have been supported by the *pr-nśwt* and *pr-ḏt* (see p. 132f.). For instance, Khufu's son Kawab was represented in his tomb viewing the offerings "brought from the king's house (and) from his towns of the funerary estate" (Simpson, 1978, 13 and Fig. 29).

Obviously, the *pr-nśwt* was an important institution directly linked with the king but what is not so obvious to us is its precise meaning and the role which it played in both the society and its economy. An opinion prevails that it was an institution which collected taxes and disposed of its own property, work force, etc. (Goedicke, 1967, 73). At the beginning, it probably denoted the 'royal household' but since the 2nd Dynasty it seems to have become a central state authority controlling and coordinating activities in the whole country (Engel, 2013, 30). Some vagueness of the institution is reflected in different translations of its name such as 'palace', 'administration of a king's property', 'king's household', etc. According to Kaplony (Kaplony, 1963, 364), the term originally, in the Early Dynastic Period, denoted a physical/actual seat of the king, a royal palace.

Kaplony's opinion is supported, and specified, by an archaeological discovery made in Elephantine. In a building lying north of a small step pyramid was found a sealing bearing, besides the Horus name of the 3rd Dynasty king Sanakht, an official's title interpreted by Seidlmayer (Seidlmayer, 1982, 303 and fig. 15; Pätznick, 2001, 142) as "the bearer of the seal of Lower Egypt with judicial authority in the King's House". The judicial authority of the King's House is attested by another title occurring on a sealing (AJ-R II,7) found in Mendes: 'one who sets right the judgement of the King's House' (Redford, 2008, 200 and Fig. 4). According to Seidlmayer, the building had an administrative and economic character, and was originally part of a royal precinct, dominated by the small step pyramid. The whole complex was a center and, at the same time, a symbol of the royal power on the southern frontier of Egypt (Seidlmayer, 1996-b, 121f.). The complex of buildings also attests to the dual, regal and economic character of the kingship (Papazian, 2012, 53). Last but not least, the complex may provide us with the meaning of several similar small pyramids from this early period, the remains of which were found scattered throughout Egypt.

The term *pr-nśwt* was examined by Helck (Helck, 1975, 96 and 173) in his seminal work on the economic history of ancient Egypt. According to him, the term denoted in the Old Kingdom "…'Liegenschaftsverwaltung' der 'staatlichen' Felder …" and (in the Middle Kingdom) even "Alles was ausserhalb der Residenz geschieht, gehört zum Bereich des *pr-nśwt*". Helck's examination of the term was continued by Martin-Pardey (Martin-Pardey, 1995, 269–285), who came to the conclusion that the *pr-nswt* "should not be in the administrative context interpreted as a king's house, a palace, and rather, that it corresponds to our modern idea of a state or, as the case might be, administrative apparatus" (Martin-Pardey, 1995, 285). A somewhat different point of view on the *pr-nśwt* is held by Andrassy (Andrassy, 2008, 27) who presumes that the term denoted personal property of the king, his estate, and that it had a broader meaning than *ẖnw* 'Residence' which pertained only to the place, the seat of the administration of the country. Papazian (Papazian, 2013, 58) assumes, on the basis of some 6th Dynasty royal decrees, that *pr-nśwt* dealt with "more tangible types of administrative requirements" such as work duties (*k3t*) while *ẖnw* was "principally concerned with actual commodity and resource management" such as imposts (*mḏd*).

Hitherto, the most thorough attention given to the term *pr-nśwt* was paid by Goelet in his previously cited dissertation. The conclusions of his research are of a primary importance for the understanding of the term. Goelet shows that the term had a multifaceted meaning in the Old Kingdom texts and could refer to:

- a source of the king's gifts to both officials and royal establishments (Goelet, 1982, 481)
- a type of property under the ruler's control, which could be expected to last from reign to reign, and which operated throughout Egypt (*o. c.* 523)
- a part of the 'central government' (*o. c.* 484)
- a source of various impositions which could be levied upon another organisation and was considered (e.g. in the royal decrees of the 6th Dynasty), together with the Residence, as the most important governmental institutions (*o. c.* 500 and 521f.).
- alongside *pr-nśwt,* or as a part of it, operated some other institutions such as *is-ḏf3*, *pr-šnʿ*, *pr-dšr*, *pr-ʿḳt*, etc. (*o. c.* 484) .

Very little can be added to the conclusions of Goelet, but perhaps the aforecited pieces of information from Raneferef's papyrus archive published after the edition of Goelet's dissertation may shed a little extra light. First of all, these documents show that the *pr-nśwt* was not such an exceptional source of offerings for the royal mortuary cult as it might have seemed from Neferirkare's archive only. Interestingly, in all the available documents the deliveries from the *pr-nśwt* included only wheat, Upper Egyptian barley and some unspecified grains known as *pẖ3*. The deliveries were organized through the administration office *gś-pr*, probably belonging to the *pr-nśwt* rather than the Residence. Anyway, the role of the Residence remains in most of these documents unclear. Were the cereals sent directly from a storeroom of the *pr-nśwt* or from central storerooms of the Residence? Undoubtedly with regard to the previously cited document **50** 1 from Neferirkare's archive, Posener-Kriéger (Posener-Kriéger, 1976, 620f.) took the position of the Residence as the exclusive distributor of offerings for the royal mortuary cult because she did not consider the direct delivery from *pr-nśwt* as probable. Though in Raneferef's documents twice occurs the date "the 23rd day", it can hardly be concluded from it that the deliveries from *pr-nśwt* had a regular character.

Eventually, the meaning and functions of *pr-nśwt* in the Old Kingdom are indirectly reflected in the contemporaneous titles of officials linked with this institution (Jones, 2000, *passim*). Last but not least, these titles also help us distinguish the *pr-nśwt* from other institutions with which it is sometimes confused namely, *pr-ˁ3* and *ẖnw*. So far attested are the following titles referring to *pr-nśwt*:

- Great one of *pr-nśwt*
- Upper Egyptian pillar of *pr-nśwt*
- foremost of the lords of *pr-nśwt*
- director of *pr-nśwt*
- overseer / (female) overseer of *pr-nśwt*
- under-supervisor of *pr-nśwt*
- inspector of *pr-nśwt*
- overseer of carpenters of *pr-nśwt*
- overseer of carpenters of the *is*-chamber of *pr-nśwt*
- overseer of the department of stores of *pr-nśwt*
- keeper of the linen of *pr-nśwt*.

Except for several ranking titles, most of them refer to the operation of *pr-nśwt*. Somewhat surprising is the general character of the titles, such as 'director', 'overseer' and 'inspector'. Can we assume that under these generally defined high officials worked other subordinated and specialised officials?

Though not a written source dating from the Old Kingdom, it might be useful to mention in conclusion the meaning of *pr-nśwt* as defined in the early New Kingdom texts known as *The Duties of the Vizier*, describing the functioning of the vizier's office and other top institutions of the country's executive. According to van den Boorn (Boorn, 1988, 310 ff.; see also Lorton, 1991, 291–316), the *pr-nśwt* in these texts:

- was a separate building complex within the residential city and one part of it was also the *pr-ˁ3* or 'Great House' – the king's private living quarters
- as an institution, it was the seat of the king and his administrative apparatus economically, it denoted the king's domain not only within the Residence but also the king's estates throughout the entire country
- administratively, it was the center of the royal government and its different departments.

From what can be inferred from the Old Kingdom written documents, it seems that some basic features of the *pr-nśwt* in this time did not much differ from van den Boorn's conclusions referring to the early New Kingdom. Obviously, the *pr-nśwt* had in the Old Kingdom a double, political and economic, character. Politically, it represented a top power institution, closely linked with the government of the country to which it was, due to the position of the king in the society, superior. Economically, it represented the king's property and its administration. The king's property could lie in any part of the country and probably involved all that was not clearly defined as a property of other physical or legal individuals. If so, in such a case the term *pr-nśwt* could correspond with the modern term "state". Because there is not available an ideal translation which could express all the aspects of the *pr-nśwt*, the most adequate translation of the term seems to be the 'King's Domain'.

II.1.3 Royal Palace (*ˁḥ*)

Though not regularly and in a rather restricted scale, the royal cult was, according to the Abusir Papyri, economically supported also by the *ˁḥ* 'Palace'. The document **5** c from Neferirkare's archive, a roster of duties, includes also "those who will bring the divine offering from the (sun temple) *Śt-ib-Rˁ*, Residence and Palace (*ˁḥ*)" (Posener-Kriéger, Cenival, 1968, pl. 5 A c). In the cited text twice occurs the preposition *m*, in front of the Residence and the *Śt-ib-Rˁ*, however in front of the Palace it is missing. The text thus seems to indicate that the Palace made part of the Residence. From an account **34** e we learn that "from the Palace were brought the breads *idꜣ*, *pꜣḏ*, *ḥṯꜣ* and *psn* and beer: 18 portions daily" (Posener-Kriéger, Cenival, 1968, pl. 34 A 1 e).

Two further pieces of evidence from Neferirkare's archive are of a different kind. On the fragment **19** A⁴, with a text referring to the feast of Hathor, occurs in a somewhat unclear meaning *ˁḥ tꜣ-nṯr* (?) (Posener-Kriéger, Cenival, 1968, pl. 19 A⁴). With regard to the context, Posener-Kriéger translated the term as "Palace of the God's Land" though the meaning of the latter remains unclear. (However, the sign following *nṯr* reads *n* rather than *tꜣ*.) The last document from Neferirkare's archive **88** B is a small fragment of the text citing "[Horus] and Seth in the palace of the *sed*-festival" and a list including one inspector of *ḥm-nṯr*-priests and eight men (Posener-Kriéger, 1976, 522). According to Posener-Kriéger, the men on the list were members of the king's mortuary temple personnel assigned to the service in the palace of the *sed*-festival. This palace, in her opinion, might have been a mere small chapel in the king's sun temple.

The *ˁḥ* 'Palace' is attested as early as in the written documents from the Early Dynastic Period. Besides titles of officials, it mostly occurs in connection with the deities (*ˁḥ Stḫ* 'palace of Seth', *ˁḥ Śšꜣt* 'palace of Seshat', *ˁḥ ḥḏ Gb* 'white palace of Geb'), sanctuaries (*ˁḥ-nṯr Šmˁ* 'sanctuary of Upper Egypt'), magnates (*ˁḥ wrw* 'palace of the magnates') and, first of all, the king who is sometimes quite explicitly expressed as

'Horus who is in the palace' or, as the case may be, 'Horus who is in the god's palace'. According to Kaplony (Kaplony, 1963, 364), the terms *ʿḥ, pr-nśwt* and *wśḫt* could in that time have been synonyms referring to the royal seat or royal court. However, Kaplony admits slight shades in the meaning of these terms: the *wśḫt* including *ʿḥ* corresponded with a palatinate and was a broader designation for the royal court whereas *pr-nśwt* and *ʿḥ* mingled if the king firmly settled in the palatinate. Concerning the Abusir Papyri and the royal funerary cult, the *ʿḥ* comes to the foreground as a seat of the king.

The Old Kingdom evidence of the *ʿḥ* 'Palace' is rather ambiguous. Besides *ʿḥ*, some other terms such as *pr-ʿ3, pr-nśwt, śtp-s3* and *ẖnw* are sometimes translated as a royal seat which is not correct since the meaning of these terms differs (Goelet, 1982 and *id.*, 1986, 85–98). Unfortunately, it is sometimes very difficult to distinguish the precise meaning of one term from each other. The Palace (*ʿḥ*) occurs e.g. in the royal annals from the time of Snofru ("making of doors of cedar/pine wood for the royal palace" in the year of the 8th cattle-count, see Schäfer, 1902, 31 Nr. 4; Strudwick, 2005, 67), inscriptions in the tombs of high officials, Pyramid Texts and titles. Athough no Old Kingdom royal palace has hitherto been archaeologically identified and examined, a common opinion prevails that in the Old Kingdom the Palace *ʿḥ* was a relatively small building of a religious and ceremonial character lacking any important economic background and, anyway, it was not the main seat of the king (Goelet, 1982, 402).

The meaning and function of the Palace (*ʿḥ)* in the Old Kingdom help us specify, to some degree, the titles of officials who served in it (Jones, 2000, *passim*). In earlier times, higher positions in the Palace were occupied by princes but since the 5th Dynasty these positions became accessible to the middle-ranking officials (Bárta, 2005-a, 119). The titles are surprisingly few and mostly of a general character such as *ḫrp ʿḥ* 'director of the palace', *ỉmy-r3 ʿḥ* 'overseer of the palace' and *sš ʿḥ* 'scribe of the palace'. Probably, to these officials were subordinated other, less important but specialized employees of the Palace. The written documents also attest that the king could have had more palaces *ʿḥ* in different parts of the country, e.g. in the Residence (Mariette, 1882, 199), broader precinct of the pyramid complex ('pyramid town'?) (Junker, 1938, 1756), etc. A specially built palace, also called *ʿḥ,* served as a stage for the *sed*-festival.

The available evidence seems to indicate that the *ʿḥ* was not a building of one standard plan but that different types of structures might have been called *ʿḥ* or, at least, determined with the sign *ʿḥ*. It also seems that the palace was a building constructed by means of light materials such as mudbricks, timber and reed mats. Of wooden poles, reeds and mats was in that time almost certainly built such a temporary structure as a *sed*-festival palace. For instance, in Nyuserre's sun temple in Abu Ghurab the palace *ʿḥ* is repeatedly represented as a tower-like building to which is adjacent a court (Kees, 1923, Blatt 9). The two structures, clearly made of light materials (reeds, matting, wooden poles), are topped with the *ẖkr*-ornaments.

There is no need to emphasize how important for our better understanding of the ancient Egyptian royal palace, its shape and meaning, its archaeological evidence would be. Unfortunately, although the written evidence for royal palaces dates as early as from the First Dynasty (for instance, inscriptions on two stone vessels mention Andjib's palace *Sꜣ-ḥꜣ-Ḥr* 'Andjib's Protection' (lit. Protection around Andjib, see Kaplony, 1963, 817 n. 810), their contemporaneous archaeological evidence is very scarce to date. The remains of a niched-façade mudbrick gateway, taken to be a palace entrance (Weeks, 1971, 29–33) has been reinterpreted by O'Connor as a temple enclosure (Adams, 1995, 65). Even more regrettable is the almost total absence of archaeological evidence in regard to the Old Kingdom royal palaces (Arnold, Palast, 1982, 646), even though their existence is attested by contemporaneous written documents; the remains of a palatial complex were, for instance, found under the Middle Kingdom palace in Tell Basta (Bietak, Lange, 2014, 7). For the time being, only from the Middle Kingdom onwards our knowledge of archaeological evidence of royal palaces begins to increase. Despite such a disappointing legacy, some features in the contemporaneous pyramid complexes give us at least a partial idea about the architecture of the Old Kingdom royal palaces. For instance, the columned hall in Raneferef's pyramid temple in Abusir – a very unusual feature in the plan of a pyramid complex – might have been inspired by contemporaneous royal palaces (Verner *et al.*, 2006, 146–152).

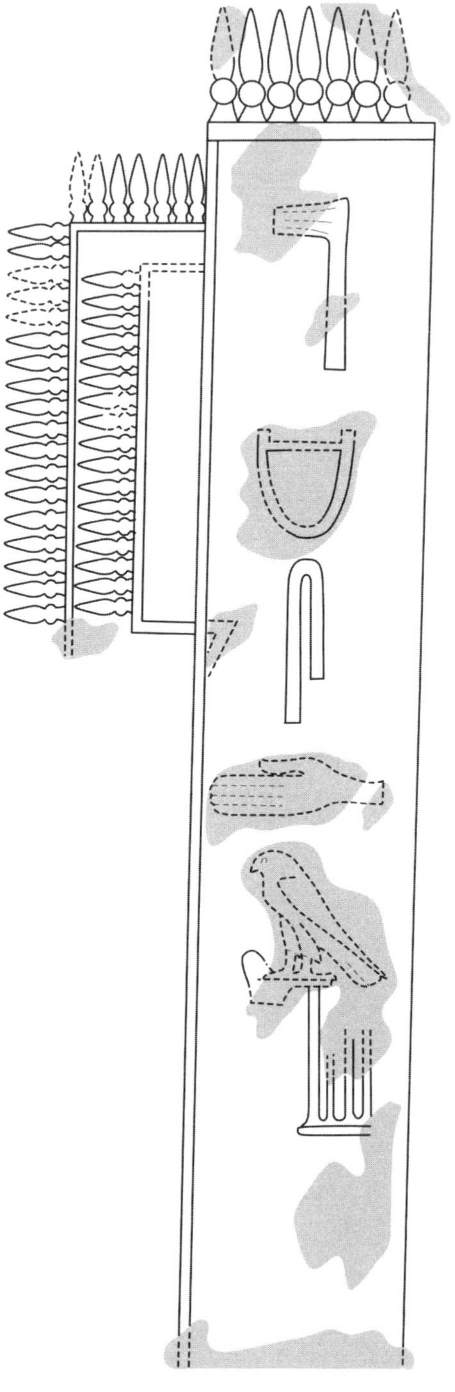

Fig. 20 Depiction of the *ḥb-śd*-palace in the reliefs of the sun temple of Nyuserre, see Kees, 1923, Blatt 16; drawing Jolana Malátková

We also can find some inspiration from our knowledge about private residences, too. A rare example of such an architecture represents the palace of governors of the Western Desert oases in Ain Aseel in Dakhla (Vallogia, 2004, 80–86).

An important Old Kingdom document referring to the royal palace is present in a cone-shaped object of red granite nearly one and half metres tall, which was found by Henri Gauthier near a small 3rd Dynasty pyramid in Elephantine in 1909 and is now deposited in Egyptian Museum in Cairo (JE 41556) (Delange, 2012, 200 no. 505). The cone, dating from the time of the last king of the 3rd Dynasty, Huny, was published by Goedicke (Goedicke, 1956, 18–24). The oval base of the cone bears an inscription in sunk relief which, according to Goedicke, reads *Śšd-Ny-Swtḥ* 'Nysutekh's (Huniys) Diadem'. As the determinative indicates, it was the name of a palace (rather than a fortress as some authors assume), and it was built by the king on the southern border of Egypt. However, the archaeological meaning of the cone is more important than it might seem at the first sight. In the area adjacent from the north to the pyramid were revealed the previously mentioned remains of a building dating from the early 3rd Dynasty. This dating is based on a sealing found in the building and bearing the Horus name of Sanakht. Besides the King's name, the text on the sealing includes the title of an official: "the bearer of the seal of Lower Egypt with judicial authority in the King's House" (Seidlmayer, 1996-a, 198). The pyramid thus probably made part of a larger complex of the King's Domain in Elephantine which included royal palace and also administrative and economic facilities. It is possible that also other similar small step pyramids dating from the 3rd to early 4th Dynasty found in different parts of Egypt (Athribis, Seila, Zawiyet el-Meiytin, Sinki, Naqada, Kula, Edfu), the meaning of which has been discussed (most recently by Bock, 2006, 20–29) since their discovery, marked the center of the King's Domain and included the King's Palace in the respective province.

Probably, the most often cited written document pertaining to an Old Kingdom royal palace is a letter sent by King Djedkare to the vizier Senedjemib Inti. The letter is recorded in the official's tomb. A not quite accurrate copy of the inscription by Kurt Sethe led to a misunderstanding, according to which, the palace, with whose construction Senedjemib Inti was entrusted, was called 'Djedkare's Lotus Flower' and its dimensions were interpreted to have been 1,220 x 220 cubits (see e.g. Stadelmann, 1981-a, 158). The inaccurrate data based on Sethe's copy of the inscription were corrected by Brovarski in his edition of the tomb of Senedjemib Inti. Brovarski (Brovarski, 2001, 97) succeeded in reconstructing the damaged signs in the relevant part of the inscription which he then reads as:

"...My Majesty has seen this ground plan {which you sent} to be considered in the court council for the precinct of the broad court of the keep of Izezi of the jubilee festival. Moreover, {you} say to My Majesty that you have made {i}t {to} a length of 1,000 cubits and {to} [a width] of 440 cubits, in accordance with what was commanded to you in the court council..."

The palace, constructed on the occasion of Djedkare's *sed*-festival, also attested e.g. by an inscription on a little calcite vase, now in Louvre (E 5323) (Ziegler, 1997-a, p. 464 and fig. 1 on p. 470), must have been a large building, since it covered the area of about 525 × 231 metres, nearly the same as Djoser's pyramid complex (544 × 277 m). As a palace built to host Djedkare's jubilee festival, the palace must have probably been a temporary construction built of light materials such as mudbrick, wood and reeds. A certain idea of such a building give us fragments of reliefs with the scenes of Nyuserre's *sed*-festival found in the king's sun temple in Abu Ghurab (Kees, 1928, *passim*). We can only surmise that it was erected in the vicinity of the king's pyramid, rather than directly in the capital, possibly at the edge of the desert near the building site of Djedkare's pyramid complex.

Another Old Kingdom royal palace is mentioned on the false door of the physician Nyankhsakhmet (*Urk* I, 38.14) namely, Sahure's palace *Ḫ*ʿ*-Wrrt-Ś*ꜣ*ḥw-R*ʿ 'Sahure's (*Wrrt*) Crown Appears in Glory'. The inscription describes how Sahure complied with Nyankhsakhmet's wish and ordered that a double false door be brought from the quarry in Tura and laid "in the audience hall of the house (called) Sahure Shines with Crowns" (as translated by Breasted) (Breasted, 1906, 109 § 239). Obviously, 'Sahure's (*Wrrt*) Crown Appears in Glory' was a type of palace different from that in which Djedkare's jubilee festival was celebrated. The mention of the Upper Egyptian crown *Wrrt* (Seeber, 1980, 812) in the name of the palace might suggest that this building stood somewhere in Upper Egypt. However, the reference to Tura and the fact, that Nyankhsakhmet was buried in Saqqara, indicate that the palace 'Sahure's (*Wrrt*) Crown Appears in Glory' is to be found near or within the capital.

However, 'Sahure's (*Wrrt*) Crown Appears in Glory' was not the only Sahure's palace. In the mid 1980s, during the excavation of Raneferef's pyramid complex in

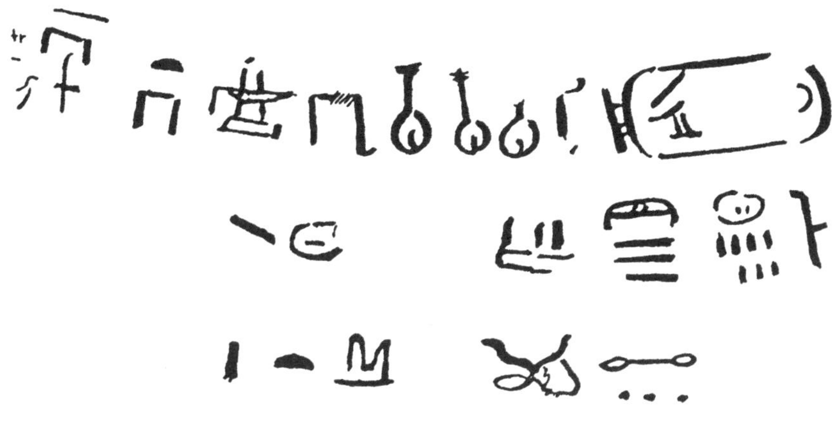

Fig. 21 Fragments of a vessel for beef fat bearing the name of Sahure's palace Extolled is Sahure's Beauty, see Posener-Kriéger, 1993, Fig. 2

Abusir, jar dockets were revealed with a reference to the slaughterhouses of Sahure's palace *Wṯś-nfrw-Ś3ḥw-Rꜥ* 'Extolled is Sahure's Beauty' (Posener-Kriéger, 1993, 8; Verner *et al.*, 2006, 272–283). The dockets, coming mostly from the time of Nyuserre, are formal dispatch notes referring to the sender of meat products to the phyles of Raneferef's mortuary temple. It is rather surprising information that the slaughterhouses of Sahure's palace were the exclusive suppliers of meat products for Raneferef's temple personnel, particularly if we take into account the existence of a large slaughterhouse called House of the Knife (*ḥwt-nmt*) adjacent to Raneferef's mortuary temple built originally to cover the needs of that king's mortuary cult. However, we need to remember that this slaughterhouse of Raneferef's pyramid complex did not function for very long. After the expansion of the early stage of Raneferef's mortuary temple in the early reign of Nyuserre, the House of the Knife was converted into a magazine. Apparently, from this time onwards, Raneferef's mortuary cult was dependent on the supplies of meat products from the slaughterhouses of Sahure's palace and Neferirkare's sun temple.

The plural *ḥwwt-nmt* indicates that the slaughterhouses of Sahure's palace 'Extolled is Sahure's Beauty' must have been a large and economically important institution. Originally, it was established to supply with meat and meat products – and perhaps only for – Sahure's palace and the royal court. Later, it apparently began to play an important role in the mortuary cult of the king and, in the course of time, some other royal mortuary cults of the kings buried in Abusir, too. Surprisingly, no jar dockets pertaining to this slaughterhouse were revealed during Borchardt's excavation of Sahure's mortuary temple. Moreover, the previously mentioned slaughterhouses indirectly indicate that to Sahure's palace there might have been attached also some other economic facilities and administrative institutions. The titles of officials operating these institutions obviously did not include the term *ꜥḥ* which would explain the relative scarcity of the titles directly linked with the royal palace *ꜥḥ* (such as *ḫrp ꜥḥ, imy-r3 ꜥḥ, sš ꜥḥ, ḥm-nṯr Ḥr ḥry-ib ꜥḥ*) (Jones, 2000, *passim*).

The palace called 'Extolled is Sahure's Beauty' took a somewhat more concrete shape in the late 1990s when new blocks from the causeway of Sahure's pyramid complex in Abusir were found. In the relief decoration on some of these blocks there is a sequence of scenes which took place precisely within this palace (Awady, 2009, 160–184). The scenes depict the return of the Egyptian expedition from Punt, the planting of a rare frankincense tree brought from Punt in the garden of the royal palace, the royal family admiring the tree and a subsequent banquet in the palace, during which distinguished officials were rewarded. The context of these scenes seems to indicate that just this palace must have been a favourite residence of Sahure's. Judging by the ships returning from Punt, and apparently anchored not far from the palace, the latter must have been lying near the capital and close to the Nile, probably at the channel linking it with the Nile, either directly or via the Lake of Abusir. Regular supplies of meat products from the slaughterhouses of this palace for the royal mortuary cults in the Abusir pyramid complexes seem to suggest that the palace also lay not far from these monuments. Theoretically, the palace might have made part of the pyramid town near the valley temple of Sahure's pyramid complex. Or, the palace might have stood at the Lake of Abusir, a natural depression filled annually with the water of the Nile flood, whose remains survived until the 19th century. The lake was called in the Ptolemaic Period documents *šỉ n Pr-ꜥ3* 'Pharaoh's Lake' (Ray, 1976, 150); in the Old Kingdom, the lake might have been called *š Pḏw* (Gaballa, Kitchen, 1969, 5 n. 6). The lake is already mentioned in the Pyramid Texts, for example, "… I am Sokar of *Ra-setau*, I turn my steps to the place in which dwells Sokar, who rules over the Lake *Pedju* …" (Faulkner, 1969, 89 Utterance 300 § 445). Be it as it may, the context of the dockets (transportation of fat and meat products) seems to indicate that the palace very probably stood in the vicinity of the Abusir pyramids.

Last but not least, the dockets found in Raneferef's mortuary temple yielded one more surprising historical information: Sahure's palace 'Extolled is Sahure's Beauty' not only physically existed but also functioned as an economic and administrative institution at least until the reign of Nyuserre. We can only surmise that the palace served as a local seat to Sahure's descendants – kings buried at Abusir and members of their families. It might have lost its meaning and fallen in oblivion only after Menkauhor's decision to abandon Abusir, the necropolis of his ancestors, and establish his pyramid complex in Saqqara.

Eventually, a question arises from the previous discussion: from which of the palaces *ꜥḥ* of a king was supplied his funerary cult? Because the cited papyri mostly date from the reign of Djedkare, was the Palace cited in the Abusir Papyri the king's main palace in the residential city or his country palace nearest to Abusir? Or, as the case might be, one of palaces of his predecessors still operating in that time such as 'Extolled is Sahure's Beauty'? From the logistic reasons, the supplies from the palace nearest to the pyramid complexes would be very practical and, moreover, there already exists evidence that Sahure's palace supplied the royal cults in Nyuserre's time. However, from the bureaucratic point of view of the central administration of the royal cults, the king's palace in the Residence seems to be more logical.

II.1.4 The *r3-š*

Among the institutions which, according to the Abusir Papyri, economically supported the royal funerary cult was also the *r3-š* or, as the case might be, *r3-šw*. The precise meaning of the term – which we meet in only Neferirkare's (not in Raneferef's) papyrus archive – is not readily apparent.

In the cited archive, the term occurs in several documents. In the monthly account **33** 1 b (Posener-Kriéger, Cenival, 1968, pl. 33 1 b), the *r3-š K3k3i* is the source of the divine daily offering sent from the King's sun temple to his pyramid complex, and it seems to have consisted of the breads *ḥtt* and *ḫ3ḏ*. In another part of the same monthly account, **34** 2 (Posener-Kriéger, Cenival 1968, pl. 34 2), the *r3-š K3k3i* was a place which only four times a month contributed the cake *psn* and the bread *bŝt,* and three jugs of the beer *ḥḏt* to the shipment of offerings from the Residence to the king's complex.

In the monthly account **36** (Posener-Kriéger, Cenival, 1968, pl. 36 A) concerning the delivery of offerings, mostly different pieces of meat from the king's sun temple *Ŝt-ib-Rˁ*, the *r3-š K3k3i* took part, but only on two different days with 17 and 20 pieces of the bread *ḥṯ* or the bread *ḥṯt* and one day with 1 jug of the beer. According to the fragment of a daily account **42** b (Posener-Kriéger, Cenival, 1968, pl. 42 b), three jugs of beer, one cake *psn* and one unidentified item were delivered from the storeroom of the *r3-š K3k3i*. It seems that this delivery came directly from the *r3-š K3k3i* and not via the Residence or the sun temple, *Ŝt-ib-Rˁ*. As a matter of fact, the two latter institutions are explicitly given as the source of offerings in other sections of the account and all the sources of offerings were separated from each other by vertical lines. This assumption seems to be supported by an individual offering of one bird presented to the king's cult by a chief physician named Khnumhotep, a fact which is recorded in the same section as the *r3-š K3k3i*. Eventually, the *r3-š K3k3i* also occurs as a source of offerings together with the domain of the King's Mother Khentkaus in the daily account **46** A^1 and A^3 (Posener-Kriéger, Cenival, 1968, pl. 46 A). Owing to the incompleteness of the text, it is not clear whether the delivery came directly from the *r3-š K3k3i* or via the Residence.

Interestingly, in the above cited monthly account **33,** the term also occurs in a plural form, *r3-šw*, as a source of the daily offerings of the breads *ḥṯ, ḥṯt* and *psn*. These offerings were sent to the king's pyramid complex via the Residence.

Besides Neferirkare's archive, we meet the term *r3-š* also in some other contemporaneous texts. For instance, according to the annals of the Palermo stone, on the occasion of the 2nd cattle-count, Sahure donated land to 'Hathor in Sahure's *r3-š*' and '(Hathor in the pyramid complex) Sahure's Soul Appears in Glory'. Wilkinson (2000, 160f.) translated the text not quite correctly as "Hathor in *r-š* of (the pyramid) Sahura is risen as a *ba*", whereas Strudwick (Strudwick, 2005, 71) did so correctly as "Hathor in the *ra-she* of Sahure and Hathor in the pyramid of Sahure". Wilkinson interprets a partly missing and partly damaged beginning of the third column of the text referring to Shepseskaf's first regnal year as *ḫntyw-š* and assumes that the latter were "... closely linked with the *r-š* and may have played a part in choosing the location of Shepseskaf's funerary apartment..." (Wilkinson, 2000, 150f.). If so, this would be the earliest Old Kingdom occurrence of the title. (The hitherto earliest evidence of the title dates from the 5th Dynasty, see Fettel, 2010, 34.) However, the reading *ḫntyw-š* is uncertain and, consequently, the suggested conclusion is arguable. In the Dahshur decree of Pepy I, the king forbade anyone "to dig in the *r3-š* of the '(pyramid complex) Divine Are the (Cult) Places of Ikauhor'" (Goedicke, 1967, 56 X; Berlandini, 1979, 13f.).

The *r3-š* also occurs in the titulary of two officials, Kha(f)isesi and Meru, from the time of Pepy I, each of whom was a '*ḥm-nṯr*-priest of the *mrt*-sanctuary of Pepy's/

Meryre's *r3-š*' (Borchardt, 1937, 120 Nr. 1438; Lloyd, Spencer, Khouli, 1990, 7 (11), 13 and pl. 8). Obviously, the *mrt*-sanctuary could have been located in the precinct of the *r3-š*. The *mrt*-sanctuary of the *r3-š* of Meryre is also referred to in the inscription from the Saqqara tomb of Duaenre (Mariette, 1882, 456 – H 10).

Finally, the term *r3-š* occurs also in the Pyramid Texts in which it is interpreted by Faulkner (Faulkner, 1969, § 2103) as 'meadow' whereas by Fettel (Fettel, 2010, 110f.) it is seen as a place in front of the pyramid complex.

The meaning of the term *r3-š* in Neferirkare's archive was examined by Posener-Kriéger (Posener-Kriéger, 1976, 616–619). She excluded the idea that it could be a toponym, the name of a funerary domain, because of the absence of the determinative for a 'locality', though she admits that a similarly constructed name of the funerary domain called *r3-š Ḫw.f-wi* is once attested (in the late 4th Dynasty tomb of Merib, see Jacquet-Gordon, 1962, 231). In her opinion, the *r3-š* was a place ('lieu', 'débouchement') in which were concentrated products from different sources of the king for his funerary cult: "*R3-š K3k3i* était un organisme économique centralisant les vivres originaires du bien foncier de Néferirkare" (Posener-Kriéger, 1979, 142). It was rather an administrative institution with its own storage, control and distribution facilities. Surprisingly, and contrary to this, the plural form of the term, *r3-šw*, she (Posener-Kriéger, 1976, 263) translates as "la porte des domaines agricoles" and adds that it undoubtedly denominated funerary domains which had no obligations in regard to Neferirkare's cult. This assumption of hers was based on the document **43** A[1] (Posener-Kriéger, Cenival, 1968, pl. 43 A[1]) in which a delivery of offerings from the previously cited *r3-š Ḫw.f-wi* was sent to Neferirkare's funerary cult via the Residence. At the same time, however, she admits that the *r3-šw* might have served to mark the origin of the bread or flour, or quality of the bread.

The interpretation of the terms *r3-š* and *r3-šw* are not easy to explain, due to the ambiguous meaning of the component *š*. On the other hand, a common opinion prevails that the meaning of the second component in the term, *r3*, is 'entrance' as a 'place of control' (see *Wb* s.v. *r3*). The term *š* was examined by Brovarski (Brovarski, 2001, 97f.) who specified its meaning in the Old Kingdom in different contexts as:

- lake, basin, water pool
- garden, plantation of trees, market garden, plantation (along the Nile levees, or on high ground on the edge of the cultivated area which was out of reach of annual inundation and therefore required artificial irrigation or were located on low lands which were protected from flooding)
- ground, precinct ('die Anlage').

To this list should be added one more meaning, namely, *š* as an area measure of 2750 m^2 (corresponding with 1 arura in the New Kingdom) (Helck, 1975, 43).

Other scholars have also examined the term *š* and helped specify its meaning. For instance, Berlev and Khodjash (Berlev, Khodjash, 2004, 65 n. d) assume that *š*, in the title *ḫnty-š*, often determined with the sign for 'desert', designated in the Old Kingdom "artificial implantations" at the edge of the desert with "each wood (put) in a special hole".

According to Stadelmann (Stadelmann, 1981, 154–164), *r3-š* was the "entrance to the precinct *š*", a zone in the transition of the Nile valley and the desert which served the inhabitants of the pyramid town as fields and gardens. It was on the outskirts of the necropolis – including the channel leading to the valley temple – but it did not include the latter. Lehner (Lehner, 1985, 136) agrees with Stadelmann's interpretation: he sees the *r3-š* as the area at the divide of the desert and the Nile valley, one in which were concentrated, stored and distributed different deliveries and which also included "check-points, docking areas for supplies and commodities separate from the quays designed to receive materials for the construction of the pyramid complex". Lehner further specifies: "It is tempting to see the entire area generally defined by the large southern boundary wall and the northern causeway foundation of Khufu as the referent for the *r3-š* of Khufu."

However, the term *š* for the precinct of the pyramid complex may have overlapped with the term *š* for the basin which served as a harbour and made part of the complex.

To *š* in relation to the territory of the pyramid complex explicitly refers the following passage from the previously cited biographic inscription of Washptah (Kloth, 2002, 330–333 Abb. 4a–4d): … *ḥḏ ḥr š ḏt nt m H̯ꜥ-b3-Ś3ḥw-Rꜥ*… "… (the tomb? of) the white stone on the funerary territory belonging to (lit. which is in) the (pyramid complex) Sahure's Soul Appears in Glory…" Blocks with the text from the as yet undiscovered tomb of Washptah are now in Egyptian Museum in Cairo (Grdseloff, 1951, pl. I on p. 141), some of them are also in the Museum of Aberdeen (Picardo, 2010, 93–104). If this interpretation of the term *š ḏt* is correct, the tomb of the vizier Washptah might have lain in Abusir or in its immediate vicinity.

However, the term *š* does not occur in relation to the pyramid complex only, it can also – in the same meaning of 'territory, precinct' – refer to the royal court *pr-ꜥ3* 'Great House'. (Concerning a brief overview of evidence for *š* in the titles referring to *pr-ꜥ3*, see Jones, 2000, 987f.) However, *š* as the 'Great House precinct' can sometimes be confused with the meaning of *š* as 'lake'. For instance, *Rꜥ ḥry š pr-ꜥ3* translated by Goelet (Goelet, Jr., 1982, 545) as "Re upon the lake(?) of the *pr-ꜥ3*", in the inscription on a stone vessel with Wenis's cartouche from Byblos, should more probably be interpreted as 'Re within the precinct of the King's House'. Sometimes, *š* can be completely misinterpreted as *mr* 'weaving workshop'. With the suggested interpretation of *š* as 'precinct' also agrees Andrassy (Andrassy, 1994, 5). She further assumes that in relation to the king, the *š* means more than a ground on which the pyramid, palace or cult structures could have been built: *š* also had a more abstract meaning of an administration unit.

After weighing up both all the cited pieces of evidence and the relevant discussion, we may sum up that, in relation to the pyramid complex *š* included not only the territory of the latter, but also the adjacent approach area from the Nile valley. The area between the Nile and the local valley temple or, in the case of the pyramids at Abusir, between the canal Bahr el-Libeini (The Pyramids Canal) (see e.g. Sanussi, Jones, 1997, 243 Fig. 1) and the local valley temples of Sahure and Nyuserre, was very probably called the *r3-š*. Obviously, *š* was a relatively large, annually flooded area of a fertile land which could easily have been used for agricultural purposes.

Obviously, the term *r3-š* had a not only a geographic but also a functional meaning. Fettel (Fettel, 2010, 113) also came to a similar conclusion. On its territory might also have stood different economic, production and administration facilities, as well as a *mrt*-sanctuary, a pyramid town (Verner, 2012, 407–410) and, exceptionally, a royal palace: Nysutnefer, for instance, was 'overseer of the *ˁḥ*-palace of the (pyramid complex) Great is Khafre' (Junker, 1938, 1756). Therefore, it seems that rather than one administrative office or building, *r3-š* was an overall name for the local economic-administrative infrastructure of the pyramid complex. Concerning the plural form of the term, *r3-šw*, it seems to have been the name for an unspecified group of several *r3-š* areas of pyramid complexes. Apparently, the offerings coming from the *r3-šw* were firstly concentrated in the Residence and only then distributed further.

Due to the character of the *r3-š* and its vicinity to the pyramid complex, one would expect that some minor deliveries of offerings produced locally would have been sent directly to the mortuary temple and not via the Residence and the sun temple. Such an assumption might be supported by the document **42** in which all the deliveries were sent via either the Residence or the sun temple *Śt-ib-Rˁ*, except for those from the *r3-š*. However, this assumption is doubted not only by the aforecited *r3-šw* but also by document **33**, in which the delivery from *r3-š K3-k3.i* was sent via the Residence.

The above suggested meaning of *r3-š* may not be in disagreement with the papyri discovered recently in Wadi Jarf. The papyri, dating from the time of Khufu, refer to the transportation of fine limestone blocks from Tura to the building site of Khufu's pyramid complex *3ḫt-Ḫw.f-wi* in Giza (Tallet, 2014, 25–49). A preliminary report on the papyri Jarf I–III with the "diary of Merer" will be published by IFAO at the end of 2014 (Tallet, in press). The discoverer of the papyri and author of the report Pierre Tallet (Pierre Tallet kindly sent the text of the paper in press to the author of this monograph) shows how important Merer's diary is, for example, for the better understanding of the way in which the blocks were transported from the quarries in Tura to the building site of the pyramid of Khufu. In the text of the diary repeatedly occur different toponyms, among them *š Ḫw.f-wi* and *r3-š Ḫw.f-wi*. The cited text seems to support the above suggested meaning of *r3-š Ḫw.f-wi* as a main administrative checkpoint and logistic background of the builders of Khufu's pyramid in Giza.

Finally, there is one more remark to be made concerning the *r3-š K3-k3.i* as the territory adjacent from the east of the king's valley temple. We know that the pyramid complex of Neferirkare Kakai had never been finished and lacked both the valley temple and the causeway. The place for the two latter components of the king's complex was reused by Nyuserre, Neferirkare's son and the second successor (after his brother Raneferef), for his own pyramid complex. Where then lay that king's *r3-š*? We can only assume that, because of the administrative reasons, Nyuserre respected the originally planned territory of Neferirkare's *r3-š*. Maybe, in this territory there existed next to each other the *r3-š K3-k3.i* and the *r3-š Ini*. But it is also possible that, in the end, there existed in this area only one *r3-š* for all the Abusir pyramid complexes the western part of its enclosure wall is still visible till now (Verner, 2012, 407–410).

II.1.5 Temple of Ptah

There is still no agreement among scholars on whether temples of gods had a direct role in the royal mortuary cult. An inscription on a block from the tomb of Persen (now in the Egyptian Museum in Berlin, no. 15004) (*Urk* I, 37: 12.) mentions Persen's share in the offerings provided by the temple of Ptah (Ptah South of His Wall) in Memphis to the Royal Mother Neferhetepes. This is a case of what is known as reversionary offering, but it is not clear from the text whether the temple of Ptah provided these offerings from its own sources or was just an intermediary in the process of their distribution. In the archive of Neferirkare's mortuary temple there is no surviving record of a consignment of offerings from Ptah or any other god's temple, but in the archive of Raneferef's mortuary temple there are two account documents that mention Ptah's temple as a source of offerings.

Document **47** A[1,2] – **48** A[3] of Raneferef's archive (Posener-Kriéger, Verner, Vymazalová, 2006, 264–266 and pl. 47 A – 48 A) is incomplete, missing the beginning and end. The document, which probably dates from the reign of Djedkare, originally consisted of at least four sections. In the heading of the second section, most of which has been preserved, is the explicit statement that it concerns a "Donation (that has been brought) from the temple of Ptah South of His Wall". Specified in the text of this section are daily allocations of different commodities for 17 successive days. The total quotas for the period of 17 days are given in red in the heading of the account document. The occasion for which the donation is provided is not stated. The list sets out these daily items for the period of 17 days:

- bread *ḥṯ3*: 56
- cake *psn*: 54
- cake *p3t Śt-ib-Rˁ*: 10
- beer: 24
- big poultry: 4
- small poultry: 8
- ox *iw3*: 13.

The following less well preserved part of the same document (**48** A[3]) concerns Raneferef's mortuary temple. Because part of the text in the heading is missing, it is

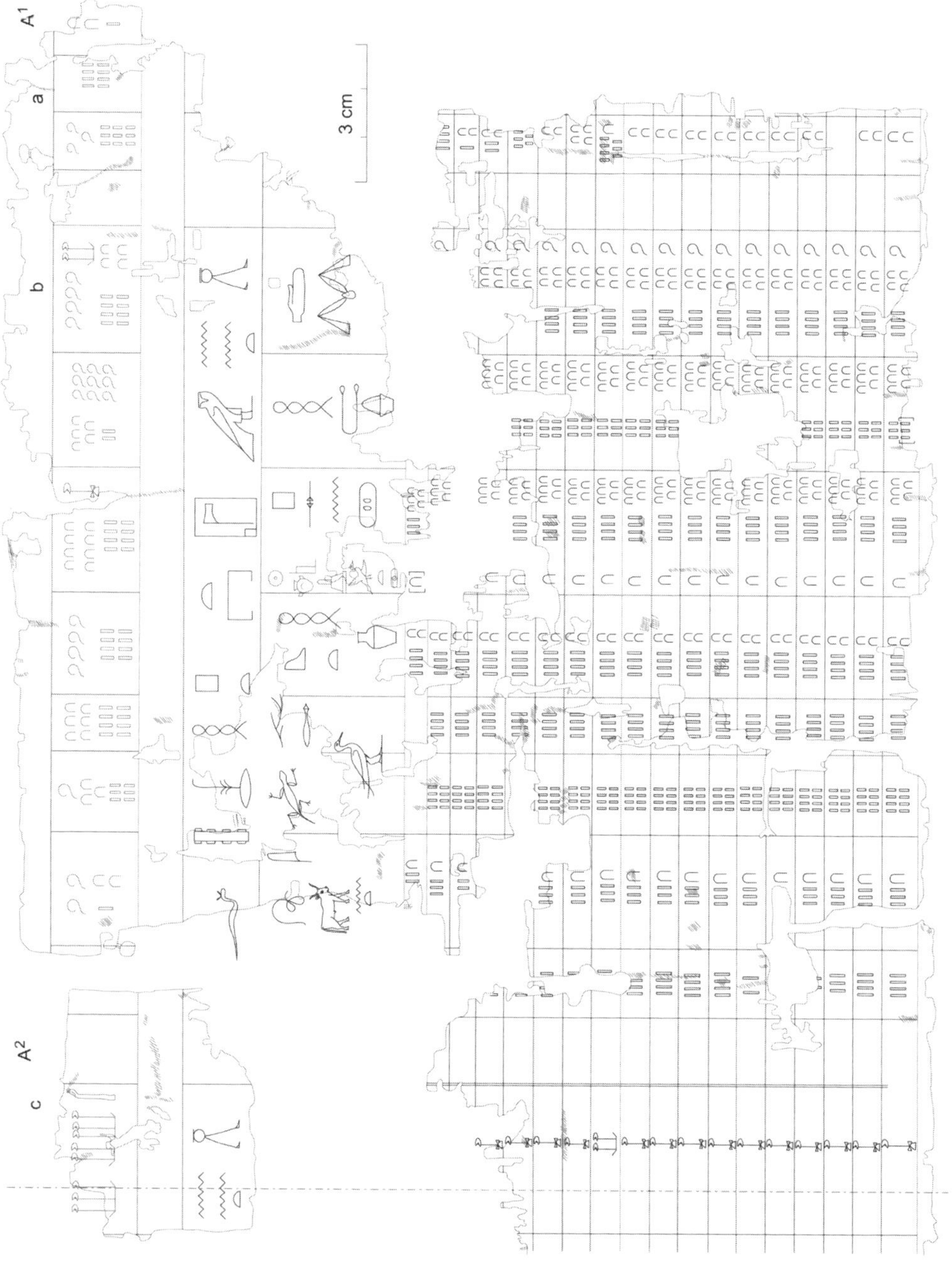

Fig. 22 Fragment of papyrus no. 47 A from Raneferef's archive mentioning the donation of a large amount of offerings sent from the temple of Ptah, see Posener-Kriéger, Verner, Vymazalová, 2006, 159, pl. 47 A

not clear, however, whether it refers to a donation to or from Raneferef's temple (we do not know whether the missing part of the text contained the preposition *m* 'from' as in the preceding part referring to the temple of Ptah, or *r* 'to').

'Donation (that has been brought) for/from the mortuary temple of Raneferef. Total delivery for 17 days (except for oxen which were delivered for 8 days only):
- [bread *ḥṯꜣ*]: 6,800 + *x*
- [cake *psn*]: 4,400 + *x*
- beer: 3,200 (in accord with prescribed quota)
- ox *ỉwꜣ*: four times 1 ox daily and four times 2 oxen daily
- big poultry: 6
- small poultry: 49 + *x*.

The editors of the document have preferred to read the missing preposition here as *m* 'from', i.e. "donation from the mortuary temple of Raneferef", as in the preceding section, because in the context of the whole document the preposition *r* would mean that it concerned a donation from the temple of Ptah and this is unlikely, given the relatively large quantities of some of the offerings then listed – e.g. bread *ḥṯꜣ*, cake *psn* and beer – as compared to the quantities that in the earlier passage were definitely sent from the temple of Ptah. In the case of beer, the overall quantity of beer donated from the temple of Ptah for 17 days was 352 beer jugs very much less than the 3,200 beer jugs mentioned in reference to Raneferef's temple. The latter could not then have been a consignment from the temple of Ptah to that of Raneferef as supposed, for example, by Papazian (Papazian, 2010, 147).

The second document, designated **64** A c, is again an accounts document, with remnants of text in three sections divided by vertical lines (Posener-Kriéger, Verner, Vymazalová, 2006, 287 and pl. 64 A a–c). The text in the third section (c) concerns deliveries of some further unspecified supplies from the temple of Ptah in an anticipated quantity of 3,300, of which 3,000 + *x* had actually been received (but it is possible that there was no further figure in the text after 3000 and only 3000 had in fact been received). Whatever the commodity referred to (grain, beer, portions of bread etc.), this high figure suggests an important and very large delivery. The preceding, second section of the account (b) concerns a consignment of some cereal from a store of products from the marshes (?) (*pr-šy ?*) for the phyle *wr*, and that of '1 *heqat* by a *wꜥb*-priest'.

In view of the fact that the first document cited **47** $A^{1,2}$ – **48** A^3 relates to a 17-day period, it appears that this was not a daily, monthly or one-year account but most probably refers to the gift of offerings for an important festival. One possibility is that the gift related to the feast of Sokar (see text further on p. 145). Sokar was a chthonic god worshipped in Memphis and the ruler of its necropolis, where he perhaps had his original underground seat in the caves by the previously mentioned lake *Pḏw* which is usually identified with the Lake of Abusir. The feast of Sokar was the greatest festival in the Memphite necropolis; it began on the 26th day of the 4th month of inundation, lasted several days and involved the distribution of a large amount of offerings. It would not be surprising that the temple of Ptah contributed a significant amount of offerings for the feast, since in the Old Kingdom at the very latest Sokar in Memphis was already being worshipped together with Ptah (Sandman-Holmberg, 1946, 124ff.). The quantity of offerings sent from the temple of Ptah would also be indirect evidence of the extent of its own economic hinterland and resources, and this too would hardly be a surprise. For example the annals on the Palermo Stone testify to large donations of land repeatedly made by the rulers of the Old Kingdom to various gods.

What is surprising in the donation from the temple of Ptah is one particular item, a total of 221 bulls. The meat of these bulls alone would be enough to bring gifts to the royal and private tombs throughout the Memphite necropolis and to feed thousands of participants at the offering rituals. Posener-Kriéger estimated that as many as 1,400–2,000 portions could be prepared from just one bull (Posener-Kriéger, 1976, 271 n. 4). (Do not 1,300 pieces of bread, repeatedly occuring in allocations in connection with 1 bull, suggest that the same number of portions of meat could have been made from 1 bull?)According to Papazian (Papazian, 2010, 150), it was the Residence that provided these oxen to the temple of Ptah, but this is not certain, for there are grounds for believing that the temple of Ptah could well have donated the 221 oxen from its own resources. The cult of Apis, for which there is evidence from as early as the 1st Dynasty (Den) (Emery, 1938, 40 and pl. 19D), was closely linked to the cult of Ptah, with the bull regarded as the embodiment of Ptah's *bꜣ*. At the very latest in the 5th Dynasty, Apis had his own temple and priests in the precincts of the temple of Ptah, as we know from a fragment of relief from the sun temple of Nyuserre in Abu Ghurab (Kees, 1928, Blatt 15 no. 251). Later, the precinct of Apis in the temple of Ptah (Amir, 1948, 51–56) was called *sékos* in Greek, and as yet only a small part of it has been excavated. Unfortunately, the older part of the temple of Ptah has not yet been archaeologically identified, although its remains are thought to lie in the nearby locality of Kom el-Fakhry (Giddy, 1990, 38–41). This means that archaeological evidence for the earliest relationship between Ptah and the cult of Apis is not yet available, but in view of the close link between Ptah and the cult of Apis we can assume that, in the 5th Dynasty at the latest, the temple of Ptah owned a large herd of cattle, from which it could chose a suitable bull that might be regarded as the embodiment of Ptah's *bꜣ*. It is nonetheless possible that the choice of a suitable bull, the future Apis, took also place on the royal cattle farms, about which we know from the annals on the Palermo Stone. For example Snofru in the year of the 7th cattle-count alone founded 35 major farms and 122 cattle farms (Wilkinson, 2000, 143).

Was the temple of Ptah just an intermediate link, an institutional heading for offerings distributed by the Residence, or did the offerings that it provided come from its own resources? Unfortunately we have very few written sources and almost no archaeological evidence about the economy of temples of the gods. It is generally believed that, until the 5th Dynasty, the temples of the gods were of relatively minor political and economic significance. On the other hand, this view may be distorted by the sheer lack of relevant written records, for the annals show that, in the 5th Dynasty, important temples of gods already had their own large-scale economic hinterland based especially on royal gifts of land. For example in just one year (the 3rd cattle-count), Weserkaf donated almost 37 aruras of land to the *bꜣw* (powers, i.e. deities) of Heliopolis, 44 aruras to Re and 44 aruras to Hathor (Wilkinson, 153 and Fig. 3; Strudwick, 2005, 70). In the 1st year of his reign Neferirkare even donated (1)10 aruras just in the 14th nome of Lower Egypt to the *bꜣw* of Heliopolis and the gods of Kheraha. In the southern part of this nome the king gave these gods another 251 aruras of land, which were exempt from taxation and put under the control of the two high priests of Heliopolis (Strudwick, 2005, 73).

From Neferirkare's decree for the temple in Abydos it is clear that, at that period, not only did the temples own lands, but these land-holdings included people obliged to work on them. By the decree the king exempted these temple lands from tax and forbade officials from taking their labour force elsewhere (Goedicke, 1967, 22–36). In the year after the 5th cattle-count Neferirkare also donated an identifiable number of aruras to Ptah South of His Wall (Strudwick, 2005, 74). Even though we do not have direct written records relating to the extent of the land holdings and other immovable property belonging to the temple of Ptah in the second half of the 5th Dynasty, from which the cited document, **47** A – **48** A, comes, we can assume that this property was considerable. After all, at this time the temple of Ptah in Memphis was – together with the temple in Heliopolis – one of the two most important in the whole country. We therefore cannot exclude the possibility that the offerings listed in this document under the heading temple of Ptah actually came from the temple's own resources. If so, however, their distribution would still have taken the form of a reversionary offering probably centrally directed by the Residence.

Unlike the situation regarding the temple of Ptah, the offerings listed in the cited document **48** A³ almost certainly did not come from Raneferef's property. Given his premature death (he reigned at the most for two years), the king did not have time to found a larger number of estates and his own resources for his mortuary cult were therefore very modest. Only three of his funerary estates were so far recorded in written sources of the time: *Mr-mꜣꜥt-Ỉsỉ*, *Śꜥnḫ-Ḥr-Ỉsỉ* and *Mr-mꜣꜥt-ꜥnḫ-Ỉsỉ* (Jacquet-Gordon, 1962, pp. 383, 392 a 394). Raneferef's archive also provides additional proof that the king's cult was subsidised via the Residence from a number of other sources, including Neferirkare's sun temple and other pyramid complexes. It is likewise evident that the offerings listed in document **48** A³ under the heading of Raneferef's mortuary temple could not have been intended just for the staff of this temple. This staff was in any case very small at the time (Posener-Kriéger, Verner, Vymazalová, 2006, 368f.) and could hardly have itself consumed for example 12 oxen during a 17-day festival. It is therefore very probable that Raneferef's temple was just a place where on festival occasions offerings were assembled, stored, checked and successively issued not just to the temple staff, but for the needs of the mortuary cult of the king's relatives and other people associated with his reign by their functions.

The important role of Raneferef's mortuary temple and, generally, of all royal mortuary temples in the system of reversionary offerings, provides an explanation for one architectural aspect of this type of temple that has not yet been accorded due attention: from the beginning of the 5th Dynasty, when there was a major change in the conception of the pyramid complex (see pp. 160–162) and the royal mortuary cult, we see a consistent rise in the number and capacity of storage chambers. The increase was particularly steep during the 5th Dynasty, and levelled off at its end. If the storage chambers in the mortuary temples of the 5th Dynasty were two-storey, as suggested in many cases by remains of staircases, then the area of these storage interiors just during the 5th Dynasty increased from approx. 150 m^2 under Weserkaf to approx. 560 m^2 under Wenis. (For more on this problem see Bárta, 2005-b, 184 Fig. 4; Verner *et al.*, 2006, 158–164.) This large storage capacity of mortuary temples might have been used to house a very large quantity of offerings all at once on certain festival occasions. The capacity would have been entirely unnecessary and incomprehensible for the ordinary operation of the temple, secured for the most part by quite small daily allocations from the Residence and the sun temple.

Apart from the Feast of Sokar, there was another festival in the Egyptian calendar of feasts in the Old Kingdom, called *ḥb wr*, or 'Great Festival', at which a large quantity of offerings was probably made. This is suggested by a text of Inscription B from the sun temple of Nyuserre (Helck, 1977, Blatt 30 no. 458), where this somewhat mysterious Great Festival is written in one column and in the following two columns we find a record of the reversionary offering of a relatively large number of animals.

As regards document **47** A – **48** A we should add that not just the temple of Ptah and Raneferef's mortuary temple but at least two other institutions, to which the front and back sections (of which little survives) of the document were probably devoted, took part in the distributions of offering at the assumed 17-day festivals. The question of how many other institutions were originally also mentioned in this document remains open. Theoretically they could have included central institutions such as the Residence, King's Domain etc., but also other pyramid complexes. It is furthermore still unclear why a document of this type should have been in Raneferef's mortuary temple at all. Is it perhaps because every institution involved in the provision of offerings received one copy of a document with an overall list of offerings intended for further distribution?

II.1.6 Pyramid Complexes

Surprisingly, as the Abusir papyri show us, among the institutions which economically supported royal funerary cults were the pyramid complexes of other kings. In these papyri, there is evidence of three complexes – those of Snofru, Menkaure and Weserkaf – which subsidized, sometimes quite regularly, the mortuary temples of Neferirkare and Raneferef.

Ḏd-Śnfrw **'Snofru Endures'**

A monthly account **34** 2 a (Posener-Kriéger, Cenival, 1968, pl. 34) attests to the delivery of different kinds of bread and beer, once a month, from Snofru's to Neferirkare's pyramid complex. According to the account **35** B (Posener-Kriéger, Cenival, 1968, pl. 35), beer and bread were sent via the Residence. The same commodities were probably also mentioned in document **39** A (Posener-Kriéger, Cenival, 1968, pl. 39), whereas in document **77** N (Posener-Kriéger, Cenival, 1968, pl. 77), only the name of Snofru's complex 'Snofru Endures' in red paint survived.

According to the documents **63** A h, **63** H and **63** I from Raneferef's archive (Posener-Kriéger, Verner, Vymazalová, 2006, pl. 63), this king's mortuary cult was also subsidized by Snofru's pyramid complex in Meidum. Document **63** A h is a fragment of an account concerning the provisions sent from Snofru's complex on selected days of the month to Raneferef's mortuary temple. The provisions consisted of different kinds of bread, flour and beverages. Tiny fragments of accounts **63** H and **63** I also refer to the delivery of breads and beverages from Snofru's complex.

An archaeological piece of evidence concerning the support rendered to Raneferef's cult by Snofru's pyramid complex in Meidum is contained in two diorite plates found in Raneferef's mortuary temple in Abusir. One plate was inscribed with Snofru's Horus name, whereas the second one contained the king's throne name. In addition to that, four fragments of diorite plates and bowls inscribed with Snofru's Horus name were revealed in the temple (Vlčková, 2006, 84–87 and Figs. 5.1, 5.2 and 5.3). Apart from the cited stone vessels with Snofru's name, three fragments of stone vessels bearing Menkauhor's name were also found in Raneferef's complex. Interestingly, not a single stone vessel bore Raneferef's name. However, vessels with Snofru's name are not a singular discovery made in Abusir: also in Sahure's mortuary temple fragments of two diorite bowls, one inscribed with Snofru's Horus and the second with his throne name, were found. (In addition to the two bowls with Snofru's name, one bowl with Khaba's name was found in Sahure's complex too, see Borchardt, 1910, 114.)

The previously cited stone vessels bearing Snofru's name were very probably gifts which were part of the cultic inventory of the recipients' mortuary temples. Obviously, it was a matter of privilege to use in the mortuary cult vessels bearing the name of the famous royal ancestor who Snofru, at that time, undoubtedly was. However, such a donation might also have had a deeper religious meaning: the offerings regularly presented in vessels inscribed with a king's name may have expressed the said king's participation in the offering ritual. We can presume that the stone vessels in question were products of a local workshop in Meidum.

Last but not least, the vessels also indirectly indicate how rich and influential Snofru's pyramid complex in Meidum was as late as in the 5th Dynasty, the time from which date the afore-cited papyri. Interestingly, the mortuary temple at the Meidum pyramid of Snofru remained unused and there is no evidence of the king's cult in it during Old Kingdom times (Petrie, 1892, 8f.). According to Wildung (Wildung, 1969, 109 and 146), Snofru was worshipped in Meidum as a god, an incorporation of Re, and his pyramid here can be considered as a precursor of the sun temples of the 5th Dynasty. Moreover, Wildung also believes that the aforesaid status of the pyramid in Meidum justifies the assumption that in the same place was also located Snofru's *mrt*-sanctuary (see p. 227). Anyway, the afore-cited evidence seems to indicate that a large economic infrastructure for the king's cult had probably been established in Meidum, prior to his decision to found a new cemetery in Dahshur. The religious meaning of Snofru's name might therefore have added some special importance to his support of other royal cults.

The stone vessels bearing Menkauhor's Horus name were also gifts which, in this case, were perhaps intended as a demonstration that the king had paid attention to the cult of his predecessor, Raneferef; it may also have been an added replenishment for the rather poor inventory contained in the latter's mortuary temple.

Nṯry-Mn-k3w-Rꜥ **'Divine Is Menkaure'**

The remains of the text on document **14** C (Posener-Kriéger, Verner, Vymazalová, 2006, pl. 14) probably refer to the donation of cloth to Raneferef's mortuary temple from the pyramid complex of Menkaure 'Divine Is Menkaure'. The text on fragment **75** E (Posener-Kriéger, Verner, Vymazalová, 2006, pl. 75) is less clear: here we find that Menkaure's pyramid complex is flanked on both sides by Raneferef's funerary domain *Śb(3?)-Ỉsi* and below each of these place names is a personal name. The presence of funerary domains may indicate that the fragment was part of a donation record.

The donations from Menkaure's pyramid complex are the more surprising that until now, due to the scarce evidence of Menkaure's funerary domains, the economic base of the king's funerary cult seems to have been weak, short-termed and only later on, from the time of Nyuserre onwards, shortly revived (see the text on p. 16). Besides the aforesaid papyri, the name of Menkaure's pyramid complex is attested, in a somewhat unclear context, on a sealing bearing Nyuserre's Horus name that had been found in the slaughterhouse adjacent to Raneferef's pyramid complex (Verner *et al.*, 2006, 225 no. 68).

Wꜥb-św t-Wśr-k3.f **'Purified Are the (Cult) Places of Weserkaf'**

The name of Weserkaf's pyramid complex 'Purified Are the (Cult) Places of Weserkaf' survived on document **75** K (Posener-Kriéger, Verner, Vymazalová, 2006, pl. 75). It is a fragment of an account referring to the transfer of six (*heqats* of grain) from Weserkaf's pyramid complex to Raneferef's mortuary temple.

It seems that Weserkaf's pyramid complex had special ties to the mortuary cult of the royal family buried in the Abusir cemetery that had been founded by the king. Stones inscribed with the name of the complex were revealed in the tomb Lepsius no. 25, which belonged to the Princess Hanebu, possibly a daughter of either Nyuserre or Raneferef (Krejčí, Callender, Verner *et al.*, 2008, 220–224 nos. 23, 31, 34, 44, 47 and 52). Very probably, the stones were gifts for the construction of this tomb in Abusir from people employed in Weserkaf's pyramid complex, which was not far away in Saqqara. The stones may also indirectly indicate Hanebu's involvement in Weserkaf's cult (Krejčí, Callender, Verner *et al.*, 2008, 229–233). Not surprisingly, Weserkaf's pyramid complex also occasionally supported the poorly funded mortuary cult of Raneferef. (The only other evidence of Weserkaf in Raneferef's pyramid complex are two fragments of a clay sealing bearing the title of a *ḥm-nṯr*-priest of Weserkaf; Verner *et al.*, 2006, 228 no. 81 and 233 no. 108.)

Ḥwt Ḥr-Śt-ib-tꜣwy **'Mortuary temple of Horus Delight of the Two Lands' (?)**
Both Neferirkare's and Raneferef's cult were probably supported by Nyuserre's mortuary temple. The term *ḥwt Ḥr Śt-ib-tꜣwy* in Neferirkare's archive, occurring on the daily account **50** 1a, was interpreted by Posener-Kriéger as "domaine 'le château de l'Horus *Śt-ib-tꜣwy*'" (Posener-Kriéger, Cenival, 1968, pl. 50 1 a; Posener-Kriéger, 1976, 332). For a more detailed discussion of the term see the text on p. 129.

The previously cited documents attest much broader and more regular contacts among the pyramid complexes than previously presumed. At the same time, however, they also ask some questions concerning the economy of the temples and the way in which the latter operated.

For instance, what position did Snofru's pyramid complex in Meidum play in the king's cult? His mortuary temple had never been used after the king had definitively decided to be buried in Dahshur, which became the major centre of his cult. Obviously, prior to his decision to move his cult, the economic background of Snofru's cult, with all the relevant production facilities, must have already been finished in Meidum and its movement to Dahshur would have been difficult and complex. Were, for instance, the provisions of bread and beverages sent directly from the reserves of Snofru's complex in Meidum, or, were they substracted from its account in the Residence and transferred to the cults in Abusir? From the documents, one has the impression that the final products – bread, flour and beverages – were sent directly from Meidum to Abusir. If so, was then the transfer recorded only in the accounts of the respective complexes in Meidum and Abusir, i.e. beyond the Residence's administration? Were such independent economic operations among pyramid complexes possible? Among such independent operations may have, for instance, ranked the previously mentioned beef fat supplied in Nyuserre's times to Raneferef's mortuary temple from the slaughterhouses of Sahure's palace which apparently lay in the near vicinity of the Abusir necropolis. Was then the control of the economy of the royal cults as absolute and bureaucratically strict as hitherto presumed?

It is rather difficult to explain why cloth, an article which was in principle supplied from the Residence (and, as the case might have been, directly from the royal palace), was sometimes sent from another pyramid complex. What was the reason for such a delivery?

Quite surprising is the common participation of the attendants of funerary domains of Raneferef and Menkaure's pyramid complex in some nebulous activity. So far, the operation of the mortuary temple personnel in the sun temple of one and the same king was considered as questionable. Unfortunately, these and many more questions pertaining to the mutual contacts among pyramid complexes remain unanswered so far. Maybe, if all the archives of the pyramid complexes would have survived, we would be surprised to learn just how frequent these contacts were.

II.1.7 Funerary Domains (*ḥwt*)

The striking absence of funerary domains (*ḥwt*) in the papyrus archive of Neferirkare led Posener-Kriéger (Posener-Kriéger, 1976, 611) to conclude that the supplies of raw materials for the royal cult did not come direct to the mortuary temples from the royal estates set up by kings for that purpose, but came via the Residence. As a primary source for the royal mortuary cult, the Residence centralised the distribution process and corrected any imbalances between the resources for the different cults. (Such imbalances might be caused by the fact that some kings reigned only briefly and had not had time to endow materially their future mortuary cults.)

Yet the absence of reference to funerary domains in the Abusir papyrus archives is not really total: there are isolated mentions and, in fact, two can be found in documents surviving in the archive of Neferirkare. Here the domain *Ỉw-Šdf-w*[*ỉ*] appears in the accounts document **33–35** as one of the sources of 'divine offering' sent from the king's sun temple to his pyramid complex. Earlier this same 'divine offering' had come to the sun temple from the Residence (Posener-Kriéger, Cenival, 1968, pl. 33–35 and Posener-Kriéger, 1976, 261). In addition to *Ỉw-Šdf-w*[*ỉ*], other sources of 'divine offering' were *r3-š K3-k3.i* and also from Snofru's pyramid complex in Meidum. Indeed, *Ỉw-Šdf-w*[*ỉ*] is recorded in inscriptions in the tomb of Nefermaat in Meidum (Jacquet-Gordon, 1962, 444). According to document **45** F (Posener-Kriéger, Cenival, 1968, pl. 45 F and Posener-Kriéger, 1976, 622), yet another source of offerings sent to the mortuary temple of Neferirkare from the stores of the Residence was from the domain of Radjedef *Bꜥḥt-Rꜥ-ḏd.f*.

There are also a few mentions of domains in the archive of Raneferef. One is the domain already known from the archive of Neferirkare, [*Ỉw*]-*Šdf-w*[*ỉ*], which is mentioned in Raneferef's account **70** L (Posener-Kriéger, Verner, Vymazalová, 2006,

70 L and p. 295). Under the name of this domain we find a list of offerings comprising bread, drinks and the *bśt*-pastry, and under all this the number 3. It is impossible to establish from the remainder of this text whether this domain sent offerings to Raneferef's mortuary temple directly or through the Residence and Neferirkare's sun temple *Śt-ib-Rʿ*. On a small fragment of accounts, **87** E (Posener-Kriéger, Verner, Vymazalová, 2006, 87 E and p. 313), there is mention of the domain *Mn-ḏf3-Ś3ḥw-Rʿ*, known from inscriptions in Sahure's pyramid complex (Jacquet-Gordon, 1962, 145 and 147; Khaled, 2008, 140f.). Under the name of the domain is the note 'remainder'. Next to the name of the domain, divided off by a vertical line, is the note 'remainder which is in the mortuary temple of Raneferef'. The third relevant record, document **75** E (Posener-Kriéger, Verner, Vymazalová, 2006, 75 E and p. 299), differs somewhat from the others described. It is a remnant of a text with a list of toponyms, including the domain of *Śb*[*3t?*]-*Ísi* 'Isi Is a Star' (?) twice, and Menkaure's pyramid complex *Nṯry-Mn-k3w-Rʿ* once, while a personal name appears under each of these toponyms. Under these names is the note *tp* in red, which can bear various different interpretations ('on ...', 'upper part ... ', 'beginning of ...', 'provision'). Did these names refer to people in different localities or institutions, who were supposed to obtain some provision or were assigned to some service in the pyramid complex of Raneferef? The domain 'Isi Is a Star' (?) is not among the few so far known estates of Raneferef, although we know of an estate with a similar name, 'Khufu Is a Star' (Jacquet-Gordon, 1962, 139).

As previously mentioned, Posener-Kriéger considers *ḥwt Ḥr-Śt-ib-t3wy* 'le château de l'Horus *Śt-ib-t3wy*', occurring in the archive of Neferirkare in daily account **50** 1a to have been a domain (Posener-Kriéger, Cenival, pl. 50 1 a; Posener-Kriéger, 1976, 332). In addition to the King's Domain (*pr-nśwt*), via the Residence, this institution participated in a consignment of wheat, the cereal *pḫ3* and 1.5 pieces of bread (*sic*). We also encounter this institution in document **14** Ad from the archive of Raneferef (Posener-Kriéger, Verner, Vymazalová, 2006, 14 Ad and p. 228). In this case, the administrative office (*gś-pr*) of this institution, together with the 'workshop of the King's Domain (?)' (*is pr-nśwt* ?), was the source of a delivery of a larger amount of select fragrant oils and materials. From this reference in particular it appears that *ḥwt Ḥr-Śt-ib-t3wy* was probably not a standard domain, i.e. a large estate devoted mainly to agricultural production. Its name consists only of Nyuserre's Horus name, which is unusual in the name of a domain (Gordon-Jacquet, 1962, *passim*; Khaled, 2008, *passim*). Also strange is that in both cases this institution is mentioned in connection with the King's Domain. A king's name in a frame does not always necessarily signify a domain, for it is also the usual designation of a mortuary temple, for example in the builders' inscriptions of Nyuserre's reign (Borchardt, 1909, 54; Verner, 1992, 115 no. 213). It is therefore possible that, rather than a large estate, *ḥwt Ḥr Śt-ib-t3wy* was just the designation of Nyuserre's mortuary temple which supplied (possibly in collaboration with the 'King's Domain', i.e. the royal personal property) Neferirkare's and Raneferef's mortuary cult with special materials. (Concerning the specific role of Nyuserre's pyramid complex in the Abusir cemetery, see p. 119.)

From all these (alas fragmentary) records from the archives of Neferirkare and Raneferef, it is clear that we cannot speak of a complete absence of funerary domains in these documents. Yet we are still faced with the question of why only a few are mentioned, and so sporadically, and why, with the sole exception of Raneferef's domain *Šb[ȝt ?]-ỉsi*, they are all domains established by other kings: Snofru (*Ỉw-Šdf-w[ỉ]* for Nefermaat), Radjedef (*Bꜥḥt-Rꜥ-ḏd.f*), Sahure (*Mn-ḏȝ-Šȝḥw-Rꜥ*) and Nyuserre (*Ḥwt Ḥr Št-ib-tȝwy*)? Apart from the specific case of *ḥwt Ḥr Št-ib-tȝwy* these were probably smaller estates. Are we dealing here with special supplies from estates that were located nearby and could send offerings promptly? Only in the case of Nyuserre's estates is the reference demonstrably to a consignment via the Residence or, as the case might be, the sun temple *Št-ib-Rꜥ*. Does the repeated mention of Snofru's pyramid complex indicate that it had a special position in distribution of special consignments of offerings to other pyramid complexes? Unfortunately, the text is so incomplete that the meaning of some of these documents eludes us.

Given the first-rank importance of domains not only in the royal mortuary cult but in the entire Egyptian economy in the period of the Old Kingdom, we need here to offer at least a brief outline of research on this theme to date. The basic works on estates/domains (*ḥwt*) in the 3rd millennium BC include for example Jacquet-Gordon, 1962; Moreno García, 1999; Khaled, 2008; Fitzenreiter, 2013. The 'estate/domain' (in the context of the mortuary cult 'funerary estate'/ 'funerary domain') was already an important economic institution in the Early Dynastic Period, as is evident from their names in the titles of the high officials who ran them (Kaplony, 1963, 1224–1226 Index s.v. *ḥwt*). The hitherto earliest piece of evidence for 'estate/domain' dates from the 1st Dynasty (the time of Djer) (Engel, 2013, 27).

From the time of Egypt's unification, the domain foundations played an important part in the integration of the country, the development of its infrastructure and the consolidation of its central government. They became an important instrument of what is known as the internal colonisation of still only sparsely inhabited and economically unexploited land. It has been argued that, from the very earliest time, the founding of estates was the sole privilege of the king, who held political sovereignty over the whole country and in this way fulfilled his obligation to care both for its advancement and the prosperity of its inhabitants (Papazian, 2012, 37). Yet the theory of the original sovereignty of the king over the whole country and its natural riches is not as unchallengeable as it might seem at first sight. We have very little information about property law in the initial phases of the development of the Ancient Egyptian state, but there are grounds for believing that when the king's political sovereignty was recognised by local rulers in the course of the unification of the country, this did not entail the expropriation of their property. The founding of estates by the king would therefore have mainly concerned uninhabited and unexploited territory that was freely available and suitable for reclamation and agricultural production.

The estates established by the king were subject to his authority and often contained his name in their title, but not always. As a rule, the name of an estate was inscribed in the frame of the hieroglyphic sign *ḥwt*. Written documents from the Early Dynastic Period show that the estates were not all of the same size and importance, as is evident from the distinction between the designation *ḥwt* 'estate' and *ḥwt-ˁ3t* 'great estate' (a great estate might in some cases be the higher administrative unit bringing together several smaller estates). The administrator of an estate or great estate had the title *ḥk3* 'chief' or *imy-r3* 'overseer' (Piacentini, 1994, 235–249). According to Moreno García (Moreno García, 1999, 39 and 205) a *ḥwt* or *ḥwt-ˁ3t* might variously mean the palace, seat of the administrator and also administrative centre organising the range of activities involved in agricultural production and the storing of foodstuffs on the territory concerned. Last but not least, the *ḥwt* could also have a defensive function. From the Early Dynastic Period to the end of the 5th Dynasty there seem to have been more *ḥwt-ˁ3t* than *ḥwt*, but then the ratio turned around (Moreno García, 1999, 36). In addition to the *ḥwt* estates and *niwt* settlements (Khaled, 2008, 195 prefers the more apt Arab term *ezba* for *niwt*), in texts from the Old Kingdom we also find the term *grgt* 'foundation' in connection with both private persons and the king (Moreno García, 1996, 116–138).

At the beginning of the 3rd Dynasty the stabilisation of political conditions in the country and consolidation of the central power of the state and the instruments of its government contributed to an economic boom and a striking rise in the number and productivity of estates and their importance in the Egyptian economy. Indirect evidence for this boom includes the emergence of monumental stone architecture, Djoser's pyramid complex. The increasing efficiency of the economy and government during the 3rd Dynasty was also eventually reflected by a change in the method of collecting taxes. Up to the end of the 3rd Dynasty, taxes were collected (and other royal competences exercised) biennially during the 'Following of Horus' (*šmśw Ḥr*), when the king and his entourage would travel round Egypt (for example, inscriptions on vessels from Elephantine dating from the reign of Huni still bear dates calculated by the 'Following of Horus', see Dreyer, 1987, 98–109). From the beginning of the 4th Dynasty, although not consistently, a new mostly biennial system of *ṯnwt/ipt* 'cattle-count', i.e. census of moveable property in the country, came into use (Verner, 2001, 124–128).

In the reign of Snofru at the beginning of the 4th Dynasty there was an important change in the concept of the royal tomb and mortuary cult, and a related stepping up of the founding of estates: for example, in the annals on the Palermo Stone we find a reference relating to the year of the 7th cattle-count under Snofru to the "setting up of 35 estates with people and 122 cattle farms" (Strudwick, 2005, 66), many of which were supposed to provide for the king's building activities and of course his mortuary cult as well. A procession of personifications of these estates (Fakhry, 1961/II Pt.1, 17–58; Jacquet-Gordon, 1962, 125–137) bringing offering gifts adorns the walls of Snofru's valley temple. (For the new interpretation of the valley temple as a *sed*-festival temple see Stadelmann, 2010, 736–746.) The high official Metjen, who started his career under Huni and died sometime in the first half of Snofru's reign, was involved in the founding and running of many estates at this time (Gödecken, 1976, *passim*). The fact that the officials entrusted with management of the states were buried at the political centre, in the Memphite Necropolis, reflects the firm control of the state over the economy of the provinces. It is also at this time that records multiply relating to the material endowment of the king's closest relatives, including their personal mortuary cults, not directly from the king's property but by the allocation either of entire royal estates or just a portion of their yield to specific members of the king's family.

Besides estates (*ḥwt*/*ḥwt-ʿ3t*), settlements (*niwt*) and foundations (*grgt*) in the course of the 5th Dynasty, there appear other economic facilities of various types, founded mainly by the king but sometimes also by important private persons. These include what are known as the 'new settlements/colonies' (*niwwt m3wt*) (Moreno García, 1998-a, 38–55; Papazian, 2012, 54–56) and also 'towers' (*śwnw*) (so-called points of support) (Moreno García, 1997, 124). The social structure of people working in all these economic facilities is not quite clear. We can presume that an important part of the workers represented people known as *mrt*, who were, according to the 5th Dynasty decree of Neferirkare for the temple in Abydos, subject to obligatory labour (but they are thought to have existed at latest from the period of transition from the 3rd to the 4th Dynasties, as shows the inscription of Metjen). (On the rather divergent views on the status of *mrt* people see e.g. Helck, 1975, 102f.; Andrassy, 2008, 65f.; I. Hafemann, 2009,106; Moreno García, 1998b, 75f.) One specific social group was known as 'the king's people' (*nśwtjw*), who, for example, took part in the reclamation of unexploited land. (The suggestion from Müller-Wollermann, 1987, 263–267 that this term be interpreted as *św.tjw* 'people belonging to the plant *św.t*', i.e. those who used to remove weeds on the edge of fertile land and convert it into arable land has not been generally accepted.) These were quasi 'colonists' who had the right to own land, to be in the army and to carry weapons (Savelyeva, 1962, 187f. See also Wenig, 1963, 66–69 and Gödecken, 1976, 294f.). As can be indirectly deduced from their name, this was land very probably subject to the king's direct sovereignty.

In inscriptions and scenes in non-royal tombs of the Old Kingdom, estates sometimes appear with the indication that they pertain to a *pr-ḏt*. This term, in most cases not quite adequately translated as, for example, '(Land)besitz' or 'Stiftungsgut' (Gödecken, 1976, 305ff.), has been the subject of discussion for many years and has no simple definition (see e.g. Helck, 1975, 57–61; Moreno García, 1999, 210–225). We know from contemporary written sources that, for services rendered, the king might reward an official with land, including cattle and the people who worked on it, and/or a share in the yield of an estate, but that no official was ever granted actual ownership of a royal estate. The mention of some such estates as belonging to a *pr-ḏt* would seem to fly in the face of this principle, and the whole problem is further complicated by the fact that a settlement (*niwt*) could be included within the property of a *pr-ḏt* (*Urk* I, 15: 7). It appears, however, that the official receiving such a grant could not treat the property provided by the king entirely at will, since it had a special legal status distinguished from that of property acquired by an individual in a different way. According to Fitzenreiter (Fitzenreiter, 2004, 70 and 87–91), the socio-economic institution of the *pr-ḏt* served as a way of maintaining particular social and professional functions. Much more than a 'funerary endowment' for the private owners of tombs, the institution regulated the legal relationship of the dead man's heirs towards the community. The core of the term, *ḏt*, denoted a legal union in which everyone with a lawful claim to the property of the deceased found himself. The institution *pr-ḏt* had its own distinctive function in society and its own organisational structure. Evidence of the activity of one such *pr-ḏt* is provided for example by papyri from Gebelein (Posener-Kriéger, 1975, 211–221).

In addition to estates and villages originating from royal gifts of land and identified as part of a *pr-ḏt*, in texts in private tombs of the period we also find depictions of estates with an even more obscure origin or status. Understanding their significance is complicated by the fact that they include estates that sometimes have a royal name in their names, but sometimes one also finds the name of the tomb owner, and sometimes the same estates appear in different tombs. Furthermore, in some instances, the lists of estates are long, suggesting extensive private property. Jacquet-Gordon (Jacquet-Gordon, 1962, 35–37) and some scholars before her considered that many of the estates mentioned in the tombs never existed in reality. Most recently this problem has been studied in detail by Moreno García (Moreno García, 1999, 116f.) and he too concluded that these estates were not part of private property and played no role in materially securing the mortuary cult of private persons – they were fictive. Apart from having a decorative function the lists of these fictive estates were primarily meant to emphasise the social status of the tomb's owner and his role in the ideal order of Egypt and the world. This conclusion cannot remain unqualified, however, because there is evidence that some of these allegedly fictive estates did exist (Papazian, 2012, 38f.). We can not exclude, for instance, that the tomb owner may have been given a token amount from a certain royal estate, not the produce of the entire estate. In this way the king could confer his graciousness on more servants or relatives.

In his presentation of the domains recorded in private tombs, Fitzenreiter (Fitzenreiter, 2013, 40f.) makes a distinction between two basic, chronologically successive forms:

- in the early Old Kingdom there are the so-called 'old', 'spontaneous' domains, villages (*niwt*), which usually bear the autochthonous name of the locality; there are also less

numerous estates (*ḥwt*) which, without exception, bear the king's name and can be regarded as the local centres of the early state;
- in the high Old Kingdom the task of securing access to the production of specific localities for the elite was delegated to the supply institutions of the Residence; through these central facilities the products were redistributed to individuals, with the distributive key being institutionalised in accounts in the form of domains; so-called 'systematic' domains were founded, with names that now tended to be based on terms from the list of offerings and the name of the owner.

Question-marks over the reality of the estates depicted in private tombs definitely do not arise in the case of the lists of estates in the royal pyramid complexes of the time. The recent discovery of blocks with scenes of long processions of personified royal funerary domains from the causeway of Sahure's complex in Abusir have made this very clear (Khaled, 2008, *passim*; 2013, 363–372). It has so far proved possible to identify around 200 domains (146 are safely identified, the remainder is an estimate of their number on only a partially excavated but not yet raised block) depicted on the northern wall of the causeway, estates (*ḥwt*) and villages (*niwt*), which the king had founded in the western part of the 7th nome of Lower Egypt (*Wꜥ-m-ḥww: gš imnty*) and in the 10th nome of Lower Egypt (*Km wr*).

Khaled estimates that, assuming the average extent of a domain to be 4–6 aruras (1 arura = 2,750 m^2), this would mean 11,020 – 14,200 m^2, i.e. a total area of about 1,2 ha, including arable land, grazing land (?) and settlement. The extent of the 146 domains of Sahure so far identified on these blocks would then be between 1.6–2.4 km^2. Khaled further believes that just as the Lower Egyptian domains were depicted on the north side of the corridor of the causeway, so the domains founded by Sahure in Upper Egypt were depicted on the south side. Khaled's assumption would mean that the overall number of domains founded by this king could have been around 400. Given the above estimate of the average size of one domain the total extent of the domains founded by Sahure alone could have been somewhere between 3.2–4.8 km^2. According to Khaled the overall extent of the domains founded during the Old Kingdom could have been as much as around 98 km^2. Khaled's assumption and calculations, however, are questionable since the founding of domains was primarily determined by economic and administrative reasons, not by balancing their number between Upper and Lower Egypt.

This great economic hinterland created through the founding of funerary domains by successive kings for the building of their pyramid complexes and their eternal funerary cult was not at the direct disposal of their mortuary temples, however, and as has already been noted in the previous text, the institution that centralised the greater part of the output of the domains (a substantial part would have remained on the estates to support their employees), and distributed it to individual cults, was the Residence. Furthermore, during the Old Kingdom, as social and political conditions changed, a new institution – the divine temple – became ever more significant. It is generally thought that, during the 3rd and 4th Dynasties, the divine temples were still of little importance and that it was only during the 5th Dynasty that their economic and political standing rose. This view may, of course, merely reflect a shortage of relevant surviving written sources for the earlier period, but from the 5th Dynasty there is a striking increase in evidence for quite large royal gifts of land to important gods such as Re, Hathor, the gods of Buto, *bꜣw* of Heliopolis and others (Schäfer, 1902, 34 Nr. 2), as well as less important local deities, for example Hathor of *Rꜣ-int* (Tehna) (*Urk* I, 24–25). Although Hathor's cult in Tehna had been founded in the reign of Menkaure, it was only in the early 5th Dynasty, under Weserkaf, that it acquired its own economic base (Goedicke, 1970, 131–148; Edel, 1981, 38–64). Dating from the time of Neferirkare is what is, so far, the earliest known royal decree concerning the temple in Abydos, granting the temple itself property and its priests immunity. Although the decree does not specify the size of the temple land holding, the property seems to have been substantial (Goedicke, 1971, 22–36; Papazian, 2012, 129–130).

According to Moreno García (Moreno García, 1999, 267ff.) the domains played an important role in the crisis at the end of the Old Kingdom. In an attempt to make government more effective, at the end of the 5th Dynasty the country was divided into two zones: Lower Egypt and the environs of Memphis, which were administered directly from the capital, while governors of the provinces administered the remaining part of Upper Egypt. Great estates (*ḥwt-ꜥꜣt*) and fortified places (*śwnw*) were increasingly replaced by smaller estates (*ḥwt*), better able than great estates to exploit free land and local resources. Moreno García believes that this led to an increase in bureaucracy and the influence of the governors of the provinces and increasingly heavy taxes, and that all this meant a deterioration in the economic position of the rural population. Eventually the estates fell into decline and lost their importance.

Whether or not we accept Moreno García's conclusions, it is clear from this brief outline that the institution of the *ḥwt* was of key significance in the economy of Egypt in the period of the Old Kingdom and that its development in this period was dynamic. This makes the many remaining questions surrounding this important economic and consequently social and political institution all the more urgent. The scenes and inscriptions which survived in the Old Kingdom tombs inform us sometimes in vivid detail on the life in rural estates, the agricultural works, pastoral environment, animals, management of the estates, etc. (Swinton, 2012, *passim*). In spite of this, we still know little, for example, about the actual administration and social-economic model of the estates and their relationship with other economic facilities at local level. What are as yet just isolated written documents such as the Gebelein papyri (Posener-Kriéger, 1975, 211-221), or relevant archaeological evidence from research in sites such as Kom el-Hisn (Wenke *et al.*, 1988, 5–35), suggest the importance of discovering more about these relationships. New evidence about the domains from the pyramid complex of Sahure shows that at the beginning of the 5th Dynasty the system of domains was hierarchic (estate/*ezba* – domain – nome – political centre of the country) and securely anchored in the government of the country. We do not know, however, how communication, the assembly and distribution of production, or more precisely of surplus production, was organised between the different levels of management within the domains.

Another set of questions, relating to the land ownership and economies of temples in the Old Kingdom generally, concerns the *ḥwt* only indirectly, because divine temples did not found these institutions. It would nonetheless be important to compare the social-economic model in temple fields and establishments (as it emerges for example from decrees delivered at the end of the Old Kingdom concerning the temple in Koptos) with that of the other estates. In the case of large temples, for example in Heliopolis and Memphis, the prevailing view that the temple economy originated only during the 5th Dynasty is very much open to doubt. And of course there are a number of other similar questions that relate to one degree or another to the institution *ḥwt*.

III. FEAST DAYS IN MORTUARY AND SUN TEMPLES

Mortuary temples not only served the purposes of routine daily rituals but were the setting for many festivals, some very important and others less so. Unfortunately, only few remains of these festivals survived in the 5th Dynasty mortuary temples. Among them are, for instance, two fragments from the relief decoration of Sahure's pyramid complex (Borchardt, 1913, 72 bottom part). Some festivals were repeated at regular intervals during the year, and others held only once a year. The dates of festivals were determined by the lunar calendar.

We find evidence about these feast days, albeit in fragments, in the papyrus archives of the temples of Neferirkare and Raneferef. The feast days recorded in the Neferirkare archive have been the subject of a detailed study by Posener-Kriéger, (Posener-Kriéger, 1976, 544–563) but there are several further references to festivals in the Raneferef archive, providing important new information about their real character and course (Posener-Kriéger, Verner, Vymazalová, 2006, pls. 11–13). Papyri evidence from the mortuary temples has been supplemented significantly by what is known as the 'founding (dedicatory) inscription' of the sun temple of Nyuserre, which includes a calendar of feasts – unfortunately, incomplete. Posener-Kriéger (Posener-Kriéger, 1976, 549 n. 3) has expressed doubts as to whether all the feasts in the calendar of feasts from the sun temple of Nyuserre were actually celebrated: she believes they were not – or at most only verbally.

The founding inscription of Nyuserre is divided into two inscriptions, known as A and B according to the circumstances of the find. Except for the 'Great Feast', the festivals are all set out in inscription A (Kees, 1928; Helck, 1977-a, 47–78). However hypothetical and questionable Helck's reconstruction of both inscriptions may be, their testimony is very valuable in view of the close religious and economic connection between the sun and mortuary temples; feasts taking place in a sun temple of its builder had direct and indirect consequences for his mortuary temple. Indeed, these feast days probably had a wider meaning, because they concerned not only the cult of the king's ancestors, but indirectly for their contemporaries as well.

(*ḥb*) *ꜣbdw* **'(Feast of the) Month'**

The 'Feast of the Month', a regularly repetitious feast day on the turn of the lunar month, is mentioned on papyrus fragment **5** f from the Neferirkare archive (Posener-Kriéger, Cenival, 1968, pl. 5 f). With reference to the chronological data (*pśḏntyw*) emphasised in red on the papyrus, Posener-Kriéger (Posener-Kriéger, 1976, 52–56 and 546) has suggested that the festival lasted from the first night of the invisibility of the moon (i.e. the 1st day of the lunar month, which began with this night, to the appearance of the first sickle moon). The festival centred on the cult of the royal statues. In the night of the invisibility of the moon (*pśḏntyw*) the statues were disrobed (*śḥ3*) and purified (*ỉr-ʿbw*). How the ritual continued was on the missing piece of the papyrus. The ritual was conducted by the lector-priest, and two higher-ranking *ḥm-nṯr*-priests, and one *ḫnty-š* was also to hand. The evidence of document **5** f is supplemented by a text on papyrus fragment **4** h from the same archive (Posener-Kriéger, Cenival, 1968, pl. 4 h), which likewise refers to the royal statues. According to this text, on the day of the new moon the statues were re-clothed (*nmś*), purified, adorned (*ḏb3*) and fumigated with incense (*ỉr-śnṯr*). In addition to the *ḥm-nṯr*-priest, the ceremony involved three *ḫnty-š*, while the lector-priest and another five *ḫnty-š*, who had evidently already performed their share of work in the preparation of the ritual and had no role in the closing rites, stood some way away by the entrance (i.e. to the chapel containing the statues). It is odd that the 'opening of the mouth' was not performed in this context as part of the ritual.

Unfortunately, our evidence about similar rituals performed on statues of Khentkaus II, whose cult was closely linked to that of Neferirkare, consists only of tiny fragments of texts found in the mortuary temple of this royal mother (Vymazalová, Coppens, 2011, 777–791).

The text of document **4** h in fact has a broader historical significance noticed by Posener-Kriéger: it is that here the statues are specified. They are three statues of the king depicted seated on a throne: the first statue shows the crown of Upper Egypt on his head and the king holds a flagellum on his lap; the second statue differs only in wearing the crown of Lower Egypt, while the third image has a *nmś*-headdress and in his hands, crossed on his breast, he holds a flagellum and the *ḥķ3*-sceptre. Posener-Kriéger (Posener-Kriéger, 1976, 52–55) considers this last statue to be Osirian. Two statues of the king seated on the throne are also recorded in the text on fragment **5** f, but the third image was on a missing part of the papyrus. The first figure has an Upper Egyptian crown and holds the flagellum, and the second has a Lower Egyptian crown and holds

Fig. 23 Three enlarged representations of the king from the papyrus fragment 4 h from the archive of Neferirkare, see Posener-Kriéger, Cenival, 1968, pl. 4

the flagellum and the *ḥḳꜣ*-sceptre. Posener-Kriéger (Posener-Kriéger, 1976, 55) believes that the actual statues were placed in the chapel with five niches: the Osirian statue in the middle niche and the other two in niches on each side of it. She does not speculate on the type of statue in the remaining two niches, and even thinks it possible that there may only have been three statues.

The statue types could, however, be interpreted in a different way. They need not necessarily have been a trio of statues of which one is Osirian. The *ḥḳꜣ*-sceptre and flagellum are not exclusively attributes of Osiris; for example as early as Snofru's time we encounter a depiction of the king during the *sed*-festival holding a sceptre and flagellum in hands crossed on his breast (Fakhry, 1961, 90 Fig. 75). The determinative of the three royal statues with different symbols of power may therefore be the expression of plurality, and in the texts concerned may include all the statues that were the subject of the ritual (see Vymazalová, Coppens, 2013-a, 371). This would explain the paradox of three statues in five niches.

The texts open up other related questions, even though we shall not go into them in depth here in this discussion: how many statues were there in mortuary temples of the time that did not have chapels with five niches, and in which of these temples did the ritual then take place? For example, the mortuary temple of Raneferef, situated immediately beside Neferirkare's temple, had no chapel with five niches, but from written documents found in it we know that there was a special 'room of the statue(s)' (*pr-twt*) (Posener-Kriéger, Verner, Vymazalová, 2006, 344–346). In Raneferef's temple, we can probably identify this room as the columned hall, in the immediate vicinity of which a large number of fragments of statues of the king have been found including six complete portraits carved in different kinds of stone (Verner, in press). It has proved possible to identify more than ten mostly seated statues of the king (Benešovská, 2006, 360–437). The statues are either without a crown, or wear an Upper Egyptian crown or sometimes a *nmś*-headdress, but they include no Osirian type as proposed by Posener-Kriéger on the basis of her interpretation of fragment **4** h.

wp-rnpt 'New Year'

The important feast of *wp-rnpt* 'New Year' (lit. opening of the year), mentioned on fragment no. 462a of the founding inscription of the sun temple of Nyuserre (Kees, 1928, Blatt 28), was undoubtedly celebrated in mortuary temples as well as sun temples. According to Helck's hypothetical reconstruction of the inscription, this feast involved the offering of "1,000 *pesen* bread, 1 ox, 10 fowl, honey, milk and all sweet things". The feast was held at the beginning of the civil year on the 1st day of the 1st month of inundation, which ideally synchronised with the heliacal rising of Sothis (*prt Śpdt*) which took place around the 19th of July (by the Julian calendar) once in 1,441 years (see e.g. Parker, 1950, 33f.; S. Schott, 1950, 79f.; Daumas, 1982, 466–472; Spalinger, 1994, 297–308).

The festival of the New Year (like the festival *tpy rnpt* 'the beginning of the year', see below in the text) was associated with important celebrations of the renewal of royal power. The rituals are described in detail for example in texts from the Ptolemaic period (J. G. Goyon, 1972). According to these texts, on the eve of the New Year, in the last hour of the last epagomenal day, the ritual of 'uniting with the solar disc' was performed, to ensure the regeneration of the statues of the gods before the new cycle for the exercising of their powers began (see e.g. Sauneron, 1964, 119). A ceremonial banquet was also held on the same evening.

Ḏḥwtyt - *w3g* **'(Feast of) Thoth' – '(Feast of)** *w3g***'**

In a few, alas incomplete, documents from the papyrus archive of Raneferef, there are mentions of the 'Feast of Thoth' and 'Feast of *w3g*' (Posener-Kriéger, Verner, Vymazalová, 2006, pls. 11–13). It is interesting that the two festivals are mentioned together (as they are in the offering lists of private persons), and in the order indicated, for although the interval between them was short they were not held on the same day, and their sequence changed over time. The combination of the feasts Thoth – *w3g* and its implications was discussed by Spalinger (Spalinger, 2013-b, 622–624). According to Parker (Parker, 1950, 36), the Feast of Thoth was originally the feast of the inserted month (Thoth was god of the Moon), which appeared at three- or sometimes two-year intervals. In the lunar calendar the 18th day of the 1st month of the season of inundation was the fixed date for the Feast of *w3g*, and its place in the civil calendar moved about (Luft, 1994, 42). Although the Feast of Thoth was celebrated the very next day, in lists of festivals from the Old Kingdom, the feast of the First day of the year (*tpy rnpt*) was inserted between the Feast of Thoth and the Feast of *w3g*.

Some of the cited documents from the papyrus archive of Raneferef offer further information about the celebration of these festivals in the king's temple. The accounts document **11** A (Posener-Kriéger, Verner, Vymazalová, 2006, pl. 11 A and 220f) concerns different kinds of fabrics and their amounts intended for cult purposes, and their allocation between five temple phyles and phyle sections on the Feast of *w3g*, whereas document **11** B is of a similar kind (Posener-Kriéger, Verner, Vymazalová, 2006, pl. 11 B and 221), but relates not to the Feast of *w3g*, but to the Feast of Thoth as well. The Feast of Thoth is also the subject of small fragments of the document **11** C and **11** D, but they offer no clear further information. These documents have been studied in detail by Posener-Kriéger (Posener-Kriéger, 1985, 35–43). Document **13** A also relates to these feasts.

Document **11** E (Posener-Kriéger, Verner, Vymazalová, 2006, pl. 11 E) is also important, although the fragmentary nature of the text does not permit a more detailed interpretation. The original text probably concerned the allocation of different clothes to the temple staff for the festival of Thoth and the *w3g* feast. What is noteworthy here is the date, which raises some questions concerning the precise timing of the celebration of the feast. We know that in the Middle Kingdom the *wꜣg* feast was celebrated on the 18th day of the 1st month of inundation. Furthermore, the Abusir papyrus archives indicate that the activities of the mortuary temples for both Neferirkare and Raneferef were regulated by the civic calendar. On the other hand, our incomplete document **11** E refers to the 28th day of the 3rd month of a season with a missing name, and this seems to support the idea of a movable *wꜣg* feast as discussed by Posener-Kriéger in her article cited below. Posener-Kriéger's publication of the documents **11** A, B and C, including her commentary, prompted Luft (Luft, 1994, 39–44) to attempt to fix the dates in terms of absolute chronology to ca 2430 BC. Luft's conclusions were then challenged by Krauss (Krauss, 1998, 53–57) whose own calculations resulted in a date somewhere between the years 2450–2335. Regardless of the differences between these scholars in their understanding of the *wꜣg* dates in the fragments **11** A, B and C, all have reconstructed the missing season in the text of fragment **11** C as 'inundation' (*ꜣḫt*). Later on, the dates referring to the *wꜣg* feast in Raneferef's papyrus archive were re-examined by Depuydt (Depuydt, 2000, 167–186). Unlike previous scholars, and on the basis of his own calculations and arguments, Depuydt (p. 173) thought the season referred to would have been the winter season (*prt*), and he suggests that this season could be "a possible restoration"; he adds that the date of document **11** C could have been written "not too far from 2302 B.C.E.". His second option was the season of inundation for which he suggested the date 2495 BC. Nevertheless, Vymazalová (Vymazalová, 2008, 141f.) accentuated that any discussion on the Old Kingdom absolute chronology based on the previously cited documents is speculative due to their fragmentary state of preservation and, above all, the missing season on the fragment **11** E; moreover, even though an absolute date could be calculated from these texts, it could not be safely attributed to any particular king of the 5th Dynasty.

The evidence of documents **11** A and **11** B is supplemented by fragments **12** A and **13** A (Posener-Kriéger, Verner, Vymazalová, 2006, pl. 12 A and 222f. and 225f.), from which we not only learn more about the kinds and quantities of textiles (for more detail on the different kinds and qualities of the materials mentioned see Posener-Kriéger, 1976, 429–438), given to the temple staff for these feast days, but we also discover that the materials were supplied by the treasury of the Residence. In both cases an official of the treasury of the Residence, Khenti, was responsible for supply. It is interesting that, in this list of materials in document **12** A, the type of material (*šfḫ: šḫt šri*[*t*]) intended just for the 'temple' (*rꜣ-pr*) marked in red colour, which is specified more precisely in the similar document **13** A as the 'temple: abode of the statue' (*rꜣ-pr: pr-twt*), is specially divided off from the preceding text by a double red line. This then was very probably the material used to dress the statues of the king during various rites.

From fragment **13** A it is likewise evident that with the materials for the phyles, Raneferef's temple also obtained materials for the lector-priest serving in 'the abode of the statue', which can very probably be identified with the columned hall in the south-west part of the temple.

It is probably the Feast of Thoth that is referred to on fragment no. 442 of the calendar of feasts for the sun temple of Nyuserre (Kees, 1928, Blatt 29, 446). According to Helck's (Helck, 1977-a, pl. II.1) reconstruction of this calendar, cited above, on the Feast of *w3g*, and the Feast of Thoth, 1,300 portions of bread and beer and 1 ox were offered.

tḫi **'(Feast of) Intoxication'**

On fragment no. 442 (Kees, 1928, Blatt 29) of the founding inscription of the sun temple of Nyuserre, Helck (Helck, 1977-a, pl. II.1) reconstructs the Feast of Intoxication, held on the 20th day of the 1st month of inundation, immediately after the Feast of Thoth (Daumas, 1970, 75 n. 2; Brunner, 1986, 773). The festivals of Toth and *tḫi* were fixed when the Egyptian civil calendar replaced the lunar (Spalinger, 2013-a, 115f.). To this popular religious festival Helck hypothetically attributes the offering of 1,300 portions of bread and beer and 1 bull. Intoxication was associated with the celebration of Hathor, but also with the beginning of the inundation (Daumas, 1977, 1034–1039). Gardiner (Gardiner, 1955, 25), on the other hand, has associated this feast with Thoth and proposed that its name be interpreted as "(Feast of) Balance" but this interpretation was not generally accepted.

mnḫt Ỉnpw **'Dressing Anubis'**

Fragments nos. 440a and 464 (Kees, 1928, Blatt 29 an 30) of the founding inscription of the sun temple of Nyuserre, show remnants of the name of the festival of Dressing Anubis (*mnḫt Ỉnpw*). This festival was held in the 2nd month of the season of inundation and according to Helck's (Helck, 1977-a, pl. II.10) reconstruction of the calendar, it involved the offering of 1,300 portions of bread and beer and 1 ox. According to the calendar from Medinet Habu (Schott, 1950, 104), the feast of Dressing Anubis took place on the 10th day of the 1st month of harvest and preceded the feast of the 'Forthcoming of Min (on the staircase)'. We know little about its meaning and course, but it may have been a special feast of the cemetery during which the statue of Anubis was adorned. A similar feast, the Forthcoming of Anubis (*prt Ỉnpw*) was held in the Middle Kingdom on the 24th day of the 2nd month of inundation and was also sometimes associated with the 'dressing of Anubis' (Altenmüller, 1977, 177).

Document **31** C from the Raneferef papyus archive is connected with the feast of Dressing Anubis. The text gives a list of cult objects, including a "face (mask) of Anubis (of lapis lazuli in a sealed chest of electrum", see Posener-Kriéger, Verner, Vymazalová, 2006, pl. 31 C and p. 249). The mask of Anubis adorned with lapis lazuli, a rare mineral symbolising protection and resurrection, was evidently used at temple rituals but these are not further specified in the text (Woliński, 1986, 5–30; Sweeney, 1993, 101–104; Quesne, 2001, 5–30).

š3ḏ **'(Feast of)** *š3ḏ*'

In the founding inscription of the sun temple of Nyuserre we find the *š3ḏ* feast appearing twice, on fragments no. 462 and no. 432 (Kees, 1928, 30). In Helck's (Helck, 1977, pl. II.2 and II.12) reconstruction it appears once in the season of inundation and once in the season of harvest. It was evidently celebrated more than once during the year, although Altenmüller (Altenmüller, 1977, 179) believes it was held only once, in the 3rd month of the season of harvest, and that the rites associated with it were comparable to those of the feast of Hathor in the season of inundation. Helck, on the other hand (Helck, 1977-a, 57f), argues that it was celebrated in every season of the year and Barta (Barta, 1968, 10 n. 8) believes it was held every month. It was a mortuary feast (Verhoeven, 1986, 645), at which offerings were brought to the dead. The meaning of the name of the feast is not quite obvious. Was it derived from *św3ḏ* 'to refresh'?

ḫnt Rˁ m Šsp-ib-Rˁ **'Voyage (Periplus) of Re in (the Sun Temple) Delight of Re'**

It seems that the feast of the 'Voyage/Periplus of Re' (*ḫnt Rˁ*) was celebrated every month on the 29th day. The feast is mentioned on several fragments of the founding inscription of Nyuserre's sun temple (Kees, 1928, Blatt 28 and 31, nos. 432, 475, 476 and 477). Helck (Helck, 1977-a, pl. II) in his reconstruction of this calendar considers it to fall in the 2nd month of inundation, the 2nd and 3rd months of winter and the 1st, 2nd, 3rd and 4th months of harvest. According to Helck the festival always involved the offering of one bull and 1,300 portions of bread and beer.

There is no satisfactory explanation for this repeated feast of the sailing around of the sun god (see e.g. S. Schott, 1950, 36). Posener-Kriéger has considered the possibility that this festival was connected to the feast of the Night of Re, mentioned in the papyrus archive of Neferirkare (Posener-Kriéger, 1970, 136f.; *id.*, 1976, 552f.). The repeated character of the feast rules out its connection with celebration of the New Year, but not its connection with the Night of Re, which may have been "a banal event and could have been repeated in the same way as the 'Voyage of Re'". Janák, Vymazalová and Coppens (Janák, Vymazalová, Coppens, 2011, 441f.) have also commented on the feast of the Voyage of Re: in their view it may have been connected with renewal rituals and have coincided with regular administrative inspections. The biographical inscription of the boat pilot Kaemtjenenet, in which there is a mention of the voyage of Djedkare in unfavourable weather, might be of interest in the context of this feast. When the boat managed to get back to the Residence safely, the king declared: "It was like the voyage of Re on the great lake (i.e. in the heavens) …" (E. Schott, 1977, 450).

The shortage of records relating to the feast day in other written accounts is another reason why it is difficult to understand the meaning of the Voyage of Re. We are left just to speculate and formulate questions – for the moment without satisfactory answers. From the date of the feast – the penultimate day of the month of the lunar calendar – it seems that it might relate to the first day of the coming new month (which already had begun on the preceding day, i.e. the last day of the preceding month, in the evening). This was the time when the moon disappeared and not even a sickle shape was visible on the eastern horizon (Spalinger, 2001, 226). Was this moonless state the suitable moment when the sun god was able to assert complete dominance in his voyage across the sky? It is also interesting that, in the full name of the feast, there is an emphasis on its local character: *ẖnt Rꜥ m Šsp-ib-Rꜥ* 'The Voyage of Re in (the Sun Temple) Delight of Re'. Does this mean that it was symbolically celebrated only inside the temple and the voyage took place in the open temple courtyard? Was the sun sanctuary seen as the point of beginning and end of the sun's periplus? Was this a reason for each pharaoh building his own sanctuary, where he and the sun god had an intimate connection? If so, the presence of the sun barques would only underscore this idea. We can only speculate that an important part in the rituals was played by the models of the day and night barques that were part of the cult inventory of the sun temple, as recorded in the annals of the Palermo Stone referring to the year of the 5th cattle-count in the reign of Neferirkare. Or was another cult object used in the rites – a barque with a lotus blossom, a symbol of the sun (Nefertem) at its centre or figurehead which appears in the founding inscription of Nyuserre's sun temple? Nor can we theoretically exclude even the less likely possibility that the Voyage of Re took place on the temple pond, which can be assumed on the basis of fragments of the founding inscription to have lain somewhere close to the entrance gate into the temple. It is probable that this feast took place only in the sun temple and not in the cemetery as a whole.

wꜣḥ ꜥẖ **'Laying Down the Brazier'**

On fragment no. 519 of the founding inscription of the sun temple of Nyuserre (Kees, 1928, Blatt 32) there is a remnant of the name of the feast, Laying Down the Brazier, which took place in the 3rd month of the season of inundation (Helck, 1977-a, II.3). As its name suggests, the festival involved a burnt offering (Verhoeven, 1986, 645). According to Helck's reconstruction, during this feast 1,300 portions of bread and beer and 1 ox were offered in the temple.

šspt itrw **'Reception of the River (Inundation?)'**

A remnant of the name of the feast *šspt itrw* has been preserved on fragment no. 417 of the founding inscription of the sun temple of Nyuserre (Kees, 1928, Blatt 28; Helck, 1977-a, pl. II.3). The name and meaning of this feast which, according to Luft, took place on the evening of the "....? day of the 3rd month of the season of inundation", are not entirely clear (Luft, 1992, 189). From the name *šspt itrw* "Empfang der Überschwemmung" (Hannig, 1995, s.v. *itrw*) and subsequent text we might deduce an evening voyage in little boats along the Nile or, as the case might be, on canals (and rites directed to obtaining a fertility of fields, abundance of fish or favourable voyage).

On the occasion of this feast a large number of reversion offerings (*wdn*) were brought: 30,000 portions of bread and beer, and 10 oxen.

ḥb Skr **'Feast of Sokar'**

The 'Feast of Sokar' is mentioned on fragment no. 442 of the founding inscription of the sun temple of Nyuserre (Kees, 1928, Blatt 29; Helck, 1977, pl. II.3), and in the papyrus archive of Neferirkare (Posener-Kriéger, 1976, 549–553). The name of the feast is followed in the text by its specification as the 'Dragging out of (the statue of) Sokar'. On the basis of three tiny fragments Helck (Helck, 1977-a, 59) hypothetically reconstructs the text following the name of the feast as: "His Majesty undertook a procession on a boat of He that is in his Cave" and associates the feast with the bringing of an offering of 1,300 portions of bread and beer and 1 bull. The feast took place on the 25th (in later periods the 26th) day of the 4th month of the season of inundation.

On document **13** A^{1} a–c from the Neferirkare archive, dated to the 26th day of the 4th month of the season of inundation of the year of the 3rd occasion (of the cattle-count) in the reign of Djedkare, there is a list of tasks relating to the feast of Sokar (Posener-Kriéger, 1976, 61–62, 549–553). The section *w3š* of the phyle *t3-wr* was entrusted with the task of cleaning the temple, preparing a pair of floral cult objects: *wẖ* and cult object *tb3*, making ready the mortuary feast in the hall of offering, bringing the appropriate cult vessel of electrum and Asian copper etc.

At the ceremony these cult objects represented the king, and the glorifying texts were then recited by the lector-priest. Six men were allocated to the two objects *wẖ* called 'One who rises up to Re' and 'One who unites with Re'. Posener-Kriéger sees these symbols as evoking the dead king in his solar aspect, symbolising two phases of the daily identification of the king with Re. The *wẖ* has sometimes been considered a fetish, and at other times a papyrus sceptre with a strip of material wound around its stem and two ostrich feathers mounted on its flower. The origin of this fetish has often been associated with the Upper Egyptian town of Qusae and the cult of the local goddess Hathor (Behrens, 1986, 820; Beinlich, 1984, 73). In the Neferirkare archive the *wẖ* appears again on the fragment of papyrus **14** A, where it is mentioned as one of the gold cult objects used at the recitation rite of 'the presentation of the eulogy' (*wdnt iḥy*). More obscure is the meaning in the Feast of Sokar of the cult object *tb3*, responsibility for which is entrusted in the text cited to two men. It is interesting that the object *tb3*, considered a kind of sceptre, is also mentioned in the latter Coffin Texts in connection with Hathor.

The original character of the Feast of Sokar remains the subject of debate. Sokar was probably originally only a local god, whose seat may have been located in the hollows of the rocky outcrop of Northern Saqqara above what is known as the Lake of Abusir (see p. 113f.). Sokar quite early became a god of the dead and merged with Ptah and Osiris.

We know the course of the Feast of Sokar in relative detail from texts of the Late and Ptolemaic Periods (Chassinat, 1966–1968), but we do not know what concrete form it took at the Memphite necropolis. It is very likely that part of the feast was a procession headed by priests bearing the cult likeness of the god in his typical *hnw* barque, with the head of an antelope turned backwards on the tip of the prow. The procession would successively visit the valley temples of the pyramid complexes and, in this way, the god Sokar would symbolically meet the kings to whom the complexes belonged. According to the calendar of feasts on the south wall of the temple of Ramesses III in Medinet Habu, the main phase of the Feast of Sokar started on the 21st day of the 4th month of the season of inundation with the 'opening of the eye in Shetyet' (the name of the original shrine of Sokar in Memphis) and ended on the 30th day of the same month with 'the raising of the *ḏd* pillar'. The feast was accompanied by prayers and a series of rituals, including for example the offering of an onion and its symbolic 'binding' around the neck of the dead, where it acted as a powerful protection. The feast culminated on the 25th day, with the already mentioned procession of Sokar in the *hnw*-barque, during which honour was paid to the god, other rituals performed and offerings distributed in the mortuary temples and tombs (Wohlgemuth, 1957, 18–23). The preparatory and final phase of the course of the Feast of Sokar extended it to at least 11 days, perhaps even longer.

The bringing of offering gifts to the dead during the Feast of Sokar may also be deduced from the task of preparing the *prt-ḫrw* 'funerary repast' mentioned in the already cited document **13 A**[1] a–c in the Neferirkare archive. The pyramid complexes played an important role in the celebration of this mortuary feast and subsequent distribution of offerings throughout the entire cemetery. It is therefore one of several possibilities that a rather mysterious incomplete text on a previously cited fragment of papyrus, **47** A – **48** A**,** from the Raneferef archive refers to the Feast of Sokar (Posener-Kriéger, Verner, Vymazalová, 2006, pls. 47–48; 265–266, 352–353;Vymazalová, 2006, 261–265). The account text mentions a great quantity of offerings distributed via the temple of Ptah in Memphis, and probably also the mortuary temple of Raneferef. It would be difficult to conceive of an important event in the Memphis cemetery requiring such a quantity of offerings if not its greatest, the Feast of Sokar.

Apart from bulls at this important event, a quantity of other offerings would be brought from the temple of Ptah: thousands of various kinds of bread and pastries, hundreds of jugs of beer and many pieces of poultry. According to the document cited, although only twelve bulls were part of this offering this time, an even greater quantity of other offerings, went through the mortuary temple of Raneferef on this occasion. The sheer amount of offerings raises a whole series of questions, some relating to the temple of Ptah, its property and role in the Feast of Sokar, but also its role in other feasts held in the necropolis. The papyrus also sheds new light on the role of the mortuary temples in the redistribution of offerings in the necropolis and the probably connected, relatively large storage capacity of these temples, which progressively increased from the beginning of the 5th Dynasty. A thorough treatment of these questions is not, however, the subject of this text.

ḥb wr **'Great Festival'**

The cited document **47** A – **48** A from the Raneferef archive very probably relates to a major 17-day event, which was probably the Feast of Sokar, but not necessarily so. This is an important caveat because, apart from the Feast of Sokar, there was another festival in the Egyptian calendar of feasts in the Old Kingdom, called the 'Great Festival' (*ḥb wr*), at which a large quantity of offerings was likely to have been made. This is suggested by a text on fragment no. 458 of Inscription B from the sun temple of Nyuserre (Kees, 1928: Bl. 31; Helck, 1977-a, pl. III.1–13), where the Great Festival is written in one column while, in the following two columns, we find a record of the reversion offering of a relatively large number of animals: 1 fat bull *iwꜣ*, another 11 bulls, 1 gazelle, 1 other bull and another 2 fat bulls *iwꜣ*, 100 bulls and 2 gazelles. Unfortunately the preceding and following text in these columns is missing, and so we do not know if the offerings relate to the Great Festival or represent an overall total of offerings or suchlike. In the lists of feasts from the Old Kingdom, the Great Festival is usually listed between the Feast of Sokar and the Feast of the Burnt Offering (*rkḥ*). In later times the Great Festival was celebrated on the 4th day of the 2nd month of the season of winter.

tpy rnpt **'First Day of the Year'**

This feast is what is probably documented on fragment no. 474a from the calendar of the sun temple of Nyuserre (Kees, 1928, Blatt 31). According to Helck's (Helck, 1977-a, pl. II.4) reconstruction of this calendar, 1,300 portions of bread and beer and 1 ox were offered in this temple. Parker (Parker, 1950, 61f.) rejected the earlier opinion of H. Brugsch and Sethe that the feast took place on the 1st day of the 1st month of the season of winter (*prt*). Instead, he has argued that the "*Tpy rnpt* originally applied only to the first day of the lunar calendar, may similarly in later times have been applied to the first day of any year, such as the civil or regnal year; but for this there is as yet no conclusive evidence. The interpretation that it was ever limited specifically to I *prt* 1 should be abandoned." Nonetheless, the dating of the feast *tpy rnpt* to the 1st day of the 1st month of the season of winter continues to prevail. The feast *Nḥb-kꜣw* was celebrated on the same day.

According to Spalinger (Spalinger, 1996, 162–165), the list of principal feasts stabilised in the tombs of the 5th and 6th Dynasties, and the sequence of the first four was *wp rnpt*, *Ḏḥwtyt*, *tpy rnpt*, *wꜣg*. Immediately after these festivals came the Feast of Sokar. The specific mention of the civil New Year (*wp-rnpt*) and its counterpart, the First Day of the Year (*tpy rnpt*), in combination with *Ḏḥwtyt* and *wꜣg* shows the primary significance of these four festivals. Because in the lists of festivals from the

Old Kingdom *tpy rnpt* follows *wp-rnpt*, Spalinger further believes that *tpy rnpt* was the original term for the heliacal setting of Sothis.

rḳḥ '(Feast of) Burning'

Preserved on fragment no. 519 of the founding inscription of the sun temple of Nyuserre (Kees, 1928, Blatt 32) is a remnant of the name *rḳḥ* '(Feast of) Burning' (Verhoeven, 1986, 645). According to Helck's (Helck, 1977-a, pl. II.4) reconstruction of this calendar, 1,300 portions of bread and beer and 1 ox were offered in the sun temple. It was a mortuary feast which took place on the 9th day of the 2nd month of the season of inundation.

prt Mnw 'Coming Forth of Min'

The text on the fragment of papyrus **82** b, c from the Neferirkare archive undoubtedly relates to the Feast of Min (Posener-Kriéger, Cenival, 1968, pl. 82 b, c). The superscription of the text *h3w r ẖtyw ... Mnw*, with vertical lines down each side, is written in red. Posener-Kriéger (Posener-Kriéger, 1976, 109) translates the superscription as "ceux qui descendent vers le reposoir … de Min". Under this text is a list of six men to whom the instruction in the superscription relates. It is unclear whether the preceding list of men and their deputies from the temple staff is connected with the passage about the feast of Min, but the subsequent, concluding part of the text on the fragment of papyrus, concerning a consignment of 'divine offerings', transported by boat from the Residence, is certainly connected to the Feast of Min. Posener-Kriéger has argued from the fact that phyles are not mentioned in the text that the subject of the text is not a cult object belonging to the mortuary temple of Neferirkare; she also says that this occasion is not a celebration of the Feast of Min held in this temple, but the visit of a cult statue of a god to the temple on the occasion of the Feast of Min (Posener-Kriéger, 1976, 561f.).

There is evidence of Min's feast, 'Coming Forth of Min' from the Early Dynastic Period. It was connected with celebration of the harvest and fertility and, according to the calendar of feasts from the temple of Ramesses III in Medinet Habu, it was held on the eve of the new moon of the 1st month of the season of harvest. It was a very important festival and attested from as early as the 3rd Dynasty (Gauthier, 1931, 22). According to later descriptions and scenes of the festival it was made up of several episodes and involved the participation of the king himself. During the celebration, the king would ascend a stepped podium (*ẖtyw*), on which stood a naos containing a statue of the god, walk round the naos and perform prescribed rites. It is highly doubtful that the Feast of Min was conducted in the mortuary temple of Neferirkare in full and with the participation of the ruling king. All the same, the Feast of Min was celebrated in the Memphite necropolis and depictions of it were part of the decorative programme of the pyramid complexes – as is shown for example by episodes from this feast, including the 'raising of the Pole of Min', in the temple of Pepi II in Saqqara (Jéquier, 1938, pl. 12).

What is probably a remnant of the name of the Feast of Min (*prt Mnw*) is preserved on fragment no. 482a of the founding inscription of the sun temple of Nyuserre (Kees, 1928, Bl. 31). If Helck's reconstruction of this calendar (Helck, 1977-a, pl. II.10) is correct, and fragment no. 432 did in fact follow on from this fragment, then on the occasion of the Feast of Min, held on the 11th day of the 1st month of the season of harvest (S. Schott, 1950, 104), offerings of 1,000 portions of *psn* bread, 1 bull, 10 geese, wheat, honey and all kinds of delicacies were made in the temple.

ḥryw rnpt **'The Five Epagomenal Days'**

On fragment no. 432 of the founding inscription of the sun temple of Nyuserre there is reference to the five epagomenal days (Kees, 1928, Blatt 28), at the very end of the civil calendar. These days were dedicated to five gods (Osiris, Horus, Seth, Isis, Nephthys). On the last day in the evening there was a procession with torches (Poethke, 1975, 1231–1232).

wdnt-ỉhy **'Feast of Adoration'**

From the text of document **14** from the Neferirkare archive (Posener-Kriéger, Cenival, 1968, pl. 14 A) we learn that on the 21st day of the 4th month of the season of summer in the year of the 10th occasion (of the cattle-count, probably in the reign of Djedkare) (Posener-Kriéger, 1976, 490), the feast *wdnt-ỉhy*, the 'adoration' was held in the king's pyramid complex. Performed by the lector-priest, the ceremony was one of praise and glorification and involved the reading of eulogies by the priest. The text does not indicate who or what was the object of adoration. In view of the date, which is towards the end of the year, Posener-Kriéger (Posener-Kriéger, 1976, 552f.) has associated the feast day *wdnt-ỉhy* with celebration of the New Year and also with the Night of Re (see text below). But this is mere conjecture. More is suggested about the character of this feast by the set of cult objects used in it, although not all have been unambiguously identified. There were five of them, all were made of gold, and four were directly connected with the solar cult: the *wẖ* sceptre, the solar disc, a pair of uraei and a pole-shaped support. There are therefore grounds for thinking that the *wdnt-ỉhy* was probably a feast of the sun god, worshipped in this case in the form of the sun disc.

grh Rʿ **'Night of Re'**

On the small fragment of papyrus **60** A from the Neferirkare archive (Posener-Kriéger, de Cenival, 1968, pl. 60 A) the 'Night of Re' is emphasised in red, as are the evidently related supplies of offerings from the Residence and the king's sun temple *Śt-ỉb-Rʿ*. The delivery from the sun temple included various drinks, while the supplies from the Residence are not specified. According to Posener-Kriéger (Posener-Kriéger, 1970,

131ff.), the Night of Re was a feast celebrated on the eve of the New Year, whether lunar or civil. According to the text cited, the Night of Re was celebrated in the mortuary temple and may have involved the representation of the king by the cult object *wḫ*. The following feast of Re connected with the New Year was, in Posener-Kriéger's opinion (Posener-Kriéger, 1976, 117f.), celebrated in the sun temple. One unsolved question is whether we might connect the Night of Re with the previously discussed Feast of the Periplus of Re, which was probably held at the end of each month in the sun temple.

Ḥwt-Ḥr **'(Feast of) Hathor'**

Recorded on the fragment of papyrus **19** A from the Neferirkare archive (Posener-Kriéger, Cenival, 1968, pl. 19A) is a mention of the preparation for the Feast of Hathor, or, to be more precise, the preparation of the ceremonial boat of the goddess on the occasion of this feast. It is not indicated when the feast was held, but Posener-Kriéger (Posener-Kriéger, 1976, 557) associates it with celebrations of the flood and so, in her view, it did not have a fixed date in the civil calendar. However, her suggestion was rejected by Spalinger (Spalinger, 2013-b, 617) who believes that the feast of Hathor was an eponymous one. Unfortunately, the text referring to the Feast of Hathor is preceded by a not entirely clear passage interpreted by Posener-Kriéger (Posener-Kriéger, 1976, 101 k) as *ꜥḥ n Tꜣ-nṯr* "palais de la terre divine (?)". *Tꜣ-nṯr* as the cosmographic and geographical term used to denote "liminal easterly lands such as the Eastern Desert, Syropalestine, Sinai and Punt" and, particularly, "the land of the rising sun", was discussed by Cooper (Cooper, 2011, 61).

There were several feasts of Hathor held at different times and some were just local or regional in character (see e.g. Desroches-Noblecourt, 1995, 21–45). Posener-Kriéger (Posener-Kriéger, 1976, 554ff.) has taken the view that in document **19** A the reference is to the falcon aspect of the goddess, depicted for example in bird form with a human head and cow's horns with sun disc on her head in her Ptolemaic temple in Dendera and designated 'the female falcon Hathor' (*Ḥwt-Ḥr bikt*). Hathor, 'the dwelling of Horus', would thus have been worshipped in the mortuary temple of Neferirkare as the generic counterpart of Horus. This would have been quite unusual because according to contemporary texts and depictions Hathor was worshipped in a different form in Memphis and the Memphite necropolis, in mortuary and especially sun temples. What was widespread here was the cult of 'Hathor, Lady of the Sycamore' (*Ḥwt-Ḥr nbt nht*), whose shrine had already existed in the Old Kingdom in the southern part of Memphis (Brovarski, 1977, 107–115). The aspect of Hathor which was worshipped in the pyramid complexes, was of fundamental importance in the *mrt*-shrines, and was no less important in the sun temples (see below the text). In all these places (on reliefs, sealings etc.) Hathor was depicted as a woman, standing or seated, often with cow's horns and sometimes also with a sun disc on her head.

This part of the text can bear a rather different interpretation from that proposed by Posener-Kriéger. It does not speak explicitly of the Feast of Hathor as *bikt* 'the female falcon' but of the preparation of the barque of Hathor for the festival, and the fixing of her symbol in this falcon form with cow horns and sun disc on her head to the prow of the barque and, specifically in this particular text, the current dilapidated state of this symbol. The symbol of Hathor in the form of a female falcon fixed to the prow of the barque does not necessarily mean that the goddess was worshipped in this form in the mortuary temple of Neferirkare. It could have been of merely decorative importance on the barque prow which was due for repair.

As regards the setting of this Feast of Hathor, which the goddess attended in her barque, we might most plausibly imagine it as a voyage along the canal linking Neferirkare's valley temple with the quayside of the king's sun temple. The goddess would be represented by her statue set in a naos in the middle of the barque. We can only speculate whether the voyage of the goddess in her barque was accompanied by the little boats of the inhabitants of the surrounding villages with little lamps, as was the case in later times – for example, in Dendera. As the probable goal of her voyage, in the sun temple the goddess most likely visited her partner, the sun god Re in his falcon form of Re-Harakhty. Re-Harakhty, Hathor and the king between them, holding each others hands, is e.g. a favourite decorative heraldic element on sealings.

Feast of the Divine Symbols

Depicted on the remnant of papyrus **18** A (recto of fragment **19** A relating to the feast of Hathor) from the Neferirkare archive, are two incomplete rows of divine symbols (Posener-Kriéger, Cenival, 1968, pl. 18 A). In each row the symbols are always in a pair and the same in both rows. The following pairs are depicted: a griffin on standard, a cobra (female), a scorpion and a seated baboon. Two men representing sections of individual phyles are assigned to each pair of symbols. In the upper row the name of the phyle and its section featuring the pair of griffins has not survived, two representatives of the *ỉr* section of the *w3ḏt* phyle are assigned to the pair of cobras, two representatives of the *wśr* section of the *nḏś* phyle to the pair of scorpions, and to the pair of baboons, two men from the *ḳ3* section of the *ỉmy-nfrt* phyle. In the lower row only a remnant of the name of the phyle *w3ḏt* has survived under the two cobras. It therefore seems that this important event involved all five phyles, each represented by one man from their two sections. If this was the case, at least five pairs of symbols pertained to five representatives of phyles. It is possible, however, that there were even more symbols.

The griffin embodied power, and we encounter it at the head of the royal procession or on the royal boat. The cobra represented the Lower Egyptian goddess Wadjet or the uraeus, and the pair of cobras represented two crowns, the Lower and Upper Egyptian. The scorpion symbolised the deadly power of the king, but at the same time offered a potent magical protection. The seated baboon, Benet, represented the son of the sun god. The material from which the symbols were made is not stated. From the character of the surviving symbols, they were clearly related to the king.

Posener-Kriéger (Posener-Kriéger, 1976, 558–560) considers that this fragment of text refers to a festival of divine symbols that must have been an important event in the life of Neferirkare's mortuary temple because it involved representatives of all the sections of the five phyles serving in the temple. It is hard to find a parallel to this feast. For Posener-Kriéger the fact that the names of the men below the individual symbols are the same in both rows suggests two phases of the feast. She argues that the deities cited are solar while the griffin indicates a voyage and so the feast might relate to Hathor (whose feast day is the subject of the text **19** A on the verso of this fragment of papyrus); if it does not, the feast might relate to Re.

It cannot be ruled out, however, that these divine symbols had a different significance. It looks more as if they relate to the king and the different aspects of his essence and power, even though two of them, the uraeus and the baboon, are also undoubtedly solar in character. The procession of divine symbols to which the text on fragment **18** A refers might then have been part of any kind of major festival, not only that of Hathor or Re.

śd '(Feast of) *sed*'

On a small fragment of papyrus **88** B from the Neferirkare archive (Posener-Kriéger, Cenival, 1968, pl. 88 B) there is a remnant of text concerning the *sed*-festival. Under the superscription '[Horus and] Seth in the palace of the *sed*-festival' there is a list of the names of seven men headed by the inspector of *ḥm-nṯr*-priests. The fragment of papyrus dates from the reign of Djedkare and according to Posener-Kriéger is from a roster of services or accounts (Posener-Kriéger, 1976, 119 and 491).

Since Neferirkare reigned for a relatively short time, the inscription cannot refer to Neferirkare's real *sed*-festival. It could however refer to the symbolic celebration of this festival either in the king's mortuary temple (for example, in Sahure's mortuary temple, remnants of relief decoration have survived relating to the king's symbolic *sed*-festival, when Sahure was also a king who failed to rule long enough to have a real *sed*-festival, see Borchardt, 1913, Blatt 45) or his sun temple, i.e. that part of it which seems from the decoration to have been reserved for a *sed*-festival (as is convincingly shown particularly by the preserved fragments of the decoration of the sun temple of Nyuserre).

It is also theoretically possible that the text on the fragment **88** B refers to the king from whose time the fragment comes, in this case Djedkare. Posener-Kriéger brought up this possibility (Posener-Kriéger, 1976, 119 and 561) only to reject it on the grounds that the people in the list are mentioned in other texts as employees of Neferirkare's temple, and so the feast must have been a local one relating to Neferirkare. However, which part of Neferirkare's mortuary temple should be identified with the 'palace of the *sed*-festival' explicitly mentioned on fragment **88** B? Or, does it refer to the king's sun temple? If this reference to a palace was not metaphorical, for example, as the place in a sun temple reserved for the holding of the *sed*-festival, it might mean a real palace. This possibility cannot be overlooked, especially when we remember that in the reign of Djedkare a real royal *sed*-festival was actually celebrated (Brovarski, 2001, 97).

IV. STANDARD AND IMPROVISATION: REMARKS ON THE DEVELOPMENT OF THE PYRAMID COMPLEX IN THE FIFTH DYNASTY

This chapter does not present a detailed account of the individual pyramid complexes of the 5th Dynasty, but simply an outline of the basic features of their architecture and a brief interpretation of changes and innovations in their plan within a broader historical context. It also shows that efforts to standardise the plan of the royal tomb at this time were not inflexible; whenever particular political, economic or topographic conditions demanded it, the builders would modify the plan and improvise.

The decoration of the pyramid complex in this period is discussed in a separate section at the end of this chapter.

IV.1 *Wꜥb-iśwt-Wśr-kꜣ.f* 'PURIFIED ARE THE (CULT) PLACES OF WESERKAF'

For political reasons (for more detail refer to the text on p. 30) and, above all, to strengthen his legitimacy, Weserkaf chose an architecturally very inconvenient but symbolically very important site for his tomb between the north-east corner of the enclosure wall of Djoser's pyramid complex in Saqqara and the roughly 40 metre wide eastern section of the trench known as the Dry Moat (Swelim, 1988, 12–22; Kuraszkiewicz, 2011, 141–142), which surrounds the complex. Another small pyramid complex, very probably belonging to Weserkaf's wife, Neferhetepes, adjoins his complex on its southern side. The two complexes differ significantly in plan and basic orientation.

Weserkaf's pyramid complex has been the subject of archaeological research since the 1920s (Labrousse, Lauer, 2000/I, 1–35; Maragioglio, Rinaldi, 1970/VII, 10–43 and pls. 1–4), but some parts of it have not yet been excavated, including the causeway and valley temple, the locations of which are only approximately estimated on the basis of Perring's observations in the 1830s (Perring, 1842, 42, pl. 7). The core of the pyramid, the northern chapel and other elements have not been thoroughly investigated either, and the precise length of the side of the pyramid and its precise height have yet to be established (49 m^2 ?, see Maragioglio, Rinaldi, 1970/VII, 12).

Weserkaf's pyramid and some other parts of the complex were designed in accordance with what is known as the sacred triangle: a vertical cross-section on the axis of the pyramid consists of two right-angled triangles placed back-to-back with their sides in the ratio of 3 : 4 : 5 (Lauer, 1977, 66–68). The builders seem to have been inspired by the pyramid of Khafre (Labrousse, Lauer, 2000/I, 143 n. 335). Unlike the pyramids of the 4th Dynasty, the access passage into the substructure (Perring, Vyse, 1842, 39f.; Maragioglio, Rinaldi,1970/VII, pl. 1 fig. 1 and pl. 3 figs. 1 and 5) opens in the paving of the courtyard at the foot of the north side of the pyramid. The passage, which lies on the north-south axis of the pyramid, initially slopes downwards and then gradually becomes horizontal before opening into the vestibule of the burial chamber. In the eastern wall of the corridor, between the granite portcullis with one slab and the vestibule, a narrow passage turns off into a chamber orientated north-south with a ground plan in the shape of an inverted letter T. The meaning of the chamber is not quite obvious; the king's funerary equipment was probably stored here. A similar chamber in Khafre's pyramid lies to the west, not the east, of the passage leading to the burial chamber (Maragioglio, Rinaldi, 1970/VII, pl. 6). The funerary apartment consists of a vestibule set in the vertical axis of the pyramid and the burial chamber, roughly twice as long as the vestibule and west of it. The six niches in the plan of the substructures of his immediate predecessors (Menkaure, Khentkaus I and Shepseskaf) are absent in Weserkaf's pyramid. The basalt (dark greywacke?) sarcophagus, partly sunk into the floor, originally stood by the west wall of the burial chamber (Perring, Vyse, 1842, 40).

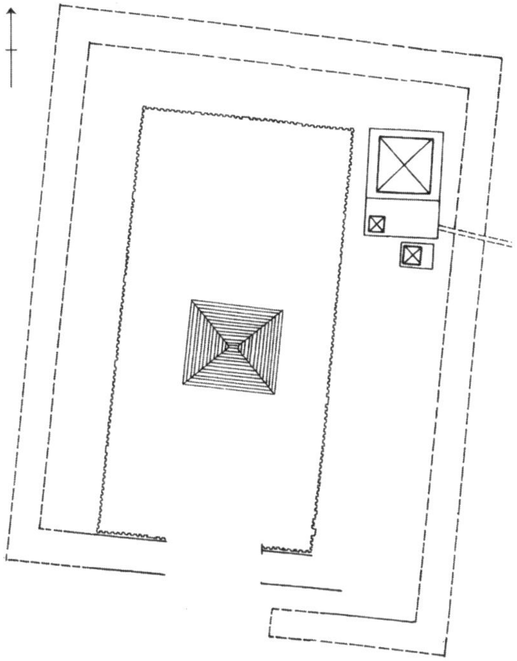

Fig. 24 Plan showing the position of Weserkaf's pyramid wedged between the north-east corner of Djoser's Enclosure and the eastern wing of the Dry Moat, see Swelim, 1988, 18, Fig. 3 and Labrousse, Lauer, 2001, 12 Fig. 39

Reconstruction and interpretation of the original plan of the mortuary temple must partly rely on conjecture because of the damage caused by shaft tombs built here in the Late Period. The temple plan was strongly influenced by its non-standard location: it lies not on the east but on the south side of the pyramid and so it is turned 90° from east to south relative to the pyramid. Despite this shift of orientation, the builders took inspiration from the royal pyramid complexes in Giza, especially Khafre's. Ricke (Ricke, 1950, 69) even suggested that Weserkaf adopted and realised the original plan ('Urplan') for Menkaure's mortuary temple.

According to Labrousse and Lauer (Labrousse, Lauer, 2000/I, 40–60 and 2, 14 Fig. 41), the temple has the following basic parts:

- entrance rooms (one peculiarity is the double gate in the entrance)
- a fore-temple, consisting mainly of a courtyard with 20 granite pillars
- a transversal corridor and storerooms (10 small and 3 large storerooms in the south-east and 7 small storerooms in the north-west part of the temple)
- an intimate temple including a hall with 8 pillars and (hypothetically) a chapel with 5 niches
- an offering hall.

In the effort to keep to religious principles the offering hall was not shifted to the south with the temple but remained on the eastern side of the pyramid. The separation of the offering hall from the temple had precedents in some earlier complexes (Snofru, Khafre, Menkaure) and would not have been a major conceptual problem. The ceiling of the hall was supported by two granite pillars, and the false door was inset in its western wall (Labrousse, Lauer, 2000/II, 37 Fig. 66). There was a storeroom on either side of the hall.

Interestingly, despite the shifting of the mortuary temple, it is the pillared courtyard that directly adjoins the pyramid. The chapel with 5 niches was moved south of the courtyard. Another innovation was a colossal seated granite statue of Weserkaf (only the head has survived of the originally 4.2-metres-high statue (now in the Egyptian Museum in Cairo, JE 52501), which probably stood by the south wall of the courtyard with its face turned into the courtyard and towards the pyramid. The statue and its location may have been inspired by the nearby seated statue of Djoser at the northern foot of the Step Pyramid, and with its back to the pyramid, placed as if to watch the ceremonies in the courtyard in front of it. The cult pyramid was shifted to the south-west corner of the king's pyramid complex. Only fragments of the high-quality relief decoration of the temple have survived (see text below) (Labrousse, Lauer, 2000/I, 72–140 Doc. 15–268; see also Stockfisch, 2003). The relatively large number of finds of fragments of statues in various types of stone (granite, diorite, quartzite, green-black greywacke, etc.) suggest that the temple originally had a lavish statue programme (Labrousse, Lauer, 2000/I, 5ff.).

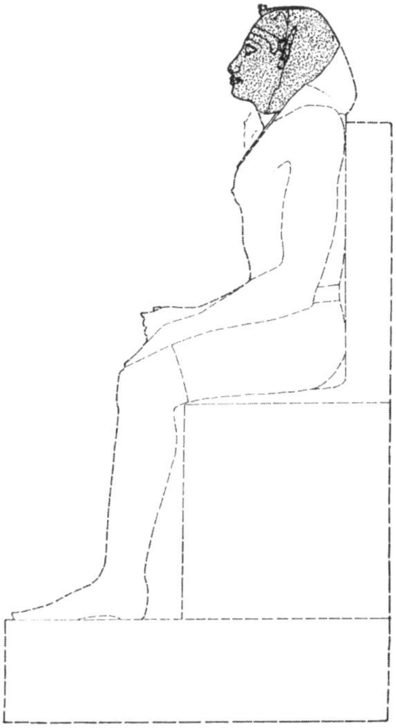

Fig. 25 – Head of the red granite colossal seated statue of Weserkaf, wearing the nemes-head covering, found in the king's mortuary temple. Egyptian Museum Cairo, JE 52501. (Courtesy Egyptian Museum in Cairo, photo Milan Zemina) – Reconstruction of the size of the seated statue, see Labrousse, Lauer, 2000, 25 Fig. 53

The Pyramid Complex of Neferhetepes

The small pyramid complex adjoining the south side of Weserkaf's mortuary temple has been attributed to the king's wife Neferhetepes on the basis of indirect evidence: an inscription from the tomb of Persen (*Urk* I, 37) and scenes from Sahure's causeway (Awady, 2009, 240–244). It has its own enclosure wall and unlike Weserkaf's complex is orientated east-west. The complex consists of a pyramid with a mortuary temple in front of its eastern side. While its overall orientation is different, the pyramid is a reduced copy of the king's. The access passage into the substructure, which runs on the north-south axis of the pyramid, starts at its foot and opens into the first of two chambers of the same size: the vestibule which is on the vertical axis of the pyramid and the burial chamber to the west of it.

The queen's mortuary temple, which is still orientated north-south in the tradition of the 4th Dynasty, consists mainly of a courtyard with two rows of limestone pillars and three storerooms. The offering hall with false door adjoins the east side of the pyramid, and to the south of the door lie three niches for statues – the earliest instances of such niches in the temple of a queen. Access to the courtyard and temple was from the south-east through a columned hall (we first encounter columns a little earlier in the courtyard of the mortuary temple G III c (Jánosi, 1996, 133 and Fig. 66). Given that the column was a typical architectonic element (with important religious connotations) in the immediately following period, especially in the royal buildings in Abusir, and given that only pillars were used in Weserkaf's own temple continuing the 4th Dynasty tradition, it is possible that this final phase of the queen's temple was built in the reign of Weserkaf's successor, Sahure. The theory is supported by the finds of the already mentioned fragment of relief from Weserkaf's mortuary temple, showing the head of a male figure on which a ritual beard has been secondarily carved, and another fragment with the remnant of a royal name in cartouche ending with the sign *w*, which Labrousse and Lauer (Labrousse, Lauer, 2000/I, 117 doc. 177 fig. 249) reconstruct as Sahure.

Although there was no space for the pyramids of his successors in the area surrounding Weserkaf's pyramid complex, a cemetery of tombs of high-ranking officials under the 5th Dynasty grew up in its vicinity between the north enclosure wall of Djoser's complex and the northern section of the Dry Moat (Baud, 1997, 69–88).

The Founding of the Cemetery in Abusir

Sahure is usually credited with the founding of the royal cemetery in Abusir, but while his pyramid complex is undoubtedly the oldest in it, there is indirect evidence that it was probably Weserkaf who chose the area of Abusir/Abu Ghurab as the site for a new cemetery for his successors. First of all, the site was in that time a relatively empty part of the Memphite necropolis (Krejčí, 2010, 95–100). Importantly, Abu Ghurab was on the western side of the Nile Valley the southernmost site of a direct optical connection with Heliopolis (see e.g. Kaiser, 1956, 114 n. 8). Moreover, it was precisely in Abu Ghurab that the imaginary line linking Abu Ghurab with Heliopolis was crossed by another symbolical line which linked Weserkaf's pyramid in Saqqara with Khufu's in Giza (G. Goyon, 1970, 88; Goedicke, 1995, 31–50; *id.* 2000, 397–412; Belmonte, Shaltout, Fekri, 2009, 258f. and Fig. 8.38; Verner, Brůna, 2011, 286–294). Very probably, the higher levels of the desert to the west of Abu Ghurab helped the ancient surveyors to discover the exceptional position of the hill on which stands Nyuserre's sun temple for the visual connection with Heliopolis.

Very probably, Weserkaf also seems to have found inspiration in Giza, where the kings Khufu and Khafre had expressed their devotion to the solar cult by siting their tombs in relation to Heliopolis, the cult centre: the south-east corners of their pyramids touch an imaginary line leading precisely to the sun temple in Heliopolis (where the later obelisk of Senwosret I still stands today) approximately 23 kilometres away and at the time probably visible from Giza with the naked eye. By choosing the area of Abusir/Abu Ghurab, and building here a sun temple, Weserkaf probably wanted not only to show symbolically his relationship to the solar cult but also to give a chance

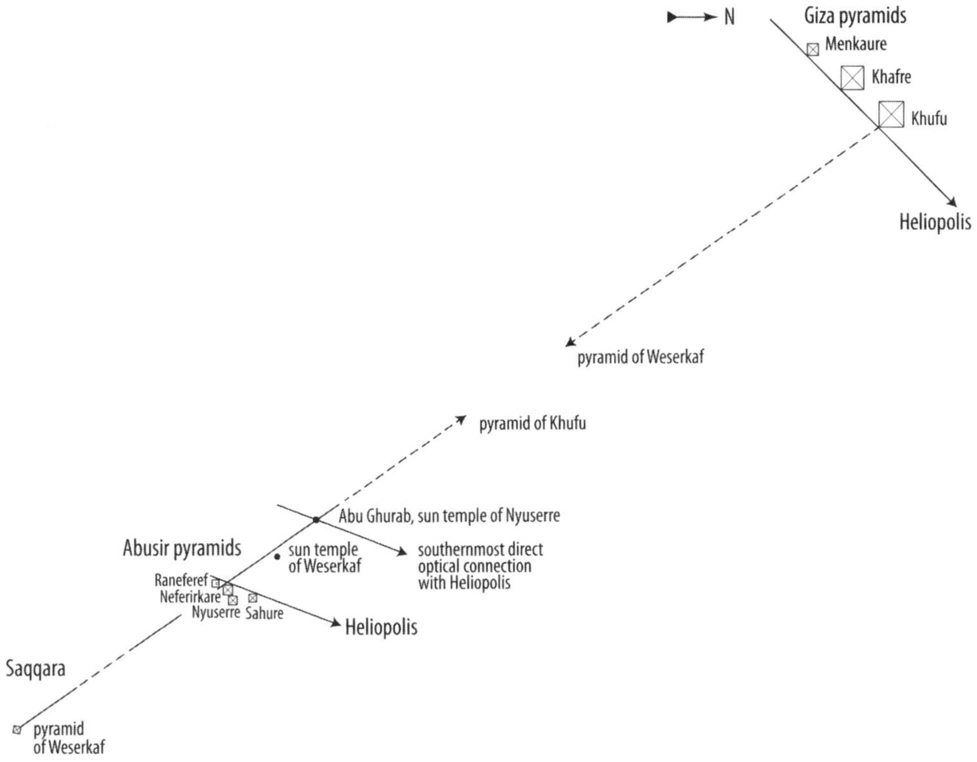

Fig. 26 Lines linking symbolically:
– the pyramid of Weserkaf with the pyramid of Khufu
– the pyramids of Giza (Khufu's and Khafre's) with Heliopolis
– the sun temple of Nyuserre in Abu Ghurab with Heliopolis
– the pyramids of Abusir (Sahure's, Neferirkare's and Raneferef's) with Heliopolis

to his successors to orientate their pyramids to Heliopolis in a similar symbolic way as Khufu and Khafre in Giza. In Abu Ghurab, however, the building and arrangement of the pyramids along the line pointing to Heliopolis was not feasible due to the local configuration of the terrain. Therefore, the pyramids of the 5th Dynasty rulers were built in a suitable site ca 1 km to the south of Abu Ghurab and subsequently arranged in a row in such a way that their north-western corners touched an imaginary line leading to Heliopolis (Verner, 2001-a, fig. on p. 303; Verner, Brůna, 2011, 290f. and Fig. 4). Weserkaf' sun temple lies approx. halfway between these pyramids and Abu Ghurab.

As pointed out by Nuzzolo, Weserkaf might have had one more reason for building his sun temple in the Abusir/Abu Ghurab area: the site chosen for his sun temple lies nearly exactly midway between Snofru's Red Pyramid in Dahshur and Khufu's pyramid in Giza (Nuzzolo, in press).

These ideas may seem speculative, but thorough investigation of the spatial relationships between the buildings in pyramid cemeteries is revealing that the Ancient Egyptians considered spacial relationships a very important aspect of this sacred ground.

IV.2 *Ḫ*ʿ*-b*ꜣ*-*Ś*ꜣḥw-R*ʿ 'SAHURE'S *b*ꜣ APPEARS IN GLORY'

Undoubtedly, the 5th Dynasty was altogether a time of major transition and sometimes dramatic change in political, economic and social conditions of Egypt. Somewhat in the shadow of all these changes remains a major reform of the architectural concept of the royal tomb linked with the ascension of the new dynasty. Obviously, the lay-out of the royal tomb was not fully stabilized and standardized during a relatively long period of the previous 4th Dynasty, the optimal plan of the pyramid complex was then only searched for. Moreover, in the political turbulence that marked the final phase of the 4th Dynasty and start of the 5th Dynasty, previous ideas on the dimensions and form of the royal tomb seem to have been shaken: Menkaure's pyramid was planned on a much smaller scale than earlier pyramids but, even so, was not completed; Shepseskaf chose a type of tomb other than a pyramid, while the plan of Weserkaf's pyramid complex was radically affected by its architecturally inconvenient but politically desirable location.

It was only under Sahure that conditions in the country regained stability and the architectural conception of the royal tomb could also stabilize in an optimal form. The more so that Sahure was the first king to build his monument in a new cemetery, at Abusir, which doubtless offered him an oportunity to rethink the concept of the royal tomb. The new concept of the pyramid complex introduced under Sahure then became a standard and source of inspiration for his successors. An important role in Sahure's decision played the culminating solar cult and the introduction of the sun temple and its interconnection with the royal funerary cult by his predecessor. Needless to emphasize that an important role also played Sahure's desire to definitely legitimate the new ascending dynasty.

The basic components of the complex – valley temple, causeway, mortuary temple and pyramid – remained, but there were a number of significant changes. They can be summarised as follows:

- The entire pyramid complex was thoroughly and symmetrically arranged along its main, east-west axis, imitating the course of the sun across the sky. This arrangement contributed to the architectural and functional harmonization of the whole and its separate parts.
- The economising trend towards reduction in the size of the pyramid, which started with Menkaure and continued with Weserkaf, became established practice. This created the basis for a better proportional balance of the whole pyramid complex.

- Poorer quality material was used for the core of the pyramid, but not for its casing or the other parts of the complex. The standard of some of the building work also declined. For example, a mistake in measurement meant that the corner of Sahure's pyramid core was nearly 3 metres too far to the east, and the error was simply covered up only by the casing of the pyramid (Maragioglio, Rinaldi, 1970/VII, pl. 6).
- The plan of the pyramid's substructure was simplified and reduced to a descending passage, vestibule, level passage interrupted by a portcullis (in the north-south axis of the pyramid) and opening into an anteroom, to the west of which lay the burial chamber (both chambers on the east-west axis of the pyramid).
- The plan of the mortuary temple underwent a major change. The previously separated offering hall was definitely incorporated into the mortuary temple (for the first time it was so in Shapseskaf's mortuary temple) and placed in the rear part of the temple directly adjoined the pyramid. In line with the religious ideas and practical needs of the cult, the mortuary temple (*ḥwt nṯr* 'god's abode'), its front cult section ('Verehrungstempel') and rear mortuary-offering section ('Totentempel'), were arranged in a functionally optimal way. In the new arrangement, the meaning of some of the spaces may have been specified (for example, the courtyard, see below the text).
- Certain practical components such as a porter's lodge, side entrance, etc. found their place in the plan either. The cult pyramid retained its location by the south-east edge of the mortuary temple. An enclosure wall on a right-angled plan defined the border of the courtyard with the pathway surrounding the pyramid, while also separating the mortuary temple and pyramid from the outside world.
- From the beginning of the 5th Dynasty we also see a consistent rise in the number and capacity of storage chambers. If the storage chambers in the mortuary temples of the 5th Dynasty were two-storey, as suggested in many cases by remains of staircases, then the area of the these storage interiors just during the 5th Dynasty increased nearly 4 times (Bárta, 2005-b, 184 Fig. 4; Verner *et al.*, 2006, 158–164).
- The column replaced the pillar as roof support. In Sahure's complex, three types of column inspired by botanical forms were used – palm, papyrus and plain, all with shapes inspired by the plant kingdom but each with a specific religious-symbolic meaning. The palm symbolized peace, protection and fertility; the papyrus regeneration and eternal life; and the simple trunk stability. Columns inspired by botanical forms had already been parts of religious and secular architecture and fine craft earlier, but their striking adoption in royal funerary architecture had the deeper purpose of promoting the principles of the solar religion in the mortuary cult.

The increasing influence of the solar religion on the royal cult was expressed in yet another important innovation: the illumination of the mortuary and valley temple and the causeway corridor by skylights. The roof terrace, which also served for astronomical observation, was no longer constructed on just one level, but on different levels above the individual temple interiors. Multi-level subdivision of the roof made it possible to use lateral skylights set close to the ceilings of selected temple chambers to light up significant interior details, especially statues and wall reliefs (F. Arnold, 2010, 212). This lighting played an important part in the temple cult, for example in rituals conducted at dawn, at night during the New Moon and so on. On certain days, the rays of the sun could fall directly on a specific statue or relief scene.

- The statue programme was optimized. The number of statues seems to have been reduced as compared to the 4th dynasty complexes of Khafre or Menkaure, for example. This conclusion can be inferred from only a few fragments of the statues that were found in Sahure's pyramid complex (Borchardt, 1910, 111f. and Figs. 142 and 144) and in the complexes of his 5th Dynasty successors. Most of the 5th Dynasty royal statues, about ten, were discovered in Raneferef's mortuary temple (see below the text).
- The decoration of the individual rooms in the complex was enhanced by the use of different materials, above all stone. Like the columns, each different stone had a particular symbolism (see e.g. Barta, 1980, 1233–1237): alabaster and limestone represented ritual purity, the basalt used on the paving was a reminder of the fertile black soil of the Nile Valley, the red granite used on columns and on the facings of parts of the walls emphasised stability and so on.
- Very probably, also the decoration programme was reorganized in the time of Sahure in compliance with the modified concept of the royal tomb. It is nonetheless hard to say to what extent because only negligible remains of the decoration of the preceding pyramid complexes have survived. But it seems that the previous decoration programme of the 4th dynasty pyramid complexes has not yet been fully standardized judging by the largely fluctuating plan of their mortuary temples. The mostly missing valley temples of that time do not allow us any clear conclusions as far as their decoration is concerned. Despite Herodotus's claim that animals were painted on the walls of Khufu's causeway, the decoration of the 4th Dynasty causeways is not quite obvious.

The presupposed standardization of the decoration programme for the pyramid complex under Sahure primarily concerned the mortuary and valley temples. On the other hand, the fluctuating length of the causeway – from 200 m in Sahure's to 720 m in Wenis's complex – certainly required a flexible decoration programme.

As far as the pyramid of Sahure is concerned, its core was constructed in six horizontal steps from rough blocks of low-quality local limestone from South Abusir and North Saqqara. However, the casing of the pyramid (blocks from the lowest layer of casing have survived in situ close to the pyramid entrance) was in fine white limestone from the area of Tura and Ma'sara (D. Klemm, R. Klemm, 2010, 131–134; Krejčí, 2010, 40f.).

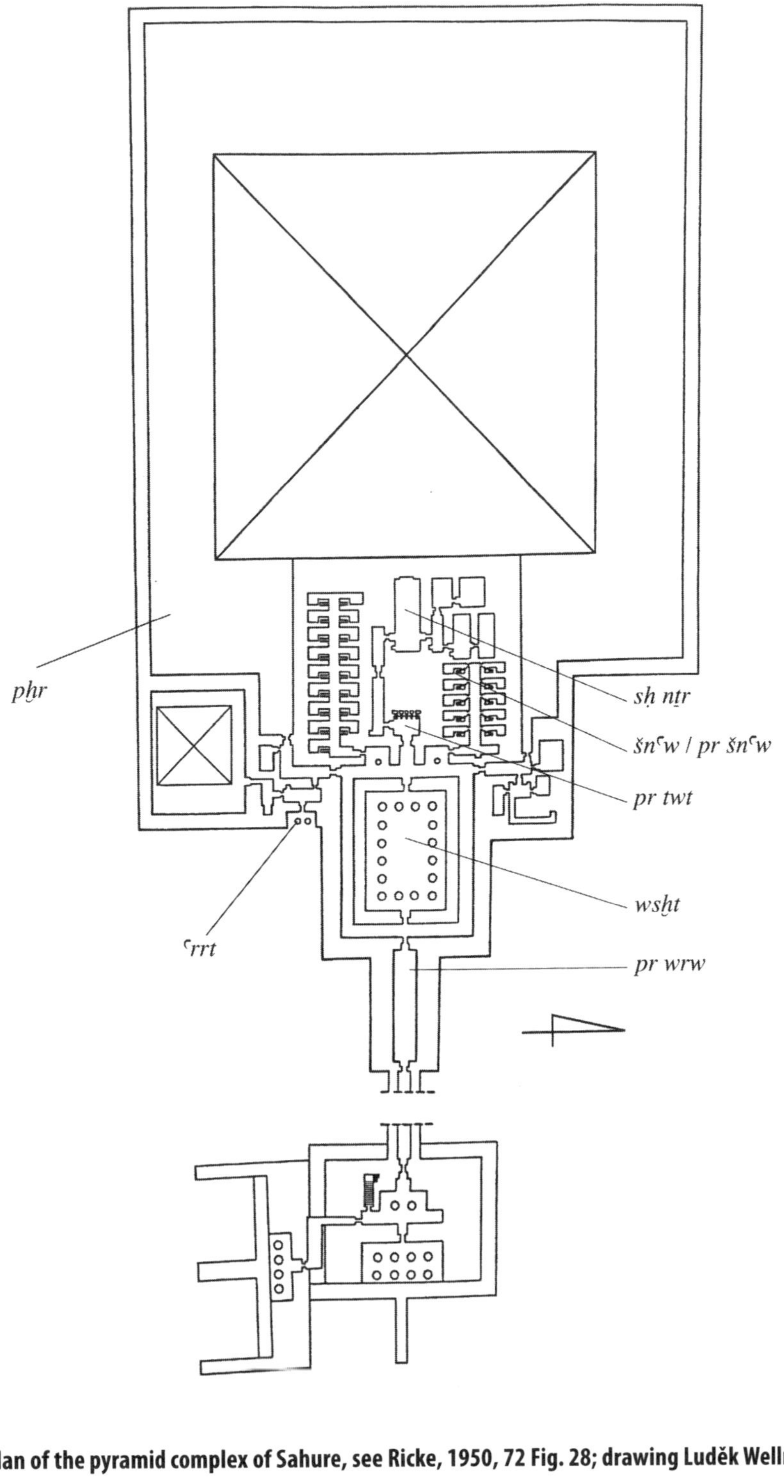

Fig. 27 Plan of the pyramid complex of Sahure, see Ricke, 1950, 72 Fig. 28; drawing Luděk Wellner

As in all the Abusir pyramids, the substructure was built in an open pit. The relatively simple plan of the substructure (Borchardt, 1910, 70–73, Abb. 94–96 and Blatt 7 and 12; Maragioglio, Rinaldi, 1970/VII, 48–52, pls. 8–9) did not differ substantially from that of Weserkaf's pyramid, but lacked a chamber east of the access passage. The passage, interrupted by a granite portcullis with one slab designed to descend and block access, opens into the vestibule. This room, which is positioned on the vertical axis of the pyramid, is located at the level of the pyramid's base. According to Perring (Perring, Vyse, 1842, 16), remnants of a basalt (dark greywacke?) sarcophagus were found in the burial chamber, which lay west of the vestibule. The shared saddle ceiling of the two chambers consists of three layers of high-quality limestone blocks.

The mortuary temple (Borchardt, 1910, 50–96 and Blatt 28; Maragioglio, Rinaldi, 1970/VII, 54–76, pl. 6) was entered from the causeway through a long hall with a vaulted ceiling (concerning the decoration of the hall and the entire mortuary temple, see the text below). The hall opened into a peristyle courtyard with 16 red granite palm columns bearing the king's name and titles. An alabaster altar, decorated by scenes of gods bringing gifts and used for the presentation of the offering *ỉmyt-wsḫt* 'what is in the open court' originally stood in the north-western part of the courtyard. Between the peristyle courtyard and the four outside walls of the temple there was a wide passage. An entrance from the courtyard on the axis of the temple led into the transverse corridor separating the front section of the temple from the rear, where the offerings were made. This corridor was also an important crossroads, providing an exit from the temple, access to the courtyard surrounding the pyramid, and access to the temple's roof terrace.

The importance and religious separation of the rear part of the temple was accented by the suggestion of a façade with a pair of columns and by the somewhat higher level of the floor. A short flight of steps, still on the axis of the temple, led from the transverse corridor to the chapel with 5 niches for the king's statues (concerning the types of statues, see the discussion on p. 138). The niches were equipped with doors, and light fell into the niches from small apertures in the ceiling above them. Because the chapel was closed off, access to the heart of the temple – the offering hall – had to be routed around it, and access to the offering hall runs not along the axis of the temple but through a passage and then a vestibule (converted in Nyuserre's mortuary temple into a so-called 'antichambre carée') situated a little to the south of the axis. In the offering hall itself, plunged in shadow, the large roughly worked block of the false door, made of quartzite and perhaps originally covered in coppered (or even gilded) foil bearing decoration, was set in the western wall (Borchardt, 1910, 57f.). The hall probably also contained a statue of the king in black granite. Two-storey storage chambers were positioned symmetrically north and south of the chapel.

Under the paving of the courtyard around the king's pyramid, there may be still undiscovered boat graves as in the complex of Neferirkare (Verner, 2013, 714–718).

The cult pyramid with a simple substructure stood in the standard position by the south-east corner of the mortuary temple and had its own enclosure wall. An ingenious drainage system with reservoirs for rain and run-off water, including metal pipes, was installed in the temple.

The causeway, with its originally lavishly decorated corridor (see below the text) linking the valley and mortuary temple, ran along the axis of the pyramid complex.

The valley temple had two harbour ramps, an eastern ramp (main, ceremonial), and a southern ramp (secondary, utilitarian). The eastern ramp led up to a portico with two rows of palm columns in red granite, and the southern ramp to a smaller portico with just one row of similar columns. The paths from both porticos met inside the columned vestibule in the centre of the temple and, having merged, continued on into the corridor of the causeway (Borchardt, 1910, 31–39; Maragioglio, Rinaldi, 1970, 78–83, pl. 6).

A pyramid town, protected by a massive enclosure brick wall, spread out around the valley temple (Verner, 2012, 407–410, pl. 38).

IV.3 *Bꜣ-Nfr-ỉr-kꜣ-Rꜥ* 'NEFERIRKARE IS *bꜣ*'

The pyramid of Neferirkare was built on a site higher than Sahure's and it therefore dominates the entire Abusir cemetery. Its siting is further indirect evidence of the previously mentioned original plan for the founding and arrangement of a pyramid cemetery in Abusir. Yet this pyramid remained unfinished. Lepsius (Lepsius, 1843, 192 and Blatt III, Fig. 8) erroneously considered its core to be proof of its construction using the method of accretion layers, but Maragioglio and Rinaldi (Maragioglio, Rinaldi, 1970/VII, 146) later showed it to have been built in 6 horizontal steps, later secondarily extended, with another two steps added. The red granite casing survives only on the first row of blocks on the eastern side of the pyramid. The steeper angle of the wall of the pyramid was probably the consequence of its secondary enlargement. The casing of the lowest step of the pyramid with smaller blocks (ashlars) of white limestone started under Nyuserre, but this work was not completed either.

The substructure of the pyramid is so devastated that it has never been thoroughly investigated and reconstruction of its plan is merely hypothetical. From the findings of Perring (Perring, 1842, pl. 6; Vyse, 1840/II, 19F) and later Borchardt (Borchardt, 1909, 39–48), there appear to have been a number of significant changes in its plan compared to the plans of the preceding pyramids. Although the entrance was on the north side and positioned on the axis of the pyramid, it was about 2 metres above the pyramid base. According to Maragioglio and Rinaldi (Maragioglio, Rinaldi, 1970/VII, pl. 11), the descending passage did not keep to the north-south axis of the pyramid but diverged from it slightly (with two bends) to the east. The passage was notable in structure: to reduce the pressure from above the builders installed an extra relieving saddle vault above the flat ceiling, with a layer of rushes placed on the vault. Beyond the vestibule was a granite portcullis with one descending slab. However, Maragioglio's and Rinaldi's suggestion that the antechamber was longer than the burial chamber seems unlikely.

There are three different views on the original plan for the mortuary temple. According to Borchardt (Borchardt, 1909, 50 fig. 50), the temple was originally planned to resemble Sahure's. It included a corridor around the courtyard with 16 columns but, at the time of Neferirkare's death, only the core of the intimate part of the temple (the offering hall with adjoining storerooms and the chapel with 5 niches) had been built; the rest of the temple was constructed in stages under Raneferef and then Nyuserre. Ricke (Ricke, 1950, 75–77 and n. 150, 237f.) rejected Borchardt's reconstruction, arguing that the plan of the mortuary temple in its existing form dated in principle from the reign of Neferirkare, including its use of light materials (with the exception of the intimate stone section) and the north-west orientation of the columned courtyard inspired by the orientation of the courtyard of Shepseskaf's mortuary temple. The third view, from Maragioglio and Rinaldi (Maragioglio, Rinaldi, 1970/VII, 164), rejected both Borchardt's and Ricke's theories of the building phases of the temple, arguing that only the stone part of the temple was completed and decorated under Neferirkare, while the rest of the temple was not built (and modified in various ways) until the reign of Nyuserre.

More recently, a survey of Neferirkare's pyramid and reconstruction of the building development of Raneferef's mortuary temple in fact suggested that none of these three views on the building of Neferirkare's mortuary temple are correct. Very probably, at the time of Neferirkare's premature death, work had not yet started on the construction of his mortuary temple, and so at least the most important part of the temple – the offering hall, the chapel with 5 niches, and storage chambers – had to be built in haste in time for the burial ceremonies. Enlargement of the core of the pyramid had taken up the part of its foundation platform originally reserved for the pyramid casing, and so this area could not be used as the platform for the construction of these cult rooms – as in the case of Raneferef's pyramid. A small foundation platform was therefore built for these rooms in front of the east side of the pyramid. Another sign of haste and improvisation in construction is the fact that the offering hall's axis does not lie precisely on the axis of the pyramid, but 1.5 m away from it (Maragioglio, Rinaldi, 1970/ VII, pl. 10 A). The stone platform and rooms above it were very probably built in the reign of Neferirkare's son and successor, Raneferef, who had to ensure the burial of his father (this is also the view of Krejčí, 2008, 127). Further construction of the temple, using mainly mudbricks and wood and with only a few architectonic elements in limestone, took place in the reign of Nyuserre. Nyuserre's decision to build his own pyramid close to the north enclosure wall of Neferirkare's mortuary temple had a major impact on the final stages of building, including the orientation

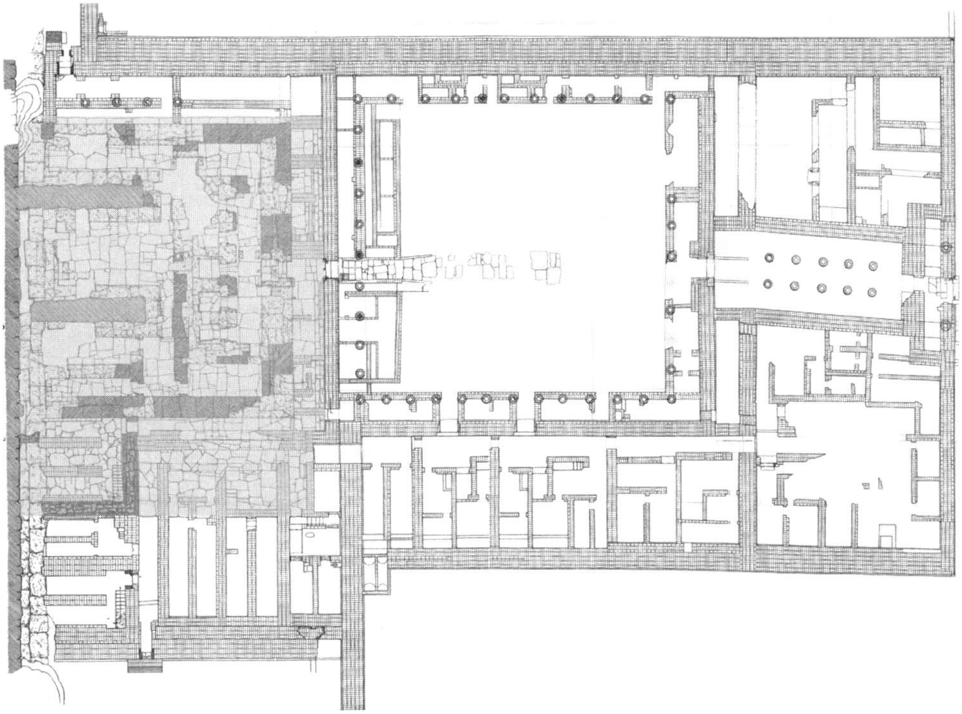

Fig. 28 Building stages of the mortuary temple of Neferirkare (concerning the final plan of the temple, see Borchardt, 1909, Blatt 10):
I. Raneferef (shade)
II. Nyuserre

of the courtyard north-south rather than east-west. Neferirkare's temple was probably completed under Nyuserre in parallel with the completion of Raneferef's mortuary temple, as may suggest the use of the the same type of wooden six-stemmed lotus columns in both structures.

In Nyuserre's reign Neferirkare's pyramid complex was equipped with yet another important component of a royal burial: two wooden funerary boats. One was buried on the north and the other on the south side of the pyramid. The boats are mentioned in papyri (Posener-Kriéger, 1976, 430) found in Neferirkare's mortuary temple. Archaeological evidence has been uncovered for the around 10-metres long south boat (Verner, 1980, 168f.). It lay on the north-south axis of the pyramid in a brick building shaped like a boat.

By the reign of Djedkare at the latest, the southern and eastern tracts of Neferirkare's mortuary temple were rebuilt and filled with the simple dwellings of the mortuary priests (Borchardt, 1909, 11f. and Blatt 10). Similar simple dwellings were also built in the area between Neferirkare's mortuary temple and the pyramid complex of his wife,

Khentkaus II. Together with the dwellings in the court of Raneferef's temple, these simple houses formed parts of the pyramid town *B3-K3-k3.i*, also mentioned in written sources of the time (Verner, 2012, 407–410, pl. 38). The town existed at least into the reign of Pepy II.

The site originally intended for the valley temple and causeway of Neferirkare's pyramid complex was exploited by Nyuserre for the building of his own complex. During the latter's reign a brick enclosure wall was built around Neferirkare's pyramid and mortuary temple.

The Pyramid Complex of Khentkaus II

It was probably shortly before the end of the reign of Neferirkare that work commenced on the small pyramid complex of his wife Khentkaus II. A symmetrical arrangement of the building, after its expansion, with pyramid and mortuary temple constructed along an east-west axis as in a king's pyramid complex, reflects high social standing of the queen (in a similar way was also reorientated, after its expansion, a chapel in front of the pyramid G III c, originally a cult pyramid, see e.g. Jánosi, 1996, 130 Abb. 62). The complex, lying on the south side of the king's pyramid, was built in two major construction phases (Verner, 1995, 38–41). As builders' inscriptions from the complex show, in the initial stages the building was for the 'King's wife' but later it was enlarged for the 'King's mother'/'Mother of two (both?) Kings of Upper and Lower Egypt'.

In dimensions the pyramid was almost identical to that of Neferhetepes (Labrousse, Lauer, 2000/I, 143). Its core was originally formed of three steps built of small blocks of local grey limestone, the casing was in fine white limestone, and there was a black granite pyramidion at the apex. No evidence has been found for a north chapel in front of the pyramid entrance, which is shifted slightly east of the pyramid's north-south axis. The access passage, opening at the foot of the pyramid, first sloped down, then became horizontal and opened directly into the burial chamber (in contrast to the pyramid of Neferhetepes, Khentkaus's funerary apartments had no anteroom). In the horizontal section was a portcullis provided by a single granite slab. The burial chamber was destroyed by robbers and only tiny fragments of funerary equipment and bandages have been found.

The devastation of the mortuary temple means that reconstruction of its 1st building phase, dated in part to the reign of Raneferef, is only hypothetical. The entrance, with two red painted pillars bearing the name and titles of Khentkaus II, was in this phase still in the south-east corner of the temple façade. The temple's central section consisted of a pillared courtyard, in which just two of the originally eight red painted pillars bearing the name and titles of the owner have survived. There was probably a hall for statues between the courtyard and the offering hall in the rear section of the temple. Some of these statues were in wooden shrines and may also have been placed in the pillared courtyard. Fragments of texts on scraps of papyrus found in the temple concern rituals involving these statues (Posener-Kriéger, 1995, 133–142; Vymazalová, Coppens, 2011, 785–799). The false door (only fragments of it have been found) in the offering hall was fixed directly to the east wall of the core of the pyramid, which means that the temple was built at the same time as the casing of the pyramid.

In the 2nd building phase, dated to the reign of Nyuserre, the temple on its lower level was extended eastwards just in mudbrick. A new entrance with two limestone pillars was built on the east-west axis of the whole complex, and behind it a broad entrance hall with an S-shaped ramp to bridge the difference in elevation between the 1st and 2nd building phases of the temple was erected. Adjoining the hall on the south were five storage chambers, and on the north the dwelling of the temple guard. Later a small cult pyramid (concerning the earliest evidence of the cult pyramid in a queen's pyramid complex, see p. 176) was built from fragments of limestone by the south-east corner of the temple of the 1st phase. The complex was surrounded by a new, mudbrick enclosure wall continuing on from the enclosure wall of Neferirkare's pyramid complex and with no barrier between the two complexes (the mortuary cults of Khentkaus II and Neferirkare were integrated). After its enlargement, and re-orientation in the east-west direction, the mortuary temple of Khentkaus II gained the status of a *ḥwt-nṯr* 'god's abode', reflecting the queen's exceptional social standing as 'Mother of two (both?) Kings of Upper and Lower Egypt'.

IV.4 THE HYPOTHETICAL PYRAMID OF SHEPSESKARE

Either Neferirkare's or, more probably, Raneferef's premature death may have been followed by the very brief reign of Shepseskare, a ruler known only from a few sealings and the Saqqara List of Kings dating from the New Kingdom. So far neither his pyramid nor any other building monuments associated with Shepseskare has been found. An

Fig. 29 Text on a sealing (Ägyptisches Museum Berlin 16277) with the alleged name of Shepseskare's pyramid, see Kaplony, 1981/IIB, pl. 82 no. 4

unfinished building on the northern edge of Abusir, halfway between Sahure's pyramid and Weserkaf's sun temple, may possibly have belonged to him (Verner, 1982, 75–77), but it seems to consist of nothing more than preliminary, and soon abandoned, earthworks. On the basis of a fragment of text on a sealing (Berlin 20396), Kaplony (Kaplony, 1981, 293) supposed that Shespseskare's pyramid was called *Rś-Špśś-k3-Rᶜ* 'Shepseskare is vigilant', but this reading and the very existence of the pyramid are disputed.

IV.5 *Nṯry-b3w-Rᶜ-nfr.f* 'DIVINE IS RANEFEREF'S POWER'

Raneferef's pyramid complex is a striking example of the ability of Ancient Egyptian builders to react flexibly to an unexpected situation, to improvise and fundamentally modify the plan of the complex under pressure of time without compromising the basic architectural and cult requirements expected of a royal tomb of the period.

The pyramid was originally planned as a smaller monument than Neferirkare's (before its enlargement) and smaller even than Sahure's. Raneferef nonetheless failed to finish it. As one of the builders' inscriptions indicates, upon the event of Raneferef's premature death, building work came to a halt roughly at the level of the first step of the core, not more than one and half years after the start of work (Verner *et al.*, 2006-a, 190 no. 8). The exposed masonry of the unfinished 1st step of the pyramid's core clearly showed that it was not constructed using accretion layers as Lepsius and Borchardt had presumed for the pyramids at Abusir. The core was made of local limestone from the quarries in south Abusir and north Saqqara, and the structure was cased in smaller blocks of fine white limestone from the area of Tura and Ma'sara (D. Klemm, R. Klemm, 2010, 127). The roof terrace was built in an original way to minimise the effects of erosion: desert pebbles were packed into a thin layer of clay. In the end, the superstructure of Raneferef's tomb had the appearance of a mastaba. As we know from papyri found in Raneferef's mortuary temple, the building was called *i3t* 'the hillock' (Posener-Kriéger, Verner, Vymazalová, 2006-b, 336–338).

The substructure was built with unavoidable modifications. The pyramid entrance (remains of a vaulted mudbrick entrance chapel were found in front of it) lay on the axis of the pyramid at the foot of its north wall. The reduction of the casing from a planned thickness of 5 metres to just 1 metre meant that the passage had to be shortened; this is why it initially descends steeply before opening into a vestibule with a horizontal floor. Instead of a portcullis, immediately beyond the vestibule there is a section of corridor built in granite and filled with roughly worked pieces of granite. Beyond the vestibule the corridor deviates slightly from the axis to the east, and gradually descends before it opens into the antechamber of the burial chamber. The burial chamber was almost double the length of the antechamber, while both rooms had the same width and the same type of saddle ceiling composed of just one layer of blocks. Small pieces of the king's mummy (e.g. the left hand), fragments of the red granite sarcophagus and remnants of funerary equipment were found in the burial chamber.

Raneferef's premature death meant that his mortuary temple was built in an improvised fashion and in several stages under his successor Nyuserre (Verner *et al.*, 2006-a, 100–112). In the 1st stage a simple chapel was hastily erected in front of the east side of the pyramid, on its axis, on a platform originally reserved for the pyramid casing. Its plan was inspired by the offering chapel at the eastern foot of Weserkaf's pyramid (Labrousse, Lauer, 2000/II, 37 Fig. 66). The chapel consisted of an offering hall with a storage chamber on its north side and a stairway, terrace and vestibule on its south side. The hall ceiling was supported by two limestone pillars; the false door (probably of limestone) in the west wall of the hall was contiguous with the core of the pyramid, which means that the casing of the pyramid and the building of the chapel took place at the same time.

In the 2nd stage, a north-west orientated temple was built in mudbrick along the entire eastern side of the pyramid. The entrance, with a pair of four-stemmed limestone lotus columns, was on the temple axis in the eastern façade. The central part of the temple, apart from a small dwelling for the guard just by the entrance, was filled with five deep chambers opening towards the pyramid and used as storerooms – another inspiration derived from the plan of Weserkaf's mortuary temple (Labrousse, Lauer, 2000, 15 Fig. 42). In a standard mortuary temple of that time there would have been

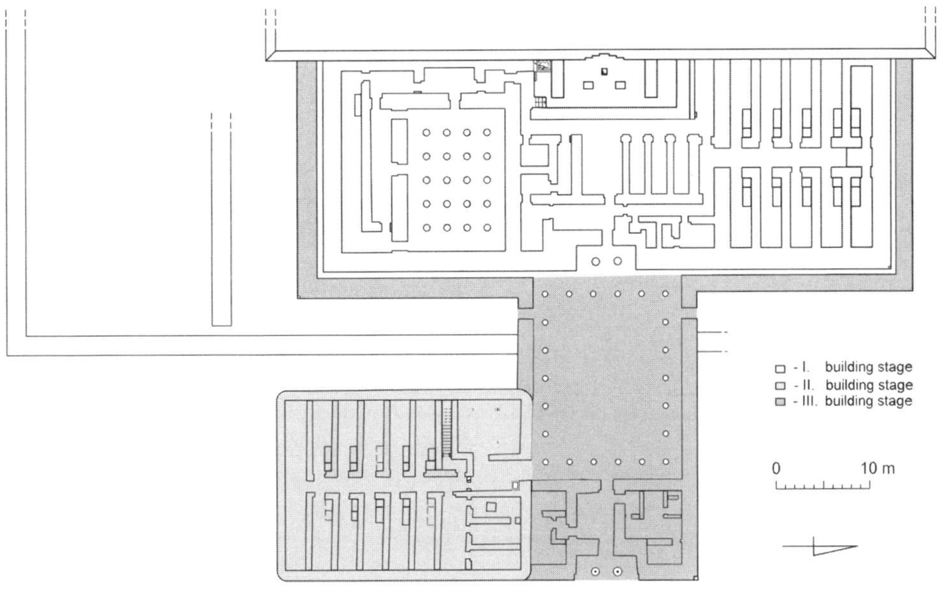

Fig. 30 The reconstruction of the plan of Raneferef's mortuary temple and its principal building stages (CUP FA CEI, drawing Luděk Wellner)

a chapel with 5 niches for the king's statues in this space. The northern part of the temple consisted of five symmetrically arranged pairs of storage chambers run by the five phyles of priests (in Nyuserre's mortuary temple each storeroom was marked with a phyle's name, see Borchardt, 1907, 54). Remains of papyri from the temple archives were among finds in some storage chambers.

An important part of a standard mortuary temple, the columned courtyard, was evidently replaced by a hypostyle hall, with twenty wooden polychrome six-stemmed lotus columns, taking up most of the southern section of the temple. The walls of the hall were whitewashed but the ceiling, painted throughout in blue, might have originally been adorned with yellow stars to evoke the night sky. Pieces and fragments of statues found in the immediate vicinity of the hall suggest that it very probably was the place where the cult of the king's statues was conducted and can be identified with the *pr twt* 'house of statue', mentioned in the papyrus archive of Raneferef. (There were at least ten statues of different types and sizes and in different materials, see Benešovská H., 2006, 360–405.) The hall – the oldest example of its kind in a mortuary temple – may have resembled the throne hall of the royal palace of the time (Di. Arnold, 1996, 39–54). The absence of the decoration programme in the temple was substituted by wooden panels inlaid with faience tablets and bearing scenes referring to the king's role in the world: legitimization of the king, his acceptance by deities, the king guaranteeing the world order, the sustenance provided for the king's afterlife, apotropaic scenes, etc. (Landgráfová, 2006, 16–23). The original location of the panels is not quite obvious, it might have been the columned hall where also the remains of a large wooden shrine were revealed. The significance of the chambers around the columned hall is not as yet clear; they may have been a stylised and reduced imitation of the circular passage around the courtyard in Sahure's mortuary temple. The first of the three rooms on the western side of the columned hall has a square groundplan and may have been the immediate precursor of the so-called 'antichambre carée', which appears in mortuary temples in the following period (starting from Nyuserre and lasting up to Senwosret I) between the chapel with 5 niches and the offering hall, but it lacks a column.

The pyramid and the mortuary temple of the 1st stage were originally surrounded by a brick enclosure wall. Unlike Neferirkare's pyramid complex, Raneferef's complex was equipped merely with wooden models of boats about 3 metres long. It is not clear where they were originally located, but after having been damaged by fire, they were ritually buried in one of the rooms in the middle part of the temple.

Concurrently with the 1st stage of the temple, and parallel to it, a north-south orientated slaughterhouse accessible from the north and called the 'house of the knife' (*ḥwt nmt*) was built in mudbrick in front of the south-east façade of the temple (Verner, 1987, 181–189). The beasts were slaughtered in an open courtyard in the north-west section of this building, the meat was processed in rooms in the north-east section, and the rest of the slaughterhouse consisted of symmetrically arranged storerooms.

The existence of this slaughterhouse, whether long-term or brief, has raised several questions about the function of the sun temple (see p. 219–226).

During the final building stage the temple was extended to the east in mudbrick, and given a columned courtyard and new entrance with a pair of six-stemmed limestone papyrus columns. Prior to these works, a passage was constructed in front of the temple of the 1st building stage that partially took over the function of the transverse corridor in a temple of standard type: this became the main crossroads for access to different parts of the pyramid complex. In the east-west orientated courtyard, its walls originally just whitewashed and without decoration, stood 22 simple wooden cylindrical columns (just a few of their limestone bases have survived in situ). At the latest in the reign of Djedkare, a small dwelling complex of priests grew up in the courtyard, as was the case with Neferirkare's mortuary temple.

IV.6 *Mn-iśwt-Ny-wśr-Rʿ* 'STABLE ARE THE (CULT) PLACES OF NYUSERRE'

The very atypical plan of Nyuserre's pyramid complex was the result of unusual historical circumstances. Nyuserre ascended the throne in the difficult situation following the premature death of his predecessor Raneferef, and immediately faced a challenging task in the royal cemetery: the pyramid complexes of three of his closest relations (Neferirkare, Khentkaus II and Raneferef) were all still incomplete and in one of them, Raneferef's, he had to organise the actual burial and cult within a short period. He combined this task with the construction of his own pyramid complex. Taking advantage of the existing technical infrastructure in situ and the chance to exploit the unfinished parts of Neferirkare's complex (the valley temple and causeway) more effectively, as well as desiring to remain close to his family, Nyuserre decided to build his pyramid close to the northern wall of Neferirkare's mortuary temple. He could have chosen a site lying on the line (described above) linking the Abusir pyramids symbolically with Heliopolis, but this would have meant lengthening the causeway from the edge of the Nile Valley by a kilometre, which would have immensely, technically and economically, complicated the building works. As it was, the site he chose had a fundamental effect on the plan of his pyramid complex.

Nyuserre's pyramid (Borchardt, 1907, 96–108) was much the same size as Sahure's, with the same length of side but a slightly steeper angle of inclination of the walls that initially made it a little taller. The core had seven steps and the materials used for the building came from the same sources as those of the preceding pyramids in Abusir. If Sahure's pyramid was the model for the superstructure of Nyuserre's pyramid, then for the substructure the model was probably the original plan for Raneferef's pyramid. Borchardt found no entrance chapel but did not even look for one. The access passage deviated from the axis of the pyramid south-east all the way from the vestibule, through a granite portcullis with two falling slabs up to its opening into the antechamber of the burial chamber. The shared saddle ceiling of the antechamber and burial chamber was constructed from three layers of limestone blocks. To reduce the pressure from above limestone rubble was spread between the two lowest layers (Maragioglio, Rinaldi, 1977/VII, 12–13, pl. 2).

The plan of the mortuary temple (Borchardt, 1907, 50–96 and Blatt 28) was radically affected not only by the siting of the pyramid and effort to exploit the area prepared for Neferirkare's causeway and valley temple, but also by a decision to leave in place a group of older mastabas from the time of Sahure that stood east of the pyramid. The plan of the temple was therefore not symmetrical along the east-west axis of the pyramid but in the form of a reversed letter L. Only the offering hall and chapel with 5 niches lay on the pyramid axis. In addition to the standard, if rather differently arranged interiors, two entirely new elements appeared in the intimate part of the temple: the 'antichambre carée' and a deep niche in the western wall of the transverse corridor.

The precise meaning of the square antechamber is unclear. So far the most suggestive evidence comes from remnants of relief decoration found in the square antechamber in the mortuary temple of Pepi II: they show the gods of Upper and Lower Egypt wishing the king eternal power, health and prosperity (Jéquier, 1938, 34–53 and pls. 36–60). Ricke (Ricke, 1950, 34f.) connected the antechamber with the courtyard of the *sed*-festival in Djoser's pyramid complex, while Di. Arnold (Di. Arnold, 1977, 10) associated it with the 'Upper Egyptian palace'. Most recently, the meaning of the square antechamber was examined by Megahed who took it for a symbolic 'fortress of the god' (Megahed, in press).

The second important innovation represented the aforementioned deep niche, where Borchardt had hypothetically placed the statue of a recumbent lion in red granite, found broken into pieces in the adjacent area and now kept in the Egyptian Museum in Cairo. The statue undoubtedly had a magical protective meaning (Schweitzer, 1948; Wit, 1951), and may have been inspired by the Great Sphinx in Giza. Goedicke (Goedicke, 1957, 57ff.) argued from the position of this statue and the title '*ḥwt-nṯr* of *Rw*(*ty?*)' that the term *ḥwt-nṯr* relates only to the intimate part (Totentempel) of the temple, but his view has not been generally accepted. Fragments of a sphinx were also found in Djedkare's mortuary temple (see p. 180).

The modification of the plan of the temple meant that the storerooms were shifted from the temple's western to its eastern part and symmetrically arranged along both sides of the entrance hall. In the open courtyard stood 16 red granite six-stemmed papyrus columns bearing the king's names and titles. The sign of a water surface at the lower edge of the column shafts evokes the idea of the courtyard as a papyrus swamp, the place of birth and the eternal cycle of life. An alabaster altar with depictions of personified nomes and fecundity deities bringing the king offering gifts (Borchardt,

1907, 68f. and Blatt 14 and 15) originally stood in the north-west part of the courtyard, but only fragments of it have survived in situ (on the decoration of a similar altar from the temple of Teti see Malek, 1988, 23–34). Ricke proposed a few justified corrections to Borchardt's plan of the eastern part of the temple relating to the passage around the columned courtyard (Ricke, 1950, 82). The plan of the cult pyramid at the south-east corner of the king's pyramid did not basically differ from Sahure's.

The north-east and south-east corners of the stone enclosure wall around the pyramid and mortuary temple were strengthened by two, high massive blocks of stone masonry, called 'Eckbau' by Borchardt and accessible from the courtyard by a staircase. They may have been meant to add emphasis to Nyuserre's pyramid, rising up between them, as viewed from the Nile Valley. These 'Eckbau' are considered the prototypes of the towers of pylons (Sourouzian, 1982, 143). Very probably another element of Nyuserre's pyramid complex, but likely to have originated elsewhere, was a ca 15-m high red granite obelisk that stood on the north side of the north-eastern 'Eckbau' (Verner, 1978, 111–118). Its pyramidion was originally cased with coppered (and gilded?) plate. The significance of this obelisk in Nyuserre's complex and its origin are not entirely clear (see text on p. 208). Borchardt did not look for boat graves, but they may well exist under the paving of the courtyard around Nyuserre's pyramid.

The causeway of Nyuserre's complex was bent for reasons already explained. It had to cope with a steeper rock escarpment and greater difference in elevation than Sahure's causeway and so an artificial terrace was needed to support its upper section, together with the front section of the mortuary temple. No remains of the causeway corridor have been found, but blocks with relief decoration may one day be discovered under the sand in its vicinity – as they were in Sahure's complex.

The plan of the valley temple resembled Sahure's with some modifications, for example the palm columns were replaced by six-stemmed papyrus columns in red granite, and the secondary harbour ramp lay on the west side of the temple not the south etc. In the west wall of the hall in the middle of the temple there was one larger niche with a smaller niche on each side of it. We can assume that there was, as in the valley temple of Wenis, a statue of the king in the larger niche and statues of Hathor and Bastet in side niches. Borchardt (Borchardt, 1907, 42) believed that the limestone statue of a kneeling bound Nubian, fragments of which were found in the hall, stood in one of the smaller niches, but it is more likely that statues of captives stood in the courtyard of the mortuary temple (Lauer, Leclant, 1969, 55–62).

The Pyramid Lepsius no. 24

The building designated Lepsius no. 24 on the south-eastern edge of the cemetery in Abusir is the last pyramid complex to have been built there. It consists of just a pyramid with a small temple on its eastern side. The pyramid core probably had only three steps, and the plan of the substructure did not differ substantially from the pyramid of Khentkaus II. The remains of a mummy, probably of a queen who died at the age of perhaps 21 to 23 years (Krejčí, Callender, Verner *et al.*, 2008, 247), were found in the burial chamber but no indication of her name has yet been found.

The temple was so devastated by stone thieves in the New Kingdom and Late Period that its original plan cannot be reconstructed but, from remains of the enclosure wall and paving, it is clear that the entrance in the eastern façade was slightly shifted towards the south-eastern corner and was not adorned with a pair of columns or pillars. The find of the remains of a cult pyramid in the south-eastern part of the temple is very important. This is the earliest occurence of a cult pyramid in the pyramid complex of a queen, and also influenced the name (perhaps only the working name?) of the complex, entirely exceptional at the time in the case of a queen: 'Two vigilant (pyramids): the small one and the big one' (Krejčí, Callender, Verner *et al.*, 2008, 144). A small cult pyramid was added to the pyramid complex of Khentkaus II, as also shown by the stratigraphy of the complex, only after the erection of a cult pyramid in the pyramid complex Lepsius no. 24.

The pyramid complex may have belonged to Nyuserre's wife, Reputnebu, only known from written sources. Whoever the anonymous queen was, not only her tomb complex but also the first example of a cult pyramid in it shows that her social status was exceptional (see the discussion on p. 58f.).

IV.7 *Nṯry-iśwt-Mn-k3w-Ḥr* 'DIVINE ARE THE (CULT) PLACES OF MENKAUHOR'

The pyramid Lepsius no. 29, known as the 'Headless Pyramid' on the eastern edge of the desert plateau not far from Teti's mortuary temple, is most often attributed to Menkauhor (on conflicting opinions on the location and owner of the pyramid see Stadelmann, 1985, 179; Berlandini, 1978, 23–35; Malek, 1994, 203–214; Di. Arnold, 1998, 7–10).

According to Lepsius (*LD Text* I, 1897, 188), the remains of the valley temple, from which a causeway rises up the side of the cliff, lie south-east of the pyramid in a place now called 'Joseph's prison'. Excavation of the pyramid started in 2006 by Hawass confirmed that it was not precisely orientated to the points of the compass (Hawass, 2010, 153–160). The access passage ran from the entrance at the foot of the north wall on the north-south axis of the pyramid as far as the vestibule, beyond which was a granite portcullis (only one descending slab had survived). From the vestibule, the passage bends south-east and opens into the antechamber of the burial chamber, which is the same width as the antechamber but about twice as long. A pit in the bedrock east of the antechamber suggests the original existence of a serdab. This would be the first instance of a serdab in the substructure of a pyramid (the link between the serdab and 6 niches in the funerary apartments of Menkaure, Khentkaus II and

Shepseskaf is open to debate, see p. 178f.), with important religious implications. We can only speculate that Menkauhor aimed at reforming funerary ideas. No remains of the burial have been found in the burial chamber except for fragments of a sarcophagus made of greywacke nor any written record that would allow us to identify the owner of the pyramid. Hawass dates the pyramid to the 5th Dynasty on the basis of the plan of the substructure and the building materials.

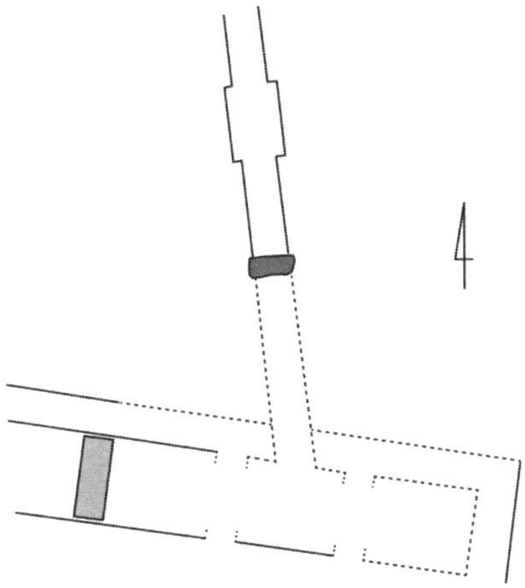

Fig. 31 Plan of the substructure of the pyramid of Menkauhor including a serdab, see Hawass, 2010, 164 Fig. 4

Hawass's so far unfinished research has hardly put an end to the long debate on the Headless Pyramid and controversy continues. Silverman (Silverman, 2009, 47–101) has tried to date the Headless Pyramid to the Middle Kingdom, citing inscriptions from the nearby tombs of Ihy and Hetep (Firth, Gunn, 1926, 61–65 and 273–288) that mention a pyramid belonging to Amenemhet I. It is still possible, that the Headless Pyramid actually dates from the Old Kingdom and was re-used by Amenemhet I. Wegner suggested in a personal communication to Hawass (Hawass, 2010, 158) that Teti's causeway may have been built at an angle because of the terrain and not in order to avoid the Headless Pyramid, and also drew attention to the inwardly slanted groove of the sarcophagus lid, which likewise appears on the sarcophagi of Pepi II and Senwosret III (Abydos). He therefore favours the theory that Amenemhet I built the Headless Pyramid. Yet whether or not speculation that the latter usurped the pyramid is confirmed, its building features seem to confirm its dating to the 5th Dynasty by Hawass and also by Maragioglio and Rinaldi (Maragioglio, Rinaldi, 1977/VIII, 62). In that case it may be most plausibly attributed to Menkauhor. This attribution is also indirectly supported by the New Kingdom revival of Menkauhor's cult in North Saqqara (Berlandini, 1979, 16–22). If so, one more puzzling question still remains to be answered: why did Menkauhor build his pyramid complex in such an unsuitable building site, at the very edge of the North Saqqara escarpment?

IV.8 *Nfr-Ḏd-kꜣ-Rꜥ* 'DJEDKARE IS BEAUTIFUL'

This pyramid complex was investigated by a series of archaeologists from the mid 1940s, for example by Varille, Abd es-Salam Husein and Fakhry (Fakhry, 1959, 30; *id.* 1961, 181), but their results were not published. Nor did anyone excavate the valley temple and causeway, which deviates slightly towards the south (Morgan, 1897, map no. 8). New research in this pyramid complex has been underway since 2010 under Megahed (Megahed, 2011, 616–634; *id.* 2014, 8–19).

Djedkare's pyramid shows some significant departures from the earlier pyramids of the 5th Dynasty. The construction material for the originally six-stepped core was no longer large blocks of the local limestone but small, irregular pieces of limestone, quarried in nearby Wadi Tafla and joined using clay mortar (D. Klemm, R. Klemm, 2010, 136). Compared to the beginning of the 5th Dynasty, this is a period in which we can observe a general decline in the use of high quality building materials difficult to quarry, for example, in Djedkare's complex the usual basalt paving was replaced by alabaster (Maragioglio, Rinaldi, 1977/VII, 96 obs. 15). There were also important changes to the plan of the pyramid's substructure. Although the entrance remained from the north, it was not placed as before at the foot of the pyramid, nor was it situated in the wall of the pyramid, but in the paving of the courtyard (as in the pyramid of Weserkaf). An entrance chapel originally stood over the pyramid entrance, but all that remains of it are imprints in the courtyard paving. The entrance was not on the axis of the pyramid but around 2.4 m west of it – a change related to the addition of a serdab to the substructure. The descending passage at first deviates slightly towards the east, levels out from the vestibule, continues in a north-south direction and opens into the antechamber. The portcullis of red granite between the vestibule and the antechamber has three descending slabs.

The funerary apartment now consisted of three rooms, rather than two, showing an important change of concept: apart from the antechamber and the burial chamber, east of the antechamber lay what was known as a serdab formed by three niches (Maragioglio, Rinaldi, 1977/VII, pl. 12 Fig. 1). This innovation may well have already been introduced under Djedkare's predecessor Menkauhor. The significance of the serdab in the substructure of the royal tomb has been the subject of scholarly debate for many years (see e.g. Ricke, 1950, 108 and Fig. 47; Stadelmann, 1985, 146; *id.* 1991, 386f.). It may have been used to store funerary equipment, but may also have had a deeper religious meaning as the seat of Osiris, the god of the dead, whose importance in the mortuary cult began to increase from the mid 5th Dynasty. For instance, Mathieu (Mathieu, 1997, 294ff.) has argued that the anepigraphic serdab with low horizontal

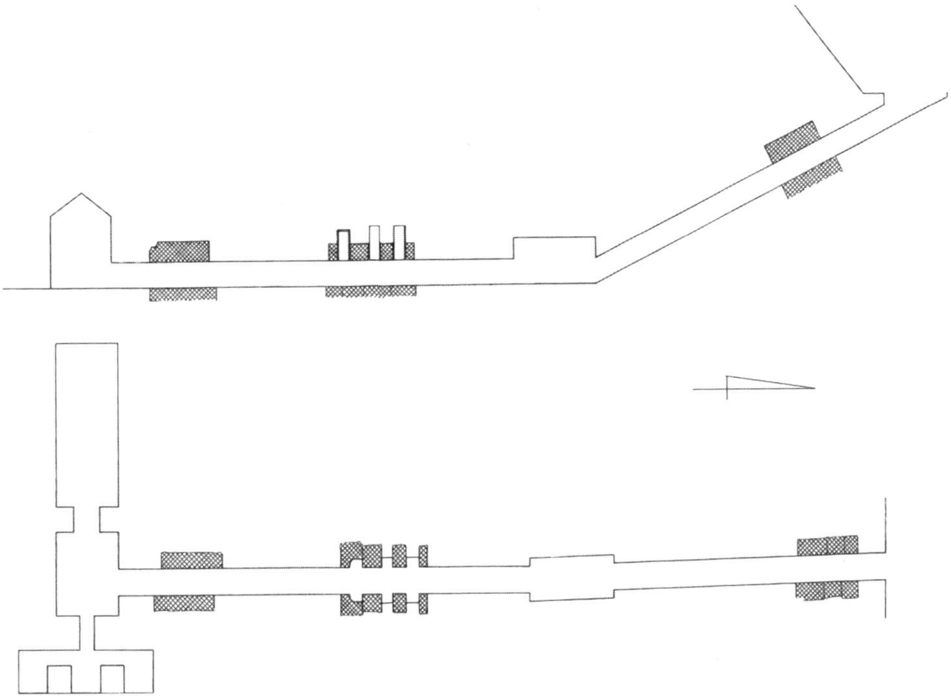

Fig. 32 Plan and section of the substructure of Djedkare's pyramid based on the plan by Maragioglio, Rinaldi, 1977/VIII, pl. 12

ceiling without stars corresponds perfectly to the place known in the Pyramid Texts as *Igeret*, 'The Place of Silence', the Underworld ruled over by the 'Lord of Silence'. The deceased had to pass through this place, the dwelling of Osiris, before ascending to heaven.

The antechamber and burial chamber shared a saddle ceiling composed of three layers of limestone blocks, while the serdab had a flat ceiling. A grey-black basalt (greywacke?) sarcophagus originally stood by the west wall of the burial chamber, where the remains of the mummified body of a man of 50–60 years old were found. Since the descending passage is still partially closed by the original blockade (the thieves squeezed around it), these mummified remnants may well be the actual remains of Djedkare and not those of a later secondary burial (Batrawi, 1947, 98–102; Strouhal, 2002, 127–132).

Extensive damage to the mortuary temple by stone thieves means that reconstruction of its plan proposed by Maragioglio and Rinaldi (Maragioglio, Rinaldi, 1977/VIII, pls. 16 and 17) is in places hypothetical, although new archaeological research may throw more light on the problem. The uneven terrain meant that the foundation of the south-east part of the temple had to be strengthened by a caisson terrace. Although in basic features the plan follows the established pattern of its predecessors, it has some important new elements. For example, the eastern façade of the temple is composed of two massive tower-like buildings of slightly different size reminiscent of a pylon and probably inspired by the two 'Eckbau' in Nyuserre's pyramid complex. In front of them, at the upper end of the causeway, were small side entrances on both sides for the use of priests.

Instead of basalt, cheaper alabaster was used for the paving of the entrance hall and the courtyard was also paved in the same material. Opposite each other, on both sides of the hall, were six storage chambers, as in Nyuserre's temple, but it was Sahure's temple that provided the inspiration for the plan of the courtyard with its sixteen palm columns in red granite bearing the ruler's titles and names on their shafts. In Djedkare's temple the circulation passage around Sahure's courtyard was modified into a long single hall on the southern and two shorter halls on the northern side of the courtyard. The decorated alabaster altar that originally stood in the north-west part of the courtyard has recently been reconstructed (Megahed, 2014, 54–62).

The intimate part of Djedkare's temple, separated from the rest of the complex by the transverse corridor, was inspired by Sahure's mortuary temple. In contrast to the latter, however, it included the 'antichambre carrée' the ceiling of which was supported by one red granite palm column bearing Djedkare's name and titles. Apart from the king, the goddess Nekhbet was depicted here. In its disposition and decoration the mortuary temple probably did not differ substantially from the preceding mortuary temples of the 5th Dynasty. This remark will be demonstrated by the forthcoming assessment of the remains of relief decoration from Djedkare's temple by Megahed.

Among the remains of statues were also revealed fragments of a sphinx that was part of Djedkare's pyramid complex. It is unclear where this was located but it may have guarded the entrance to the intimate part of the mortuary temple, as in Nyuserre's complex. The sphinx must have been large because its base alone was around 2.5 m high, as we learn from a biographical inscription of Kaemtjenenet, who conveyed the sphinx by boat to the temple building site (E. Schott, 1977, 450).

The king's pyramid and mortuary temple were surrounded by a limestone enclosure wall, while the cult pyramid in front of the south-east corner of the king's pyramid had its own enclosure wall.

Pyramid of the Unknown Queen (Djedkare's wife ?)

The smaller pyramid complex with its own enclosure wall by the north-east corner of Djedkare's mortuary temple consists simply of a pyramid and mortuary temple. Given the type of the temple and location of the complex it is most probably the tomb of the queen, Djedkare's wife, whose name is still unknown (for more detail see p. 81f.). There are no good grounds for the view that it was originally Djedkare's *sed*-festival temple (Rochholz, 1994, 255–280). The size and especially the plan of the complex, completed probably at the same time as Djedkare's pyramid complex (personal communication of Megahed), suggest that its owner had an important social position.

As yet this complex has only been partially examined or excavated (Fakhry, 1961, 31; Moursi, 1987, 185–193; *id.* 1988a, 65–66; *id.* 1988b, 65–72; Maragioglio and Rinaldi, 1962, 38–43; Jánosi, 1989, 187–202; Megahed, 2011, 616–634). The pyramid originally had a three-step core built in the same way as the neighbouring pyramid of Djedkare. Its substructure has not so far been investigated.

The plan of the mortuary temple on the east side of the pyramid differs markedly from the established pattern for a queen's temple and has elements typical for a king's mortuary temple. It does not follow the east-west axis of the pyramid and was entered from the west. The entrance hall had a row of six-stemmed papyrus columns in limestone running through its centre, and exits into both the transverse corridor and the columned court in the eastern part of the temple. The walls of the courtyard were originally decorated with scenes in low relief, some of which appear to have been secondarily altered. According to one fragment the owner of the pyramid was probably the 'mother of the king of Upper and Lower Egypt'. If so, she may have been the mother of Djedkare's successor Wenis. North of the courtyard were a group of five symmetrically arranged pairs of storage chambers.

In the intimate part of the temple, the offering hall is not on the east-west axis of the pyramid, but south of it, while the 'antichambre carrée' (in fact, this antechamber is not square shaped but rectangular) is north of it. The occurrence of the 'antichambre carrée' in the plan of the temple is another piece of evidence of the high social standing of the owner of this pyramid complex. Between the offering hall and the 'antichambre carrée' are three niches for statues. The complex also included a small cult pyramid by the south-east corner of the queen's pyramid.

IV.9 *Nfr-iśwt-Wniś* 'BEAUTIFUL ARE THE (CULT) PLACES OF WENIS'

This pyramid and its significance for the dead Wenis are directly mentioned in § 1657 of his Pyramid Texts:

"This pyramid of Wenis is Osiris and his building (as well). Approach thyself to Wenis; be not far from him in his name Pyramid."

The pyramid, under which lay the mummy of the king, was thus considered to be his body (Piankoff, 1968, 4).

As previously mentioned, Wenis's pyramid complex surround several as yet unanswered questions. The first concerns the site chosen for the complex. Although there were more convenient sites from the technical point of view, Wenis chose a site in the immediate proximity of Djoser's complex in Saqqara, very close to the southern stretch of the Dry Moat. Moreover, the site chosen for Wenis's pyramid lies on the imaginary line linking Djoser's pyramid with that of Sekhemkhet (Dobrev, 2006, 128

Fig. 1). Two large and already previously damaged royal tombs of the 2nd Dynasty, one ascribed to Nynetjer and the other to Hetepsekhenwy or Raneb (Munro, 1993, 1), had to be removed to make way for it, as did several relatively recently completed tombs of high officials. Wenis, in contrast with one of his predecessors, Nyuserre, in Abusir, did not hesitate to remove these earlier buildings. This all clearly shows that Wenis had an overriding interest in the symbolism of the location of his tomb next to that of the famous Djoser, just like Weserkaf at the start of the 5th Dynasty in the cause of strengthening his legitimacy. Wenis's pyramid is the smallest of all pyramids built by rulers of the Old Kingdom, possibly because of limited resources, but it is nonetheless exceptional for the fact that it was on the walls of its underground rooms that the Pyramid Texts – a collection of different religious texts reflecting a vision of the royal afterlife – were first recorded. However, besides religious meaning, the Pyramid Texts also have the political dimension reflecting the social conditions of the time. Though the dead king figures in them as an absolute ruler, the Pyramid Texts reflect, according to Kákosy (Kákosy, 1981, 27–46), the weakening position of the king in the society.

The core of the pyramid consisted of six steps of lower quality limestone from the eastern outcrop of the Saqqara desert plateau, but the casing was made of high-quality limestone from Ma'sara (D. Klemm, R. Klemm, 2010, 140). In the 19th Dynasty the restoration inscription of Prince Khamwaset was carved into the casing, preserved partly in situ in the lowest layers. As in Djedkare's complex, the entrance to the substructure is set in the paving of the courtyard north of the pyramid. Unlike the preceding pyramids from Neferirkare to Djedkare, the access passage kept to the north-east axis of the pyramid for its whole length. Originally, a chapel stood over the entrance: inside it, a stela was inset right in the pyramid wall and placed in front of it was an offering table in the shape of the sign *ḥtp*.

The plan of the pyramid's underground chambers was inspired by that of Djedkare's pyramid, including the portcullis of red granite with three descending slabs. The serdab, antechamber and burial chamber lay on the pyramid's east-west axis, and in the antechamber all three axes – east-west, north-south and vertical – of the pyramid intersected. The antechamber and the burial chamber shared a saddle ceiling decorated with yellow stars on a blue background, while the ceiling of the serdab with 3 niches was flat and unadorned. The dark graywacke sarcophagus stood by the west wall of the burial chamber, which was decorated in the pattern of the palace façade, and at the south-east corner of the sarcophagus there was a pit in the floor for the canopic jars. The remaining walls of the burial chamber and antechamber were covered with Pyramid Texts carved in sunk relief and painted in green-blue symbolising both mourning and faith in rebirth.

Mathieu (Mathieu, 1997, 292–298) develops Allen's (Allen, 1994, 5–28 and fig. 5) interpretation of the underground chambers in pyramids on the basis of the Pyramid Texts and adds the following ideas:

- the burial chamber represented the 'Duat'
- the passage between the burial chamber and the antechamber was 'the gate of the horizon'
- the antechamber represented the 'horizon'
- the passage between the antechamber and the serdab corresponded to 'the gate of the dwelling of Osiris'
- the serdab was 'the dwelling of Osiris'
- the passage out of the pyramid was 'the wings of the gate of heaven'.

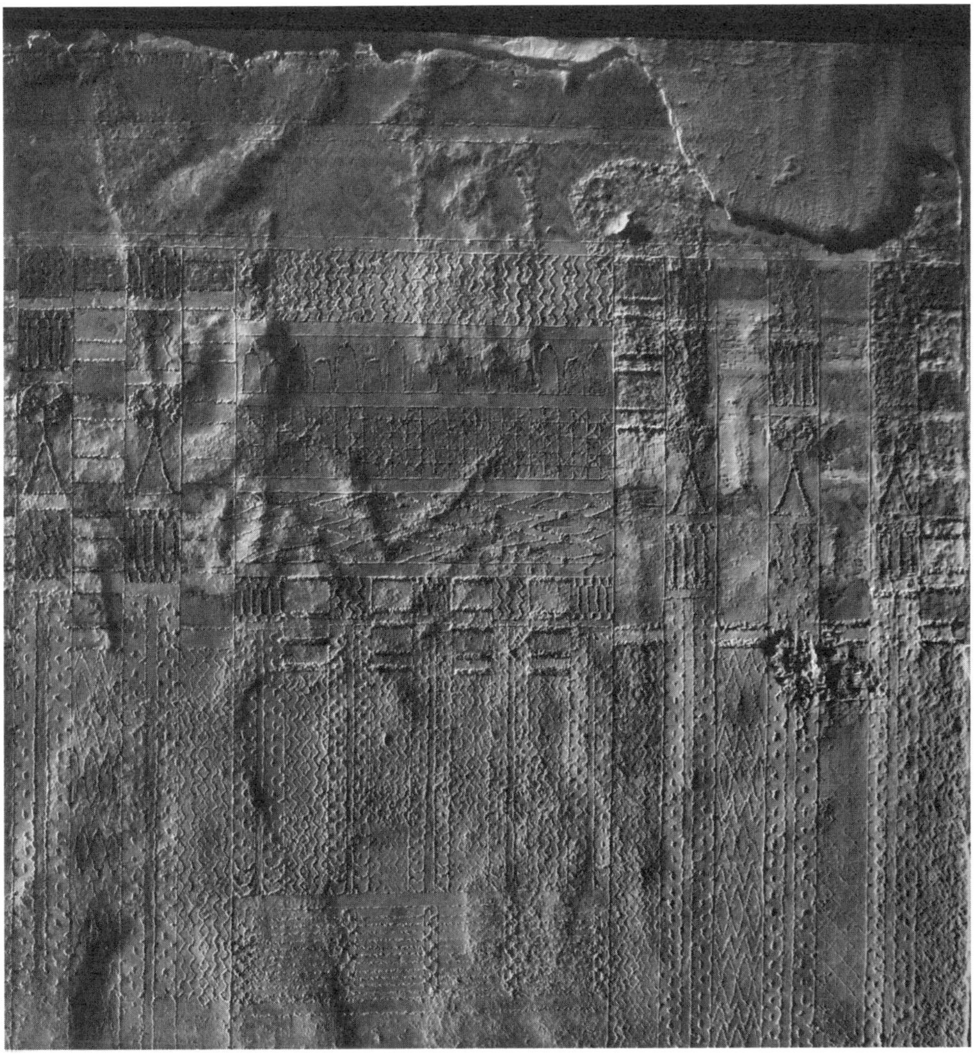

Fig. 33 The western part of the northern wall of Wenis's burial chamber with the remains of an earlier representation of a harpooning king. In front of the king's head are the remains of his Horus name, see Yousef, 2011, 820–822 and pls. 43–45. (Courtesy Mohammed Youssef, photo Sandro Vannini)

How far the Pyramid Texts can be used to interpret architectural details and rituals in the different rooms of the pyramid complex has been the subject of sometimes quite speculative debate for many years.

During recent photodocumentation (by S. Vannini) of the burial chamber in the pyramid of Wenis it was discovered that blocks originally from another, as yet unidentified building, had been used in the facing of its north and south wall (Yousef, 2011, 820–822 and pls. 43–45; 2014). Under the decoration there are discernible outlines of an original scene depicting a king in the act of harpooning. In the *serekh* by the king's head we can see the remains of his Horus name which very probably reads *Ḥr Mḏdw*. Obviously, the blocks come from a building of Khufu which might have lain in the vicinity and been in a dilapidated state in the time of the construction of Wenis's pyramid.

The mortuary temple (Labrousse, Lauer, Leclant, 1977) was completed only after Wenis's death, as is evident from the red granite entrance gate in the middle of the eastern façade of the mortuary temple bearing the name of Wenis's successor Teti. In basic features the temple plan respects established tradition, with just minor modifications – particularly in its front section. Access was along the axis of the complex through a vaulted entrance hall, paved in alabaster, led into an open courtyard with 18 red granite palm columns (two more than in Sahure's or Djedkare's temple), bearing the king's name and titles. (Concerning the transportation of the columns and architraves from Aswan in the biographical text of Henu, see Edel, 1981, 72ff.) In contrast to the earlier, usually symmetric, arrangement of the storage chambers in pairs on both sides of the entrance hall, there were five on the south side, twelve on the north side, and another five on the north side of the courtyard. This change corresponds to the existing trend to increase ever greater storage capacity in mortuary temples, which is observable from the beginning of the 5th Dynasty and connected with the redistribution of offerings.

The location of the chapel with 5 niches, the 'antichambre carrée' (which originally had one palm column in brownish quartzite) and the offering hall in the western, slightly elevated part of the temple, were all much the same as in Djedkare's temple. The remaining space around these three important cult rooms and connecting passage were again filled with storage chambers. Part of an inscription surviving on a fragment of the false door in the west wall of the offering hall mentions the *b3w* of Nekhen on the south side and the *b3w* of Buto on the north side.

The causeway (see Hassan, 1938, 519–521; Hassan, 1955, 136–139; Raslan, 1973; Labrousse, Moussa, 2002) is approximately 720 m long, bends twice and overcomes a difference in elevation of 34 metres. At its upper end there were probably exits on the north and south side, with the north exit leading to the mastabas of Wenis's wives Nebet and Khenut. Part of the original relief decoration of the corridor on the causeway has been preserved (see text further on). Wenis's complex also included a pair of boat pits,

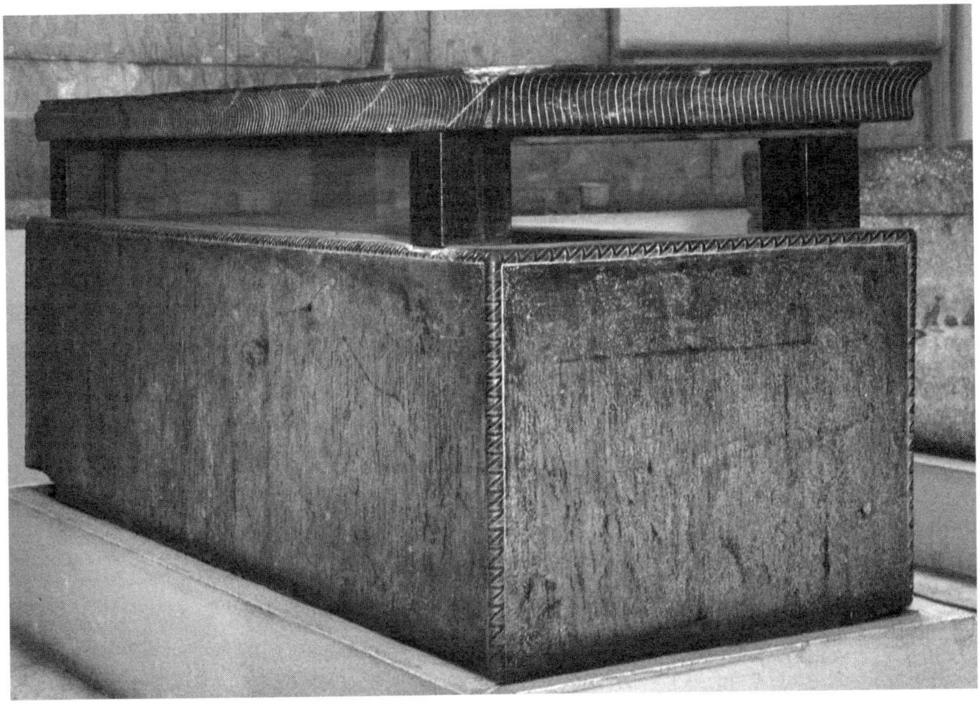

Fig. 34 Dark greywacke sarcophagus of the prince Shepes(pu)ptah discovered in the valley temple of Wenis. Egyptian museum Cairo, JE 870077. (Courtesy Egyptian Museum Cairo, photo Sameh Abdel Mohsen)

cased with white limestone blocks, on the south side of the upper part of the causeway. Evidently, the pits originally contained two wooden boats.

The north-south orientated valley temple differed in plan from both Sahure's and Nyuserre's temples. It had three porticos with harbour ramps, the main ramp on the eastern side and the secondary ramps on the north and south side. The main portico was adorned with 8 red granite palm columns, and the secondary porticos with just two of these columns each. The paths from the porticos converged in the hall, from which there was one exit west to the causeway and one exit south into a chapel with three niches. A statue of the king probably stood in the middle, larger niche, and a statue of Bastet in the north niche and Hathor in the south niche (Labrousse, Moussa, 1996, 60 n. 61). Beyond the chapel, further south, lay a trio of storage chambers.

IV.10 BETWEEN THE MYTH AND REALITY: THE DECORATION PROGRAMME OF THE PYRAMID COMPLEX

The architecture of three parts of the pyramid complex – valley and mortuary temple and causeway – was complemented by decoration in polychrome low relief on the walls of the interiors and sunk relief on the exteriors. (In the time of Wenis, the Pyramid

Texts appeared on the walls of the underground chambers of the king's pyramid.) Interpretations of the subjects depicted, what is known as the 'decorative programme', often diverge, especially since only fragments of scenes survive and we cannot reliably reconstruct them individually, let alone assess their long-term development in the Old Kingdom.

The largest numbers of fragments of decoration (but no more than several percent of the original decoration) have survived from the complexes of Sahure (Borchardt, 2013; Awady, 2009; *id.* 2010, 197–208; Khaled, 2008; Stockfisch, 2003, 5–7 and 41–48; Wildung, 2010, 183–196) and Wenis (Labrousse, Moussa, 1996; Labrousse, Lauer, Leclant, 1977, *passim*; Labrousse, Moussa, 2000, *passim*), and only smaller numbers have survived from the complexes of Weserkaf (Labrousse, Lauer, 2000/I–II, *passim*), Neferirkare (Borchardt, 1909, 28–30), Nyuserre (Borchardt, 1907, *passim*) and Djedkare (Moursi, 1987, 185–193; *id.* 1988a, 65–66; *id.* 1988b, 65–72; Megahed, in press). Some complexes may have had no relief decoration (Raneferef's), and in some cases what remains has not yet been fully uncovered and published (Weserkaf, Menkauhor and Djedkare). Only a small proportion of the fragments found were discovered in situ; furthermore, stone thieves often dragged decorated blocks or their fragments away from their original locations, making them therefore hard to identify. Some decorated blocks from the pyramid complex of Wenis may have been re-used in the pyramid of Amenemhet I at Lisht (Goedicke, 1971, 24, 59–74, 86–94, 97–99).

The following text presents a brief (and inevitably incomplete) overview of the basic subjects of the decoration of the different parts of the 5th Dynasty pyramid complexes, so providing a basis for some partial conclusions.

The Valley Temple

Sahure

- the king as a griffin trampling down the enemies of Egypt on both sides of the exit from the temple to the causeway
- the royal boat with sails called *Nṯry-bꜣ* 'Divine-*bꜣ*' and running boatmen
- fragments of the founding inscription of the temple
- an historical inscription, of which only a small fragment has been found.

We cannot be sure that the temple was the original location of other fragments of scenes found here, such as a hunt in the swamps, Khnum, other gods and their shrines, the seated king wearing a Lower Egyptian crown at the *sed*-festival, etc. These could have been dragged here from other parts of the complex when those parts were destroyed.

Nyuserre

- life in a papyrus thicket
- a palm and the shrine *pr-nw*

– the king standing with a pearled apron and a sceptre in his hand
– the lion goddess Sakhmet suckling the king, etc.

Here too it is not certain that the scenes came specifically from this location.

Wenis
– the king during his run at the *sed*-festival
– deities
– offering bearers
– boat scenes
– inscriptions, etc.

There are grounds for doubt about the origin of some decorated loose blocks and fragments of scenes found in the aforecited valley temples. They may come from other parts of the pyramid complex and could have only been left here during their movement to the Nile valley. On the other hand, a block with Wenis's cartouches and part of a historical inscription, used in the pyramid of Amenemhet I in Lisht (Goedicke, 1971, 24–26) most probably comes from Wenis's valley temple and shows that, at the beginning of the 12th Dynasty, this building must already have been seriously damaged.

Causeway

Sahure
South wall of the corridor (upper part)
– return of Egyptian expedition from Punt
– banquet to celebrate the return of the expedition from Punt
– the king with his family and courtiers admiring the exotic incense trees in the garden of the royal palace 'Extolled is Sahure's Beauty'
– the king taking a voyage on big state boats with sails, and a visit to the shrines of Wadjet in Lower and Nekhbet in Upper Egypt
– rows of running boatmen, rewarding the boat crews
– procession of personified mortuary estates from the regions of Upper Egypt bringing the king offering gifts

North wall of the corridor (upper part)
– gods bringing foreign captives to the king
– men bringing furniture and offerings
– butchers
– celebrations of the end of work on the building of the pyramid, including sports competitions (wrestling, archery, combat with poles), and performance by female dancers
– procession of officials and foremen of building works

- transportation of the pyramidion, sheathed with electrum, and the representation of a group of starving Bedouin (as proof of the hardships involved in obtaining the pyramidion in quarries in the mountains)
- the king, during fishing, pulls out with a rope 10 nets, full of fish, at one time
- the king during a hunt in the Nile swamps
- a number of processions featuring personified mortuary estates from the regions of Lower Egypt

Nyuserre

- the king as a griffin, crushing defeated enemies from all foreign lands.

The original decoration of the causeway probably did not differ substantially from that of Sahure, and may simply have been thematically richer in historical events, given the greater length of Nyuserre's causeway and his reign.

Wenis

Lower section

- opposite each other on the northern and southern wall the king in the form of a griffin crushing a Libyan chief
- captives and booty

Central section

- battle with Asians
- boats with raised masts and Asians paying homage
- boats bringing palm columns and concave cornices from Aswan
- a market, goldsmiths, metal beaters, production of metal vessels
- wild animals and hunting in the desert
- life and work in different seasons of the year
- bringing in the herds

Upper section

- procession of gods
- courtiers
- bearers of offerings
- the festive completion of building works, female dancers, wrestlers
- starved Bedouin
- a procession of personified mortuary estates

This account can be supplemented with remnants from other scenes documented by Černý in his diaries, now kept in the Griffith Institute in Oxford (Espinel, 2011, 50–70). They include fragments of scenes already mentioned, but also some quite new ones, such as:

– transport of the pyramidion
– combat with poles
– the return of a boat expedition from an unknown land (Punt ?)
– the siege of a fortress (?), etc.

Right at the top on both sides of the causeway were probably pictures of the king seated on his throne watching the procession of mortuary estates and everything depicted on the walls of the causeway corridor. It is these pictures of the king that give the decoration of the central and upper part of the causeway a clear meaning as a pictorial display of Wenis's main achievements and the daily life during his reign.

The Mortuary Temple

Weserkaf

Entrance hall

– the royal sailing boat
– oarsmen, freight boats
– the king on a hunt with a harpoon and throwing stick in the swamps
– the papyrus thicket

Pillared court, east side

– a procession of personified mortuary estates from Upper Egypt

Pillared court, west side

– a procession of personified mortuary estates of Lower Egypt
– bringing the herds of farm animals before the standing king
– bringing wild beasts and bulls to the king
– butchers
– the bringing of offerings

Pillared court, north side

– a procession of wild animals and bulls
– butchers
– the bringing of offering gifts
– hunting birds with net

Pillared hall and ***transverse corridor***

– hunting a hippopotamus with a harpoon
– the defeat of enemies
– the goddess Seshat recording the booty

Offering hall
– offering gifts

Fragments ***without*** identified original ***location***
– inscriptions
– scenes of the *sed*-festival
– gods, courtiers
– archers
– the transportation of a colossal statue (?)
– the production of vessels
– a herd of cattle crossing a ford
– hunting fish

Neferhetepes (?)
– a procession of personified mortuary estates (among them the domain of Khufu)
– the presentation of herds and poultry
– the bringing of offerings
– sailing in the swamps (?)

Sahure
Columned courtyard
– scenes of Sahure triumphing over enemies, four on the north and four on the south side of the courtyard
– also on the north side: Asian captives, Asian booty, gifts from Syria (amphorae with wine, bears)
– also on the south side: captive Libyans, the chieftain Ash with his family and Libyan booty

Passage around the courtyard
– east wing: the king with his retinue and standard bearer; the king making an offering to Bastet
– west wing: boats (with lowered masts) departing and returning, boatmen
– north wing: hunting in the swamps
– south wing: procession of gods, the king with his retinue, the bringing of offering beasts, the king and protective gods, the king hunting in the desert

Transverse corridor, northern part
– the king giving gifts to courtiers
– female dancers

Transverse corridor, southern part
– the bringing of cabinets and temple equipment
– offering gifts

Lateral (southern) columned entrance
– southern half: funerary domains bringing offerings from Upper Egypt, butchers
– northern half: funerary domains bringing offerings from Lower Egypt, butchers

Vestibule of the offering hall
– a procession of personified mortuary estates with gifts

Offering hall
– Nile deities, *b3w* of Nekhen and Pe
– list of offerings

Precise original ***location not established***
– ceremonies of the *sed*-festival
– title of a queen
– princes and courtiers
– butchers

Neferirkare
Offering hall and ***adjacent rooms***
– list of offerings
– Nile deities
– members of the royal family
– the king's titulary

Khentkaus II
Mortuary temple
– the queen's titles
– the funerary repast
– list of offerings
– offering bearers
– members of the royal family
– a procession of mortuary estates

Nyuserre
The precise original ***location*** of the fragments of scenes is ***uncertain***.
– statue of king seated on his throne (it was resting on runners and so moveable)

with the *atef*-crown on his head, Anubis standing in front of him gives him the *ankh*-symbol by holding it to his nose, Wadjet with her right arm embraces the king around the shoulders
- boatmen with poles in their hands
- courtiers
- processions of personified mortuary estates
- offering bearers
- a list of offerings
- founding rituals (a run around the future building site)
- processions of gods
- the king killing enemies

Djedkare

All that survive are fragments of scenes that are only now being conserved and catalogued.
- a procession of gods
- a procession of personified mortuary estates
- circumcision scene, probably part of a scene of the divine birth of the king
- *sed*-festival
- bringing offerings
- captured enemies
- desert animals
- names of foreign countries
- courtiers

Wenis

The original ***location*** of the scenes ***is not*** entirely ***clear***.
- the king and his titles
- the king killing a kneeling enemy
- *sed*-festival
- the king is embraced from one side by Nekhbet and from the other by Wadjet
- Horus and Seth place the crowns of Upper and Lower Egypt on the king's head
- the king being suckled by an unidentified goddess
- the king bringing Hathor four calves
- a procession of gods
- captured enemies
- offering bearers

It will be evident from this brief list that the decorative programme of the 5th Dynasty pyramid complexes is largely incomplete, that the survived scenes are fragmentary and that their original location on the walls of the buildings concerned and the rooms within them can rarely be precisely established. This is why discussion on the decorative programme cannot be conclusive and why we often encounter quite contradictory views on both the meaning of the decoration as a whole and the sense of the decoration of individual spaces. To give one example: according to Schott (Schott, 1950, 135), who was influenced by Ricke's (Ricke, 1940; *id.* 1950, 1–128) religious interpretation of the architecture of royal tombs of the Early Dynastic Period and Old Kingdom, not only did the pyramid complex serve the rituals of the mortuary cult, but the actual funeral ritual took place within its individual parts, including the valley and mortuary temple. He tried to localise the different stages of the burial and subsequent cult to particular spaces in the pyramid complex and their decoration and to link them also with particular passages in the Pyramid Texts. Schott (Schott, 1950, 137) himself claimed: "Mann kann so vermuten, das in den Pyramidentexten die Stimme erhalten ist, die einst die Pyramidentempel erfüllte."

Schott and Ricke's views were challenged by Dieter Arnold (Di. Arnold, 1977, 1–14), who pointed out, that there were no burial scenes in the surviving decoration of the pyramid complexes. Arnold also argued from the architecture of the mortuary temple, showing for example that the width of the doors and direction in which they opened would have made it impossible for a funeral procession with coffin to move through the temple interiors. His view was that the architecture and decorative programme show that the pyramid complex was the magical residence of the dead king in the other world, and intended to secure him eternal life and an everlasting monument to his important deeds and the divine nature of his rule forever.

A rather different view of the decoration of the pyramid complex has been proposed by O'Connor (O'Connor, 1998, 135–144), who builds on Allen's (Allen, 1994, 5–28 and fig. 5) cosmographic interpretation of the underground chambers in the pyramid using the Pyramid Texts recorded on their walls. Emphasising the solar cycle, O'Connor sees the pyramid complex as the place where the dead king identifies himself with the divine forces that create, daily renew, and forever govern the cosmos (O'Connor, 1998, 140). It is within this framework that he explains the decorative programme, defining the meaning of the individual spaces of the mortuary temple and its decoration as follows:

- sanctuary: nourishment via offerings
- 'antichambre carrée': rebirth and resurrection
- vestibule: overthrow of chaotic, hostile forces via the imagery of the desert hunt
- transverse corridor: symbolic rebirth via the *sed*-festival and defeat of chaotic forces
- court: the court's floor equates with the surface of Nun, and the darkness of Duat, from whence the sun emerges, while the side columns recall the flooded primeval landscape
- the process of solar emergence is shielded by a massive high feature on the east, a 'proto-pylon'.

In his dissertation Ćwiek (Ćwiek, 2003, 325–343) takes Arnold's theories a step further, arguing that the pyramid complex was not just a static 'Jenseitsarchitektur', but a dynamic 'Resurrection Machine' to secure the king's divine transfiguration and eternal life. On the basis of the orientation of the figures of the king in the decoration of the complex Ćwiek even reconstructs what he considers to be the 'King's Path', i.e. the route of the king's *kꜣ*, which during the rituals of the mortuary cult would leave the sarcophagus in the burial chamber, enter the offering hall through the false door and then proceed through the different rooms of the temple, experiencing the events depicted on their walls (for example in the open courtyard the king's *ka* united with the sun god). This theory has encountered some scepticism for several reasons, and Ćwiek himself admits to leaving unanswered questions surrounding e.g. the journey of the king's *kꜣ* back to the sarcophagus.

Recently, Steiner (Steiner, 2012, 35) argues that in the rituals of the mortuary cult the king was manifested in his mortuary temple in three places, i.e.
- the court, in his relationship with the sun-god
- the room with niches, in his royal office
- the offering chamber, as a private person.

So far, it is Stockfisch who has produced the most thorough study of the decoration of the royal tomb complexes and mortuary cult in the Old Kingdom (as for a summary, see Stockfisch, 2003, 390–400). According to Stockfisch, in the decorative programme themes of the world of men are entwined with themes of the world of the gods. In the front part of the temple ('Verehrungstempel'), the main figure in the decoration is the king acting in accordance with the royal dogma as the guarantor of the order of the world, which he maintains by his constant contact with the gods, cultivation of the cult and performance of rituals. In contrast to the front part, in the rear part of the temple ('Totentempel') the king is passive: he himself is the object of cult and recipient of offerings. Stockfisch rightly considers that earlier theories, such as the idea that the valley temple was the place of burial preparations, or mummification of the dead king and so on, to be outdated, but admits that the cultic significance of the valley temple is still unclear. However, if it is a doorway, as she says (Stockfisch, 1999, 8), does it need to have cultic significance?

Obviously, the scholarly discussion and dispute will continue, largely because of the gaps in the evidence. Many questions concerning the relationship between the architecture, decoration, and the function of the different rooms of the pyramid complex remain open. For instance, relevant written sources, above all papyri from the pyramid complexes in Abusir, show that certain parts of the complex had their own practical names such as *ꜥrrt* 'entrance space', *wśḫt* 'courtyard', *pr twt* 'abode of the statue', *pr šnꜥ* 'store' and so on (Posener-Kriéger, 1976, 493–518; Posener-Kriéger, Verner, Vymazalová, 2006, 336–350). Although the names accurately describe the physical setting of these rooms and spaces, the religious meaning of those areas is still being debated.

As an example of such a debate can serve the columned courtyard (*wsḫt*) in Sahure's mortuary temple and the scholarly dispute centering around the problem of how to interpret its religious meaning. Arguing from the palm-shaped columns, and also the decoration on one 3rd Dynasty wooden coffin, Ricke (Ricke, 1950, 21 fig. 4 and 73) considered the courtyard to be a stylised archaic "national cemetery in Buto", where according to later depictions the tombs of the early Lower Egyptian rulers lay in a palm grove on the banks of a Nile canal. By contrast, for O'Connor (O'Connor, 1998, 143) this columned court is the place where the sun emerges from the darkness of the underworld, symbolised by the black basalt paving, and the columns round the edge recall the land submerged by water at the beginning of the world. Dorothea Arnold regards the courtyard as a representation of the hill that emerged from the primeval waters during the creation of the world (Do. Arnold, 2010, 94f.). In her view boat scenes on the wall of the west wing of the passage around the court support the theory (regardless of the fact that these are seagoing commercial sailing vessels with Syrian crews).

None of these interpretations, unfortunately, pay enough attention to the surviving decoration of the columned court of Sahure's mortuary temple, and this makes them doubtful. The columns in the form of palm, the symbol of protection, peace, refreshment and fertility, evoke the idea of the courtyard as a place abounding in these characteristics. In the mortuary temple of Neferirkare, Sahure's immediate successor, the columns are lotus-shaped, which can be associated with the idea of the lotus as the solar symbol of resurrection. The papyrus columns in the courtyard of Nyuserre, with the undulating symbol of water on their lower edge, conjure up the idea of the papyrus swamp which was for the ancient Egyptians the place of the origin and eternal cycle of life. The ceiling of the peristyle around the courtyard, however, accentuated another idea: it was adorned with yellow stars, vividly evoking the sky of the underworld. Moreover, according to Borchardt (Borchardt, 1910, 17 and Blatt 6), in the decoration of the peristyle walls, images of the king triumphing over defeated enemies predominate, with four on the north and four on the south side.

Taking the aforesaid aspects of the columned courtyard into consideration, the religious meaning of this space seems to offer another interpretation. The columns surrounding the courtyard can be said to suggest a stylised Egyptian landsape, the earthly world transposed into the underworld. Their shape – whether palm, lotus or papyrus – accentuates the idea of the eternal cycle of life. Moreover, the columns as such refer to the notion of the stability and order of the world (like the pillars for example in the courtyard of Weserkaf's mortuary temple, or the pillars supporting the sky's canopy), with the king as its guarantor of perpetuity. Just as the king had magically protected his earthly realm through rituals and in union with the gods, so he protected his stylised underworld realm against internal and external evil and chaos and maintained its order. In carrying out this task he was strengthened by the offerings brought to him regularly on an altar usually placed in the north-west corner of the

Fig. 35 Borchardt's reconstruction of the rear part of the columned court in the mortuary temple of Sahure, see Borchardt, 1910, Blatt 6

courtyard. The aforesaid role of the king was accentuated by statues of the kneeling bound enemies of Egypt arranged around the courtyard (Lauer, Leclant, 1969, 55–62).

The duality of the mortuary temple is already suggested in its architecture, and further emphasised by the decoration. This duality is in line with the dual, human and divine, nature of the king. In the front part of the temple, the main figure in the decoration, the king, is presented in harmony with royal dogma as the guarantor of the order of the world through his contact with the gods, the maintenance of cults and performance of rituals. As the list in the text above shows, the relevant mythological scenes could have been complemented by scenes from the king's real life. This active, externally acting king in the front part of the temple gives place in the rear, a little raised part of the temple, following after the transverse corridor, to the king, who himself becomes the object of the cult and rituals. He was worshipped in his different aspects through his statues in the chapel with five niches. In the most intimate space of the whole temple, the offering hall, the king's *k3* used to come regularly from the pyramid, the eternal body of the king as Osiris (Utterance 600, § 1657, see Faulkner, 1969, 247), to receive the offerings needed to sustain his eternal life.

It was originally assumed that the decoration of the causeway would be mythical and apotropaic in character, but excavation of Wenis's and most recently Sahure's causeways has changed this view. The decorative themes in the long corridor on the causeway from the valley to the mortuary temple may have largely been determined by its structure and length. Where it began, by the exit from the valley temple, the ascent had to be again protected by apotropaic images. The immense surface of the walls of the corridor, up to several hundred metres long, was an opportunity to depict scenes from the real life of the king and his reign, albeit in rather heroic form, alongside mythological subjects. The pictures of the king at the upper edge of the corridor, receiving processions of funerary domains bringing offerings and looking down on all the real and mythological subjects in front of him, was the logical culmination of the decoration of the causeway.

The decoration of the valley temple was influenced by its function and site on the border between the Nile Valley and the desert, the world of the living and the kingdom of the dead. Primarily, the valley temple was a monumental gateway to the king's posthumous residence. As such, the valley temple is not a temple in true sense of the word, but a forecourt to a sacred space. It was also an anchorage for boats where an artificial water canal terminated, it was the end of one journey and beginning of another.

Such a place required special protection, provided by pictures of protective deities and apotropaic images of the king destroying enemies. There was probably once an historical inscription in the valley temple about the founding and building of the pyramid complex, and there may also have been a calendar of the festivals that were supposed to be celebrated in the pyramid complex. Naturally, it was around the valley temple and its harbour that the economic and administrative infrastructure of the mortuary cult in the pyramid complex would have been concentrated, i.e. what was known as the pyramid town. Except on ceremonial occasions, however, the priests and temple staff did not use the valley temple, and to fulfil their daily duties they used the side pathway by the causeway and secondary entrance into the mortuary temple.

The function of the valley temples in Abusir (Sahure's and Nyuserre's) and Saqqara (Wenis's) has been recently questioned by Jeffreys on the basis of the EES survey carried out at the foot of the Saqqara escarpment (Jeffreys, 2001, 15f. and 2006, 14f.). According to the results of this survey, the floor level of the cited valley temples is too high to allow them to function as true harbours. This finding would refute the common assumption that the Nile flood sediments reached in the pharaonic times about one metre every one thousand years. These temples might have been, in Jeffreys's opinion, only symbolic, dummy buildings, whereas the true harbours of the pyramid complexes lay farther to the east.

The suggested theory provokes a number of questions: for instance, were the temples accessible all the year or only during the Nile floods? Did a basin supplied with the Nile water, as one discovered in Giza near the tomb of Khentkaus I and the valley temple of Menkaure, also exist around other valley temples, and was it supplied with water by means of a canal? Had two or, as the case might be, three landing ramps in these temples only a symbolic meaning, and if so, what was it? These and many other questions are linked to the survey results as published by Jeffreys and we certainly need further thorough field research around the valley buildings to resolve these issues.

What then can be said in conclusion on the role of the decorative programme in the pyramid complex, the eternal residence of the king and his *k3*? The earlier architectural-archaeological researches of Lauer in Djoser's pyramid complex (Lauer, 1936) and the work of a series of other archaeologists (for example Kaiser, 1969, 1–21 and Arnold, 1977, 1–14) already demonstrated that both fictive and functional parts existed alongside each other in the architecture of the complex. It is therefore not surprising that we encounter both mythological subjects and pictures of the real world in the decorative programmes of the pyramid complexes. Here the two worlds, the mythic and the real, mutually complement and permeate each other and reflect the dual, human and divine, nature of the king. However, though represented in the decoration of the three parts of the pyramid complex – the valley and mortuary temple and causeway – the two worlds were accentuated in them in different ways.

V. SUN TEMPLES

V.1 *Nḫn-Rʿ* 'RE'S-NEKHEN / RE'S STOREHOUSE (?)'

Borchardt (Borchardt, 1910, 149f.) was the first to suggest that the ruins of a building on the northern edge of the cemetery in Abusir hid a sun temple; he confirmed this theory by two probes conducted in 1907 and 1913. What he discovered was the sun temple of Weserkaf, although he mistakenly read its name as *Sp-Rʿ* and not *Nḫn-Rʿ*. His excavations were followed up and completed in the years 1954–1957 by a German-Swiss team led by Ricke (Ricke, 1965–1969).

The plan of Weserkaf's sun temple represents an entirely new type in the development of the Egyptian temple. Its creators clearly found inspiration in other buildings of the period, particularly the plan of pyramid complexes, as is evident in the division of the sun temple into three parts: a valley temple, a causeway, and what is known as an upper temple. As we shall see below, the inspiration for the valley temple was Snofru's *sed*-festival temple, built on the causeway between the Nile Valley and the Bent Pyramid in Dahshur. Identifying the models for the upper temple is harder; it is probable that the architects of the sun temple were inspired by buildings of the solar cult centre in Heliopolis, but the site of Heliopolis is still so under-explored and little excavated that the theory cannot yet be proved. The same applies to the dominant architectural element of the upper temple, an obelisk, but according to Ricke it was not erected in the sun temple until the 2nd construction phase (on the obelisk see below).

Ricke (Ricke, 1965, 35) believed that originally the sun temple had only a simple entrance gate in the valley – a structure that cannot be found today because of ground water. In his view (Ricke, 1965, 42) the valley temple was erected later in the reign of Nyuserre, during the 3rd construction phase of the upper temple. The valley temple stood on a massive foundation platform constructed of three layers of blocks, from which the causeway rose without a gap. Both the valley temple and the causeway are orientated north-east, while the upper temple is orientated east-west.

Ricke thought that the plan of Weserkaf's valley temple had been inspired by the mortuary temple of Khafre. Three pillars and smaller remnants of walls or in some cases just their imprints are all that have survived of Weserkaf's valley temple and so it has proved possible to reconstruct only the middle and rear part of the groundplan. Ricke (Ricke, 1969, 140) hypothesised that the front section consisted of an entrance hall with storage chambers on each side of it and also one room for the temple guard.

According to his reconstruction there was a court with a total of 16 pillars along its sides in the middle section, and at the rear seven chapels.

As regards the cult significance of the valley temple, Ricke (Ricke, 1965, 46) thought it could have been a temple of the *ḥwt-k3* or *mrt* type – in which case the chapels would have contained either statues just of the king, or statues of Hathor, Ihy and the king as well. Ricke even theorised that it could have been a temple of Neith – since in front of the temple entrance he found the head of a dark greywacke statue (Egyptian Museum in Cairo, JE 90220) that he believed was of Neith (Ricke, 1969, 139–148). Today it has been conclusively identified as a head of Weserkaf, and the consensus on the cult significance of this valley temple is also different.

The causeway did not rise from the rear section of the temple but, as in Shepseskaf's tomb complex, for example, it was built along the south side of the valley temple. It was open and lined on both sides by low mudbrick walls.

The upper temple went through four construction phases. From the little that survives of the first phase it is clear that the upper temple originally had a rectangular ground-plan orientated east-west; the temple was enclosed by a massive mudbrick wall with rounded corners, plastered on both sides and white-washed. The rounding of the corners may have been intended, according to some scholars, to evoke either the primeval hill or the oval sign for *Nḫn* 'Hierakonpolis'. But it could just have been routine construction technique, familiar from other mudbrick buildings, to protect the vulnerable corners. From the determinative sign of the temple's name in an inscription on a limestone tablet found in the temple Ricke believed that a wooden column with a cross-beam had originally stood inside the temple on a pedestal (Ricke, 1965, 5). There had probably been an altar at the foot of the pedestal. According to Ricke, in this 1st phase the building had resembled the temple of Re in Heliopolis.

During the 2nd building stage the temple was enlarged and acquired a square ground plan, and the mudbrick pedestal with the wooden column was replaced by a massive square limestone base (its lower section was clad in quartzite and red granite) around 6–7 metres high. An obelisk faced in red granite was raised on the base, but since only fragments of the obelisk have survived its height cannot be precisely determined. It is unclear whether the apex of the obelisk, the pyramidion, was covered by metal (copper? gold?), or whether a symbol of the solar disc was fixed to the top. In a hieroglyphic inscription from the tomb of Neferiretenef (Walle, 1930, 53), a priest in both Weserkaf's and Nyuserre's sun temples, the name of Weserkaf's temple is determined by an obelisk with a solar disc, and Nyuserre's temple only by an obelisk.

At the foot of the obelisk ceremonies were conducted. Inside the eastern section of the base there may also have been a small chamber accessible from the courtyard. In front of the east side of the base there were probably two chapels, each containing a dark greywacke cabinet and decorated on the outside by an intertwined pattern.

Ricke believed that a statue of Hathor had stood in the south chapel and a statue of Bastet in the northern chapel. In Ricke's view the cabinets date from the reign of Nyuserre, in whose sun temple a fragment with a similar pattern has been found.

In the 3rd phase the temple was enlarged further towards the east and west. What were probably storerooms were built in the western part of the temple, while the causeway was shortened on the eastern side and a new entrance created. In this phase a brick building, entered from the temple courtyard, was built adjoining the southern wall of the temple. The building had rooms with vaulted ceilings and probably served as a dwelling for priests.

In the 4th phase a mudbrick altar, surrounded by a small wall with regular apertures, was constructed in the courtyard in front of the east side of the base. In the eastern part of the temple, on its axis, there were a row of low benches made of clay and pieces of limestone: offerings were probably placed on these benches during ceremonies. In this phase a few narrow chambers were built in the southern part of the court.

The last building works in Weserkaf's sun temple evidently took place in the reign of Djedkare, probably as part of the king's efforts to renovate the monuments of his ancestors in Abusir and Abu Ghurab (Borchardt, 1907, 158; *id.* in: Bissing, 1905, 73). On the basis of a rock inscription in Wadi Maghara from the year after the 4th cattle-

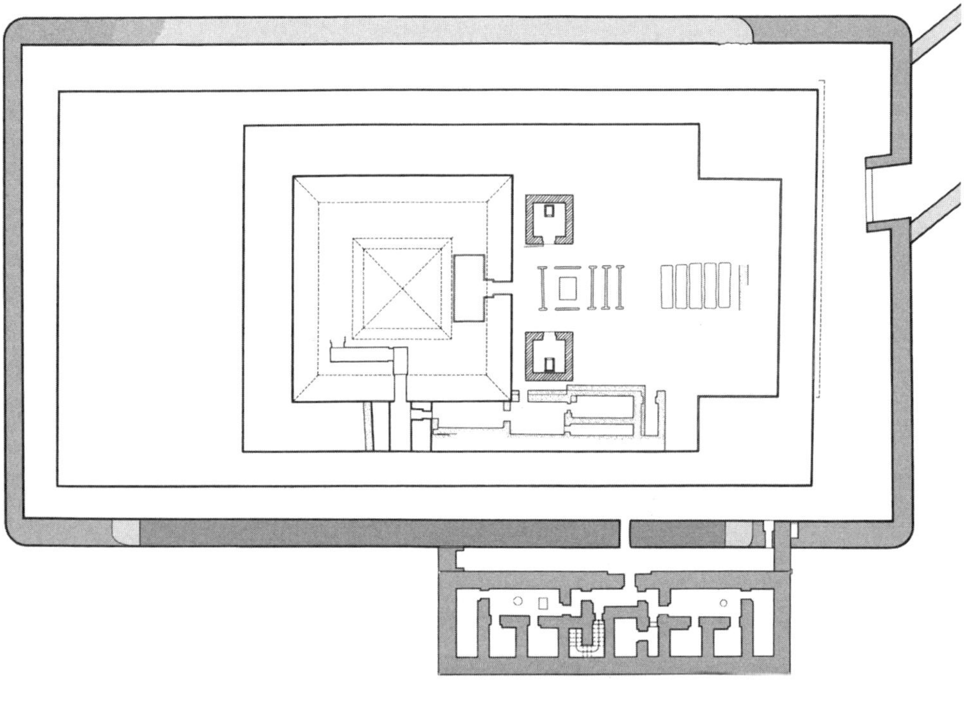

Fig. 36 Plan of the 3rd and 4th (final) building stage of the upper temple of Weserkaf's sun temple complex, see Ricke 1965, Plan 3

count, Kammerzell (Kammerzell, 2001, 153–164) argues that the king had the older brick altar in Weserkaf's sun temple replaced by a stone altar reminiscent of the altar in Nyuserre's sun temple in shape.

The Palermo Stone tells us that in the year of the 3rd cattle-count in the reign of Weserkaf the king assigned to the gods of his sun temple 2 bulls and 2 geese daily. In addition he allocated to each of the deities worshipped in his sun temple, Re and Hathor, 44 aruras of fields in the nomes of Lower Egypt (Schäfer, 1902, 34 no. 2; Strudwick, 1985, 70). These gifts are indirect evidence of the temple economy and the people involved in running the temple. These were hardly minor gifts over just a single year, for the flesh of two bulls daily could alone have sated the appetites of hundreds of people, not to speak of the yield from the fields. In this period the temple was already fully functional and took the form resulting from the 2nd building phase, i.e. not yet with stone obelisk.

From sealings found in Weserkaf's sun temple it is clear that the cult continued in the temple at least up to the end of the 5th Dynasty. The latest sealings discovered so far bear the name of Wenis (Kaplony, 1969, 90 and 96).

Both the sealings, and especially inscriptions in private tombs from the 5th and 6th Dynasties, suggest that a hierarchically organised priesthood served in Weserkaf's sun temple (Voss, 2004, 48–53; Nuzzolo, 2007, 247). As in mortuary temples, the staff of the sun temple was undoubtedly organised in phyles. It can neither be proved nor disproved that these phyles worked on an alternating basis in the royal pyramid complex and the sun temple (Posener-Kriéger, 1976, 572; Kaplony1981, 333), but some records, such as the sealings, suggest that several priests may have served in both places.

The priesthood of Weserkaf's sun temple included two categories, *ḥm-nṯr*-priests and *wꜥb*-priests who, as the case may be, also held some other titles (Voss, 2004, 52f.). Attested are the titles of

- *ḥm-nṯr*-priest of Re in *Nḫn-Rꜥ*
- *ḥm-nṯr*-priest of Re and Hathor in *Nḫn-Rꜥ*
- *ḥm-nṯr*-priest of Re and secretary in *Nḫn-Rꜥ*
- *ḥm-nṯr*-priest of Re and Hathor in *Nḫn-Rꜥ* and Sahure, as well as [*ḥm-nṯr*]-priest of Sahure [of *Nḫn*]-*Rꜥ* (*?*), may attest to the cult of Sahure in Weserkaf's sun temple.

The second category of priests in Weserkaf's sun temple is represented by the titles of a *wꜥb*-priest of Re in *Nḫn-Rꜥ*and inspector of *wꜥb*-priests of Re in *Nḫn-Rꜥ*.

Besides the priests also different administrative officials worked in Weserkaf's sun temple, such as:

- overseer of the storehouse
- overseer of the house of *šmꜥt*-linen of *Nḫn-Rꜥ*
- overseer of the scribes in *Nḫn-Rꜥ*
- scribe of all the sealed royal documents which are in *Nḫn-Rꜥ*

– secretary in *Nḫn-Rʿ*
– sealer of the god's book in *Nḫn-Rʿ*.

The previously cited archaeological research on Weserkaf's sun temple has thrown light on its building development, but left many questions surrounding this monument unanswered. The very name *Nḫn-Rʿ* is still an unresolved problem, for scholars do not agree on its precise interpretation. Obviously, the term *nḫn* can have different meanings including the original one – 'fortress'. Like several before them, Janák, Vymazalová and Coppens (Janák, Vymazalová, Coppens, 2011, 432f.), translate the name as "Re's *Nekhen*", and see in this and all the other names of the six documented sun temples of the 5th Dynasty the encoded idea "of the sun god's rest, nourishment, renewal and resurrection". It is an essentially persuasive view but very broadly conceived. As regards the specific name 'Re's *Nekhen*' it would seem

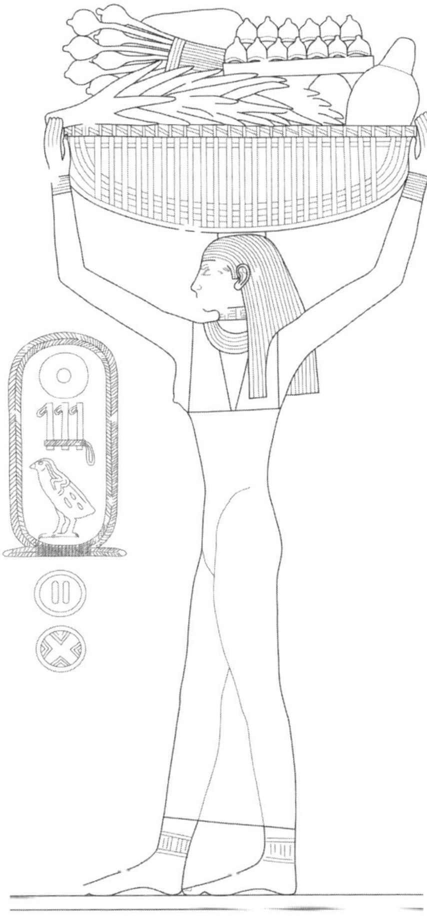

Fig. 37 Personified funerary domain *Nḫn-Rʿ* from the causeway of Sahure, see Khaled, 2008, p. 121

to be associated with the meaning of the name of the Upper Egyptian locality *Nḫn*, which McNamara (McNamara, 2008, 922f.) interprets as meaning a place for royal ceremonies and "the setting for various major royal occasions, such as the reception of offerings". Indeed, the name of Weserkaf's sun temple expresses the idea not so much of a site for the reception of offerings as of a permanent source for those offerings (Loret, 1935–1938, 856 f.; Pfirsch, 1997, 351–354). Bárta (Bárta, 2013-a, 25), on the other hand, assumes that Weserkaf decided to call his sun temple *Nḫn* to demonstrate on a symbolical level his supremacy over all Egypt and present himself as a true successor of his royal ancestors from Hierakonpolis. The trouble is, that it is hard to find a direct connection between *Nḫn,* centre of the falcon cult, and the solar cult. In any case, *nḫn* appears in the Pyramid Texts (a food-spell, Utterance 409 § 718) as the place (*nḫn*-shrine), from which the king gets five meals daily (Faulkner, 1969, Utt. 409: § 717). A further argument in favour of this interpretation of the term *nḫn* is that we repeatedly encounter it as a place name in the contemporary procession of funerary estates. Indeed, in profane names for such small agricultural settlements as 'Sahure's-*nḫn*' (Khaled, 2008,121), specialising in production of food for the needs of the cult of Sahure, the meaning of *nḫn* could hardly be that of a setting for royal rituals.

Questions of building history and cult significance go deeper than problems of interpretation concerning the name of Weserkaf's sun temple. For example, Ricke's theory (mentioned above) that the valley temple was erected in the 3rd building phase on the site of an original simple entrance gate, cannot be archaeologically proven. A more likely theory might be that it was constructed in the 2nd building phase which, according to Ricke, included the raising of the obelisk. Either way, in its ground plan this valley temple was inspired not by Khafre's mortuary temple (despite several similar features) but by Snofru's temple (Fakhry, 1961/II, 2 Fig. 1) roughly half way along the causeway to the Bent Pyramid. On the basis of further archaeological research, and the find of building inscriptions bearing the date of the 15th cattle-count, as well as fragments of relief decoration, Stadelmann (Stadelmann, 2011, 732) has concluded that this so-called valley temple of Snofru was in fact a *sed*-festival temple built on the occasion of the royal jubilee. Voss (Voss, 2004, 23) reached a similar conclusion (recently doubted by F. Arnold, 2014, 12). In this case the valley temple of Weserkaf would not have had the character of a mortuary cult building, but would have been the setting for *sed*-festival rituals, although of a symbolic kind because there is no evidence that Weserkaf ever celebrated a real *sed*-festival during his relatively short reign. That sun temples were closely associated with the performance of the ritual *sed*-festival is attested by Nyuserre's sun temple, but there a monumental gate replaced the valley temple and the site of the *sed*-festival was shifted to a part of the upper temple.

All the same, there is a striking difference in orientation between Snofru's *sed*-festival temple and Weserkaf's valley structure: Snofru's *sed*-festival temple is orientated north-south while the valley temple of Weserkaf's sun temple, together with its causeway, is orientated northeast-southwest. The reason for this peculiar orientation, which is shared by the valley temple and causeway of Nyuserre's sun temple located about half a kilometre to the north, is unclear. Was it towards some unknown larger settlement in the Nile Valley? If the intention was to orientate temple and causeway towards Heliopolis, then its axis should have been angled rather further north. Unfortunately, the idea that these valley buildings of the sun temples may have helped by their orientation with observation of the stars and the determination of the precise time, i.e. that they served as stellar clocks, sheds no light on the problem (Wells, 1990, 104). Ultimately it is possible that this peculiar orientation was just the result of an effort to build the upper temple as near to the Nile Valley as possible, which given the relief of the edge of the Nile Valley, meant compromise to ensure that the causeway was not impractically steep.

Unlike the valley temple, the upper temple, before as well as after the addition of the dominant obelisk, was unambiguously associated with the solar cult. To judge by the titles of the priests serving in the temple, it was the cult of Re, a specific form of the sun god, and rites involved in veneration of Hathor alongside Re. The link between the cult of Re and Hathor and the mortuary cult of the king in the sun temple has already been pointed out by Winter (Winter, 1957, 228). Earlier, the scholarly consensus was that the cult of Re as sun god was of later date and that it did not come to the fore until the beginning of the 5th Dynasty (Helck, 1984, 69), but arguments based on the absence of relevant evidence of the cult of Re and its symbols in the centre of the solar cult, Heliopolis, are very misleading. For example, while the oldest obelisk so far discovered there dates from the beginning of the 6th Dynasty, and so the obelisks in the sun temples of the 5th Dynasty kings are considered to be the earliest of their kind, Heliopolis is still waiting for thorough archaeological investigation, if indeed that ever proves possible. Meanwhile, the recent study by Kahl (Kahl, 2007) convincingly shows that the cult of Re was much older, going back to the 2nd Dynasty, and that its importance was progressively rising from that time.

Overall, the whole complex of Weserkaf's sun temple indicates an attempt to give the integration of the royal with the solar cult solid, architectural expression. The effort to combine the architectural elements of a pyramid complex with a divine temple shows signs of initial experimentation and the sun temple gives the impression of a certain architectural heterogeneity. Indeed the very fact of its repeated renovation and alteration is indirect evidence of a search for an optimal architectural form. We can regret that we know only Weserkaf and Nyuserre's sun temples and not the other four recorded as having existed, and so we cannot trace the architectural evolution of this type of temple.

The dating of the building phases of the temple is also still an open question. The 1st phase undoubtedly fell into the reign of Weserkaf himself. On the Palermo Stone the name of the sun temple in the 'year of the 3rd occasion (of cattle-count)', i.e.

towards the end of Weserkaf's reign, is determined merely by the pedestal without an obelisk. In a cursive inscription on a limestone tablet (Edel, 1969, pl. 2A) found in the temple and dated to the 5th cattle-count of the reign of a king not further specified, the determinative of the temple's name already has a different form. Ricke (Ricke, 1965, 5) interpreted this form as a pedestal supporting a wooden column with a short crossbeam at the top, but it is more probable that this is a cursive form denoting an obelisk (see paleographic variants of the sign O 24 in Posener-Kriéger, Cénival, 1968, Paleography Pl. VIII.), and that the 'crossbeam' is in fact a stylised sun disc, as is clear on a more careful scrutiny of the sign. In fact Edel (Edel, 1969, 5 and 8) had already expressed doubts about the 'crossbeam' and considered the sign to be a cursive writing of obelisk. He also realised that the tablet dated from a time when the obelisk had already been raised in the temple. This is anyway borne out by the aforesaid chronological information on the tablet, which does not relate to Weserkaf, but to one of his successors (unfortunately the tablets were found in excavated waste, and not in a stratified situation permitting dating).

As regards which successor, the theory that the obelisk in Weserkaf's temple was raised in the reign of Neferirkare, proposed by Kaiser (Kaiser, 1956, 112) and Ricke (Ricke, 1965, 18), is weak. It is true that what is so far the highest documented year of the reign of Neferirkare is the year after the 5th cattle-count, the fact that his pyramid complex remained so incomplete raises doubts as to whether this king could have carried out extensive renovation of the sun temple of his distant ancestor in addition to building his own sun temple *Śt-ib-Rʿ*.

It is much more likely that the reconstruction of Weserkaf's sun temple, including the addition of obelisk, had already taken place under Sahure (Verner, 2000, 387–389). The same conclusion was reached by Voss (Voss, 2004, 29), who finds indirect support for it in the relatively large number of sealings (Kaplony, 1981/IA, 340) relating to Weserkaf's sun temple and bearing Sahure's name. Moreover, some of the sealings (Kaplony, 1981/IIB, no. 19, no. 24 etc.) indicate that Sahure was worshipped in Weserkaf's sun temple, but this does not necessarily mean that the temple was either temporarily (Nuzzolo, 2007, 231) or in the long-term (Stadelmann, 2000, 542) usurped by Sahure. The paucity of written references to Sahure's sun temple *Śḫt-Rʿ*, and the fact that – where we find them at all – they are always determined only by a pedestal without an obelisk, suggests that his building was never completed. It is therefore possible that (as in the case of Raneferef's unfinished sun temple) the cult of Sahure was attached to the already functioning sun temple of his father and predecessor Weserkaf (see the text below).

Another question still open concerns the statues originally housed in the temple. The greywacke statue of the king mentioned earlier, of which only the head with Lower Egyptian crown has been found, was probably placed in the valley temple. As regards the upper temple, there are good grounds for doubting Ricke's theory that there were statues of Bastet and Hathor in the two dark greywacke chapels in front of the obelisk. Instead, we can only agree with Stadelmann (Stadelmann, 1985, 164) that these shrines probably contained statues of Re and Hathor, whose cults are recorded by written sources in the temple. There were also statues of the king here for, in the upper temple, Borchardt found fragments (mouth, ears and a *nmś*-headdress) of an alabaster statue in almost life size (now in Berlin, Egyptian Museum no. 19774) that is considered to be an image of the king, although it is not yet clear where it originally stood.

V.2 *Śḫt-Rˁ* 'RE'S FIELD'

The meaning of the name of Sahure's sun temple is not quite obvious. It can be interpreted as a reference to either the 'Fields of Re' (Utt. 436 § 792) or the 'Field of Offerings of Re' (Utt. 519 § 1206), both of them being the toponyms of the Other World mentioned in the Pyramid Texts (see Faulkner, 1969, 143 and 192). Archaeologists have not yet located the remains of Sahure's sun temple, and our evidence for it comes only from the 5th Dynasty written sources, e.g. on the Palermo Stone (Schäfer, 1902, 36), in the Mastaba of Tjy (Épron, Daumas, 1930, pls. 20 and 37; Wild, 1953, 170, 183) and elsewhere. For example, from the text on the Palermo Stone we read that in the year after the 2nd cattle-count, Sahure donated 4 measures of divine offerings daily to Hathor of *Śḫt-Rˁ* and 24 arouras of land in the tenth nome of Lower Egypt to Re of *Śḫt-Rˁ*. In all these records its name is always given without an obelisk, leading scholars to conclude that the temple was not completed. The priests and officials of Sahure's sun temple, in which the categories of '*ḥm-nṯr*-priest of Re in *Śḫt-Rˁ*' and '*wˁb*-priest of Re in *Śḫt-Rˁ*' were represented, were also not numerous (Voss, 2004, 139; Nuzzolo, 2007, 247). Attested is the title of 'overseer of *Śḫt-Rˁ*' whose holder was e.g. the previously mentioned Tjy.

Borchardt (Borchardt, 2009, 54f.) made the very interesting discovery of building inscriptions with the name of Sahure's sun temple *Śḫt-Rˁ* on a few blocks in the core of the south wing of the enclosure wall of Nyuserre's pyramid. This finding led Kaiser (Kaiser, 1957, 112 n. 2) to the hypothesis that Sahure's sun temple may have stood on the site chosen by Nyuserre for the building of his own pyramid, and so the temple was removed and its remains used in Nyuserre's building. Kaiser's theory was accepted also by Voss (Voss, 2004, 136) in her dissertation on the sun temples.

In theory, Kaiser's ideas might find support in finds of numerous fragments of a large granite monolith obelisk, including a pyramidion originally covered in coppered plates, not far from the north-eastern corner of Nyuserre's mortuary temple (Verner, 1978, 111–118). The obelisk probably stood on a stone platform that from the north adjoined what is known as the northern 'Eckbau', a massive corner of the temple that resembles the tower of a pylon. It is extremely unusual to find a large obelisk in a pyramid complex, and from its position it seems to have been joined to the complex only secondarily. The present author, who originally believed (Verner, 2002, 82f.) that this find of an obelisk might well support Kaiser's theory of the location of the sun temple, today takes a different view. As has already been noted (see p. 158f.), there are some indications that the site for a new cemetery for his successors, Abusir, was chosen because it enabled the setting of a symbolic line for the orientation of the future pyramids in the cemetery towards Heliopolis. The hypothetical location of Sahure's sun temple suggested by Kaiser would not fit into this concept. Moreover, if built in this place Sahure's sun temple would have hindered already the construction of Neferirkare's pyramid complex. Its destruction as early as in the time of Nyuserre, and recycling its remains in the latter king's own pyramid complex, is therefore hard to believe. The aforesaid blocks bearing the name of *Śḫt-Rʿ* might have rather been leftovers of an unfinished building of this temple which might have lain not far from here. Be it as it may, the occurrence of the obelisk in Nyuserre's pyramid complex is very strange. Whether originally intended for Sahure's sun temple or Nyuserre's pyramid complex, why was the obelisk erected only at the norther Eckbau; at the southern Eckbau Borchardt found no platform for an obelisk. Had this obelisk something to do with the position of Nyuserre's pyramid off the symbolic line linking the Abusir pyramids with Heliopolis? Was the obelisk intended to establish in a symbolic way a substitute connection of Nyuserre's pyramid with Heliopolis via the king's sun temple in Abu Ghurab?

Kaiser (Kaiser, 1957, 113) put forward another idea relating to Sahure's sun temple, however, this time based on the discovery of an older brick building in Abu Ghurab under the upper (stone) temple of Nyuserre's sun temple complex (Borchardt, 1905, 68f.). According to Kaiser this older building could be the unfinished sun temple of one of Nyuserre's predecessors, Sahure or Raneferef. Nuzollo (Nuzollo, 2007, 230–232) opted for the first of these two possibilities, arguing from a fragment of a restoration inscription of Khamwaset found in the upper temple by Borchardt (Borchardt, 1905, 72 Fig. 61i), bearing the remnant of a cartouche with part of the sign *š3ḥ* and supposedly also the sign *w*. However, this cannot be Sahure's name, for in that case the sign *š3ḥ* would have to be preceded by the sign *rʿ*, and the interpretation of the second sign is also erroneous, since what was taken for a *w* is in fact part of the sign *bit* or *m* (see further discussion of the problem on p. 212).

According to Stadelmann (Stadelmann, 2000, 542), it is possible that Sahure not only completed Weserkaf's sun temple but even appropriated it under the title *Śḫt-Rʿ*, and that Neferirkare then did the same in turn under the title *Śt-ib-Rʿ*. It is a theory that would solve the mystery of the missing sun temples of these two kings, and it builds on some earlier speculation by Ricke. It is not persuasive, however, because there is no evidence either from Weserkaf's sun temple or from contemporary archaeological and written sources to support the identification of these three sun temples within a single building. The theory is also indirectly excluded by the passages in the papyrus archives of the mortuary temples of Neferirkare and Raneferef that concern their operating relationship with the sun temple *Śt-ib-Rˁ* (see below).

From all this evidence we can indirectly conclude that Sahure's sun temple was probably never completely finished and that it only functioned on a limited basis for just a short period, and no later than the end of the 5th Dynasty. The unfinished temple may have lain near Abusir and would soon have become a source of material for other buildings, which would help to account for its evident 'vanishing without trace'. It remains to ask why Sahure never finished his sun temple. Perhaps in the first years of his reign he gave priority to building his own pyramid complex. Perhaps he also wanted first to complete the sun temple of his father and predecessor on the throne Weserkaf. Later on, Sahure's mortuary cult was possibly joined with the sun temple of his father just as later, in a similar situation (an unfinished sun temple), Raneferef's mortuary cult was joined with the sun temple of his father Neferirkare. Had the papyrus archive of Sahure's mortuary temple survived it would probably have answered our questions.

V.3 *Śt-ib-Rˁ* 'PLACE OF RE'S PLEASURE'

Neferirkare's sun temple 'Place of Re's Pleasure', has not yet been archaeologically located, but of all the sun temples of the 5th Dynasty it is the most frequently mentioned in written sources. This has sometimes prompted scholars to believe that it was a very important building, but the inference may be misleading, because we owe the large number of references to the find of fragments of the papyrus archives of the mortuary temples of Neferirkare and Raneferef, which both had close links with the temple *Śt-ib-Rˁ* economically and religiously (Posener-Kriéger, 1976, 519–526; Posener-Kriéger, Verner, Vymazalová, 2006, 351f.). In all the written records the determinative of the name of Neferirkare's sun temple is an obelisk, and this can be considered another indication that it was a finished and evidently large building, still functioning at the beginning of the 6th Dynasty.

The papyrus archive of Neferirkare in particular provides us not only with important administrative and economic records, but also valuable information on the architectural arrangement of the king's sun temple (Posener-Kriéger,1976, 493–518). We learn from the papyri that the temple had an *ˁrrt* 'entrance area' and *pr-šnˁ* 'storerooms', which apart from the general designation were also specified geographically, for example as 'eastern storerooms'. One important place in the temple was 'the altar of Re', on which offerings were placed before their distribution to the mortuary temples mentioned. It is possible that the part of the temple reserved for the symbolic celebration of the *sed*-festival was metaphorically called 'palace of the *sed*-festival', but this may refer to a completely different building (see p. 109). More information about Neferirkare's sun temple is provided by a text on the Palermo Stone, according to which in the year of the 5th cattle-count the king had a solar boat of *Maat* set up by the southern side of his sun temple and also dedicated two copper boats, *mꜥnḏt* and *mśktt*, each 8 cubits long, to the Re-Horus of this temple (Schäfer, 1902, 41; Strudwick, 2005, 73).

The information that a service boat *bit* (Posener-Kriéger, 1976, 631–634) was used to transport offerings between Neferirkare's sun and mortuary temples suggests that the temples were not located in the close proximity that would have made land transport possible. A waterway was also used for transportation between the *Śt-ib-Rꜥ* temple and the Residence in the centre of Memphis. The offerings were probably shipped along canals on the western edge of the Nile Valley, including Bahr el-Libeini (The Great Memphis Canal) used by the pyramid builders (G. Goyon, 1977, 131–135). The Palermo Stone also mentions a canal in connection with Neferirkare's sun temple (Strudwick, 2005, 72–74). The natural water reservoir fed by the Nile flood and later called the Lake of Abusir may likewise have been exploited for transport. The Nile itself was almost certainly not used for transport between sun temples and pyramid complexes, because in this period its course ran east of Memphis, although around 4 kilometres further to the west than it does today.

The titles that appear in contemporary written records and show that Neferirkare's sun temple had a relatively large staff of priests and officials have been collected by Voss (Voss, 2004, 150f.). All these titles are at the same time evidence of the deities worshipped in the temple *Śt-ib-Rꜥ*. The priests were hierarchically organised and the following categories were represented among them:

- *ḥm-nṯr*-priest of Re of/in *Śt-ib-Rꜥ*
- *ḥm-nṯr*-priest of Re and Hathor in *Śt-ib-Rꜥ*
- under-supervisor of *ḥm-nṯr*-priests of Re, Hathor and Neferirkare in *Śt-ib-Rꜥ* and *Bꜣ-[Kꜣkꜣi]* (The title evidences the cult of Neferirkare in his sun temple. It also supports the presumption that some priests and officials served in both the sun and mortuary temple of the king.)
- *ḥm-nṯr*-priest of Re-Harakhty in *Śt-ib-Rꜥ*
- *ḥm-nṯr*-priest of Horus
- *ḥm-nṯr*-priest of Akhty (?) of *Śt-ib-Rꜥ* (Verner *et al.*, 2006, 218 no. 36). (The reading of the god's name as *Akhty* on a sealing from Raneferef's pyramid complex is not quite clear. No such name is attested from the Old Kingdom, and it may instead be part of the name Harakhty.)
- scribe of the secret books of the King of Upper and Lower Egypt Neferirkare – Horus *Wśr-ḫꜥw*, Golden Falcon *Śḫmw-nbw*, Hathor and Re of *Śt-ib-Rꜥ*
- *wꜥb*-priest
- under-supervisor of *wꜥb*-priests
- under-supervisor of *wꜥb*-priests and secretary of Hathor, Re and the King of Upper and Lower Egypt Neferirkare in *Śt-ib-Rꜥ*.

There are also attested purely official administrative titles referring to *Śt-ib-Rʿ* such as:
– overseer of *Śt-ib-Rʿ*
– overseer of the storeroom of *Śt-ib-Rʿ*.

The fact that no one has yet managed to find the remains of the sun temple *Śt-ib-Rʿ*, or even a secondarily used fragment of a block with an inscription from the building, is surprising but may itself be significant, for the temple may well have been built mainly of mudbricks with only its obelisk and pedestal base in stone. This is indirectly suggested by two circumstances. The first is that Neferirkare did not finish his own pyramid complex but only the pyramid core during his reign. The second is what is known as the founding inscription of Nyuserre's sun temple, from which it seems that the latter was probably first built (at least partly) of mudbricks and only subsequently (re)constructed from stone (see text below). Perhaps Neferirkare only managed to finish the first, brick version of his sun temple. If this temple lay north of Abusir, somewhere between Abu Ghurab and Zawiyet el-Aryan, we may never find it because of the widespread devastation of this area.

V.4 *Ḥtp-Rʿ* 'RE'S OFFERING TABLE'

The only records of Raneferef's sun temple are in inscriptions in the tomb of Tjy in Saqqara, in which 'overseer of the sun temple Re's Offering Table' (theoretically, the temple's name could also be interpreted as 'Re is Satisfied') appears four times in Tjy's titles. This temple is referred to twice on the false door (to the right, north), once as *Ḥtp-Rʿ* and once, probably by a scribe's error, as *Ḥtp-ib-Rʿ* (Wild, 1953, pl. 183). In both cases the name of the temple is determined by the sign of a pedestal without obelisk. In the entrance into Corridor I (Épron, Daumas, 1930, pl. 37) the name of the temple appears in the same title of Tjy likewise twice and is determined not just by the pedestal without obelisk but by the sign for 'town' as well. This ought logically to be referring to a settlement on the edge of the Nile valley adjoining the entrance gate of Raneferef's sun temple, but it seems unlikely that such a town could have grown up during Raneferef's short reign. Perhaps the differences in the writing of the name of the sun temple indicate no more than that the inscriptions were made by different scribes.

In the contemporaneous written sources only two titles refer to Raneferef's sun temple, '*ḥm-nṯr*-priest of Re in *Ḥtp-Rʿ* ' and 'overseer of *Ḥtp-Rʿ*', both of them dating from the time of Nyuserre (Voss, 2004, 154f.). Another two alleged records of the name of the temple in titles on sealings from the reign of Nyuserre (Kaplony, 1981/I, 341 and *id.* II^{B}, pl. 72 no. 8 and pl. 77 no. 37; this inaccurate data was repeated in Voss, 2004, 154) are citations very probably based on mistaken interpretations. One case (no. 8) seems in fact to be an incomplete name of a temple [*Śt-ib*]-*Rʿ* with a determinative of obelisk, and the other (no. 37) is probably not the abbreviated writing of the names of three sun temples one after the other – *Šsp-ib-Rʿ*, *Śḫt*-[*Rʿ*], *Ḥtp*-[*Rʿ*] – but just faulty writing of the name of the temple *Šsp-ib-Rʿ*. Kaplony himself admits that the copy of the text on the sealing shows errors (Kaplony, 1981/II^{A}, 266). Not only would it have been miraculous if Raneferef had managed to build his sun temple during his reign of around just a year and a half, but it would be surprising indeed had a priest of the cult of Re still existed in such a temple in the time of Nyuserre. By that time Raneferef's mortuary cult had for long been dependent on offerings from Neferirkare's sun temple (Posener-Kriéger, Verner, Vymazalová, 2006, 351f.).

As previously noted, under the stone structure of Nyuserre's sun temple Borchardt (Borchardt, 1905, 68f.) found the remains of an earlier brick building, also with a relatively large courtyard, massive enclosure wall and chambers not further specifiable as to function. Borchardt distinguished between two phases in this earlier building itself, and concluded that it was probably the earlier brick version of the sun temple. This theory is further supported by a mention in the so-called founding inscription, remnants of which were found in the entrance building to the temple complex on the edge of the valley: "His Majesty constructed this temple of *Šsp-ib-Rʿ* in stone, for His Majesty had found its columns had been erected in wood and its walls of brick ..." (Strudwick, 2005, 88). It is theoretically possible that the older brick version of the temple was based on the scarcely begun and soon abandoned building of the sun temple of one of Nyuserre's predecessors. According to Kaiser's theory (Kaiser, 1956, 113) mentioned earlier the possible candidates are Sahure or Raneferef. If the theory is correct (for further discussion see the text below), then Raneferef would be more likely to have been the builder of this structure than Sahure, as suggested by the alabaster altar of Nyuserre's sun temple, constructed from parts designed as signs together forming *Ḥtp-Rʿ*, the name of Raneferef's sun temple (Verner, 1987-a, 293–297).

V.5 *Šsp-ib-Rʿ* 'RE'S DELIGHT'

If the building plan of Weserkaf's sun temple gives the impression of experimentation and the search for an optimal form, then the stone version of Nyuserre's sun temple already represents a mature design on an integrated plan. In its final form the temple was built of limestone – apart from a few elements in other kinds of stone: limestone from the quarries of north Saqqara was used for the core of the wall, for the casing fine white limestone from Tura, while the quartzite came from Kom el-Ahmar, the red granite from Aswan and the greywacke from Wadi Hammamat (D. Klemm, R. Klemm, 2010, 118).

As in Weserkaf's, so in Nyuserre's sun temple the basic elements – valley temple, causeway and upper temple with obelisk – have different orientations (Borchardt,1905,

Blatt 1). Adjoining the lower temple (more precisely the monumental entrance gate) was a dwelling complex, relatively large to judge by its 300-metre long western enclosure wall reaching right to the foot of the small hill on which the upper temple stood. The valley temple had three porticos and three quayside ramps: the main portico with four palm columns of red granite was set in the centre of the façade and the other two porticos flanked it on either side, each with two red-granite palm columns. From the hall, in which paths from all three porticos converged, there was access to a long open causeway – which stretched approximately 100-metres up to the upper temple with its obelisk. The inscription (see the text below) about the founding and equipment of the temple, including a calendar of festivals to be celebrated in it, was probably carved on the wall of the lower temple. Although only fragments of the inscription have survived it offers a very valuable testimony (Kees, 1923 and 1928; Helck, 1977, 47–77).

The natural hillock chosen for the upper temple with the obelisk was evidently too small for an extensive building and had to be enlarged and strengthened with terraces before the temple foundations were laid. Not particularly suitable technically, the site for the construction of the temple was very probably chosen for religious-political reasons: it was precisely on this hillock that two symbolic lines met, for here the southernmost limit of the sightline between the Memphite necropolis and the sun temple in Heliopolis, intersected with the line connecting the apex of Weserkaf's pyramid in Saqqara with Khufu's pyramid in Giza (see p. 159). The temple had a rectangular plan on a main axis orientated east-west. It was entered from the causeway through the massive so-called upper gate, from which paths led in three directions: directly into the open courtyard and into passageways along the north and south sides of the courtyard.

The eastern part of the north passage originally had relief decoration, but only remnants have survived (for more detail see Voss, 2004, 83f.). There was access from this passage to two storerooms arranged one after the other along the north side of the temple. The storerooms, their doorjambs made of quartzite and bearing the king's name and titles, were connected by a long passage opening into the antechamber and the courtyard. The storerooms seem to have been just one-storey high, for no fragments of stairs have been found in them. Re-examination of this space led Nuzzolo and Pirelli (Nuzzolo, Pirelli, 2011, 677f.) to conclude that these were not ordinary storerooms but a set of rooms with cult as well as practical functions. In front of the first storeroom was a flight of steps leading up to the roof terrace. A secondary entrance in the northern enclosure wall also provided direct access to the storerooms.

Between the storerooms and the altar, in the middle of the large courtyard, was an area that Borchardt characterised as the Great Slaughterhouse, and between the stores and the western wall of the temple was what he called the Small Slaughterhouse. The paving of both these areas was inset with channels, so that liquids could be run off from here into circular calcite basins arranged along the eastern side of the courtyard. In fact it is unlikely that animals were really slaughtered here, directly in the temple.

There have been no finds by these so-called slaughterhouses of the stone blocks set into the ground with tethering holes to which cattle would be tied before slaughter (as discovered in the slaughterhouse that was part of Raneferef's pyramid complex, see Verner, 1987-b, 181–189). Nor have any butchers' flint knives been found here. In any case, by what route could the cattle with broad horns have been led here? This was most probably a place where various offerings (meat, vegetables and fruit, etc.), were assembled and cleansed before being placed on Re's altar. The theory may be lent further support by an inscription found on one of the stone basins and referring either to the workshop where the basin was produced or to clensing area in the sun temple: *wꜤbt nśwt: gś-pr* 'royal workshop (place of the purification?): administration office' (Borchardt, 1905, 48).

The southern passage had skylights and its walls were adorned with scenes of the so-called 'Grosse Festdarstellung', which continued on the circular passage inside the base of the obelisk (Voss, 2004, 81). Between the southern passage and the entrance to the base was a chapel, entered from the western end of the southern passage. The chapel may have served for the re-robing of the king during the rituals of the *sed*-festival. On its walls were scenes from what is known as the 'Kleine Festdarstellung', with themes including foundation rituals, the procession of Min, the procession of Wepwawet, visits to the shrines of Upper and Lower Egypt, etc. The chapel was also accessible from the courtyard, where there were two granite steles, one on each side of the entrance, and at their foot a small round basin with water for purification set into the paving.

Beyond the chapel, between the end of the southern passage and the base of the obelisk, was the so-called 'Weltkammer' (Hall of Seasons, taken to Germany, where it was partially destroyed during the Second World War), lavishly adorned with scenes and inscriptions, showing the creative power of the sun in the eternal cycle of life and nature (Edel, Wenig, 1974). The scenes are only of the seasons of the inundation and summer. The season of winter is absent – either because scenes of it have not survived or else because it was never depicted here – and was left out to preserve the symmetry of the decor in the corridor-like chamber that had only two walls for decoration.

As Voss points out (Voss, 2010, 232), "the static canonisation and anonymity of the protagonists" in the scenes suggests to scholars today that they are not depictions of real events taking place in the temple. In any case, according to Voss, Nyuserre's reign was not long enough for him to reach his thirtieth year, in theory the requisite condition for the holding of a real *sed*-festival. However, there can be another explanation for the fact that except for the king the participants of the *sed*-festival rituals in the scenes are unnamed and in some cases represented only by titles: the names might have been left out deliberately to convey the eternal, repeated character of a festival relating exclusively to the king which the names of commoners would only disturb. Whatever the case, the argument that the king did not in fact reach the thirtieth year of his reign and so cannot have had a real *sed*-festival is debatable (on the discussion of the length of Nyuserre's reign see the text on p. 62). (In arguing the improbability of Nyuserre having had a real *sed*-festival, Voss misunderstood the papyrus fragment 88 B from the Neferirkare's archive; on this papyrus see the text on p. 152). Pobably to Nyuserre's *sed*-festival also refers an inscription on the fragment of an alabaster vase found in the court of the tomb of Weserkaf in Abusir and deposited now in the Egyptian Museum in Berlin (no. 16623) (Borchardt, 1907, 139 Fig. 119).

From the Hall of Seasons the way continued into a crooked, gradually narrowing passage on the rising ramp inside the 20-metre high base of the obelisk, which had the shape of a truncated pyramid. The passage was probably unlit, its ceiling decorated with stars and its walls with scenes from the 'Grosse Festdarstellung'. The lowest level of the outer casing of the base was made of red granite, and the remaining casing in fine white limestone. It is possible that the rising passage circled the base of the obelisk not once, as Borchardt (Borchardt, 1905, plan on Blatt 2) assumed, but twice (Nuzollo, Pirelli, 2011, 651). The passage came out at the foot of the 36-metre high obelisk (if we add to it the height of the hillock and base, its apex was 72 metres above the valley), which surprisingly was not positioned precisely on the long axis of the temple. The obelisk was constructed of blocks of white limestone. Borchhardt did not exclude the possibility that there were inscriptions on the obelisk and that its pyramidion was made of a different stone or covered with shining metal. We can assume that rituals took place at the foot of the obelisk.

In the courtyard which was in front of the base of the obelisk stood an altar (ca 6 × 5.5 m) lying on the east-west axis of the temple. Its name, 'Re's offering table' was a rebus, in the form of an altar (Borchardt, 1905, 43 Fig. 33). The altar was made up of five alabaster blocks: in the centre was one block rounded into the shape of the sign *Rˁ*, 'Re', and around it four blocks in the form of the sign *ḥtp*, 'offering', arranged into a nearly square and orientated to the four points of the compass. The altar was surrounded by a low wall on a square plan, which has left only its imprint in the paving and the granite plinth of its eastern side with openings for metal pins (perhaps for securing cult objects).

Outside the temple, along its southern side, stood a large model of a solar boat made of mudbricks. The walls had no solid foundations, however, and were built directly on the desert sand. Findings of remnants of whitened and gilded woods, copper nails etc. suggest that the model of the boat was enhanced with details in various different materials and decorated.

What archaeological sources have revealed about Nyuserre's sun temple is significantly augmented by written sources, especially fragments of the 'founding inscription' discovered on the site of the entrance gate on the edge of the Nile Valley. While this testament is incomplete, and its reconstruction by Helck (Helck, 1977,

47–77) is controversial, it gives us good grounds for thinking that after a certain time the king had ordered an originally brick temple to be rebuilt in stone even if we do not precisely know when the reconstruction took place. From the inscription we can conclude that the king also had an artificial pool built not far from the sun temple and that sycamores were probably planted in its vicinity. The reference in the inscription to a structure 20 cubits long, 20 cubits wide and … ? … cubits high is most probably to the obelisk. By contrast, although we have no reason to doubt its veracity, the reference to a building 7,000 cubits long, …22 cubits broad and … ? … cubits high is immensely hard to interpret for purposes of even a very hypothetical reconstruction.

According to the inscription, the inventory of the temple was also renewed and enlarged in important ways. The king donated statues of Re and Hathor (out of gold?), 107 (gold?) and 19 (silver?) vessels, 8 bronze altars, a cult boat inlaid with green stone, 10 *wḫ*-standards ornamented with lapis lazuli, 100 vessels in cedar wood and evidently many other cult objects. It even seems that some building elements of the temple were decorated with fine gold.

Another very valuable piece of evidence provided in the inscription is that on the occasion of the reconstruction of the temple the king allocated estates (the names of almost ten of these have been preserved) to serve the needs of the temple with their produce and revenues. In comparison with the hundreds of mortuary estates enumerated in contemporary pyramid complexes, however, their number is small. It was from these estates that it was possible to secure the huge quantity of products intended by the king as offerings 'for his father Re' at the many festivals enumerated on the foundation inscription (for more detail on the calendar of festivals see the text on p. 137). According to Helck's reconstruction of the inscription, in annual total this was more than one hundred thousand portions of bread and beer, thousands of pieces of various kinds of pastry, more than a thousand head of cattle, a thousand pieces of poultry, wild animals (e.g. gazelles), milk, honey and suchlike. All these offerings went first to Re's altar in the temple, but obviously the priests of the sun temple could only have consumed a small proportion of them, and most of the offerings would have been distributed further to the king's mortuary temple, to the mortuary temples of his ancestors, and then to other places in accordance with the system of what was known as 'the reversal of offerings'. From the organizational and administrative point of view it is not entirely clear whether the products from the estates belonging to the sun temple were taken there directly, or first to the Residence and only then to the temple. In the case of the production of the mortuary estates listed in the pyramid complexes, the Residence was the place where they would have been concentrated, and from which they would be distributed, as is shown by the Abusir papyrus archives. In the case of sun temples, which had facilities where products from the estates were processed, the system may have been different for practical reasons, even if under some form of supervision on the part of the Residence.

The quantity of listed festivals relating to a varied range of deities should not obscure the chief gods to whose cult the temple was dedicated. From contemporary written sources we know that these were Re, Hathor and Nyuserre, but also Re-Horus (regarded as the temporary form of Re-Harakhty), worshipped here as 'Re-Horus of *Šsp-ib-Rʿ*' with the epithets 'Lord of Heaven', 'Lord of Truth', 'Lord of the Gods' and 'Lord of the Two Lands' (Edel, Wenig, 1974, Taf. 24 Nr. 571). More detailed information is lacking, for example, on the locations of the cult statues of these gods in the temple; in the founding inscription there are only fragments with references to a 'chapel' (*ṯpḥt*), and a 'golden shrine' (*ḥwt nbw*), where the ritual of the opening of the mouth was performed on the statues, and suchlike.

Because the papyrus archive of Nyuserre's sun temple (undoubtedly very carefully kept) has not survived in this instance, it is hard to estimate the number of temple staff that there were engaged in service. The employees of the temple were probably organised in phyles, as in the contemporary royal pyramid complexes, but their numbers would have varied, depending on the size of the economic hinterland of the temple. We can only speculate on whether service in the mortuary and sun temples was strictly separate or whether the staff of both would supplement each other, as perhaps suggested by some of the titles of the priests. The titles of the priests and officials of Nyuserre's sun temple did not differ much from those serving in the other sun temples. The following priestly titles (Voss, 2004, 123) are represented:

- *ḥm-nṯr*-priest of Re of/in *Šsp-ib-Rʿ*
- *ḥm-nṯr*-priest of Re and Hathor in *Šsp-ib-Rʿ*
- under-supervisor of *ḥm-nṯr*-priests of *Šsp-ib-Rʿ*
- under-supervisor of *ḥm-nṯr*-priests of Re, Hathor and the King of Upper and Lower Egypt Nyuserre in *Šsp-ib-Rʿ*
- *wʿb*-priest of *Šsp-ib-Rʿ*
- under-supervisor of *wʿb*-priests and secretary of Re, Hathor and the King of Upper and Lower Egypt Nyuserre in *Šsp-ib-Rʿ*.

The following titles of officials are represented:

- overseer of *Šsp-ib-Rʿ*
- overseer of commissions of *Šsp-ib-Rʿ*
- inspector of the storeroom of *Šsp-ib-Rʿ*
- singer of the Great House (in) *Šsp-ib-Rʿ*.

It is evident that most of these titles related only to service in the temple itself and not in the whole temple complex which included the large production facilities already mentioned and a settlement by the entrance gate on the edge of the Nile Valley. The Abusir papyri record that the sun temples had slaughter houses where animals were slaughtered and their meat processed daily, and also bakeries producing special kind of bread, facilities for the production of beer and other drinks, etc. There were storehouses for honey, corn, natron and various materials necessary for the maintenance of operations not only in the sun temple but in the mortuary temple as well. There were facilities for the cleaning and processing of fresh vegetables and fruit, evidently supplied directly from nearby estates (rather than from distant provinces only after their inspection and redistribution via the Residence). We can assume that when the cult of Nyuserre was at its height, the production, storage and transport capacities of the temple employed many workers and officials of whom no record has survived, except (in the case of officials) perhaps just here and there in general-sounding titles without specific reference to Nyuserre's sun temple.

After Nyuserre's death his sun temple probably started to decline relatively soon. The remnants of what is known as a restoration inscription found in the temple show that as early as in the reign of Djedkare the temple was damaged and the king had it repaired. In the time of the New Kingdom the temple was already in ruins, but the obelisk still stood (Borchardt, 1905, 73f.). The remains of an inscription with a fragment of a Ramesside cartouche suggest that Khamwaset may also have conducted some kind of repair.

Archaeological research on the temple at the very end of the 19th century threw light on much from its past, but much remains obscure. The brick building, the remains of which Borchardt found under the upper temple, deserves to be more fully investigated. This older building had itself been preceded by consolidation and terracing of the hillock and was constructed in at least two phases, during which time some internal walls were built of brick which had a limestone casing (Borchardt, 1905, 68f.). It remains an open question whether this older brick temple of Nyuserre was built on the basis of an even older structure erected by one of his predecessors.

Another important and still unanswered question is why Nyuserre was the first king to decide to build his sun temple in Abu Ghurab. From indirect evidence we gather that this was a site of key importance for the founding of the royal necropolis in Abusir (see p. 159). Was Nyuserre's decision influenced by the presence here of an older unfinished building of one of his predecessors (Sahure, Raneferef)? Or was it because there were serious reasons why the king had to build his pyramid away from the symbolic line connecting the royal pyramids in Abusir and Heliopolis? Was the sun temple in Abu Ghurab then supposed to provide the king's pyramid with a substitute symbolic connection to Heliopolis? Was the raising of an obelisk by the north-east corner (by the northern 'Eckbau') of Nyuserre's pyramid complex meant to assist in this connection (see text on 175)?

V.6 *ꜣḫt-Rꜥ* 'RE'S HORIZON'

The last of the six sun temples of the 5th Dynasty was built by Menkauhor. Like that of Sahure, Neferirkare and Raneferef this sun temple has not yet been archaeologically located. It is known only from written sources, the latest dating from the beginning of the 6th Dynasty (Voss, 2004, 156). The name of the temple is written in one case without an obelisk and in the remaining cases with an obelisk (Nuzzolo, 2007, 246). On a sealing found by Borchardt (Borchardt, 1907, 132) in the Mastaba of the Princesses in Abusir, the name of the temple in the title of the priest of Re of Menkauhor's sun temple is written without an obelisk. Voss (Voss, 2004, 155) argued from this that Menkauhor's sun temple was supplied with offerings from Nyuserre's pyramid complex, with which the Mastaba of the Princesses was linked. However, the title is only one of several titles of the seal-bearer and does not justify such a conclusion. Moreover, the direction of the supply chain was in the reverse direction: it was the sun temple which supplied with some special offerings the mortuary temple, not the other way round.

That the temple functioned for only a relatively short period of time is indirectly suggested by the fact that, so far, we know of only two priestly titles associated with it:
- *ḥm-nṯr*-priest of Re in *3ḫt-Rꜥ*
- under-supervisor of *ḥm-nṯr*-priests of Re in *3ḫt-Rꜥ*.

Although there are no known recorded references to the priestly title referring to Hathor in *3ḫt-Rꜥ*, we can safely assume that the cult of this goddess was practised in this temple too.

With reference to the writing of the name of the temple in an inscription in the tomb of Hapdua in Saqqara (D 59), Helck (Helck, 1991, 163) has argued that the temple *3ḫt-Rꜥ* was later called *3ḫt-Ḥr*. This is definitely a misunderstanding, because Menkauhor's temple is not in fact mentioned at all in this inscription. Hapdua was a priest of Re and Re-Horus in the sun temple of Neferirkare, priest of Re in Nyuserre's sun temple, and also priest of Re-Harakhty.

V.7 THE MEANING OF THE SUN TEMPLES

Views on the meaning of the six sun temples of the 5th Dynasty have changed and developed over time and consensus among the scholars is yet to be achieved. Let us look at the most important issues one by one.

A seminal work on a particular type of an ancient Egyptian temple called the 'sun temple' we owe to Werner Kaiser (Kaiser, 1956, 104–116). He assessed all the hitherto available written and archaeological evidence of the 5th Dynasty sun temples and came to several important conclusions. For instance, he stressed the similarity between the plan of the sun temple complex and the pyramid complex. Kaiser also noticed the proximity of the two identified sun temples (they lay only ca 400 metres from each other) to Abu Ghurab, the place which represents in the Memphite necropolis the southermost limit of the direct optical connection with Heliopolis, the center of the solar cult. He stressed the proximity of the two identified sun temples (they lay only ca 400 metres from each other) and he theorised that the two types of buildings, the sun temple and the pyramid complex, had a unified priesthood. Despite the scenes in

Nyuserre's temple he believed that the sun temples were not built for the *sed*-festival and looked for their meaning in beliefs about the afterlife.

Winter (Winter, 1957, 232f.) likewise drew attention to the architectural and cult similarity between the pyramid complex and the sun temple. He was inclined to agree with Ricke (Ricke, 1969, 64 and 77f.), that the reign of Shepseskaf saw an increase in the influence of the cult of Re in the mortuary temple, in which an open court, separate from the mortuary-cult section, was now reserved for the sun god. Winter argued that this line of development culminated in the following period when in addition to his pyramid complex (his tomb as earthly ruler) the king would build another cult site in which he would be worshipped after his posthumous merger with the sun god Re. Winter also noticed that a sun temple was always associated exclusively with the cult of the particular king who had built it.

Helck (Helck, 1991, 163), on the other hand, believed that the 5th Dynasty kings built sun temples as tombs for their solar forefathers: initially, these had taken the form of a mastaba topped with a column erected to mark it as a sacred place.

According to Stadelmann, (Stadelmann, , 1094–1096; *id.*1985, 164) the sun temple was Re's mortuary temple or cenotaph, and at the same time, the material embodiment of the king's desire to identify his destiny with the sun god and his journey across the sky by day and night. Rochholz (Rochholz, 1994, 273f.) advanced the same idea in his study of the *sed*-festival and its influence on the architecture of the mortuary and sun temple.

Posener-Kriéger (Posener-Kriéger, 1976, 519–526) has made a major contribution to the understanding of the function of the sun temple on the basis of her thorough analysis of records from the papyrus archive of Neferirkare. This research has confirmed the close relationship between the king's sun and mortuary temples, and she has shown that it was in the sun temple and its production facilities that raw materials supplied for the needs of the king's cult from the stores of the Residence were processed. From the sun temple, they would then be conveyed already as offerings in the form of dishes to the mortuary temple. In particular, meat products came from the sun temple. This conclusion has been somewhat qualified and complicated, however, by the find of the previously mentioned great slaughterhouse built by Raneferef's mortuary temple; apparently it was built as a substitute for a sun temple, which Raneferef did not have the time to build in his very short reign. All the same, the slaughterhouse was only in operation for a very short time, and Raneferef's cult was supplied with meat and special breads from the sun temple of his father Neferirkare. Some meat products (e.g. fat) were also supplied to Raneferef's mortuary temple from the above cited slaughterhouses of the nearby palace of Sahure.

One very original theory about the meaning of sun temples has been put forward by Quirke (Quirke, 2001, 90), who regards them as a kind of relay station or channel for energy from the sun temple in Heliopolis to the tombs of their builders, necessary because these lay out of sight of Heliopolis. The general validity of the theory is undermined by the site of the first of the sun temples, Weserkaf's, which has no direct visual connection with Heliopolis.

Recently, Winter's basic theory has been taken up and developed by Nuzzolo (Nuzzolo, 2007, 217–247), for whom the "sun temple was a real *alter ego* of the tomb of the pharaoh". Nuzzolo argues that Khufu's aspiration to become the sun god was abandoned by his successors but revived at the beginning of the 5th Dynasty, when the Heliopolitan theology sought to harmonise the two main aspects of the royal cult, the mortuary and the solar. Nuzzolo finds additional evidence for this theory in the titles of the priests who held cult functions in the sun and mortuary temple of the kind, and from the time of Neferirkare and Nyuserre the increasing number of records of priests of the cult of Re who were also closely associated with the cults of Anubis, Sokar and above all Osiris. The process of 'popularisation' of the mortuary cult and Osiris culminated under Djedkare, these elements emerging later in the Pyramid Texts. According to Nuzzolo, the evidence for development includes the Osiris statue of the king placed in the middle niche of the five niches in the chapel of Neferirkare's mortuary temple, as suggested by Posener-Kriéger (Posener-Kriéger, 1976, 545); this suggestion, however, raises some doubts (see text on p. 138).

Nuzollo finds yet another argument (Nuzzolo, 2007, 240 n. 118) in the claim originally made by Winter that the pyramid complexes of the kings who built sun temples lack boat burials, which only reappear from the time of Wenis. Nuzzolo's claim is in fact mistaken in regard to Neferirkare's pyramid complex, for he built a sun temple and, in addition, there *were* boat burials: one on the north and the other on the south side of the pyramid (Posener-Kriéger, 1976, 430; Verner, 1980, 168f.). Raneferef also is credited with a sun temple – at least it must have been started – and two big wooden models of boats were found within his pyramid complex (Verner, 2006, 143f.). The precise meaning of these boats is another matter, however, as they were damaged by fire and subsequently ritually buried inside the central cult area. As regards the other records naming sun temples, this is an *ex silentio* argument, because no one has yet searched for boats in the other pyramid complexes of this period (Sahure's, Nyuserre's and Menkauhor's), but that they originally existed is likely (Verner, 2013, 714–718).

Among the most recent published studies on the meaning of the sun temple is that of Voss, who provides a brief summary of the basic conclusions of her dissertation on the subject (Voss, 2004; *id.* 2010, 222–233). According to Voss, in the sun temple Re was worshipped as the divine ancestor of the king in a way analogical to the cult of ancestors in the pyramid complexes, and this is why the temple was sited on the west bank of the Nile, in the necropolis. Re was the supplier of life to the earthly ancestors buried in the pyramid complexes, thus ensuring their eternal rule and regeneration. Scenes and the pair of boats – day and night barques – also recorded in written sources (the Palermo Stone mentioning Neferirkare's pair of copper barques to his sun temple *Śt-ib-Rʿ*), and the cult of Re-Harakhty are evidence that the sun temple was consecrated to the repetition of the solar cycle. The decorative scheme of the so-called Weltkammer is then an expression of the creative and regenerative aspect of the solar cycle for life on earth. By analogy, with this representation of the solar cycle and its regenerative force, the king expressed his desire to reign eternally through the power of the cult and magical pictures in the temple. Put briefly, the sun temple served the cult of ancestors, the father Re giving life to earthly ancestors in their pyramid complexes and so unending rule and regeneration.

Janák, Vymazalová and Coppens have also recently published their views on the sun temples of the 5th Dynasty kings (Janák, Vymazalová, Coppens, 2011, vol. 1, 430–442). Their conclusions are in many respects based on older ideas already cited here. They believe that the sun temple had the same function for Re as the mortuary temple for the king – it was "Re's mortuary temple". Rituals in the temple were performed in honour of the sun god in his role as creator and father of the king. Secondarily, these rituals related to the king both as living ruler (as Re's son and bearer of the royal *ka*, who himself needed the periodic renewal of royal potency) and as the dead/transformed king, resurrected into the world of the gods together with the sun. Ideologically, the sun temple not only secured the renewal of royal rule, but also expressed the role of that particular king in upholding the order of the world. In this way, it was held to have the same effect as the later Pyramid Texts. Finally, by its architecture, decoration and function it expressed religious concepts which showed how the world, including its creator and its earthly representative, were sustained and constantly renewed in being and order.

Such theories – not only these last, but also the previous opinions of the various authors cited above – may be helpful in appreciating the role of the sun sanctuaries, but they fail to pay enough attention to the particular historical circumstances of these temples. A focus on these circumstances can lead us to a better grasp of the meaning of these structures, all the more so when we speak of the introduction of a completely new type of temple.

From the surviving sources it would appear that Weserkaf, like his only briefly reigning predecessor (and perhaps his brother), Shepseskaf, very probably did not possess the 'full blood royal' qualification to become heir to the ruling royal line of the 4th Dynasty (for more detail see p. 18f.). There are hints that Shepseskaf was well aware of his lack of legitimacy in this respect: for instance, he did not build a tomb for himself in the shape of a pyramid, did not choose a site for it beside his immediate predecessors in the cemetery in Giza and, unlike those predecessors was reluctant to directly associate himself with the sun god by including Re in his throne name. His successor, Weserkaf, also seems to have not been very confident regarding his legitimacy. He decided on a tomb in the shape of a pyramid, but he chose a site for it by the north-eastern corner of the enclosure wall of Djoser's pyramid complex. This site, although technically inconvenient (to build his complex, part of the Dry Moat had to be filled in and, as a consequence of the constricted site thus available, the plan of Weserkaf's pyramid complex had to be radically altered from the standard design of the 4th Dynasty), was politically most important, because by this choice Weserkaf symbolically associated himself with the founder of the powerful royal line.

No less significant was Weserkaf's choice of site for his sun temple and, indirectly, a new cemetery for his own royal descendants. There was no space for a cemetery close to his pyramid in Saqqara, but Weserkaf did not intend to be content with any merely practical location: it had to fulfil a number of important conditions (see p. 159).

Architectural and historical analysis of Weserkaf's sun temple shows that this was not a building constructed according to a unified plan. This is not surprising, for it was the first temple of its kind (the temple in front of the Great Sphinx in Giza seems to have been dedicated to another aspect of the solar cult) and the builders were still looking for its optimal form. The plan of the temple exhibits a certain eclecticism and improvisation, and is inspired not just by the contemporary pyramid complex, but also by the design of cult places for the celebration of the *sed*-festival; very probably, it may also have derived some of its concepts from a contemporary building of the solar cult in Heliopolis, which provided the inspiration for the inclusion of an obelisk as the dominant element in the plan of the sun temple. The source of inspiration in this respect may have been the sanctuary of the *bnbn* (for different representations of the fetish stone *bnbn*, see e.g. Kemp, 2006, 139 Fig. 48; see also Bauval, 1989, 5–16) mentioned e.g. in the Pyramid Texts (Utt. 600 § 1652): "O Atum Kheper, you became high on the height, you rose up as the *bnbn*-stone in the 'Mansion of the Phoenix' in On, ..." (Faulkner, 1969, 246). As previously mentioned, it is not a serious counter-argument that as yet the oldest obelisk found in Heliopolis dates only from the beginning of the 6th Dynasty. Unfortunately, Heliopolis is a locality which has been very inadequately explored archaeologically and we can only hope that at least some of the many shrines there known from written sources (see e.g. Raue, 1999, *passim*) will one day be discovered.

Various different religious and political ideas undoubtedly came together in Weserkaf's conception of a sun temple. Here the cult of Re, a specific form of the sun god, and of Hathor, Re's partner, comes to the fore. At the latest, from the reign of Nyuserre onwards the sun god was also worshipped in the sun temple in the form of Re-Harakhty. The king was venerated together with these gods, but the relationship between the king and the sun god was that of son and father. Although the presence of a solar boat (as a building or cult object) has not been directly proven in Weserkaf's sun temple, a symbolic boat is recorded as part of the architecture of Nyuserre's sun temple, and in the equipment of Neferirkare's sun temple in the form of a pair of copper, 8-cubit long models of the sun god's day and night boats. The presence of these boats in the sun temples clearly expresses the king's wish to share the destiny of the sun god in eternity: every morning to 'sail up', to be born on the eastern horizon, to give forth life during his voyage across the daytime sky and at evening to descend into the underworld, there to experience a mystical transformation and regeneration and, at the end of the voyage through the night sky, to emerge again on the eastern horizon.

The father–son relationship between the sun god and the king was reflected in the relationship between the sun temple and mortuary temple: the primary recipient of the offerings was the sun god, and only afterwards were these gifts taken from his altar to the altar in the king's mortuary temple. The sun god was the guarantor of the eternal life of the king, and through the king, a guarantor for the prosperity of 'the people of his time'. The cult and the mutual relations of the three main protagonists of the sun temple – Re/Re-Harakhty, Hathor and the king – is recorded in its architecture (even though only remnants of stone shrines testify indirectly to the cult statues) and in written sources, especially the titles of the priests who served there. In the temple rituals the king formed a triad, together with Re and Hathor, and in this way undoubtedly legitimised his divinity and right to rule. This divine triad is also eloquently attested in inscriptions and heraldry on sealings relating to the sun temples (see e.g. Kaplony, 1981/II^{B}, pl. 88, no. 22 and no. 23).

The king was not worshipped in the sun temple only in the context of the solar cult. The sun temple was, however, the setting for the royal *sed*-festival, as we can see from the valley temple in the complex of Weserkaf's sun sanctuary. It was inspired by Snofru's *sed*-festival temple, and especially from remains of the relief decoration of Nyuserre's sun temple. Here the *sed*-festival was not a one-off event, but cyclical and symbolically celebrated in perpetuity. The sun temple was thus the place of rituals meant not only to unite the king with the sun god and secure him constant regeneration and immortality, but also to preserve his rule forever. These principles were already the basis of the king's cult in the sun temple during his lifetime, even – as indirectly documented in surviving written records – in cases when the temple was not yet complete.

If the sun temples were a way of achieving these important goals of legitimization and consolidation of the king's position during his life and after his death (*mrt*-shrines also helped to serve this purpose, see the text below), we must inevitably ask why their construction ceased so suddenly after the ascent of Djedkare to the throne. There is no simple and clear answer to that question, perhaps because there were probably several factors behind the cessation to the building of these sanctuaries.

Obviously, the social conditions had changed during the first half of the 5th Dynasty. Moreover, despite its meaning and the expectations associated with it, the institution of the sun temple seems not to have put down deep roots in the religious consciousness of the time. We can scarcely overlook the fact that of the six known sun temples only half were finished and functioned effectively. It seems that for some of their royal builders their existence was not unconditionally necessary. As the case of

Raneferef's cult shows, it was not a problem for a king's sun and mortuary cult to be combined with (and materially supplied by) the sun temple of his father. It is also very striking that the builders of the three completed and fully functioning sun temples – Weserkaf's, Neferirkare's and Nyuserre's – had serious political-dynastic reasons for building them and so consolidating their positions as ruler (see the previous discussion of these rulers). By contrast, there was less doubt about the legitimacy of the succession to the throne of Sahure, Raneferef and Menkauhor.

There may also have been entirely practical reasons behind the ending of the practice of building sun temples. The construction of a sun temple and its associated facilities for assembling, processing and distributing offering gifts as part of the royal mortuary cult may well have turned out to be too costly an intermediary link. The logistics of huge supplies of offerings for a number of the royal funerary cults must have been exhausting state treasury at a time when the revenues were diminishing in the train of an ever increasing bureaucracy, exemption of chosen temples from taxes and a general worsening of the economy due to climatic instability.

All the same, probably the most important reasons for the abandonment of sun temples are to be found in the changing religious beliefs of Egyptian society and especially its governing elite. The presentation of offerings first on the altar of Re in the sun temple, and only then their conveyance to the altar in the king's mortuary temple very eloquently expressed the dominant position of the sun god not only in his relationship to the king, but to the world in general. It would then seem that the abrupt ending of the practice of building sun temples reflects the retreat of the sun god from his previously dominant position. This retreat overlaps strikingly with the no less rapid rise in the popularity of Osiris, the ruler of the underworld kingdom of the dead, in the Egyptian vision of life after death. The situation, however, seems to have been more complex.

The origin of Osiris, his meaning, the interpretation of his name and so on, has been the subject of debate for a long time, and the scholarly controversies are far from resolved. (A summary of this discussion up to the beginning of the 1980s was provided by Griffith, 1982, 623–633. See also the fundamental work on Osiris by the same author *The Origins of Osiris and his Cult*, (Suppl. to Numen 40) Leiden 1980. More recently contributions have included Lorton, 1985, 113–126; Westendorf, 1987, 456–461; Helck, 1991, 164f.; Bolshakov, 1997, 183–185 and 286; Manuelian, 1998, 115–127; Baud, 1999, 517f.; Shalomi-Hen, 2006; and especially Mathieu, 2010, 77–107). Fragments of the relief decoration of a chapel from Djoser's time found in Heliopolis and bearing the names of several gods of the Ennead are considered the oldest indirect evidence for Osiris so far known (Curto, 1988, 48 Fig. 48). Osiris is not in fact among these gods, but from later sources we know that he was part of the Ennead, although the Osiris of the Ennead was not the god of the dead, but the god and symbol of the fertile land and eternal cycle of life. A supposed depiction of

Osiris (Griffith, *o. c.* 237; Eaton-Krauss, 1987, 233–236) on a fragment of relief from Djedkare's pyramid complex is now considered to be probably a mis-identification. It seems, for the time being, that Osiris first appears as the god of the dead in funerary formulae from the time of Nyuserre (see p. 70).

Mathieu in the recent article cited earlier has put forward new and very inspiring suggestions in discussion of Osiris. He draws attention to the strikingly short interval between the sudden appearance of Osiris and the rapid spread of his cult throughout Egypt, which he considers a matter not of chance, but of the decision made by the Egyptian central power (Mathieu, 2010, 78). He suggests that, like the Amarna religious "reformation", the "Osirian innovation" was decreed from above, by the king. The conception of Osiris as god and ruler of the dead was elaborated in Heliopolis on the basis of the "crystallisation of lunar, stellar and funerary aspects" already possessed by the Heliopolitan god-creator Re-Atum. In this way a pair of mutually complementary aspects of the god-creator emerged: the day/solar Re on the one hand and the night/lunar Osiris on the other (Mathieu, 2010, 87ff.). Only after this was Osiris introduced into principal cult places, Abydos and Busiris.

According to Mathieu, from the mid-5th Dynasty at the latest there was a *synchronicity* between the exceptional development of the cult of Re, as attested by the institutional and architectonic innovation represented by the sun temples, and the appearance of Osiris. Sources so far known, however, suggest sequence rather than synchronicity: the cult of Osiris probably appears shortly prior to the end of the era of the sun temples in the reign of Nyuserre. At the same time the cult of Osiris may have found expression in royal funerary architecture: inserted into the plan of the underground part of Djedkare's (maybe as early as Menkauhor's underground chambers, see p. 177) pyramid contained a so-called serdab made up of three niches, which according to some scholars may be interpreted as Osiris's underworld dwelling (for more detail see p. 178f.). Osiris was only to be fully introduced into the royal pyramid complex and mortuary cult under Djedkare's successor, in the Pyramid Texts in the pyramid of Wenis. It is plausible to see the relationship between these two developments as one of cause and effect, but this does not rule out Mathieu's idea of the complementarity of Re and Osiris.

Earlier in this account we suggested that the project of the sun temples was introduced at the beginning of the 5th Dynasty on the orders of the king Weserkaf. This project was very probably conceived by priests in the centre of the solar cult at Heliopolis, with the primary aim of consolidating the legitimacy of the king – and hence the new ruling line. It also seems to have been on the orders of a king, this time Djedkare, that the project of the sun temples was eventually abandoned. The primary purpose of the sun temples had been fulfilled, the power of the new ruling line had been legitimised and strengthened, and as social conditions changed, the rationale for this expensive institution had withered away.

VI. SANCTUARY *mrt* AND THE ROYAL CULT

Even less well-known than sun temples are sanctuaries called the *mrt*, not one of which has as yet been archaeologically identified. Hitherto, the earliest written evidence for these monuments refers to Snofru and dates from the 1st regnal year of Neferirkare (*Urk* I 247, 15–16). In this year, Neferirkare donated a statue of Ihy made of electrum to Hathor, Lady of the Sycamore, in Snofru's *mrt*-sanctuary. (Wilkinson, 2000, 172f. confused Snofru's *mrt*-sanctuary with the king's town known as "Beloved of Sneferu". The toponym is correctly interpreted as "*Mrt* des Snofru" by Barta, 1983, 98f., and also by Strudwick, 2005, 73 as "the *meret* temple of Sneferu".) The sanctuary may have lain near Snofru's pyramids in Dahshur, or in Meidum, as Wildung assumes (Wildung, 1969, 109), although Brovarski (Brovarski, 1977, 115) has suggested that Snofru's *mrt*-sanctuary might have lain within the precincts of the temple of Hathor, the Lady of the Sycamore House in southern Memphis.

Weserkaf's *mrt*-sanctuary is known from two written sources. One comes from the tomb of Ptahhotep, who lived approximately in Weserkaf's time (Baer, 1960, 74 [157]) and was a 'king's *wꜥb*-priest of the *mrt*-sanctuary of Weserkaf and *ḥm-nṯr*-priest of Weserkaf' (Mariette, 1882, 314; Barta, 1983, 99).

The second piece of evidence comes from the titulary of Khnumhotep, who was 'inspector of *wꜥb*-priests of the (sun temple) *Nḫn-Rꜥ*, *ḥm-nṯr*-priest of Weserkaf, *ḥm-nṯr*-priest of Hathor in front of Weserkaf 's (pyramid complex) and overseer of *ḥm-nṯr*-priests of Hathor of the House of the Sycamore (in) Weserkaf's *mrt*-sanctuary' (Mariette, 1882, 312 (D 49); Brit. Mus. Inscr. I² 1143, pl. 18; Barta, 1983, 99). Khnumhotep, who lived a little later than Weserkaf (Baer, 1960, 119 [406] dates Khnumhotep to a time later than the 5th Dynasty; however, his tomb lies east of Weserkaf's pyramid and typologically belongs to the early 5th Dynasty), concentrated in his hands priestly offices in three cult places of the king: the pyramid complex, sun temple and the *mrt*-sanctuary.

Quite questionable is the last piece of evidence for Weserkaf's *mrt*-sanctuary to which Ricke (Ricke, 1965, 46) refers, namely, Helck's reconstruction of the damaged text on a Cairo fragment of the Annals (*Urk* I 240, 13–18) which would, if correct, read as "building (the *mrt*-sanctuary) of Hathor in front of the purification pool of (the pyramid complex) Pure are the (cult) places of Weserkaf". According to this text, the sanctuary would lie near Weserkaf's pyramid complex in Saqqara. Ricke (Ricke, 1965, 46f.) also considered the possibility of identifying the valley building of Weserkaf's sun temple in Abusir with the king's *mrt*-sanctuary. Nowadays, such an assumption is outdated: it is clear from the previously cited Khnumhotep's three related titles that the places represented separate institutions. Also Helck (Helck, 1975-a, 95), with referrence to the Dahshur decree of Pepi I, tried to identify the valley temple of Snofru with the latter's *mrt*-sanctuary, but his theory has not been accepted either.

Sahure's *mrt*-sanctuary occurs in the titulary of a mid 5th Dynasty (Baer, *o. c.* 90 [256]) official, Neferirtenef, who was a '*ḥm-nṯr*-priest of Re in the (sun temple) *Nḫn-Rꜥ*, and a *ḥm-nṯr*-priest of Hathor and inspector of phyle *wr* in Sahure's *mrt*-sanctuary' (Mariette, 1882, 327; *PM* III^2, 583f.; Barta, 1983, 99; Walle, 1978, 34, 38 etc.). This text is especially significant, since it reveals that the *mrt*-sanctuary had its priesthood organized in phyles.

This sanctuary of the king also appears on a seal (now in the Egyptian Museum in Cairo, JE 72622) in the titulary of an official who lived in the time of Menkauhor and was a 'juridicial under-supervisor of those who are in charge of the reversions (of offerings), secretary, king's *wꜥb*-priest and *ḥm-nṯr*-priest of Sahure's *mrt*-sanctuary' (Kaplony, 1981/I, 305f. (no. 9); Barta, 1983, 99).

Possibly, to Sahure's *mrt*-sanctuary also relates the king's donation of land mentioned on a Cairo fragment of the Annals (*Urk* I 244, 34–35). 'Hathor in the *rꜣ-š* of Sahure', mentioned in the text on this fragment, might have been worshipped in the *mrt*-sanctuary – as can be inferred from a similar text 'the *mrt*-sanctuary of the *rꜣ-š* of Meryre' (Mariette, 1882, 456). The text attests to the location of this type of sanctuary in the *rꜣ-š* which, very probably, was an area adjacent on the eastern side of the pyramid complex (see the text below).

Menkauhor's *mrt*-sanctuary is referred to in two short texts. The first of them is the titulary of the king's contemporary, Duare (Baer, 1960, 155 [580]), who was a director of scribes of the house of the reversions (of offerings) and *ḥm-nṯr*-priest of Hathor of the *mrt*-sanctuary of Menkauhor' (Mariette, 1882, 419; Barta, 1983, 99). The second one is on a sealing dating from the time of Wenis, which belonged to an anonymous official who was a 'scribe of the secret documents of the king of Upper and Lower Egypt, Neferirkare, (and of) Re and Hathor of (the sun temple) *Śt-ib-Rꜥ*, and a phyle-member of a group of ten in the *mrt*-sanctuary of Ikauhor' (Kaplony, 1981/IIA, 350–352 (19); *id.* 1981/IIB, 96 (19); Barta, 1983, 99). The latter titulary is further evidence that the priesthood of the *mrt*-sanctuary was organized in phyles.

The only, but very important piece of evidence for Djedkare's *mrt*-sanctuary is the inscription in the tomb of the king's contemporary and vizier, Senedjemib Inti, who was in charge of building (or designing) this sanctuary in the precincts of the Great House (*mrt Ỉssi ntt ḥr š pr-ꜥꜣ*) (Brovarski, 1977, 92; see also Barta, 1983, 99). Obviously, this type of sanctuary could have existed not only near the pyramid complex but also in the Great House in the residential city.

Mention of Wenis's *mrt*-sanctuary occurs in the written sources several times. Djadjamankh, an official who lived in the time of Wenis or a little later, presents among his titles that of an 'inspector of the *ḥm-nṯr*-priests of Hathor of the *mrt*-sanctuary of Wenis'. As evidenced by Nubhetepet, of the good name Bebi, who was a '*ḥmt-nṯr*-priestess of Hathor in the *mrt*-sanctuary of Wenis' (Saad, 1941, 681 Fig. 72; Barta, 1983, 100), priestesses could have also served in the *mrt*-sanctuary. According to Gillam (Gillam, 1995, 226), the priestesses of Hathor maintained in the *mrt*-sanctuaries the relationship between the god Re and the king as the congener of Re. To the *mrt*-sanctuary of Wenis may also refer the title of an official named Hetep, who lived in the time of the king or a little later and was an 'inspector of the *ḥm-nṯr*-priests of Hathor of the *mrt*-sanctuary' (Hassan, 1975-b, 54 fig. 30). Though the king is not explicitly mentioned in the title, the relation to him can be indirectly inferred from the location of the tomb of Hetep near the king's pyramid.

Further Old Kingdom evidence for the *mrt*-sanctuary dates from the 6th Dynasty. To the three pieces of evidence referring to Teti published by Barta (Barta, 1983, 100) should be added those discovered only recently. One of them comes from the tomb of Sankhuiptah lying in the Teti pyramid cemetery (Kanawati, Abder-Raziq, 1998, 40). Sankhuiptah was a 'scribe of the *ḥm-nṯr*-priests of the *mrt*-sanctuary of Teti'. The second piece, a fragment of relief from the same cemetery, bears the title of an official who was 'he who is in charge of the lake of the *mrt*-sanctuary of Teti, the scribe of the phyle of the palace' (Kanawati, Hassan, 1996, 66, TNE94:F123). The third piece referring to Teti is represented by the titulary of Merefnebef, who was an 'under-supervisor of the *ḥm-nṯr*-priests of the *mrt*-sanctuary of Teti' (Mysliwiec *et al.*, 2004, 48).

To the three pieces of evidence of Pepy I's *mrt*-sanctuary cited by Barta (Barta, 1983, 100) can be added two recently discovered examples. One comes from the Saqqara tomb of Meru who was a '*ḥm-nṯr*-priest of Meryre's *mrt*-sanctuary of the *r3-š*' (Lloyd, Spencer, Khouli, 1990, 7 (11), 13 and pl. 8), and the second from the tomb of Pepymeryheryshef in South Abusir. Pepymeryheryshef has, among other titles, also that of an 'under-supervisor of the *ḥm-nṯr*-priests of the *mrt*-sanctuary of Pepy' (Vlčková, 2005, 169ff.). Concerning the *mrt*-sanctuary of Pepy II, there appeared no new evidence which could complete that cited by Barta (Barta, 1983, 100).

Owing to the brevity of the previously cited evidence, and the fact that so far no *mrt*-sanctuary has been archaeologically identified, our knowledge of this type of sacral building from the Old Kingdom remains very limited. Nevertheless, some conclusions can be inferred from the evidence already mentioned.

Firstly, it seems that the *mrt*-sanctuary mostly lay in the *r3-š*, a place the meaning of which is still the subject of a debate which has not yet been concluded. The available documents allow us the assumption that the *r3-š* was both a geographical and functional term denoting a zone, on the outskirts of the Nile valley, adjacent from the east to the pyramid complex. In this zone could have lain the pyramid town, administrative buildings, production facilities and, as the case might have been, also a royal palace. (Concerning a more detailed discussion of the term *r3-š* , see p. 114) Therefore, a *mrt*-sanctuary in this zone would come as no surprise. Judging by the aforecited title of an official who was 'in charge of the lake' in Teti's *mrt*-sanctuary, these sanctuaries included a pool and were probably connected with a channel leading to the valley temple. If we consider the importance of a lake in the cult of Hathor and her main feasts, the pool is of no surprise to us. Anyway, the citation of the term *r3-š* would suggest that the location of each *mrt*-sanctuary lay within the royal cemetery.

However, two documents locate the *mrt*-sanctuary elsewhere than in the *r3-š*. From the aforecited inscription in the tomb of Senedjemib Inti it is obvious that the sanctuary could have lain within the precincts of the Great House (*pr-ˁ3*), i.e. in the residential city. According to the inscription on a lintel from the chapel of queen Iput II, the *mrt*-sanctuary of Pepy II lay in the *ḏ3dw* (Jéquier, 1933, 58 Fig. 36). The term *ḏ3dw* is mostly interpreted as an audience hall or a summer palace of the king (Hannig, 1995, 1493 s.v.). Does this interpretation support Allam's comparison of the Memphite *mrt*-sanctuary with its cult of Hathor and Ihy to the later, Ptolemaic *maru* from Edfu and Dendera with the cult of Hathor and Harsomtus (Allam, 1963, 10)? In spite of some similarities, there is neither written nor archaeological evidence strong enough to support Allam's assumption that the *mrt*-sanctuary in Memphis and *maru* in Dendera had the same function. The name is different and, moreover, the gap of time between the two terms is too large to allow their direct comparison of their meaning.

Even if the remains of the *mrt*-sanctuaries should still lie under several metres of a thick layer of Nile mud sediment, the fact that not a single block of stone from any of them has as yet been found seems to be indicative of the character of these structures. Very probably, they were built of light materials such as mudbrick and wood, though some of their architectural elements might have been of stone. We can presume that at least a statue of Hathor, and possibly also that of a king and Ihy were placed in the most important room of the sanctuary. Probably, these sanctuaries had not been designed as permanent structures (perhaps except for Snofru's *mrt*-sanctuary in Memphis (?) to which Neferirkare donated the statue of Ihy about one century later), and therefore they also did not last long. The fact that evidence for these buildings is only infrequently mentioned and is, moreover, chronologically limited, also points to the same conclusion. On the other hand, the sanctuaries must have operated for at least a short period of time – as testified by their priesthoods, which included both *ḥm-nṯr*-priests (and *ḥmt-nṯr*-priestesses) as well as *wˁb*-priests. The priesthood was probably not necessarily small, as its organization into phyles indirectly shows.

In the so far only major study on the *mrt*-sanctuaries, Barta (Barta, 1983, 102) tried to identify the meaning of these buildings. He pointed out that their names do not occur independently but are always linked with either the throne or the personal name of a king – its founder. The cult in the *mrt*-sanctuaries placed near the pyramid complex began after the king's death and focused primarily on Hathor, but also on her son Ihy and the king. According to Barta, the sanctuary thus might have served as a place of *hieros gamos* 'sacred marriage' of the king with Hathor. The *mrt*-sanctuaries in the royal palace might have been the stage of annual ceremonies of the cultic joining of the ruling king with Hathor in order to increase the fertility of not only the royal couple but also all the men, animals and fields. Eventually, Barta rejected Kaplony's suggestion that the *mrt*-sanctuary might have been the precursor of the *mammisi*, or 'birth house', known from the temple complexes of the Ptolemaic and Roman Periods.

However, we might add to Barta's conclusions, with which we can in principle agree, several suggestions and open questions. Interestingly, after its first occurrence in the time of Snofru, the sanctuary seems to have recurred only as late as at the very beginning of the 5th Dynasty. If we consider the number of written documents dating from the 4th Dynasty, it is rather surprising that no further mention had been made of such structures for any of Snofru's successors. This is all the more striking if Snofru's *mrt*-sanctuary lay, as presumed by Brovarski, within the precincts of the temple of Hathor in South Memphis. Is it, therefore, possible that the *mrt*-sanctuary gained new significance, and also place, in the king's cult at the beginning of the 5th Dynasty, in the time of Weserkaf? If so, did the *mrt*-sanctuary, as well as the sun temple, become another piece of innovation designed to support the king's cult in the time of Weserkaf?

The relevant contemporaneous written documents inform us that in the cult at the sun temple, the king presented himself as a son of Re and Hathor. The worship of the triad Re – Hathor – king has already been recognized by Helck (Helck, 1984, 67–72) and discussed in more detail by Voss (Voss, 2004, 162–164). On the other hand, the previously cited sources relevant to the *mrt*-sanctuary seem to portray the king as a partner of Hathor, which would not be surprising: the king was the terrestrial incarnation of Horus and Hathor, by the definition of her name, presented herself as 'Horus's abode', Horus's spouse. The name of the *mrt*-sanctuary 'house of love' as a place of the symbolical marriage of the king-Horus with Hathor would then be quite appropriate. Horus's and Hathor's son was Ihy and, therefore, the previously cited presentation of Ihy's statue by Neferirkare to Hathor in Snofru's *mrt*-sanctuary does not lack its logic. The question is, why was Snofru's *mrt*-sanctuary chosen by Neferirkare? Maybe, due to the divinisation of Snofru and his long lasting cult (see e.g. Graefe, 1990, 257–263), maybe, just as it was the oldest sanctuary located probably in Memphis, the *mrt*-sanctuary enjoyed an especially high status and deserved the gift.

Finally, to the double cult of the king, one in the sun temple and the second in the *mrt*-sanctuary, should be added his cult in his pyramid complex in which he merged with Osiris. The king's cult in the necropolis would thus be tripled. If these assumptions are correct, the *mrt*-sanctuary became, besides the sun temple, another means among Weserkaf's efforts to legitimize his new royal dynasty. However, in the course of time, as the position of the new dynasty consolidated, the two institutions began to lose their meaning for the royal cult and, eventually, faded away: the sun temple in the time of Djedkare and the *mrt*-sanctuary had probably disappeared by the time of Pepy I.

THE FIFTH DYNASTY – A TIME OF CHANGES

It was emphasised in the foreword to this book that its aim was not to give a comprehensive account of the history of Egypt in the period of the 5th Dynasty. The book is focused primarily on the ruling royal line, its protagonists and their role in a time of complex and profound social change in Egypt. In the following text we shall try to summarise the main features of the relevant social processes and the nature of the changes in a brief overview. These processes clearly need to be set, however briefly and in rather simplified form, within a wider historical framework – especially the context of the preceding development of Egyptian society in the first half of the Old Kingdom, during the 3rd and 4th Dynasties.

The beginning of the Old Kingdom saw the consolidation of the central political power after the instability and even crisis of identity experienced at the end of the Early Dynastic Period with the unification of two such geographically, politically, economically and culturally different countries as Upper and Lower Egypt. The construction of the Step Pyramid, the technically, organisationally and economically very demanding but politically and ideologically prestigious tomb complex of the founder of the 3rd Dynasty, Djoser, is eloquent testimony to the success of the process of economic development and political integration of Egypt at the beginning of the Old Kingdom. This monumental stone building, expressing the social, religious and political pre-eminence of the ruler, is testimony not just to the high level of division of labour attained, but to the efficiency of the country's government, then firmly centralized in the hands of the narrow circle of royal family members.

The political and economic process sometimes known as 'internal colonisation' (see e.g. Jacquet-Gordon, 1980, 672f.; Helck, 1975, 34–44), which had already been initiated during the unification of the country and directed from its political centre, acquired a new momentum. Its goal was the expansion of agricultural production, the basis of Egypt's economy, and the creation of new resources through the establishment of farming estates (Helck, 1975, 37f.; Moreno García, 1999, 233f.; Papazian, 2012, 39–43; Engel, 2013, 50f.) on previously uncultivated land. There is evidence of water management from the end of the prehistoric era (K.W. Butzer, 1976, 19–21; Lepp, 1995, 197–209) but its role in the expansion of agricultural production, which had earlier been increased simply by expanding the amount of land cultivated, remains controversial; artificial irrigation was introduced only from the First Intermediate Period (Schenkel, 1978; Endesfelder, 1979, 37–51). The process of internal colonisation had not only economic (apart from agriculture it also stimulated the development of crafts, local trade and so forth) but political effects, deepening the political integration of the country and enabling the central power to consolidate its position and appropriate the surplus product.

In addition to newly established colonies and farms, usually located in flood territory (Bietak, 1979, 101f.; Redford, 1992, 8) and inhabited by early agricultural and hunter-gatherer communities on a common land basis, larger, fortified administrative and economic centres grew up as seats of regional administrations and places where agricultural products were concentrated (Moreno García, 1999, 205f.). It was during the 3rd Dynasty that the governing apparatus of the country, already divided into basic administrative regions, crystallised fully in its essential features (Helck, 1977, 385–408), but the government itself was probably still mobile up to the end of the 3rd Dynasty: once every two years the king and his retinue, the Following of Horus, would visit the regional centres to receive the taxes that had been gathered, address local problems on the spot, give court judgments and so on (Engel, 2013, 37). In the provincial regions the royal power was probably directly represented by a deputy institution, symbolised by a small pyramid and adjoining royal palace ('Pfalz'). A complex of such buildings on the southern border of the country, on Elephantine, which at this time was already surrounded by a rapidly expanding, large urban agglomeration, provides one example of this state of affairs (Seidlmayer, 1996, 108–127).

Even so, Djoser's huge Step Pyramid complex seems to have overstrained the economic resources of the country at the time, to judge by the smaller, sometimes unfinished pyramids of Djoser's immediate successors. The immense concentration of power essential for the collection of taxes and mobilisation and concentration of resources from all over the country for the big building projects, as well as the system of redistribution of the income from one political centre, also had further serious political and social consequences. For example, in the provinces it led to the weakening of local elites, as we can deduce from the fact that they ceased to build great tombs for their members in important provincial cemeteries.

Egyptian society at the beginning of the Old Kingdom is often compared to a pyramid, with the ruler at its apex. It was a complex, socially stratified structure, in which the king, regarded as the earthly embodiment of the sky god Horus, 'the highest', combined divinity (gained from the gods at coronation), and humanity in his own person and was thus the natural mediator between his people and the gods. Above all, he was the guarantor of the order of the world, which was created by divine will but constantly threatened by the forces of chaos and evil (Baines, 1995, 17). From the politico-religious point of view he was sole sovereign lord of the land, its inhabitants and natural resources. This unequivocal concept of royal supremacy persisted into the first half of the Old Kingdom, but as Egyptian society grew in complexity and sophistication it was to be diluted and qualified. At this earlier time almost all the highest representatives of the government of the land, in first place the vizier but sometimes other high ranking officials such as the overseer of all the royal works, came from the ruler's family (Strudwick, 1985, 337–346). Even though the founding of new local cults of gods increased, their material endowments were still very modest at this point and the priesthood was still small in numbers and politically relatively insignificant (Bussmann, 2010, 506–513). Soldiers were likewise an unimportant social group, since at this point there was still no standing army but only armed guards, including e.g. foreign archers, for important institutions and garrisons in the forts; an army would be called together *ad hoc* according to need (Faulkner, 1953, 32–36; Spalinger, 2013-c, 460–471).

With economic and social advance came growth in Egypt's administrative apparatus of specialised officials. At the beginning of the 3rd Dynasty the capital, the White Wall, already founded during the unification of Egypt at the geographical and political boundary between Upper and Lower Egypt, became the permanent seat of central government. It was here, around the royal seat, that the main institutions of the country were concentrated: the office of vizier and the supreme executive and judicial power associated with it, the office of the overseer of all works, the administration of the treasury, granaries and so forth. The scale of the administrative apparatus and increase in its functions at the time is evident from the period titles of officials (Jones, 2000, *passim*; Helck, 1954, *passim*; Baer, 1968, *passim*). At the latest from the beginning of the 4th Dynasty, the older mobile system of running the country and tax collection (Dreyer, 1987, 98–109) was replaced by a normally biennial (Verner, 2001, 413) inspection of property, known as the 'count (census) of all cattle and livestock', as a basis for the calculation of tax. An essential part of production from the provinces would be left to cover the needs of the local population while the rest was brought to the political centre, from which it would be re-allocated in accordance with royal interests, with a major proportion going to the building of the royal tomb complexes and their associated royal mortuary cults. This redistribution was also a form of legitimisation of royal power.

Concurrently with the building of the capital, the White Wall, a cemetery was founded not far away from it on the edge of the desert on the west bank of the Nile. Kings, members of the royal family and high-ranking officials were buried there, at first just sometimes, but later as a rule. The pyramid dominating each complex was not just the posthumous dwelling place of the king's *ka*, but conceived as his eternal body (Piankoff, 1968, 4). Even after his death, a king had a fundamental social role, for according to what was a cyclical concept of time and the continuity of kingship he continued to be the ruler of the people 'of his time' and a guarantor of stability and prosperity of the land. The grandiose tomb complex of a king thus had both a symbolic and political meaning: it helped support state ideology. According to the astral conceptions still dominant in the 3rd Dynasty, the king, after his death, became a never setting circumpolar star. This belief was embodied in the north-south orientation and arrangement of the ruler's pyramid complex. Its buildings were mainly symbolic rather than functional, since mortuary cult practices were still very limited. In line with the beliefs of the time a large quantity of offering gifts would be placed in the tomb alongside the funerary equipment. The closed and exclusive character of a king's tomb complex would be emphasised by its huge enclosure wall.

All the same, in the course of the 3rd Dynasty the solar cult, which had its origins reaching back to the Early Dynastic Period (Kahl, 2007, 61–63) if not even earlier, was already starting to spread in the circles of the governing elite. The reign of Snofru saw a basic reorganisation of the royal tomb complex and mortuary cult. Complexes would now be divided into three parts – valley temple, mortuary temple and pyramid – and orientated on an east-west axis to follow the journey of the sun across the sky. They were no longer isolated and more or less closed buildings in the cemetery, but were directly connected to the world of the living by their valley temples on the edge of the Nile Valley. Their mortuary temples became the setting for offering rituals that took place several times a day, and the whole pyramid complex became the stage for many festivals and ceremonies in the course of the year. Snofru's grandson, Radjedef, finally proclaimed himself the direct son of the sun god and adopted the title 'son of Re', which subsequent pharaohs then included in their official royal titulary after him.

To fund the building of pyramids and endow the mortuary cults of not only kings but an increasing number of high officials, more and more new estates were founded. For example in just one year during the reign of Snofru, "35 estates with people ? (and) 122 cattle farms" were founded (Wilkinson, 2000, 143). The relationship between the ruler, members of his family and high officials continued after his death and found expression in the arrangement of cemeteries. One example is the cemetery in Giza founded in the reign of Snofru's son Khufu, which was designed in a unified form so that the king's pyramid would be surrounded by the tombs of his family members and beyond them by the tombs of his officials (see e.g. Jánosi, 2005, 77–225). The close relationship of the ruler as the giver of offerings and guarantor of the eternal life and prosperity of his people is eloquently expressed in the funeral formula 'an offering which the king gives', which appears in private tombs at the end of the 3rd and beginning of the 4th Dynasty (Barta, 1968, 3).

In the first half of the Old Kingdom the rulers also devoted attention to the development of the cults of gods, although contemporary written and archaeological sources do not provide us with a comprehensive picture of the process. Only fragments of information about these cults have survived from the time in the royal annals, but they show that kings made efforts to support the cult of gods such as Min, Bastet, Anubis, Wepwawet and others, and their shrines in different parts of the country (Wilkinson, 2000, 136–151, 228, 234, 239). Major temples as yet existed only in the area of the political centre of the country, in Heliopolis and Memphis, but unfortunately our information about these is also very incomplete. In this period, the temple of Khontamenty in Abydos and of Min in Koptos may have been of more than local significance (Bussmann, 2010, 511). Most of the provincial shrines were small buildings made of clay, wood and rushes, and had only very modest economic resources, for example the cult of Hathor in Tehna, founded by Menkaure was not materially adequately endowed until the reign of Weserkaf.

In terms of social structure, the great majority of the population was rural during the time of the 3rd and 4th Dynasties, and made up mainly of farmers, but also fishermen, hunters, craftsmen, tax collectors and others, including migrating Bedouin. Evidence of the diverse composition of two such communities at the end of the 4th Dynasty is to be found for example in papyri from Gebelein (Posener-Kriéger, 2004). The authorities kept very precise records of the rural population, and these show that it was diverse in occupation and also socially stratified. The largest group, known as *mrt* (significantly the basis of the term is the sign for a pick) had compulsory labour duties (the corvée) according to the needs and instructions of the authorities, for example in the fields or on major building projects (see e.g. Moreno García, 1998, 71–83; Hafemann, 2009, 106). Some people in the rural communities had the status 'king's servant' – they served the monarch directly. There were other social groups as well including scribes, priests, etc.

Although hierarchical, Egyptian society at this time was not petrified but changing and developing. In principle, the king held absolute sovereign power over the whole country, its population and resources, but practice was more diverse and flexible. The king very probably respected existing property relationships, and he himself rewarded his subjects for services rendered by grants of property in the form of revenue from the royal estates, the gift of agricultural land, material for the building of a tomb and so forth. Ownership (Egyptian has no specific term for this concept, and instead renders it as 'share' and suchlike) required a royal decree to be legally valid (Menu, Harari, 1974, 127). Rights of ownership were more personal than private, and the king could confiscate property if its holder was disloyal.

One source that offers an illuminating picture of the relationship of high-ranking officials to property at the end of the 3rd and beginning of the 4th Dynasty is the autobiography of Metjen (Gödecken, 1976). Metjen started his career as a relatively insignificant official: he inherited his post from his father and with it an income in the form of foodstuffs, and his mother left him land in Upper Egypt. He went on to acquire more property and income by his own efforts from the title of his positions. For example Metjen increased his land ownership to 200 aruras after becoming a high official whose duties included administering several regions in Upper and Lower Egypt. His autobiography is direct evidence that in this period even people of non-royal origin could control substantial property.

Even very humble people could own property, for example a small clay house, and freely dispose of it (see e.g. Menu, 1985, 249–262). If they decided to sell their property, the transaction was accomplished using a document known as *imyt-pr* (lit. 'what is in the house', i.e. 'testament', 'Hausurkunde') (Mrsich, 1968). There were also some highly specific forms of ownership. For example what is known as the mortuary foundation (*pr-ḏt*), which could include the use of revenues from estates, was an institution that gave people individual property rights within the framework of a collective agreement (Fitzenreiter, 2004, 87–91). After the death of a holder, his individual property would be taken back into collective ownership and then re-allocated. Concepts and practices relating to property conditions were not static, but it is hard to identify and date important changes precisely, for example the shift from personal to private ownership (Römer, 2007, 73).

Social development meant not only advance, however, but mounting problems that were to come to a head at the end of the 4th Dynasty. The problems were of various kinds, and mutually interacted until eventually the outcome was a deep political and social crisis in a relatively short period. Egypt did not collapse, but the political elite and their mode of rule was shaken to the foundations. A new royal line, the 5th Dynasty, came to power, bringing new approaches to resolving the accumulating problems, and at the same time opening the way for further social change.

The successors of Djoser failed to learn the lesson of the excessive strain on Egyptian economic resources involved in the building of his pyramid complex: ideology prevailed over reality and the building of costly pyramid complexes legitimising supreme royal power continued to be a political priority. The political stabilisation of the country and an economic boom at the beginning of the 4th Dynasty, together with the full adoption of the solar cult, led to the building of even larger and more demanding royal tomb complexes. The founder of this dynasty, Snofru, built himself three whole pyramid complexes: the total volume of their masonry (3,6 mil. m^3) was never exceeded by any subsequent king (Stadelmann, 1985, 105). Apart from the pyramid complexes other economically and organisationally ambitious building projects were undertaken, such as the Sadd el-Kafara dam in Wadi el-Gerawi (Garbrecht, Bertram, 1983).

These works required not only massive material resources, but also the mobilisation of human resources, which were relatively limited and only available in large quantities on a seasonal basis. Under the 4th Dynasty there were around 1 to 1.5 million people in Egypt (Mortensen, 1991, 29; Kemp, 2006, 50). Estimates today suggest that around 20–30 thousand people were involved in the building of a pyramid, including preparation and transport of building materials (Lehner, 1997, 224). These were long-term projects, which under Snofru, Khufu, Radjedef and Khafre took anything from roughly two decades to four decades, and so, overall, around a hundred years. In the long term, the construction of gigantic tombs and their subsequent cult operation was a major burden on the Egyptian economy, tying down and 'immobilising' resources that might otherwise have been used to stimulate more growth. It is no wonder that despite sophisticated organisation and advances in logistics (see e.g. Tavares, 2011, 270–277), under Menkaure we already see a drastic reduction in the volume of the pyramid, undoubtedly in an attempt to bring down costs, and that even so, at the end of a reign estimated as at least 18 years in length, Menkaure's pyramid complex was still a very long way from complete.

The great building projects were undeniably a stimulus to the development of Egypt's infrastructure (boat transport along the Nile, the construction of artificial channels, founding of harbours, etc.), including various crafts and arts. The demands the projects placed on effective organisation and labour management also contributed to the development of the administration at central and local level. Yet this led to an expansion of bureaucracy, further exhausting the material resources of the country and putting a greater burden on their redistribution, and so became another factor making for crisis (Müller-Wollermann, 1986, 105). Directing the entire administrative machinery from a single power centre, the royal family, was becoming ever harder.

The climate, which became significantly less stable at this time, was also taking its toll. New studies have shown that at the end of the 4th and beginning of the 5th Dynasty, serious climatic anomalies were occurring at roughly four-year intervals in the period between the end of the reign of Khafre and beginning of the reign of Weserkaf. These were characterised in northern Egypt by repeated torrential rainfall, which caused floods (see e.g. K.W. Butzer, E. Butzer, Love, 2013, 3340–3365; for Lehner's opinion on the aforesaid climatic anomalies see p. 26). The economic damage must have been substantial. Nor was this just a short-term (several decades) climatic fluctuation, but a sign of a long-term trend that deepened during the 5th Dynasty and was associated with the gradual end of the Holocene Wet Phase in North Africa. The climate was becoming hot and dry, with a correlated progressive decline in rainfall in equatorial Africa, a fluctuating level of the annual Nile floods and gradually decreasing discharge of the Nile (Said, 1993, 138–142). All this has been confirmed by paleo-ecological studies in the area of the Abusir Lake (Cílek, Lisá, Bárta, 2011, 325) and Abusir necropolis (Bárta, Bezděk, 2011, 221f.). Obviously, environmental conditions must have been deteriorating, although the depiction of starving Bedouins on a block from the causeway of Wenis is not, as is sometimes suggested, a record of the problem (Vercoutter, 1985, 327–337). A similar scene also appears on Sahure's causeway. Rather than general hunger this 'famine scene' illustrates the poverty and backwardness of the inhabitants of the mountainous desert and so implicitly highlights the hardships and risks of the expeditions sent to these tough and dangerous parts to obtain rare kinds of stone for the building of the pyramids. Probably, these scenes were already standard parts of the decorative programme of the royal pyramid complex of the era.

At the end of the 4th Dynasty, deepening long-term troubles were evidently exacerbated by unexpected events in the power centre of the country – the royal family.

Menkaure seems to have left no male heir that could legitimately succeed him. Khuenre, probably his son with Queen Khamerernebty II, was either born after his death, or was too young to take his place. Although several of the sons of Menkaure's predecessor Khafre were still alive, it appears to have been the highest-ranking woman, Khentkaus I, undoubtedly a direct representative of the royal line, whose position proved crucial. She was probably a daughter of Khafre and it was to her, rather than to one of his sons, that the task of securing the continuation of the line fell. Without direct evidence we can only speculate whether the husband of Khentkaus I (it is unlikely that she was Menkaure's remarried widow) was either not of the main branch of the royal family or even of royal origin at all. Several clues give us grounds for supposing that the sons of Khentkaus I were probably the two kings following Menkaure – Shespsekaf and Weserkaf, who had to struggle to establish the legitimacy of their position. It is even possible that Shepseskaf and Weserkaf were fraternal (?) twins. Moreover, it seems that fraternal (?) twins occured three times in the royal family in the early 5th Dynasty. If so, this possibility may have lain at the root of the "birth of triplet" (for more detailed discussion see p. 10f.).

On the other hand, the chance discontinuity in the royal family at the end of Menkaure's reign and succession of rulers who were probably not of the full blood royal, was an opportunity for the adoption of new approaches to Egypt's accumulating problems. A period of apparent stability based on rigidity of kingship and the ordering of society ended, and there was a new search for pragmatic solutions. With the transition from the 4th to the 5th Dynasty, then, new forces were released that kings could not entirely control and perhaps no longer even wished to master absolutely. Henceforward kings would seek instead just to oversee, moderate and keep a balance between them. This conceptual change was reflected in the new image of the divine ruler, in his 'humanisation' including, for example, the incorporation of his birth name into his royal titulary, beginning with Neferirkare (Helck, 1991, 167). The marriages of royal daughters to powerful men of non-royal origin, for example Weserkaf's daughter Princess Khamaat to the influential official and priest Ptahshepses (another such official might have been the spouse of Khentkaus I), was another sign of the changing position of the ruler in this era of transformation, and of his search for broader consensus and support from the society he governed.

Given the circumstances in which the new royal dynasty came to power, it is not surprising that legitimising and consolidating their claim was a priority for the first kings of the 5th Dynasty. Devotion to the solar cult was a primary way of expressing legitimacy and these 5th Dynasty rulers devised new methods to do so. They initiated the building of temples of a new type – what are known as sun temples, in which they presented themselves as sons of the sun god Re and also symbolically renewed their ruling authority in society in the rituals of the *sed*-festival. The building of *mrt*-shrines was also a means to legitimise and consolidate their position, this time in rituals associated with the goddess Hathor. The rituals in both these institutions supplemented and supported the cult of the ruler in his pyramid complex.

Administrative changes were made with the aim of developing a new, better structure corresponding to the real needs of the country. They included opening the path to posts in the government, even the highest, to people of non-royal origin. In view of the character of the Egyptian society of the time it is clear that the basic impetus for these changes must have come from the ruler himself. It was not just a practical but a political move, a way of consolidating power and creating new support for it in a new bureaucracy. Nor was it just a one-off measure, but the start of a long-term 'reform process' of improvement and standardisation within the government of Egypt. The rationale was the need for a continual and flexible response to the changing needs of the country, and thus for officials who were both expert and loyal to the central power. As before, it remained the ruler who made appointments to higher posts by decree (Kanawati, 1977, 71; Meyer, 2011, 59). And so while one effect of the process was the gradual depersonalisation of kingship, another was to multiply the social obligations of the king himself (Bárta, 2013, 166). Family and clientele relations and contacts were increasingly decisive for success in gaining positions in government.

The first phase of the new dynasty saw a reduction in the political influence of the old royal political structures. The supreme office of vizier, who had direct control of the most important organs of government of the land, ceased to be the exclusive domain of members of the royal family (Schmitz, 1976, 165f.) and loyal experts of non-royal origin were now sometimes appointed to it. Although viziers were no longer blood princes, they retained some of the honorary princely titles that went with the post (Bárta, 2013, 166). In the transitional period of the end of the 4th and beginning of the 5th Dynasty, the office of vizier was probably held by two officials in tandem, one from the royal family and the other of non-royal origin, with the second being the chief and genuinely executive vizier (Strudwick, 1985, 337f.). It is from this period that we have several examples (setting aside one from the beginning of the 4th and a second from the end of the 5th Dynasty) of titles of vizier with the specific addition *ṯꜣy* (Dulíková, 2011, 327–336) and *mꜣʿ* (Callender, 2000, 371–373), the meaning of which is still a matter of debate. At the beginning of the 5th Dynasty, but at the latest under Neferirkare, new posts emerged such as 'overseer of the scribes of the king's documents', 'overseer of the great mansions', 'overseer of the six great mansions', 'overseer of the granary', etc. (Strudwick, 1985, 238). The growth of the bureaucracy and multiplication of their functions eventually required a re-ordering and standardisation of officials' titles (Baer, 1960, 300).

One politically important change at the beginning of the 5th Dynasty was the emergence of a new social group known as *ḫnty-š*, not quite precisely translated as 'land tenant' (Jones, 2000, 691f.) or sometimes 'attendant' (Roth, 1995); only much later did the term acquire the meaning 'gardener'. On the basis of the Dahshur decree of Pepy I, which mentions the *ḫnty-š*, Posener-Kriéger (Posener-Kriéger, 1976, 577–581) argued that the status already existed at the beginning of the 4th Dynasty in the time of Snofru, but the text in fact shows no more than that these officials were serving in the cult of Snofru at the time when the decree was promulgated. These officials were members of the king's retinue, who accompanied him during his life at the royal court and, after his death, took part in the maintenance of his mortuary cult (Fettel, 2010, 168f.; Baud, 1996, 13–30). The close relationship of the *ḫnty-š* to the ruler and his mortuary cult (Fettel, 2010, 168 and 279–282) found expression in their personal names, which were often basiliform, using the name of the king in whose cult they served (Roth, 1991, 179). They were probably permitted to lease land in the neighbourhood of the pyramid complex, cultivating products for the royal cult there. The direct connection between the lease and the royal mortuary cult in practice meant the long-term holding of leased land and so a guaranteed source of income, which was why the function of serving as *ḫnty-š* became attractive even for high officials.

Closely bound up with this development surrounding the royal mortuary cult was the increasing economic and political importance of the pyramid complex (which included the dwelling complex, the so-called pyramid town, of its employees situated mostly in the surroundings of the valley temple) from the reign of Neferirkare, or at the latest Nyuserre. It is suggested by the titles of the priests and officials who worked in them (Helck, 1991, 167). The overseer of the whole pyramid complex by this time was a high-ranking official, in most cases the vizier (Helck, 1957, 94). The position of the pyramid complex may well have already been changing some time before, from the beginning of the 5th Dynasty, with the appearance of sun temples in royal building schemes. Unfortunately, relevant written documents from the archives of these temples, which might confirm the theory, have not survived.

Other important changes and innovations in the government of Egypt took place in the reign of Nyuserre. One reason for this is perhaps that Nyuserre, like Djedkare after him, ruled for a relatively long period and had the chance to react more consistently to the changing situation that the dynamic development of the country was creating. Some scholars (e.g. Strudwick, 1985, 308) believe that it was under Nyuserre that the important office 'overseer of Upper Egypt' was established and Kai was its first holder, but some others believe that this introduction was probably somewhat later. This office was supposed to ensure a more effective government of Upper Egypt and, in particular, to improve tax collection and financial administration (Martin-Pardey, 1976, 155f.; Brovarski, 2013, 98).

Around the middle of the 5th Dynasty there was a significant shift in religious ideas, with the appearance of the cult of Osiris as god of the dead and ruler of the underworld. The precise dating of the quite rapid rise and spread of the cult of Osiris is still a matter of debate; the so far earliest occurrence of Osiris in a funerary offering formula dates from the time of Nyuserre. The circumstances of this change or innovation support the theory that the cult of Osiris was introduced from above, by royal decision, and so can be considered in its way a kind of religious reform (Mathieu, 2010, 78). According to Mathieu the concept of the cult originated in Heliopolis, the centre of the solar cult, with the aim of creating two mutually complementary aspects of the god-creator: the diurnal/solar Re on the one hand and the nocturnal/lunar Osiris on the other (Mathieu, 2010, 87ff.). Osiris was only then introduced into what were to be the two main centres of his cult, Abydos and Busiris.

If this account is correct, what may have been the wider social and political contexts of this theological innovation? The incompleteness of the written records of the period, and the intricacies and ambiguities of the Pyramid Texts, means that we can only speculate. It has already been noted that the rulers of the 4th Dynasty linked their destiny with the sun god and from the time of Radjedef proclaimed themselves his direct offspring with the title 'son of Re'. There are various indications that the 4th Dynasty kings sought to identify entirely with the sun god Re, and share his divine essence (for example the location of the burial chamber in Khufu's pyramid high above the level of the base is sometimes interpreted as an expression of the king's effort to rise up to the sun god and unite with him). The rulers of the 5th Dynasty, probably in view of the circumstances of their rise to power, saw their relationship to the sun god rather differently, stressing filial rather than direct identification. This emphasis was supposed to support their legitimacy as heirs–rulers, but the derivation of their kingly authority from the sun god shifted them into the role of his subordinates. The status of the ruler was thereby weakened, for it was Re rather than his earthly son who became the highest authority in the world of the living.

The shift in the relationship of the king to the sun god Re was projected into ideas of life after death and the king's role in it for his contemporaries. Earlier the king (as well as the gods of the dead, Anubis and Khontamenty) had been the giver of offerings and hence also the guarantor of the eternal life of his people, as explicitly expressed in the burial formula quoted above: 'an offering which the king gives' (Barta, 1968, 4–8; Lapp, 1986, 37). At the beginning of the 5th Dynasty, however, the king himself became the recipient of offerings provided from the altar of his father Re in the sun temple. The king would thus lose his exclusive relationship with the sun god and find himself on the same level as his subjects. It is possible that this fear contributed to the theological reinterpretation of Osiris, so that from just a deity of the earth and its fertility and the regeneration of nature (in this form Osiris appears e.g. in the Ennead coming from shrine of Djoser, the remains of which were revealed in Heliopolis by Schiaparelli, see Donadoni-Roveri, 1988, 48 Fig. 48) he now also became the god of the dead, ruler of the underworld and a symbol of resurrection. The new concept also brought the existing practice of the mortuary cult into harmony with a royal ideology in which the dead king was identified with Osiris, the mythical original ruler of Egypt. The king continued to appear in the funeral formula, but ever more frequently so did

Osiris (and also Anubis and occasionally Khontamenty and Geb). In some cases, the king was a partner with Osiris (Barta, 1968, 4–8), as we see in the phrase: 'an offering which the king gives, an offering which Osiris gives'. This conception of the mortuary cult was better suited to the new social conditions, in which the more affluent strata of officials and priests also assumed ever more importance as far as the afterlife was concerned.

Unfortunately the growth in the bureaucracy and its influence, reflected in the increasing number of official titles, was eventually, if we disregard the weakening of the king's power, counter-productive: it reduced the efficiency of the administration, swallowed up more material resources and upset the balance between social groups. A series of measures adopted in the reign of Djedkare were responses to the problem: the position of vizier was strengthened, the power of his immediate subordinates curtailed and the number of overseers of offices of the middle category reduced. At the same time a third vizierate was introduced; two viziers served in the capital, while the southern part of the country was administered by a third (Strudwick, 1985, 328 and 340; Andrassy, 2008, 38). Some offices and the titles associated with them were re-valued. For example, the titles 'king's son' and 'hereditary prince' (*iry-pˁt*), re-appeared in the titulary of high officials without having the same meaning as before. Old, sometimes unusual religious titles started to spread, in a trend that is sometimes interpreted as an expression of the increasing independence of officials, which then undermined the central power of the country (Helck, 1954, 133).

We are not entirely sure of the reasons for Djedkare's special attention paid to the royal mortuary cults, which can be indirectly deduced from a number of his decrees preserved in the Abusir papyrus archives. Sometimes the matters seem so trivial that it is amazing that the ruler himself had to address these issues by a decree. It is hard to judge the context of these decrees. Were they associated with the rise of the cult of Osiris? Or was the main reason the discontinuation of the building of sun temples (possibly interrelated with the rise of the cult of Osiris), which certainly counts as a major intervention in the operation of the pyramid complex and the royal mortuary cult? Or was it just a question of resolving routine staff and operational problems involving employees of the mortuary cults of Djedkare's royal predecessors? Or was the number of Djedkare's decrees a mere coincidence due, for instance, to the king's long reign?

In the reign of Djedkare there was a striking increase in the numbers of smaller estates at the expense of large estates, which may be interpreted as an attempt at reform of the existing model of the administration of the provinces with the aim of increasing production of resources: small estates were supposed to be more efficient than large ones (Moreno García, 1999, 231f.). It may bear some relation to other significant changes that had already been occurring in the provinces during the first half of the 5th Dynasty. Earlier their administration had been entrusted to an official, the 'overseer of commissions' (*ỉmy-r3 wpt*), who would return to the capital after fulfilling his task. Now influential official families were appearing in the centres of the economically more important areas, and not just serving there but having themselves buried there, as is evident particularly from the cemeteries in Deshasha, Hemmamiya, Bersha and Tehna. Although these officials started to accumulate priestly functions in local cults as well as administrative posts, they cannot yet be considered independent governors of the provinces (Moreno García, 2013, 114f.; Andrassy, 2008, 112). The provinces continued to be fully under royal control, which was even strengthened by the creation of the office of 'overseer of Upper Egypt' mentioned above.

In the context of these changes and long-term trends there was a further shift in property relations. As early as in the 4th Dynasty, as is clear for example from an inscription in the tomb of Khafre's son Nykaure (Goedicke, 21f.; Strudwick, 2005, 200), members of the royal family owned estates permanently and disposed of them freely, giving them to their children and so on. Over the 5th Dynasty there is ever more evidence that officials too were permanently appropriating property that had originally been entrusted to them either directly or via the institution *pr-ḏt*. Although land, the basic means of production, was probably still de iure the property of the king (Menu, Harari, 1974, 150), de facto it was inherited (like official positions); it would remain in the family, and private persons founded their own estates, which they would designated with their own names (Helck, 1975, 69; Gutgesell, 1983, 67–80). Immoveable property could also be bought and sold (*ỉni r ỉśw/rdi n ỉśw*), but anyone who incurred the king's displeasure could be stripped of his property – as we know from the already mentioned decree of Neferirkare for the temple in Abydos. In written records of the period, for example inscriptions in the tombs of officials and priests, we find phrases emphasising the full legality of property acquired (*ỉšft.ỉ m3ˁ*) (Edel, 1944, 50 § 46). This is regarded as further proof of the increasing economic independence of these social groups and one of the features of the so-called democratization of the Egyptian society.

In the course of the 5th Dynasty the political and economic importance of temples rose and the priesthood became an increasingly influential social group (see e.g. Papazian, 2012, 128). We cannot pinpoint when this process began because the historical sources relating to the preceding period, especially the royal annals, are only fragmentary, but it is clear that important temples already existed before the 5th Dynasty not only in the area of the capital (Heliopolis, Memphis) but also in the provinces, for example in Abydos, Koptos, Hierakonpolis, Elephantine and elsewhere. According to written documents, the last rulers of the 4th Dynasty, Menkaure (Urk I, 24–31; Goedicke, 1970, 131–148; Edel, 1981, 38–64) and Shepseskaf (Wilkinson, 2000, 149), actively supported local cults and it can be assumed that their predecessors also did so. At the latest, from the reign of Neferirkare, as is evident from the previously cited decree relating to the temple of Khontamenty in Abydos, priests appear as a specific, hierarchically organised professional and social group (Goedicke, 1979, 113–133). At this period priests were already enjoying privileges arising from the exemption of temples from tax, corvée obligations, etc. In a broader historical context, it appears that the rise of the priesthood and the establishment of the new dynasty were not unrelated. Support for the priesthood and the cults of gods, especially gifts of land and exemption from tax, were important political instruments in the legitimisation and consolidation of the political power held by the new ruling line. Eventually, however, this policy was to lead to the growing economic independence of the temples and their influence in Egypt.

The foreign policy of the 5th Dynasty kings seems to have been influenced by their primary interest in the stabilization of home affairs and consolidation of the key institution constituting the power center of the Egyptian state. The available contemporary historical sources create an impression of balanced, mostly peaceful policy regarding Egypt's contact with the regions on its periphery. The base of these relations were primarily commercial contacts. Egypt interest in the regions of its northern and north-eastern periphery, the Sinai and Syro-Palestine, were chiefly concerned with the mining of copper ore and importing of cedar wood, though wine, grain and luxury products (stone vessels, jewels, etc.) also made part of the commercial exchange. Byblos occupied a special position within these commercial relations.

Other areas of special interest were the relations that were carried out with the regions on the eastern and southern peripheries of Egypt. Raw materials – gold, rare and precious stones, wood, skin of wild animals, etc. – seem to have prevailed amongst those commodities at that time. During 5th Dynasty, expeditions were regularly sent to the Eastern Desert and at least two of them, one under Sahure and the second under Djedkare, were sent to Punt from whence they brought to Egypt many exotic items such as myrrh, frankincense trees etc. Obviously, these long distance commertial contacts required the relevant infrastructure which had, as evidence e.g. by the Red Sea ports (Ayun Sokhna and others), already been in use. However, the prevailing character of the Egyptian trading contacts with the regions on its petiphery did not exclude occasional conflicts, as may be evidenced by Sahure's military campaign against Libyans. These engangements were to become more numerous in the following dynasty.

On the basis of existing sources it is hard to imagine that the end of the reign of Djedkare was followed by some fundamental discontinuity in the ruling line, or that the throne was seized by a member of some influential and wealthy commoner from the north of the country, as Helck (Helck, 1991, 163–168; id. 1994, 103–106) contends. In addition to the long-term social changes the reasons for the dynastic change should instead be sought inside Djedkare's family. During his relatively very long life and reign Djedkare probably had a many-branched family, some of whom were buried north of Djoser's pyramid in Saqqara, and some in Abusir, while others can be assumed to be buried near the ruler's own pyramid in South Saqqara. In these circumstances it is likely that there was tension between competing groups within the royal family. There is no direct evidence that Wenis was Djedkare's son, but it is most unlikely that he was not from the wider royal family. He may have succeeded to the throne at a very young age, and it is possible that his claim was upheld against his rivals with the help of his mother (the still anonymous owner of the pyramid complex by the pyramid of Djedkare?). There are some clues that especially at the beginning of his reign Wenis was trying to strengthen his legitimacy. Even later he was still seeking to consolidate his position through alliance with influential families and in some cases with high officials, as we might deduce, for example, from the fact that Wenis's wife, Nebet, was not of royal origin and did not give the king an heir to the throne.

Like the end of the 4th Dynasty, the end of the 5th Dynasty is surrounded by many obscurities, although it seems to have happened under less dramatic circumstances. Trends in the development of society, especially a growing tension between the central political power and the ever more independent and influential official and priestly elites, had continued in the reign of Djedkare's successor Wenis who may have been a relatively weak ruler. In the reign of Wenis, which might not have been as long as previously believed, there was a radical change within the ranking system of the priests of the king's pyramid, which Baer (Baer, 1960, 298–302) regards as the king's attempt to solve on the religious level the problem of the growing power of the bureaucracy. A weakening of the ruler's power and a certain destabilisation of conditions in the country is perhaps suggested by some unfortunately incomplete records hinting at military clashes on the north-eastern border of Egypt in the reign of Wenis. The smallest of all in the list of 5th Dynasty royal pyramids, Wenis's pyramid seems to reflect the erosion of the monarchy's economic resources. Despite the great significance of the fact that it was in this pyramid that the Pyramid Texts first appear, Wenis's reign was more the end of one era than the beginning of another one (the 6th Dynasty), as some scholars such as Baer (Baer, 1960, 298f.) have argued.

The Horus name of Wenis's successor Teti was 'He Who Reconciles the Two Lands', suggesting that there had been disturbances not just in the ruling line but probably the entire country. Yet, despite his Horus name, Teti failed to end the disputes inside the royal family or to restore full order in Egypt. After Teti's death, which according to legend was violent, his successors, Weserkare and Pepy I, competed for control of the country until eventually Pepy I managed to stabilise conditions in Egypt.

BIBLIOGRAPHY

ABD EL-RAHMAN, M. A.

2009 The Lost Temples of Esna, in: *BIFAO* 109, 1–8

ADAMS, B.

1995 *Ancient Nekhen. Garstang in the City of Hierakonpolis*, (ESA Publication No. 3, SIA Publishing) New Malden, Sia Publishing

ALBRIGHT, W. F.

1926 Foundation of the early Egyptian temple in Byblos, in: *ZÄS* 62, 62–63

ALLAM, S.

1963 *Beiträge zum Hathorkult (bis zum Ende des Mittleren Reiches)*, (MÄS 4) Berlin

2010 Notes on the designation 'eldest son/daughter' (*z3/z3t smsw : ꜥ3/šri͗.t ꜥ3.t*), in: Hawass, Z., Der Manuerlian, P., Hussein, R. B. (eds.), *Perspectives on Ancient Egypt. Studies in Honor of Edward Brovarski* (*Suppl. ASAE* 40), Le Caire 2010, 29–34

ALLEN, J. P.

1992 Rē-wer's accident, in: Lloyd, A. B. (ed.), *Studies in Pharaonic religion and Society in Honour of J. Gwyn Griffith*, London, The Egypt Exploration Society, 14–20

1994 Reading a pyramid, in: Berger, C., Clerc, G., Grimal, N. (eds.), *Hommages à Jean Leclant. Vol. 1. Études pharaoniques*, (BdÉ 106/1) Le Caire, IFAO 5–28

ALLIOT, M.

1937–1938 Un nouvel exemple de vizier divinisé dans l'Égypte ancienne, in: *BIFAO* 37, 94–160

ALTENMÜLLER, H.

1970 Die Stellung der Königsmutter Chentkaus beim Übergang von der 4. zur 5. Dynastie, in: *CdÉ* 45, 223–235

1974 Zur Vergöttlichung des Unas im Alten Reich, in: *SAK* 1, 1–18

1990 Bemerkungen zur Gründung der 6. Dynastie, in: Schmitz, B., Eggebrecht, A. (eds.), *Festschrift Jürgen von Beckerath zum 70. Geburtstag am 19. Februar 1990*, (HÄB 30) Hildesheim, 7–20

1977 *Feste*, in: LÄ II, 171–191

1995 Die „Abgaben" aus dem 2. Jahr des Userkaf, in: Kessler, D., Schulz, R. (eds.), *Gedenkschrift für Winfried Barta*, (MÄU 4) Frankfurt am Main, 37–48

2008 Family, ancestor cult and some observations on the chronology of the late Fifth dynasty, in: Vymazalová, H., Bárta, M. (eds.), *Chronology and archaeology in Ancient Egypt (The Third*

Millenium B.C.), Prague, Czech Institute of Egyptology, Faculty of Arts, Charles University in Prague, 144–161
2010 Die Erzählungen des Papyrus Westcar. Geschichte am Hof des Königs Cheops und die Prophezeiung der Geburt der Könige der frühen 5. Dynastie als Söhne des Sonnengottes, in: Brinkmann, V. (ed.), *Sahure. Tod und Leben eines grossen Pharao*, Frankfurt am Main, Liebighaus Skulpturensammlung, 265–273
2013 Magische Riten zur Beeinflussung von Naturereignissen: Der Fall der Nilpferdjagd, in: *ÉT* 26, 44–55

AMIR, M. el-
1948 The *sekos* of Apis in Memphis, in: *JEA* 34, 51–56

ANDRASSY, P.
1993 Das *pr-šnʿ* im Alten Reich, *SAK* 20, 17–35
1994 Die *ẖntyw-š* im Alten Reich, in: Gundlach, R., Rochholz, M. (eds.), *Ägyptische Tempel – Struktur, Funktion und Programm (Akten der Ägyptologischen Tempeltagungen in Gosen 1990 und in Mainz 1992),* (HÄB 37) Hildesheim, Gerstenberg Verlag
2008 *Untersuchungen zum ägyptischen Staat des Alten Reiches und seinen Institutionen*, (IBAES Vol. 9) Berlin – London

ARNOLD, Di.
1977 Rituale und Pyramidentempel, in: *MDAIK* 33, 1–14
1982 Palast, in: LÄ IV, 646
1996 Hypostyle Halls of the Old and Middle Kingdom, in: Der Manuelian, P., Freed, R. E. (eds.), *Studies in Honour of William Kelly Simpson. I*, Boston, Museum of Fine Arts, 39–54
1998 Eine Verlorene Pyramide?, in: Kloth, N., Martin, K., Pardey, E. (eds.), *Es werde niedergelegt als Schriftstück. Festschrift für Hartwig Altenmüller zum 65. Geburtstag,* (BSAK 9) Hamburg, 7–10

ARNOLD, Do.
2010 Royal Reliefs, in: Brinkmann, V. (ed.), *Sahure. Tod und Leben eines grossen Pharao*, Frankfurt am Main, Libieghaus Skulpturensammlung, 85–97

ARNOLD, F.
1998 Die Priesterhäuser der Chentkaues in Giza, in: *MDAIK* 54, 2–18
2010 Schaffung einer neuen Architektur, in: Brinkmann, V. (ed.), *Sahure. Tod und Leben eines grossen Pharao*, Frankfurt am Main, Liebieghaus Skulpturensammlung, 209–216
2014 Ein Garten des Königs Snofru in Dahschur, in: *Sokar* 29, 6–13

AWADY, T. el-
2006 *The royal family of Sahura. New evidence*, in: Bárta, M., Coppens, F., Krejčí, J. (eds.),

Abusir and Saqqara in the Year 2005, Prague, Czech Institute of Egyptology, Faculty of Arts, Charles University in Prague, 191–218
2009 *Abusir XVI. Sahure – The Pyramid Causeway. History and Decoration Program in the Old Kingdom*, Prague, Charles University
2013 Sekhmet-Sahure: New Evidence, in: *ÉT* 26, 58–63

BADAWY, A.
1976 *The Tombs of Iteti, Sekhemankh-Ptah, and Kaemnofret at Giza*, Berkeley – Los Angeles – London

BAER, K.
1960 *Rank and Title in the Old Kingdom. The Structure of the Egyptian Administration in the Fifth and Sixth dynasties*, Chicago, The University of Chicago Press

BAGNATO, D.
2006 *The Westcar Papyrus. A Transliteration, Translation and Language Analysis*, Wien, Edition Atelier

BAINES, J.
1995 Kingship, Definition of Culture, and Legitimation, in: O'Connor, D., Silverman, D. P. (eds.), *Ancient Egyptian Kingship*, (PdÄ 9) Leiden – New York – Köln, E. J. Brill, 3–47

BAINES, J., PARKINSON, R. B.
1997 An Old Kingdom record of an oracle? Sinai Inscription 13, in: van Dijk, J. (ed.), *Essays on Ancient Egypt in honour of Herman te Velde*, Groningen, STYX Publications, 9–27

BAREŠ, L.
1985 Eine Statue des Würdenträgers Sachmethotep und ihre Beziehung zum Totenkult des Mittleren Reiches, in: *ZÄS* 112, 87–94

BÁRTA, M.
2000 The mastaba of Ptahshepses Junior II at Abusir, in: *Ä & L* 10, 45–66
2001 *Abusir V. The Cemeteries at Abusir South I* (with a contribution by Černý, V. and Strouhal, E.), Prague, Czech Institute of Egyptology, Faculty of Arts, Charles University in Prague
2005-a Architectural Innovations in the Development of the Non-Royal Tomb During the Reign of Nyuserra, in: Jánosi, P. (ed.), *Structure and Significance. Thoughts on ancient Egyptian Architecture*, Vienna, 105–125
2005-b Location of the Old Kingdom Pyramids in Egypt, in: *CAJ* 15:2, 177–191
2013-a The sun kings of Abusir and their entourage: 'Speakers of Nekhen of the King', in: Bárta, M., Küllmer, H., *Diachronic Trends in Ancient Egyptian History. Studies dedicated to the memory of Eva Pardey*, Prague, Charles University in Prague, Faculty of Arts, 24–31
2013-b Kings, Viziers, and Courtiers: Executive Power in the Third Millenium B. C., in:

Moreno García, J. C. (ed.), *Ancient Egyptian Administration*, Leiden – Boston, Brill, 153–175
--- Social change and the end of the Fourth Dynasty, in: Hein, I., Billing, N. (eds.), *The Pyramids: between life and death. Proceedings of a conference held in Uppsala, May 31 – June 1, 2012*, in press
--- 'Abusir paradigm' and the beginning of the Fifth Dynasty, in press

BÁRTA, M., BEZDĚK, A.
2011 Beetles and the decline of the Old Kingdom: climate change in Ancient Egypt, in: Vymazalová, H., Bárta, M. (eds.), *Chronology and Archaeology in Ancient Egypt (The Third Millenium B.C.)*, Prague, Czech Institute of Egyptology, Faculty of Arts, Charles University in Prague, 214–222

BARTA, W.
1968 *Aufbau und Bedeutung der altägyptischen Opferformel*, (ÄF 24) Glückstadt, Verlag J. J. Augustin
1980 Materialmagie und symbolik, in: LÄ III, 1233–1237
1981 Die Chronologie der 1. bis 5. Dynastie nach den Angaben des rekonstruierten Annalensteins, in: *ZÄS* 108, 11–23
1983 Zur Lokalisierung der *mrt*-Bauten, in: *ZÄS* 110, 98–104
1985 Bemerkungen zur Existenz der Rituale für Geburt und Krönung, in: *ZÄS* 112, 1–13

BATRAWI, A.
1947 The Pyramid Studies. Anatomical Reports. I. Season 1945–1946, in: *ASAE* 47, 97–111

BAUD, M.
1996 La date d'apparition des *ḫntjw-š* , in: *BIFAO* 96, 13–49
1997 Aux pieds de Djoser. Les mastabas entre fossé et enceinte de la partie nord du complexe funéraire, in: Berger, C., Mathieu, .B. (eds.), *Études sur l'Ancien Empire et la nécropole de Saqqâra dédiées à Jean-Philippe Lauer*, (OrMon 9) Montpellier III, Université Paul Valéry, 69–88
1999 *Famille royale et pouvoir sous l'Ancien Empire*, t. 2, (BdÉ 126/2) Le Caire, IFAO
2000 Le palais en temple. Le culte funéraire des rois d'Abousir, in: Bárta, M., Krejčí J., (eds.), *Abusir and Saqqara in the Year 2000*, Praha, Academy of Sciences of the Czech Republic, Oriental Institute, 347–360
2006 The relative chronology of Dynasties 6 and 8, in: Hornung, E., Krauss, R., Warburton, D. A. (eds.), *Ancient Egyptian Chronology*, Leiden – Boston, Brill, 144–158

BAUD, M., Dobrev, V.
1995 De nouvelles annales de l'Ancien Empire égyptien. Une «Pierre de Palerme» pour la VIe dynastie, in: *BIFAO* 95, 23–92

BAUVAL, R. G.
1989 Investigation on the origins of the benben stone : was it an iron meteorite?, in : *DE* 14, 5–16

BECKERATH, J. v.
1997 *Chronologie des pharaonischen Ägypten*, (MÄS 46) Mainz am Rhein, Philipp von Zabern
1999 *Handbuch der ägyptischen Königsnamen*, (MÄS 49) 2nd ed., Mainz am Rhein, Philipp von Zabern

BEGELSBACHER-FISCHER, B. L.
1981 *Untersuchungen zur Götterwelt des Alten Reiches im Spiegel der Privatgräber der IV. und V. Dynastie*, (OBO 37) Freiburg, Schweiz, Universitätsverlag - Göttingen, Vandenhoeck & Ruprecht, 121

BEHRENS, P.,
1986 Uch, in: LÄ VI, 820–821

BEINLICH, H.
1984 Qusae, in: LÄ V, 73

BELMONTE, J. A., SHALTOUT, M., FEKRI, M.
2009 Astronomy, Landscape and Symbolism: A Study of the Orientation of Ancient Egyptian Temples, in: Belmonte, J. A., Shaltout, M. (eds.), *In Search of Cosmic Order*, Cairo, Supreme Council of Antiquities, 215–283

BENEŠOVSKÁ, H.
2006 Statues from the Pyramid Complex of the King Raneferef, in: Verner, M. *et al.*, *Abusir IX. The Pyramid Complex of Raneferef. The Archaeology*, Prague, Czech Institute of Egyptology, Faculty of Arts, Charles University in Prague - Academia, Publishing House of the Academy of Sciences of the Czech Republic, 360–405

BERLANDINI, J.
1978 La pyramide «ruinée» de Saqqara-nord et Menkauhor, in: *BSFÉ* 83, 23–35
1979 La pyramide «ruinée» de Saqqara-nord, in: *RdE* 31, 3–28

BERLANDINI-GRENIER, J.
1976 Varia Memphitica I (I), in: *BIFAO* 76, 301–316

BERLEV, O. D.
1979 'Zolotoe imya' egipetskogo carya, in: Katsnelson, I. S. (ed.), *J. F. Champollion: deshifrofka egipetskikh ieroglifov*, Moskva, Izdatelstvo „Nauka“ glavnaya redaktsiya vostotschnoy literatury, 41–59

BERLEV, O. D., KHODJASH, S. I.
2004 Skulptura drevnjego Egipta v sobranii Gosudarstvennogo muzeia izobrazitelnykh isskustv im. A. S. Pushkina, Moskva, Vost. lit.

BERMAN, L.M. *et al.*
1999 *Catalogue of Egyptian Art*, Cleveland, The Cleveland Museum of Art

BIETAK, M.
1979 Urban Archaeology and the "town Problem" in Ancient Egypt, in: K. Weeks (ed.), *Egyptology and the Social Sciences*, Cairo, The American University in Cairo Press, 97–144
1988 Zur Marine des Alten Reiches, in: Baines, J., James, T. G. H., Leahy, A., Shore, A. F. (eds.), *Pyramid Studies and Other Essays Presented to I. E. S. Edwards,* London, Egypt Exploration Society 1988, 35–40

BIETAK, M., LANGE, E.
2014 Tell Basta: the palace of the Middle Kingdom, in: *EA* 44, 4–7

BISSON de la Roque, F.
1937 *Tôd (1934 à 1936),* (Fouilles de l'IFAO 17) Le Caire

BLACKMAN, A. M.
1998 *The Story of King Kheops and the Magicians*, Reading, Berks, J. V. Books 1988

BOCK, J.
2006 Die kleinen Stufenpyramiden des frühen Alten Reiches, in: *Sokar* 12, 20–29

BOGDANOV, I. V.
2004 Dve traditsii o proiskhozjdenii V dinastii v Egipte, in: *VDI* 2004 no. 1, 3–17

BOLSHAKOV, A. O.
1992 Princess *Ḥm.t-rˁ(w)*: The First Record of Osiris?, in: *CdE* 67, 203–210
1997 *Man and his Double in Egyptian Ideology of the Old Kingdom,* (ÄAT 37)
2001 Osiris in the Fourth Dynasty Again? The false door of Jntj , *MFA 31.781,* in: György, H. (ed.), *Mélanges offerts à Edith Varga, BMHBA Suppl.* 2002 – Budapest, 65–80

BOORN, G. P. F. van den
1988 *The Duties of the Vizier. Civil Administration in the Early New Kingdom*, London & New York, Kegan Paul International

BORCHARDT, L.
1905 Der Bau, in: Bissing, F. W. v., *Das Re-Heiligtum des Königs Ne-woser-re (Rathures). I,* Berlin, Duncker
1907 *Das Grabdenkmal des Königs Ne-user-reˁ*, (WVDOG 7) Leipzig, Hinrichs Verlag
1909 *Das Grabdenkmal des Königs Nefer-ìr-keꜣ-reˁ*, (WVDOG 11) Leipzig, Hinrichs Verlag
1910 – 1913 *Das Grabdenkmal des Königs Śaꜣ-ḥu-reˁ. I–II*, (WVDOG 14/26) Leipzig, Hinrichs Verlag

1937 *Denkmäler des Alten Reiches (ausser Statuen) im Museum von Kairo Nr. 1295–1808. I. Text und Tafeln zu Nr. 1295–1541*, Berlin, Reichsdruckerei
1938 *Ḫnt-k3w.ś*, die Stammutter der 5ten Dynastie, in: *ASAE* 38, 209–216

BOTHMER, B.
1973 A Bust of Ny-user-ra from Byblos, in: *Kêmi* 21, 11–16
1974 The Karnak Statue of Ny-user-ra, in: *MDAIK* 30, 165–170

BREASTED, J. H.
1906 *Ancient Records of Egypt I*, Chicago, The University of Chicago Press
BROVARSKI, E.
1977 The Doors of Heaven, in: *Or* 46, 107–115
2001 *The Senedjemib Complex. Part I. The Mastabas of Senedjemib Inti (G 2370), Khnumenti (G 2374), and Senedjemib Mehi (G 2378)*, (Giza Mastabas vol. 7) Boston, Museum of Fine Arts
2013 Overseers of Upper Egypt in the Old to Middle Kingdoms. Part 1, in: *ZÄS* 140, 91–111

BRUNNER, H.
1986 Trunkenheit, in: LÄ VI, 773–777

BRUNTON, G.
1940 Objects from Fifth Dynasty Burials in Gebelein, in: *ASAE* 40, 521–532
1947 The burial of the Prince Ptah-shepses, in: *ASAE* 47, 125–133

BUSSMANN, R.
2010 *Die Provinztempel Ägyptens von der 0. bis zur 11. dynastie. Archaeologie und Geschichte einer gesellschaftlichen Institution zwischen Residenz und Provinz. Teil I: Text, Teil II: Abbildungen*, Leiden – Boston, Brill

BUTZER, K. W.
1976 *Early Hydraulic Civilization in Egypt*, Chicago, The University of Chicago

BUTZER, K. W., BUTZER, E., LOVE, S.,
2013 Urban geoarcheology and environmental history at the Lost City of the Pyramids, Giza: synthesis and review, in: *JAS* 40, 3340–3365

CALLENDER, V. G.
1991 A contribution to discussion on the title of *s3t-nṯr*, in: *SAK* 18, 89–110
2000 À propos the title of *r Nḫn n z3b*, in: Bárta, M., Krejčí, J. (eds.), *Abusir and Saqqara in the Year 2000*, Prague, Academy of Sciences of the Czech Republic, Oriental Institute 2000
2011-a *n Hathor's Image*, Prague, Charles University in Prague, Faculty of Arts
2011-b Reflections on Princess Khamerernebty of Abusir, in: Callender, V. G., Bareš, L., Bárta, M., Krejčí, J. (eds.), *Times Signs and Pyramids. Studies in Honour of Miroslav Verner*

on the Occasion of His Seventieth Birthday, Prague, Faculty of Arts, Charles University, 101–120
2011-c Notes on the statuary from the Galarza Tomb in Giza, in: *BACE* 22, 35–46

CAPART, J.
1927 *Documents pour servir à l'étude de l'art égyptien. I*, Paris, Les éditions de Pégas

CHASSINAT, É. G.
1966–1968 *Le mystère d'Osiris au mois de Khoiak. I–II*, Le Caire, IFAO

CHERPION, N.
1989 *Mastabas et hypogées d'Ancien Empire. Le problème de datation*, Bruxelles, Connaissance de l'Égypte ancienne

CÍLEK, S., LISÁ, L., BÁRTA, M.
2011 The Holocene of the Abusir area, in: Bárta, M., Coppens, F., Krejčí, J. (eds.), *Abusir and Saqqara in the Year 2010. Vol. 1–2*, Prague, Czech Institute of Egyptology, Faculty of Arts, Charles University in Prague, 312–326

COOPER, J.
2011 The Geographic and Cosmographic Expression *Tꜣ-nṯr*, in: *BACE* 22, 47–66

COUR-MARTY, M.-A.
1997 Les poids inscrits de l'Ancien Empire, in: Berger, C., Mathieu, B., *Études sur l'Ancien Empire et la nécropole de Saqqâra dédiées à J.-Ph. Lauer*, (OrMon 9) Montpellier III, Université Paul Valéry, 129–145

CURTO, S.
1988 Die Königsstätten: Heliopolis und Gise, in: Donadoni Roveri, A. M. (ed.), Das Alte Ägypten. Die religiösen Vorstellungen, Torino, Istituto bancario San Paolo di Torino, 44–61

ĆWIEK, A.
2003 *Relief Decoration in the Royal Funerary Complexes of the Old Kingdom. Studies in the Development, Scene Content and Inconography*, PhD Dissertation Warsaw University, Warsaw

DARESSY, G.
1910 La tombe de la mère de Chéfren, in: *ASAE* 10, 41–49

DAUMAS, F.
1967 L'origine d'Amon de Karnak, in: *BIFAO* 65, 201–214
1970 Les objects sacrés d'Hathor à Dendara, in: *RdÉ* 22, 75 n. 2
1977 Hathorfeste, in: LÄ II, 1034–1039
1982 Neujahr (Le nouvel an), in: LÄ IV, 466–472

DAVIES, N. de G.
1900 *The Mastaba of Ptahhetep and Akhethetep at Saqqareh. I. The Chapel of Ptahhetep and the Hieroglyphs*, London, Egypt Exploration Fund
1901 *The Tomb of Ptahhetep and Akhtihetep at Saqqareh. II. The Mastaba. The Sculptures of Akhtihetep*, London, Egypt Exploration Fund

DELANGE, É. *et al.*
2012 *Les fouilles françaises d'Élephantine (Assouan) 1906–1911. Les archives Clermont-Ganneau et Clédat*, vol. 2 – Planches, (MAIBL t. 46) Paris, Académie des inscriptions et belles-lettres

DERCHAINE, Ph.
1969 *Snefrou et les rameuses, in: RdE* 21, 19–25

DESROCHES-NOBLECOURT, Ch.
1995 *Amours et fureurs de La Lointaine. Clés pour le compréhension de symboles égyptiens*, Paris, Stock-Pernoud

DESROCHES NOBLECOURT, Ch., LEBLANC, Ch.
1984 Considérations sur l'existence des divers temples de Monthou à travers les âges, dans le site de Tod, in: *BIFAO* 84, 81–109

DEPUYDT, L.
2000 Sothic Chronology and the Old Kingdom, in: *JARCE* 37, 167–186

DIODORUS SICULUS
1990 *The Antiquities of Egypt. A Translation of the* Library of History *of Diodorus Siculus. Revised and Expanded with Bibliography and Illustrations by Edwin Murphy*, New Brunswick – London, Transaction Publishers

DOBREV, V.
1993 Considérations sur les titulatures des rois de la IVe dynastie égyptienne, in: *BIFAO* 93, 179–205
1999 La IVe dynastie: un nouveau regard. Chepseskaf et le «Mastabat Faraoun», in: *EAO* 15, 3–29
2006 A new necropolis from the Old Kingdom at South Saqqara, in: Bárta, M. (ed.), *The Old Kingdom Art and Archaeology. Proceedings of the conference, Prague May 31 – June 4, 2004*, Prague, Czech Institute of Egyptology, Faculty of Arts, Charles University, 127–132

DONADONI ROVERI, A. M.
1969 *I sarcofagi egizi dalle origini alla fine dell'Antico Regno*, Roma, Istituto di studi del Vicino oriente – Università
1988 *Egyptian Museum of Turin. Egyptian Civilization. Religious Beliefs*, Torino, Istituto Bancario San Paulo

DORMAN, P.
2002 The biographical inscription of Ptahshepses from Saqqara: a newly identified fragment, in: *JEA* 88, 95–110

DREYER, G.
1986 *Elephantine VIII. Der Tempel der Satet*, (AV 39) Mainz am Rhein, Verlag Philipp von Zabern
1987 Drei archaisch-hieratische Gefässaufschriften mit Jahresnamen aus Elephantine, in: Osing, J., Dreyer, G. (eds.), *Form und Mass. Beiträge zur Literatur, Sprache und Kunst des alten Ägypten. Festschricht für Gerhard Fecht zum 65. Geburtstag am 6. Februar 1987*, (ÄAT 12) Wiesbaden, Otto Harrassowitz, 98–109

DRIOTON, É.
1944 La ceinture d'or récement découverte à Sakkarah, BIÉ 77–90

DULÍKOVÁ, V.
2008 Instituce vezirátu ve Staré říši / The Institution of Vizierate in the Old Kingdom, Praha: Filozofická fakulta Univerzity Karlovy v Praze, Český egyptologický ústav (unpublished MA thesis)
2011 Some notes on the title of 'Vizier' during the Old Kingdom, especially on the phallus-sign in the vizier's title, in: Bárta, M., Coppens, F., Krejčí, J. (eds.), *Abusir and Saqqara in the Year 2010*, Prague, Czech Institute of Egyptology, Faculty of Arts, Charles University, 327–336

DUNAND, M.
1939 *Fouilles de Byblos. I*, Paris, P. Geuthner

DUNHAM, D., SIMPSON, W. K.
Giza Mastabas. I. The Mastaba of Mersyankh III (G 7530–7540), Boston, Department of Egyptian and Near Eastern Art – Museum of Fine Arts 1974

EATON-KRAUSS, M.
1987 The Earliest Representation of Osiris?, in: *VA* 3, 233–236

EDEL, E.
1944 Untersuchungen zur Phraseologie der ägyptischen Inschriften des Alten Reiches, in: *MDAIK* 13, 1–90
1969 Die Kalksteintäfelchen, in: Ricke, H. (ed.), *Das Sonnenheiligtum des Königs Userkaf. II. Die Funde*, (Beiträge Bf 8) Wiesbaden, Franz Steiner Verlag
1978 A Comment on Professor Giveon's Reading of the New Sahure Inscription, in: *BASOR* 232, 77f.
1981 *Hieroglyphische Inschriften des Alten Reiches*, (Abh. Rheinisch-Westfälische Akademie der Wissenschaften 67) Opladen, Westdeutscher Verlag

EDEL, E., WENIG, S.
1974 *Die Jahreszeitenreliefs aus dem Sonnenheiligtum des Ne-user-re*, Berlin, Akademie Verlag

EICHLER, E.
1993 *Untersuchungen zum Expeditionswesen des ägyptischen Alten Reiches,* (GOF 26) Wiesbaden, Harrassowitz Verlag

EMERY, W.B.
1938 *The Tomb of Hemaka*, Cairo, Government Press
1963 Egypt Exploration Society Preliminary Report on the Excavation at Buhen, 1962, in: *Kush* 11, 116–120

ENDESFELDER, E.
1979 Zur Frage der Bewässerung im pharaonischen Ägypten, in: *ZÄS* 106, 37–51

ENGEL, E.-M.
2013 Organisation of a Nascent State: Egypt until the Beginning of the 4th Dynasty, in: Moreno García, J. C. (ed.), *Ancient Egyptian Administration*, Leiden–Boston, Brill, 19–40

ÉPRON, L., DAUMAS, F.
1930 *Le tombeau de Ti. Les approches de la chapelle*, (MIFAO 45) Le Caire, IFAO

ERMANN, A.
1890 *Die Märchen des Papyrus Westcar. I. Einleitung und Commentar. II. Die Märchen des Papyrus Westcar. Glossar, palaeographische Bemerkungen und Feststellung des Textes*, Berlin, W. Spemann

ERMAN, A., GRAPOW, H.
1929–1931 *Wörterbuch der aegyptischen Sprache. I–V*, Leipzig, J. C. Hinrichs'sche Buchhandlung

ERMAN, A., RANKE, H.
1923 *Aegypten und aegyptisches Leben im Altertum*, Tübingen, Mohr Verlag

ESPINEL, A. D.
2002 The Role of the Temple of Ba'alat Gebal as Intermediary between Egypt and Byblos during the Old Kingdom, in: *SAK* 30, 103–119

EYRE, Ch. J.
1999 The Village Economy in Pharaonic Egypt, in: Bowman, A. K., Rogan, E. (eds.), *Agriculture in Egypt from Pharaonic to Modern Times*, (Proceedings of the British Academy 96) Oxford – New York, Oxford University Press, 33–60

FAKHRY, A.
1959 *The Monuments of Sneferu at Dahshur. I. The Bent Pyramid,* Cairo, General organisation for Government Printing Offices
1961 *The Pyramids*, Chicago, The University of Chicago Press

FAULKNER, R. O.
1953 Egyptian military organization, in: *JEA* 39, 32–47
1969 *The Ancient Egyptian Pyramid Texts,* Oxford, Claredon Press

FAY, B.
1999 *Royal Women as Represented in Sculpture During the Old Kingdom. Part II: Uninscribed Sculptures*, in: Ziegler, Ch. (ed.), *L'art de l'Ancien Empire Égyptien. Actes du colloques organisé au Musée du Louvre par le Service culturel les 3 et 4 Avril 1998,* Paris, La documentation française

FETTEL, J.
2010 *Die Chentiu-schi des Alten Reiches*, PhD Dissertation Universität Heidelberg, Heidelberg

FINNEISER, K.
1998 Beobachtungen zu einem Kopf des Alten Reiches, in: *GM* 163, 53–70

FIRTH, C. M., GUNN, B.
1926 *Excavations at Saqqara. Teti Pyramid Cemeteries. I. - Text*, Le Caire, IFAO, 61–65 and 273–288

FISCHER, H. G.
1959 A scribe of the army in a Saqqara mastaba of the early Fifth Dynasty, in: *JNES* 18/4, 233–272
1974 *NBTY* in Old-Kingdom Titles and Names, in: *JEA* 60, 94–99
1975 Two tantalizing Biographical Fragments of Historical Interest, in: *JEA* 61, 33–37

FITZENREITER, M.
2004 *Zum Toteneigentum im Alten Reich*, Berlin, Achet Verlag
2013 Die Domänen des Ibi, in: Bárta, M., Küllmer, H. (eds.), *Diachronic Trends in Ancient Egyptian History. Studies dedicated to the memory of Eva Pardey*, Prague, Charles University, Faculty of Arts

FRANKE, D.
1988 Zur Chronologie des Mittleren Reiches (12.–18. Dynastie). Teil 1: Die 12. Dynastie, *Or* 57, 113–138

FRIEDMAN, F. D.
2008 The Menkaure Dyad(s), in: Thompson, S. E., Der Manuelian, P. (eds.), *Egypt and Beyond. Essays Presented to Leonard H. Lesko upon retirement from the Wilbour Chair of Egyptology at Brown University June 2005*, Providence RI, Brown University, 109–144

GABALLA, G., KITCHEN, K. A.
1969 The Festival of Sokar, in: *Or* 38, 24–35

GABOLD, L.
2008 Une statuette thébaine au noms de Pépi Ier et «d'Amon-Rê de la ville de Thèbes», in: Gabold, L. (ed.), *Hommages à Jean-Claude Goyon,* (BdÉ 143) Le Caire, IFAO, 165–180

GARBRECHT, G., BERTRAM, H.-U.
1983 *Der Sadd el-Kafara. Die älteste Talsperre der Welt (2600 v. Chr.)*, Braunschweig, Lichtweiss-Institut für Wasserbau der Technischen universität Braunschweig, Mitteilungen, Heft 81

GARDINER, A. H.
1955 The problem of the Month-names, in: *RdE* 10, 9–31
1959 *The Royal Canon of Turin*, Oxford, University Press
1961 *Egypt of the Pharaohs*, Oxford, At the Claredon Press

GARDINER, A. H., PEET, T. E., ČERNÝ, J.
1957 *The Rock Inscriptions of Sinai I*, London (2nd ed.), Egypt Exploration Society - Geoffrey Cumberlege, Oxford University Press

GAUTHIER, H.
1915 Quatre nouveaux fragments de la Pierre de Palerme, in: Maspero, G. (ed.), *Musée égyptien III*, Le Caire, IFAO, 29–45
1925 Le roi Zadfré successeur immédiat de Khoufou-Khéops, in *ASAE* 25, 178–180
1931 *Les fêtes du dieu Min*, Le Caire, IFAO

GIDDY, L. L.
1990 Memphis, 1989: The Ptah Temple Complex, in: *BACE* 1, 38–41

GILLAM, R. A.
1995 Priestesses of Hathor: their function, décline and disappearance, in: *JARCE* 32, 211–237

GIVEON, R.
1977 Inscriptions of Sahure and Sesostris I Inscriptions from the wadi Kharig, in: *BASOR* 226, 61–63

GÖDECKEN, K. B.
1976 *Eine Bterachtung der Inschriften des Meten im Rahmen sozialen und rechtlichen Stellung von Privatleuten im ägyptischen Alten Reich*, (ÄA 29) Wiesbaden, Otto Harrassowitz

GOEDICKE, H.
1957 A Lion-Cult of the Old Kingdom connected with the Royal Temple, in: *RdÉ* 11, 57ff
1957 A provision-jar of the time of Asosi, in: *RdÉ* 11, 61–71

1958 Ein Verehrer des Weisen *ḎDFḤR* aus dem späten Alten Reich, in: *ASAE* 55, 35–55
1961 Die Siegelzylinder von Pepi I., in: *MDAIK* 17, 69–90
1967 *Königliche Dokumente aus dem Alten Reich*, (ÄA 14) Wiesbaden, Otto Harrassowitz
1970 *Die privaten Rechtsinschriften aus dem Alten Reich*, (BWZKM 5) Wien, Verlag Notring
1971 *Re-used blocks from the pyramid of Amenemhet I at Lisht*, New York, Metropolitan Museum of Art 1971
1974 Some Remarks Concerning the Inscription of Ahmose, Son of Ebana, in: *JARCE* 11, 31–41
1979 Cult-temple and 'State' in Egypt, in: Lipiński, E. (ed.), *State and Temple Economy in the Ancient Near East. I. Proceedings of the International Conference organized by the Katholieke Universiteit Leuven from the 10th to the 14th April 1978*, (OLA 5) Leuven, Departement oriëntalistiek, 113–133
1993 Thoughts about Papyrus Westcar, in: *ZÄS* 120, 23–36
1995 Causes and Concepts, in: *BACE* 6, 31–50
2000 Abusir – Saqqara – Giza, in: Bárta, M., Krejčí, J. (eds.), *Abusir and Saqqara in the Year 2000*, Praha, Academy of Sciences of the Czech Republic, Oriental Institute, 397–412
2011 Three Small Tokens. Memphis, in: Callender, V. G., Bareš, L., Bárta, M., Krejčí, J. (eds.), *Times, Signs and Pyramids. Studies in Honour of Miroslav Verner on the Occassion of His Seventieth Birthday*, Prague, Faculty of Arts, Charles University in Prague 132–134

GOELET, O.
1982 *Two Aspects of the Royal Palace in the Egyptian Old Kingdom*, PhD Dissertation Columbia University, New York
1986 The Term *Śtp-s3* in the Old Kingdom and Its Later Development, in: *JARCE* 23, 85–98

GOYON, G.
1970 Nouvelles observations relatives à l'orientation de la pyramide de Khéops, in: *RdÉ* 22, 88
1977 *Le secret des bâtisseurs des grandes pyramides:Khéops*. Paris, Pygmalion
1979 Est-ce enfin Sakhebou?, in: Vercoutter, J. (ed.), *Hommages à la mémoire de Serge Sauneron. I*, (BdÉ 81) Le Caire, IFAO, 43–50

GOYON, J. C.
1972 Confirmation du pouvoir royal au nouvel an. [Brooklyn Museu Papyrus 47.218.50], Cairo, IFAO – Brooklyn Museum

GRAEFE, E.
1990 Die gute Reputation des Königs „Snofru“, in: Israelit-Groll, S. (ed.), *Studies in Egyptology presented to Miriam Lichtheim*, Jerusalem, The Magnes Press, The Hebrew University, 257–263

GRDSELOFF, B.
1943 Deux inscriptions juridiques de l'Ancien Empire, in: *ASAE* 42, 25–70
1951 Nouvelles données concernant la tente de purification, in: *ASAE* 51, 129–142

GREEN, F. W.
1909 Notes on some inscriptions in the Etbai district, in: *PSBA* 31, 247–254, 319–323

GRIFFITH, J. G.
1980 *The Origins of Osiris and his Cult*, (Suppl. to Numen 40) Leiden
1982 Osiris, in: LÄ IV, 623–633

GRIMM, A.
1985 Das Fragment einer Liste fremdländischer Tiere, Pflanzen und Städte aus dem Totentempel des Königs Djedkare-Asosi, in: *SAK* 12, 34–40

GUNDACKER, R.
2010 Ein Beitrag zur Genealogie der 4. Dynastie, *Sokar* Nr. 20, 30–44

GUTGESELL, M.,
1983 Zur Entstehung des Privateigentums an Produktionsmitteln im alten Ägypten, in: *GM* 66, 67–80

HAENY, G.
1969 *Die Steinbruch- und Baumarken*, in: Ricke, H. *et al.*, *Das Sonnenheiligtum des Königs Userkaf. II. Die Funde*, (BÄBA 8) Wiesbaden, 42 no. 6

HAFEMANN, I.
2009 *Dienstverpflichtung im Alten Ägypten während des Alten und Mittleren Reiches*, (IBAES 12) Berlin – London, Golden House Publications

HANNIG, R.
1995 *Grosses Handwörterbuch Ägyptisch-Deutsch (2800–950 v. Chr.)*, Mainz, Philipp von Zabern

HARPUR, Y.
1987 *Decoration in Egyptian Tombs of the Old Kingdom. Studies in Orientation and Scene Context*, London – New York, Routledge & Kegan Paul

HASSAN, S.
1939 *Excavations at Giza. Vol. II. 1930–1931*, Cairo, Government Press, Boulâq
1941 *Excavations at Giza. Vol. III. 1931–1932*, Cairo, Government Press, Boulâq
1943 *Excavations in Giza. Vol. IV. 1932–1933*, Cairo, Government Press, Boulâq
1938 Excavations at Saqqara 1937–1938. II. The Causeway, in: *ASAE* 38, 519–521
1950 *Giza. Vol. VI, Part III. 1934–1935*, Cairo, Government Press, Boulâq
1955 The causeway of *Wnis* at Saqqara, in: *ZÄS* 80, 136–139
1975-a *Excavations at Saqqara, 1937–193. Vol. I. The Mastaba of Neb-Kaw-Ḥer*, (re-edited by Zaky Iskander), Cairo, General Organisation for Government Printing Offices

1975-b *Excavations at Saqqara (1937–1938). Vol. III. Mastabas of Princess Ḥemet-Ra and Others*, Cairo, Government Press

HAWASS, Z.
2010 The excavation of the Headless Pyramid, Lepsius XXIX, in: Hawass, Z., Der Manuelian, P., Hussein, R. B. (eds.), *Perspectives on Ancient Egypt. Studies in Honor of Edward Brovarski*, (Suppl. *ASAE*, Cahier no. 40) Le Caire, Supreme Council of Antiquities, 153–160
2011 The Discovery of the Pyramid of Queen Seshseshet (?) at Saqqara, in: Callender, V. G., Bareš, L., Bárta, M., Krejčí, J. (eds.), *Times, Signs and Pyramids. Studies in Honour of Miroslav Verner on the Occassion of His Seventieth Birthday*, Prague, Faculty of Arts, Charles University in Prague, 175–189

HAYS, H. M.
2011 The Death of the Democratisation of the Afterlife, in: Strudwick, N., Strudwick, H. (eds.), *Old Kingdom, New Perspectives. Egyptian Art and Archaeology 2750–2150 BC*, Oxford, Oxbow Books, 115–130

HELCK, W.
1954 *Untersuchungen zu den Beamtentiteln des äyptischen Alten Reiches*, (ÄF 18) Glückstadt–Hamburg–New York, Verlag J. J. Augustin
1956 *Untersuchungen zu Manetho und den ägyptischen Königslisten*, (UGAÄ 18) Berlin, Akademie Verlag
1957 Bemerkungen zu den Pyramidenstädten im Alten Reich, in: *MDAIK* 15, 91–111
1975-a *Wirtschaftsgeschichte des Alten Ägypten im 3. und 2. Jahrtausend vor Chr.*, (Handbuch der Orientalistik, 1. Abt. Der Nahe und Mittlere Osten) Leiden – Köln, E. J. Brill
1975-b Ägis und Ägypten, in: LÄ I, 69–76
1977-a Die „Weihinschrift" des Neuserre, in: *SAK* 5, 47–77
1977-b Gaue, in: LÄ II, 385–408
1977-c *Die Lehre für König Merikare*, (KÄT) Wiesbaden, Otto Harrassowitz
1979 *Die Beziehungen Ägyptens und Vorderasiens zur Ägäis bis ins 7. Jahrtausend v. Chr. (Erträge der Forschung* 120) Darmstadt, Wissenschaftliche Gesellschaft
1984 Heliopolis und die Sonnenheiligtümer, in: *Studies in Honour of Torgny Säve-Söderbergh*, (BOREAS 13) Uppsala, 67–72
1991 Überlegungen zum Ausgang der 5. Dynastie, in: *MDAIK* 47, 163–168
1994-a Gedanken zum Mord an Teti, in: Bryan, B. M., Lorton, D. (eds.), *Essays in Egyptology in honor of Hans Goedicke*, San Antonio, Texas, Van Siclen Books, 103–106
1994-b Wege zum Eigentum und Bode im Alten Reich, in: Allam, S. (ed.), *Grund und Boden in Altägypten. Rechtliche und sozial-ökonomische Verhältnisse. Untersuchungen zum Rechtsleben im Alten Ägypten* II, Tübingen, Selbstverlag des Herausgebers, 9–14

HERODOTOS
1972 *Dějiny aneb devět knih dějin nazvaných Músy*, translated by Jaroslav Šonka, Praha

HILL, M.
1999 King Sahure and a Nome God, in: *Egyptian Art in the Age of the Pyramids*, New York, The Metropolitan Museum of art 1999, 329f.

HÖLSCHER, U. , MUNRO, P.
1975 Der Unas-Friedhof in Saqqara. 2. Vorbericht über die Arbeiten der Gruppe Hannover im Frühjahr 1974, in: *SAK* 3, 113–126

HORNUNG, E.
1973 Die „Kammern" des Thot-Heiligtums, in: *ZÄS* 100, 33–35
1991 Sedfest und Geschichte, in: *MDAIK* 47, 169–171

HORNUNG, E., STAEHELIN, E.
1974 *Studien zum Sedfest.* (AH I/1) Basel, Ägyptologisches Seminar der Universität - Genève, Centre d'études orientales de l'Université de Genève

HORVÁT, Z.
2003 Sahure and his Cult-Complex in the Light of Tradition, in: Popielska-Grzybowska, J. (ed.), in: *Proceedings of the Second Central European Conference of Young Egyptologists. Egypt 2001: Perspectives of Research. Warsaw 5-7 March 2001*, Warsaw 2003, 63–70

JACQUET-GORDON, H.
1962 *Les noms des domaines funéraires sous l'Ancien Empire égyptien*, (BdÉ 34) Le Caire, IFAO
1980 Kolonisation, innere, in: LÄ III, 672f.

JAMES, T. G. H.
1961 A group of inscribed Egyptian tools, in: *The British Museum Quarterly*, vol. 24 no. 1–2, 36–43
1974 *Corpus of Hieroglyphic Inscriptions in the Brooklyn Museum. I. From Dynasty I to the End of Dynasty XVIII*, Brooklyn N.Y., Brooklyn Museum

JANÁK, J., VYMAZALOVÁ, H., COPPENS, F.
2011 The Fifth dynasty 'sun temples' in a broader context, in: Bárta, M., Coppens, F., Krejčí, J. (eds.), *Abusir and Saqqara in the Year 2010/1*, Prague, Czech Institute of Egyptology, Faculty of Arts, Charles University in Prague, 430–442

JÁNOSI, P.
1994 Bemerkungen zur Regierung des Schepseskaf, in: *GM* 141, 49–54
1996 *Die Pyramidenanlagen der Königinnen. Untersuchungen zu einem Grabtyp des Alten und Mittleren Reiches*, Wien, Verlag der Österreichischen Akademie der Wissenschaften
2005 *Giza in der 4. Dynastie. Die Baugeschichte und Belegung einer Nekropole des Alten Reiches. I. Die Mastabas der Kernfriedhöfe und die Felsgräber*, Wien, Verlag der Österreichischen Akademie der Wissenschaften

2006 Old Kingdom tombs and dating – problems and priorities. The *Cemetery en Échelon* at Giza, in: Bárta, M. (ed.), *The Old KingdomArt and Archaeology. Proceedings of the conference held in Prague, May 31 – June 4, 2004,* Prague, Czech Institute of Egyptoology, Faculty of Arts, Charles University in Prague, Academia, Publishing House of the Academy of Sciences of the Czech republic, 175–183

JEFFREYS, D.
2001 High and Dry? Survey of the Memphite escarpment, in: *EA* 19, 15–16
2006 The Survey of Memphis: recent results, in: *EA* 29, 14–15

JEFFREYS, D., TAVARES, A.
1994 The Historic Landscape of Early Dynastic Memphis, in: *MDAIK* 50, 158.

JENNI, H.
1998 Der Papyrus Westcar, in: *SAK* 25, 113–141

JÉQUIER, G.
1928 *Le Mastabat Faraoun*, Le Caire, IFAO
1933 *Les pyramides des reines Neit et Apouit*, Le Caire, IFAO
1938 *Le monument funéraire de Pepi II*, t. II. *Le temple*, Le Caire, IFAO

JIDEJIAN, N.
1968 Byblos through the Ages, Beirut, Dar el-Machreq

JIMÉNEZ-SERRANO, A.
2012 On the Construction of the Mortuary Temple of King Unas, in: *SAK* 41, 153–161

JUNKER, H.
1932 Die Grabungen der Universität Kairo auf dem Pyramidenfeld von Giza, in: *MDAIK* 3, 123–149
1938 *Bericht über die von der Akademie der Wissenschaften in Wien auf gemeinsame Kosten mit Dr. Wilhelm Pelizaeus unternommenen Grabungen auf dem Friedhof des Alten Reiches bei den Pyramiden von Giza. III*, Wien und Leipzig, Hölder-Pichler-Tempsky A.G.
1951 *Bericht über die von der Akademie der Wissenschaften in Wien auf gemeinsame Kosten mit Dr. Wilhelm Pelizaeus unternommenen Grabungen auf dem Friedhof des Alten Reiches bei den Pyramiden von Giza X*, Wien, Rudolf M. Rohrer

JONES, D.
2000 *An Index of Ancient Egyptian Titles, Epithets and Phrases of the Old Kingdom. I–II*, (BAR International series 866) Oxford, Archaeopress

KAHL, J.
2007 *"Ra is my Lord". Searching for the Rise of the Sun God at the Dawn of Egyptian History*, (MENES 1) Wiesbaden, Harrasowitz Verlag

KAHL, J., BRETSCHNEIDER, M., KNEISSLER, B.
2002 *Frühägyptisches Wörterbuch. Erste Lieferung ꜣ-f.* Wiesbaden, Harrasowitz Verlag

KAISER, W.
1956 Zu den Heiligtümern der 5. Dynastie, in: *MDAIK* 14, 104–116
1969 Zu den königlichen Talbezirken der 1. und 2. Dynastie in Abydos und zur Baugeschichte des Djoser-Grabmals, in: *MDAIK* 25, 1969, 1–21

KÁKOSY, L.
1981 The Pyramid Texts and Society in the Old Kingdom, (Studia Aegyptiaca 7) Budapest, 27–40

KAMAL, A.
1910 Rapport sur les fouilles du comte Galarza, in: *ASAE* 10, 116–121

KAMMERZELL, F.
2001 „... within the Altar of the Sun". An unidentified hieroglyph and the construction of the sun temple *Nḫn-Rꜥw*, in: *LingAeg* 9, 153–164

KANAWATI, N.
1976 The mentioning of more than one eldest child in Old Kingdom inscriptions, in: *CdE* 51, 235–251
1977 *The Egyptian Administration in the Old Kingdom*, Warminster, Aris & Phillips Ltd.
1980 *Governmental Reforms in Old Kingdom Egypt*, Warminster, Aris & Phillips Ltd.
2001 *The Rundle Foundation for Egyptian Archaeology Newsletter* no. 75, January, 1–2
2003 *Conspiracies in the Egyptian palaces. Unis to Pepi I*, London – New York, Routledge
2010 The vizier Nebet and the Royal Women of the Sixth Dynasty, in: Hawass, Z., Ikram, S. (eds.), *Thebes and Beyond. Studies in Honour of Kent R. Weeks*, CASAE 41, 115–125

KANAWATI, N., ABDER-RAZIQ, M.
1998 *The Teti Cemetery at Saqqara. Vol. III. The Tombs of Neferseshemre and Sankhuiptah*, (ACE Reports 11) Warminster, Aris and Phillips
2000 *The Teti Cemetery at Saqqara. Vol. VI. The Tomb of Nikauisesi*, (ACE Reports 14) Warminster, Arris and Phillips
2001 *The Teti Cemetery at Saqqara*. Vol. 5. The Tomb of Hesi, (ACE Reports no. 13), Warminster, Aris and Phillips Ltd.
2003 Nepotism in the Sixth Dynasty, in: *BACE* 14, 39–59

KANAWATI, N., HASSAN, A.
1996 *The Teti Cemetery at Saqqara. Vol. I. The Tombs of Nedjem-em-pet, Ka-aper and Others*, (ACE Reports 8) Sydney, The Australian Centre for Egyptology

KANAWATI, N., McFARLANE, A.
1993 *Deshashah. The Tombs of Inti, Shedu and Others,* (ACE *Reports* 5) Sydney

KAPLONY, P.
1963 *Die Inschriften der ägyptischen Frühzeit. I – III*, (ÄA 8), Wiesbaden, Otto Harrassowitz
1969 Die Siegelabdrücke, in: Ricke, H. *et al.*, *Das Sonnenheiligtum des Königs Userkaf. II. Die Funde*, (BÄBA 8) Wiesbaden, Otto Harrassowitz
1981 *Die Rollsiegell des Alten Reiches I – III*, (MonAeg 3^{A-C}) Bruxelles, Fondation égyptologique Reine Élisabeth

KEES, H.
1923 Die kleine Festdarstellung, in: Bissing, F. W. von, *Das Re – Heiligtum des Königs Ne-woser-re (Rathures). II.* Leipzig, J. C. Hinrichssche Buchhandlung
1928 Die grosse Festdarstellung, in: Bissing, F. W. von, *Das Re – Heiligtum des Königs Ne-woser-re (Rathures). III.* Leipzig, J. C. Hinrichssche Buchhandlung

KEMP, B.
1968 The Osiris Temple at Abydos, in: *MDAIK* 23, 138–155
2006 *Ancient Egypt. Anatomy of a Civilization*, (2nd ed.) London and New York, Routledge

KHALED, M. I.
2008 *The Old Kingdom Royal Funerary Domains: New Evidence from the Causeway of the Pyramid Complex of Sahura*, PhD Dissertation Charles University in Prague, Prague
2013 The economic aspects of the Old Kingdom funerary domains, in: *ÉT* 26/1, 363–372

KLEMM, D., KLEMM, R.
2010 *The Stones of the Pyramids. Provenance of the Building Stones of the Old Kingdom Pyramids of Egypt*, Berlin – New York, Walter de Gruyter GmbH

KLOTH, N.
2002 *Die (auto-)biographischen Inschriften des ägyptischen Alten Reiches: Untersuchungen zu Phraseologie und Entwicklung*, (BSAK 8) Hamburg, Helmut Buske Verlag

KOZLOFF, A.
1982 Weserkaf, Boy King of Dynasty V, in: *Bulletin of the Cleveland Museum of Art*, September, 210–233

KRAUSS, R.
1997 Chronologie und Pyramidenbau in der 4. Dynastie, in: *Or*, *66*, 1–14.
1998 Wenn und aber: das Wag – Fest und die Chronologie des Alten Reiches, in: *GM* 162, 53–57

KREJČÍ, J.
2008 Several remarks on the Abusir pyramid necropolis: its minor tombs and their place in the chronology of the royal cemetery, in: Vymazalová, H., Bárta, M. (eds.), *Chronology and Archaeology in Ancient Egypt (The Third Millenium B.C.)*, Prague, Czech Institute of

Egyptology, Faculty of Arts, Charles University in Prague, 124–136
2009-a *Abusir XI. The Architecture of the Mastaba of Ptahshepses*, Prague, Czech Institute of Egyptology, Faculty of Arts, Charles University in Prague, Academia
2009-b Die Mastaba des Werkaure, in: *Sokar* 19, 30–37
2010 *Abusir XVIII. The Royal Necropolis in Abusir*, Prague, Charles University in Prague, Faculty of Arts
2013 Das Grab des Kakaibaef in Abusir, in: *Sokar* 27, 26–37

KREJČÍ, J., CALLENDER, V. G., VERNER, M. *et al.*,
2008 *Abusir XII. Minor Tombs in the Royal necropolis. The Mastabas of Nebtyemneferes and Nakhtsare, Pyramid Complex Lepsius no. 24 and Tomb Complex Lepsius no. 25*, Prague, Czech Ibstitute of Egyptology, Faculty of Arts, Charles University in Prague

KUCHMAN SABBACHY, L.,
1982 *The Development of the Titulary and Iconography of the Ancient Egyptian Queens from Dynasty One to the early Dynasty Eighteen*, PhD Dissertation University of Toronto, Toronto

KURASZKIEWICZ, K. O.
2011 An afterworld for Netjerykhet, in: Strudwick, N., Strudwick, H. (eds.), *Old Kingdom, New Perspectives. Egyptian Art and Archaeology 2750–2150 BC*, Oxford, Oxbow Books, 139–142

LABROUSSE, A., LAUER, J.-Ph.
1996 *Le temple d'accueil du complexe funéraire du roi Ounas*, (BdÉ 111) Le Caire, IFAO
2000 *Les complexes funéraires d'Ouserkaf et de Néferhétepès. I. Texte, II. Planches*, (BdÉ 130/I-II) Le Caire, IFAO

LABROUSSE, A., LAUER, J.-Ph., LECLANT, J.
1977 *Le temple haut du complexe funéraire du roi Ounas*, (*BdÉ* 73) Le Caire, IFAO

LABROUSSE, A., MOUSSA, A.
2002 *La chaussée du complexe funéraire du roi Ounas*, (BdÉ 134) Le Caire, IFAO

LANDGRÁFOVÁ, R.
2006 *Abusir XIV. Faience Inlays from the Mortuary Temple of King Raneferef. Raneferef's Substitute Decoration Program*, Prague, Czech Institute of Egyptology, Faculty of Arts, Charles University in Prague

LAPP, G.
1968 *Die Opferformel des Alten Reiches*, (SDAIK 21) Mainz am Rhein, Verlag Philipp von Zabern

LAUER, J.-Ph.
1936 *La pyramide à degrés. I. Text. II. L'architecture*, (Service des antiquités de l'Égypte. Fouilles à Saqqarah), Le Caire, IFAO
1939 Fouilles du Service des antiquités à Saqqarah. Secteur de la pyramide à degrés (novembre 1938 – mai 1939). IV. La pyramide d'Ounas, in: *ASAE* 39, 447–456
1977 Le triangle sacré dans les plans des monuments de l'Ancien Empire, in: *BIFAO* 77, 66–68

LAUER, J.-Ph., LECLANT, J.,
1969 Découverte de statues de prisoniers au temple de la pyramide de Pépi I, in: *RdÉ* 21, 55–62

LECLANT, J.
1967–1968 Fouilles et travaux, in: *Or* 38, 298f.
1969–1970 Fouilles et travaux, in: *Or* 40, 233
1971 Fouilles et travaux, in: *Or* 41, 230–234

LEFEBVRE, G.
1949 *Romans et contes égyptiens de l'époque pharaonique*, Paris, Adrien – Maisonneuve

LEHNER, M.
1985 The Development of the Giza Necropolis: The Khufu Project, in: *MDAIK* 41, 109–143
1997 *The Complete Pyramids*, London, Thames and Hudson Ltd.
--- The Name and Nature of the *Heit el-Ghurab* Old Kingdom Site: Workers' Town, and the Port Hypothesis, in: *The Pyramids: Between Life and Death*, Uppsala, in press
--- The Monument and the Formerly So-called Valley Temple of Khentkaus I: Four Observations, in: Coppens, F., Janák, J. (eds.), *Royal versus Divine Authority: Acquisition, Legitimization and Renewal of Power*, (7. Tagung zur Königsideologie), Wiesbaden, Otto Harrassowitz, in press

LEHNER, M., JONES, D., YEOMANS, L., MAHMOUD, H., OLCHOWSKA, K.
2011 Re-examining the Khentkaus Town, in: Strudwick, N., Strudwick, H. (eds.), *Old Kingdom, New Perspectives*, Oxford, Oxbow Books, 143–191

LEPSIUS, R.
1843 Über den Bau der Pyramiden, in: Monatsberichte der Akademie der Wissenschaften zu Berlin, Berlin
1897 Denkmäler aus Aegypten un Aethiopien. Text I, Unteraegypten und Memphis. Herausgegeben von Eduard Naville, unter Mitwirkung von Ludwig Borchardt, bearbeitet von Kurt Sethe, Leipzig, J. C. Hinrichs'sche Buchhandlung 1897

LEPP, J. van
1995 Evidence of Artificial Irrigation in Amratian Egypt, in: *JARCE* 32, 197–209

LEPPER, V. M.
2008 *Untersuchungen zu pWestcar. Eine philologische und literaturwissenschaftliche (Neu-) Analyse*, (ÄA 70) Wiesbaden, Harrassowitz Verlag

LLOYD, A. B., SPENCER, A. J., KHOULI, A. el-
1990 *Saqqâra Tombs II. The Mastabas of Meru, Semdenti, Khui and Others*, London, Egypt Exploration Society

LORET, V.
1935–1938 Pour transformer un vieillard en jeune homme, in: Jouget, P. (ed.), *Mélanges Maspero I3,* Le Caire, IFAO

LORTON, D.
1985 Considerations on the Origin of the Name Osiris, *VA* 1, 113–126
1991 What was the *pr-nśwt* and who managed it? Aspects of Royal Administration in "The Duties of the Vizier", in: *SAK* 18, 291–316

LUFT, U.
1992 *Die chronologische Fixierung des ägyptischen Mittleren Reiches nach dem Tempelarchiv von Illahun*, (ÖAW, Sitzungsbericht Phil.-hist. Kl., Bd. 598), Wien, Verlag der Österreichischen Akademie der Wissenschaften
1994 The date of the *wꜢgy* Feast: Considerations on the Chronology of the Old Kingdom, in: A. Spalinger (ed.), *Revolutions in Time: Studies in Ancient Egyptian Calendrics*, (*VA Supplement* 6) San Antonio, Van Siclen Books, 39–44

MACRAMALLAH, R.
1935 *Le mastaba d'Idout*, Le Caire, IFAO

MAGLI, G., BELMONTE, J. A.,
2009 Pyramids and Stars, Facts, Conjectures and Starry Tales, in: Belmonte, J.A., Shaltout, M. (eds.), *In Search of Cosmic Order*, Cairo, Supreme Council of Antiquities, 307–321

McNAMARA, L.
2008 The Revetted Mound at Hierakonpolis and Early Kingship, in: Midant-Reynes, B., Tristant, Y. (eds.), *Egypt and its Origins 2*, (OLA 172), Leuven – Paris – Dudley, M.A., Uitgererij Peeters en Department Oosterse Studies

MALEK, J.
1982-a The special features of the Saqqara king-list, in: *JSSEA* vol. 12 no. 1, 21–28
1982-b The original version of the Royal Canon of Turin, in: *JEA* 68, 93–106
1988 The "Altar" in the Pillared Court of Teti's Pyramid-Temple at Saqqara, in: Baines, J. *et al.*, Pyramid Studies and Other Essays Presented to I. E. S. Edwards, Occ. Publ. 7, London, The Egypt Exploration Society, 23–34

1994 King Merykare and his pyramid, in: Berger, C., Clerc, G., Grimal, N. (eds.), *Hommages à Jean Leclant,* vol. 4, (BdÉ 106/4) Le Caire, IFAO, 203–214
1997 The Temples at Memphis. Problems highlighted by the EES survey, in: Quirke, S. (ed.), *The Temple in Ancient Egypt. New Discoveries and Recent Research,* London, The Egypt Exploration Society, 90–101

MALEK, J., MAGEE, D., MILLES, E.
1999 *Topographical Bibliography of Ancient Egyptian Hieroglyphic Texts, Statues, Reliefs and Paintings. VIII. Objects of Provenance not Known. Part 1. Royal Statues. Private Statues (Predynastic to Dynasty XVII),* Oxford, Griffith Institute, Ashmolean Museum

MANETHO
2004 MANETHO with an English translation by W. G. Waddel, Cambridge, Mass. - London, Harvard University Press (reprinted)

MANUELIAN, P. der
1998 A Case of Prefabrication at Giza? The False Door of Intj, in: *JARCE* 35, 115–127

MARAGIOGLIO, V., RINALDI, C.
1963–1977 *L'architettura delle piramidi menfite. I–VIII. (Testo / Tavole),* Rapallo, Tipografia Canessa

MARIETTE, A.
1882 *Les Mastabas de l'Ancien Empire. Fragment du dernier ouvrage publié d´après le manuscript de l´auteur par G. Maspero,* Paris, F. Vieweg, Libraire - éditeur

MARTIN-PARDAY, E.,
1976 *Untersuchungen zur ägyptischen Provinzialverwaltung bis zum Ende des Alten Reiches,* (HÄB 1) Hildesheim, Verlag Gebr. Gerstenberg
1995 Das „Haus des Königs" *pr-nśwt,* in: Kessler, D., Schulz, R. (eds.), *Gedenkschrift für Winfried Barta,* (MÄU 4) Frankfurt am Main, Peter Lang, 269–285

MARTINET, É.
2011 *Le nomarque sous l'Ancien Empire,* Paris, Presses de l'université Paris-Sorbonne

MATTHIAE, P.
1977 *Ebla: An Empire Rediscovered,* London, Hodder and Stoughton

MATHIEU, B.
1997 La signification du serdab dans la pyramide d'Ounas, in: Berger, C., Mathieu, B. (eds.), *Études sur l'Ancien Empire et la nécropole de Saqqâra dédiées à J.-Ph. Lauer,* (OrMon 9) Montpellier III, Université Paul Valéry, 289–304

2010 Mais qui est donc Osiris? Ou la politique sous le linceul de la religion (Enquêtes dans les Textes des Pyramides, 3), in: *ENiM* 3, 77–107

McCORCODYLE, K.
2012 Reconsidering the Term 'Eldest Son / Eldest Daughter' and Inheritance in the Old Kingdom, in: *BACE 23*, 71–88

MEGAHED, M.
2010 in: Bárta, M., Coppens, F., Krejčí, J. (eds.), *Abusir and Saqqara in the Year 2010*, Prague, Czech Institute of Egyptology, Faculty of Arts, Charles University in Prague, 616–634
2011 The Pyramid Complex of 'Djedkare's Queen' in South Saqqara. Preliminary Report
2014 Die Wiederentdeckung des Pyramidenbezirks des Djedkare-Isesi in Sakkara – Süd, in: *SOKAR* No. 28, 6–19
2014 The altar of Djedkara's funerary temple from South Saqqara, in Lekov, T., Buzov, E. (eds.), *Cult and Belief in Ancient Egypt. Proceedings of the Fourth International Congress for Young Egyptologists, 25–27 September 2012, Sofia*, Sofia, New Bulgarian University / East-West, 2014, 56–62
--- Antichambre Carrée in the Old Kingdom, Its Reliefs and Function, in Landgráfová, R., Mynářová, J. (eds.), *Rich in Years, Great in Victories: Studies in Honour of Tony Spalinger*, Prague, in press
--- *The fragments of reliefs from the pyramid complex of Djedkare*, PhD Dissertation Charles University in Prague, Prague, in preparation

MENU, B.
1985 Ventes de maisons sous l'Ancien Empire égyptien, in: Geus, F., Thill, F. (eds.), *Mélanges offert à Jean Vercoutter*, Paris, Édition recherche sur les civilisations, 249–262

MENU, B., HARARI, I.
1974 La notion de propriété privée dans l'Ancien Empire Egyptien, in: Études sur l'Égypte et le Soudan anciens 2, Lille, l'Institut de Papyrologie et d'Egyptologie de l'Université

MEYER, M. de
2011 The Fifth Dynasty Royal Decree of Ia-ib at Dayr al-Barsha, in: *RdÉ* 62, 57–72

MONTET, P.
1928 Notes et documents pour servir à l'histoire des relations entre l'ancienne Égypte et la Syrie, in: *Kemi* 1, 83–93
1939 Le roi Sahurê et la Princesse lointaine, in: *Mélanges syriens offerts à Monsieur René Dussaud. I*, Paris, P. Geuthner
1998 *Byblos et L'Égypte. Quatre campagnes de fouilles 1921–1924*, (2nd ed.) Paris, Bibliothèque archéologique et historique

MORALES, A. J.
2006 Traces of official and popular veneration to Nyuserra Iny at Abusir. Late Fifth Dynasty to the Middle Kingdom, in: Bárta, M., Coppens, F., Krejčí, J.(eds.), *Abusir and Saqqara in the Year 2005. Proceedings of the conference held in Prague (June 27 – July 5, 2005)*, Prague, Czech Institute of Egyptology, Faculty of Arts, Charles University in Prague, 311–341

MORENO GARCÍA, J. C.
1996 *Administration territorial et organisation de l'espace en Égypte au troisième millénaire avant J.-C.: grgt et le titre ᶜ(n)ḏ-mr grgt, in: ZÄS* 123, 116–138
1997 Administration territoriale et organisation de l'espace en Égypte au troisième millénaire avant J.-C. (II) *swnw*, in: *ZÄS* 124, 116–130
1998 La population *mrt*: une approche du problème de la servitude dans l'Égypte du IIIe millénaire, in: *JEA* 84, 71–83
1999 *Ḥwt et le milieu rural égyptien du IIIe millénaire. Économie, administration et organisation territoriale*, Paris, (Bibliothèque de l'école des Hautes études, sciences historiques et philosophiques t. 337) Libraire Honoré Champion

MORENZ, L.
2003 Die thebanischen Potentaten und ihr Gott. Zur Konzeption des Gottes Amun und der (Vor-)Geschichte des Sakralzentrums Karnak in der XI. Dynastie, in: *ZÄS* 130, 110–119

MORGAN, J. de
1897 *Carte de la nécropole Memphite. Dahchour, Sakkarah, Abou-Sir*, Le Caire, Ministère des Travaux publics

MORTENSEN, B.
1991 Change in the Settlement Pattern and Population in the Beginning of the Historical Period, in: *Ä & L* 2, 11–37

MOURSI, M.
1972 *Die Hohenpriester des Sonnengottes von der Frühzeit Ägyptens bis zum Ende des Neuen Reiches,* (MÄS 26) München Berlin, Deutscher Kunstverlag
1987 Die Ausgrabungen in der Gegend um die Pyramide des *Ḏd-kꜣ-Rᶜ „Issj"* bei Saqqara, in: *ASAE* 71, 185–193
1988-a Die Ausgrabungen in der Gegend um die Pyramide des *Ḏd-kꜣ-rᶜ „Issj"* bei Saqqara II, in: *GM* 105, 65–66
1988-b Die Ausgrabungen in der Gegend um die Pyramide des *Ḏd-kꜣ-rᶜ „Issj"* bei Saqqara III, in: *GM* 106, 65–72
2005 *Die Hohenpriester des Sonnengottes von der Frühzeit Ägyptens bis zum Ende des Neuen Reiches,* (MÄS 26) München – Berlin, Deutscher Kunstverlag

MOUSSA, A.
1971 A Stela from Saqqara of a family Devoted to the Cult of Unis, in: *MDAIK* 27, 81–84

MRSICH, T.
1968 *Untersuchungen zur Hausurkunde des Alten Reiches. Ein Beitrag zum altägyptischen Stiftungsrecht*, (MÄS 13) Berlin, Verlag Bruno Hessling

MÜLLER, H. W.
1985 Gedanken zur Entstehung, Interpretation und Rekonstruktion ältester ägyptischer Monumentalarchitektur, in: *Ägypten. Dauer und Wandel*, (SDAIK 18) Mainz am Rhein, Verlag Philipp von Zabern

MÜLLER-WOLLERMANN, R.
1986 *Krisenfaktoren im ägyptischen Staat des ausgehenden Alten Reiches*, PhD Dissertation Universität Tübingen, Tübingen
1987 *św.tjw*-Bauern als Kolonisatoren, in: *VA* Vol. 3 No. 3, December, 263–267

MUNRO, P.
1993 *Der Unas-Friedhof Nord-West. I. Topographisch-historische Einleitung. Das Doppelgrab der Königinnen Nebet und Khenut*, Mainz am Rhein, Verlag Philipp von Zabern

MYŚLIWIEC, K. *et al.*
2004 *Saqqara I. The Tomb of Merefnebef. Text*, Warsaw, Editions Neriton

NELSON, H. H.
1934 Fragments of Egyptian Old Kingdom vases from Byblos, in: *Berytus* 1, 19–22

NICHOLSON, P. T., SHAW, I.
2000 *Ancient Egyptian Materials and Technology*, Cambridge, Cambridge University Press

NUZZOLO, M.
2007 The Sun-Temples of the Vth Dynasty, in: *SAK* 36, 217–247
--- Royal Authority, Divine Legitimization. Topography as an element of acquisition, confirmation and renewal of power in the Fifth Dynasty, in: Coppens, F., Janák, J., Vymazalová, H. (eds.), *VII. Tagung zur Königsideologie: Royal versus Divine Authority. Acquisition, Legitimization and Renewal of Power*, (Königtum, Staat und Gesellschaft früher Hochkulturen 4/4), Wiesbaden, Otto Harrassowitz, in press

NUZZOLO, M., PIRELLI, R.
2011 New archaeological investigation in the sun temple in Abu Ghurab, in: Bárta, M., Coppens, F., Krejčí, J. (eds.), *Abusir and Saqqara in the Year 2010*, Vol. I, Praha, Czech Institute of Egyptology, Faculty of Arts, Charles University in Prague, 664–679

O'CONNOR, D.
1998 The Interpretation of the Old Kingdom Pyramid Complex, in: Guksch, H., Polz, D.

(eds.), *Stationen. Beiträge zur Kulturgeschichte Ägyptens Rainer Stadelmann gewidmet*, Mainz, Verlag Philipp von Zabern

ODLER, M.
--- The chronology and morphology of adzes in the Early Dynastic Period and Old Kingdom, in *Proceedings of the Conference "Copper and Trade in South Eastern Mediterranean"*, Kraków, 5–7 May, in press

ONDERKA, P.
2009 *The Tomb of Unisankh at Saqqara and Chicago*, Prague, National Museum – Charles University

OTTO, E.
1966 *Ägypten. Weg des Pharaonenreiches*, Stuttgart, W. Kohlhammer Verlag

PÄTZNICK, J.-P.
2001 La ville d'Éléphantine et son matériel sigillaire: enquête sur un artefact archéologique, in: *Le Sceau et l'Administration dans la Valée du Nil (Villeneuve d'Ascq 7 juillet 2000)*, (CRIPEL 22) Lille III, Université Charles-de-Gaulle, 137–151
2005 *Die Siegelabrollungen und Rollsiegel der Stadt Elephantine im 3. Jahrtausend v. Chr. Spurensicherung eines archäologischen Artefaktes*, (BAR International Series 1339) Oxford, Archaeopress

PAMMINGER, P.
2000 Features of the past. A royal statuary and its secret, in: *RdÉ* 51, 153–173

PAPAZIAN, H.
2010 The Temple of Ptah and Economic Contacts between Memphite Cult Centers in the Fifth Dynasty, in: Dolińska, M., Beinlich, H. (eds.), in: *8.* Ägyptologische *Tempeltagung: Interconnections between Temples*, Wiesbaden, Otto Harrassowitz Verlag, 137–153
2012 *Domain of Pharaoh. The Structure and Components of the Economy of Old Kingdom Egypt*, (HÄB 52) Hildesheim, Gebrüder Gerstenberg
2013 Central Administration of the Resources in the Old Kingdom: Departments, Treasuries, Granaries and Work Centers, in: J. C. Moreno García (ed.), *Ancient Egyptian Administration*, Leiden - Boston, Brill, 41–84

PARKER, R. A.
1950 *The Calendars of Ancient Egypt*, (SAOC 26) Chicago, The Oriental Institute of the University of Chicago

PERRING, J. S.
1839–1842 *The Pyramids of Gizeh from actual survey and admeasurement. I–II.* London, A. J. Andrews, Esq.

PERRING, J. S., VYSE, H.
1842 *Appendix to Operations carried on at the Pyramids of Gizeh in 1837. The pyramids at Abou Roash, and to the southward, including those in the Faiyoum. Vol. III*, London, John Weale, High Holborn – G. W. Nickisson, 215 Regent street

PETRIE, W. M. F.
1892 *Medum*, London, D. Nutt
1898 *Deshashah*, London, The Egypt Exploration Fund
1902 *Abydos I*, London, The Egypt Exploration Fund
1903 *Abydos II*, London, The Egypt Exploration Fund
1927 *Objects of Daily Use*, London, British School of Archaeology in Egypt
1990 *The Pyramids and Temples of Gizeh*, (new and revised ed.) London, Histories & Mysteries of Man Ltd.

PFIRSCH, L.
1997 À propos du titre *mḏḥ nḫn* attribué à Imhotep, in: Berger, C., Mathieu, B. (eds.), *Études sur l'Ancien Empire et la nécropole de Saqqâra dédiées à J.-Ph. Lauer*, (OrMon 9) Montpellier III, Université Paul Valéry, 351–354

PIACENTINI, P.
1994 On the titles of *ḥḳ3w ḥwt* , in: Allam,S. (ed.), *Grund und Boden in Altägypten. Akten des internationalen symposiums, Tübingen 18.–20. Juni 1990*, Tübingen, Selbstverlag des Herausgebers, 235–249

PIANKOFF, A.
1968 *The Pyramid of Unas. Texts Translated with Commentary*, (Bollinngen Series XL 5) New York, Princeton University Press

PICARDO, N. S.
2010 (Ad)dressing Washptah: Illness or Injury in the Vizier's Death, as Related in His Tomb Biography, in: Hawass, Z., Wegner, J. H. (eds.), *Millions of Jubilees. Studies in honor of David P. Silverman*, vol. 2, Cairo, Supreme Council of Antiquities, 93–104

POETHKE, G.
1975 Epagomenen, in: LÄ I, 1231–1232

PORTER, B., MOSS, R. L. B., BURNEY, E. W., MÁLEK, J.
1974–1981 *Topographical Bibliography of Ancient Egyptian Hieroglyphic Text, Reliefs, and Paintings. III. Memphis. Part 1. Abû Rawâsh to Abûsîr – Part 2. Saqqara to Dahshûr*, (2nd edition, revised and augmented), Oxford, Griffith Institute Ashmolean Museum

POSENER-KRIÉGER, P.
1969 Sur un nom de métal égyptien, in: *UGARITICA VI* (Mission de Ras Shamra), Paris,

Libraire Orientaliste Paul Geuthner, 419–426
1975 Les papyrus de Gébélein. Remarques préliminaires, in: *RdE* 27, 211–221
1976 *Les archives du temple funéraire de Néferirkare-Kakaï. Traduction et commentaire. I–II*, (BdÉ 65) Le Caire, IFAO
1993 Un nouveau bâtiment de Sahourê, in: *SEAP* 12, 8
1995 Fragments de papyrus, in: Verner, M., *Abusir III. The Pyramid Complex of Khentkaus* (with contributions by P. Posener-Kriéger and P. Jánosi), Praha, Universitas Carolina – Academia, 133–142
1997 News from Abusir, in: Quirke, S. (ed.), *The Temple in Ancient Egypt. New discoveries and recent research,* London, British Museum, 17–23
2004 *I papiri di Gebelein – Scavi G. Farina 1935*, Torino, Ministero per i beni i le attività culturali – Soprintendenza al Museo delle antichità egizie

POSENER-KRIÉGER, P., CÉNIVAL, J. L. de
1968 *The Abusir Papyri,* (HPBM Fifth Series), London

POSENER-KRIÉGER, P., VERNER, M., VYMAZALOVÁ, H.
2006 *Abusir X. The Pyramid Complex of Raneferef. The Papyrus Archive*, Praha, Czech Institute of Egyptology, Faculty of Arts, Charles University in Prague

POSTEL, L.
2004 *Protocol des souverains égyptiens et dogme monarchique au début du Moyen Empire*, (MRE 10) Brepols, Fondation égyptologique Reine Élisabeth

QUESNE, T. du
2001 Concealing and Revealing: The Problem of Ritual Masks in Ancient Egypt, in: *DE* 51, 5–30

QUIBELL, J. E., HAYTER, A. G. K.
1927 *Teti Pyramid. North Side*, Le Caire, IFAO

QUIRKE, S.
2001 *The Cult of Ra. Sun-worship in Ancient Egypt*, London, Thames and Hudson

RASLAN, M. A.
1973 Academic and Applied Paper on the History of Architecture. The Causeway of Ounas Pyramid, in: *ASAE* 61, 151–196

RAUE, D.
1999 *Heliopolis und das Haus des Re: Eine Prosopographie und ein Toponym im Neuen Reich.* ADAIK 16. Berlin, Achet-Verlag

RAY, J. D.
1976 *The Archive of Ḥor*, London, Egypt Exploration Society

REDFORD, D. B.
1986 Egypt and Western Asia in the Old Kingdom, in: *JARCE* 23, 125–144
1992 *Egypt, Canaan, and Israel in Ancient Times*, Cairo, The American University in Cairo Press
2008 Some Old Kingdom Sealings from Mendes: I, in: D'Auria, Sue H., *Servant of Mut. Studies in Honor of Richard A. Fazzini*, (PdÄ 28) Leiden - Boston, Brill, 198–203

REEVES, N.
1992 *Egyptian Medicine*, Shire Egyptology 15, Haverfordwest

REISNER, G. A.
1931 *Mycerinus. The Temples of the Third Pyramid at Giza*, Cambridge, Mass., Harvard University Press
1942 *A History of the Giza Necropolis. I*, Cambridge, Mass., Harvard University Press

RICKE, H.
1935 Der Hohe Sand in Heliopolis, in *ZÄS* 71, 107–111
1950 *Bemerkungen zur ägyptischen Baukunst des Alten Reichs. II*, (BÄBA 5) Kairo, Schweizerisches Institut für ägyptische Bauforschung und Altertumskunde in Kairo
1965–1969 *Das Sonnenheiligtum des Königs Userkaf. I. Der Bau. II. Die Funde*, (BÄBA 7–8) Kairo, Schweizerisches Institut für ägyptische Bauforschung und Altertumskunde in Kairo

ROCCATI, A.
1982 *La litérature historique sous l'Ancien Empire égyptien*, Paris, Édition du Cerf

ROEHRING, C. H.
1999 Fragmentary Head of a King, in: O'Neill, P. O. (ed.), *Egyptian Art in the Age of Pyramids*, New York, The Metropolitan Museum of Art, 316f.

ROCHHOLZ, M.
1994 Sedfest, Sonnenheiligtum und Pyramidenbezirk. Zur Deutung der Grabanlagen der Könige der 5. und 6. Dynastie, in: Gundlach, R., Rochholz, M (eds.), *Ägyptische Tempel – Struktur, Funktion, Program. (Akten der ägyptologischen Tagungen in Gosen 1990 und in Mainz 1992)*, HÄB 37, 255–280

RÖMER, M.
2007 Die Aussagekraft der Quellen für das Studium ägyptischer Wirtschaft und Verwaltung, in: *ZÄS* 134, 66–81

ROTH, A. M.
1991 The Distribution of the Old Kingdom title *ḫnty-š*, (BSAK 4) Hamburg, Helmut Buske Verlag
1995 *A Cemetery of Palace Attendants*, (Giza Mastabas vol. 6) Boston, Museum of Fine Arts

ROWE, A.
1936 *A Catalogue of Egyptian Scarabs, Scaraboids, Seals and Amulets in the Palestine Archaeological* Museum, Le Caire 1936, IFAO, 283–289 and pl. 36
1938 Additional references to the article Provisional Notes on the Old Kingdom Inscriptions from the Diorite Quarries, in: *ASAE* 38, 678–688

RYDSTRÖM, K.
1994 *ḥry sštȝ* "In charge of Secrets": the 3000-year Evolution of a Title, in: *DE* 28, 1994, 53–94

SAAD, Z. Y.
1940 A Preliminary report on the Excavations at Saqqara 1939–1940, in: *ASAE* 40, 675–714
1941 A preliminary report on the excavations at Saqqara 1939–1940, *ASAE* 40, 683–685

SAID, R.
1993 *The River Nile. Geology, Hydrology and Utilization*, Oxford – New York – Soeul – Tokyo, Pergamon Press

SANUSSI, A. el-, JONES, M.
1997 A Site of the Maadi Culture near the Giza Pyramids, in: *MDAIK* 53, 241–250

SANDMAN-HOLMBERG, M.
1946 *The God Ptah*, Lund, C. W. K. Gleerup – Copenhagen, Ejnar Munksgaard

SAUNERON, S.
1950 La ville de *Sȝḫbw*, in: *Kêmi* 11, 63–72
1955 Sakhebou, in: *BIFAO* 55, 61–64
1959 *Esna I. Quatre campagnes à Esna*, Le Caire, IFAO
1964 Le 30 Mesorè à Esna, in: *BIFAO* 62, 115–119

SAVELYEVA, T. N.
1962 Dannye nadpisi Mecena o charaktere tschastnogo zemlevladeniya v drevnem Egipte v konce III i natschale IV dinastii, in: *Akademiku Vasiliu Vasilievitchu Struve. Drevniy mir. Sbornik statey*, Moskva, Izdatelstvo vostotchnoy literatury

SCHÄFER, H.
1902 *Ein Bruchstück altägyptischer Annalen*, Berlin, Verlag der königlichen Akademie der Wissenschaften
1908 *Priestergräber und andere Grabfunde vom Ende des Alten Reiches bis zur Griechischen Zeit vom Totentempel des Ne-user-rê*, Leipzig, J. C. Hinrichs

SCHEELE-SCHWEITZER, K.
2007 Zu den Königsnamen der 5. und 6. Dynastie, *GM* 215, 93f.

SCHILD, R., WENDORF, F.
2013 Early and Middle Holocene Paleoclimates in South Western Desert of Egypt – The World Before Unification, in: Marks, L. (ed.), *Studia Quaternaria*, vol. 30, no. 2, Warsaw, Polish Academy of Sciences, 153–133

SCHMITZ, B.
1976 *Untersuchungen zum Titel S3-NJŚWT „Königssohn"*, Bonn, Rudolf Habelt Verlag

SCHNEIDER, T.
1996 *Lexikon der Pharaonen*, München, Deutscher Taschenbuch Verlag

SCHOSKE, S.
1995 *Eine ägyptische Kunstgeschichte. Rundgang durch die Ägyptische Sammlung München*, München, Staatliche Sammlung ägyptischer Kunst

SCHOTT, E.
1977 Die Biographie des Ka-em-Tenenet, in: Assmann, J., Feucht, E., Grieshammer, R. (eds.), *Fragen an die altägyptische literatur. Studien zum Gedenken an Eberhard Otto*, Wiesbaden, Dr. Ludwig Reichert Verlag, 443–462

SCHOTT, S.
1950 *Altägyptische Festdaten.* (AWL Mainz, Abh. der Geistes- und Sozialwiss. Kl. 50) Wiesbaden, Franz Steiner Verlag GMBH

SCHENKEL, W.
1978 *Bewässerungsrevolution im Alten Ägypten*, Mainz am Rhein, Verlag Philipp von Zabern

SCHWEITZER, U.
1948 *Löwe und Sphinx im Alten Ägypten*, (ÄF 15) Glückstadt und Hamburg, Verlag J. J. Augustin

SEEBER, Ch.
1980 Krone, in: LÄ III, 812

SEIDEL, M.
1996 *Die königlichen Statuengruppen. Band I: Die Denkmäler vom Alten Reich bis zum Ende der 18. Dynastie*, (HÄB 42) Hildesheim, Gerstenberg Verlag

SEIDLMAYER, S.
1982 Nekropole, Keramikwerkstatt und königliche Anlage in der Nordweststadt, in: Kaiser, W. *et al.*, Stadt und Tempel von Elephantine. Neunter / Zehnter Grabungsbericht, in: *MDAIK* 38, 284–306

1996-a Die staatliche Anlage der 3. Dynastie in der Nordweststadt von Elephantine. Archäologische und historische Probleme, in: Bietak, M. (ed.), *Haus und Palast im alten Ägypten*, Wien, Österreichische Akademie der Wissenschaften, 195–215
1996-b Town and State in the Early Old Kingdom: A view from Elephantine, in: Spencer, J. (ed.) *Aspects of Early Egypt*, London, British Museum Press, 108–128

SEIPEL, W.
1980 *Untersuchungen zu den ägyptischen Königinnen der Frühzeit und des Alten Reiches. Quellen und historische Einordnung*, PhD Dissertation Universität Hamburg, Hamburg

SETHE, K.
1913 Die Inschriften, in: Borchardt, L., *Das Grabdenkmal des Königs Śaꜣ-ḥu-reʿ. II*, (WVDOG 26) Leipzig, Hinrichs Verlag, 73–132
1916 Der Name der Phönizier, in: *Orientalische Studien, Fritz Hommel zum sechsigsten Geburtstag, am 3l Juli 19l4: gewidmet von Freunden, Kollegen und Schülern. I–II*, Leipzig, Hinrichs Verlag, 305–322
1917 Ein ägyptisches Denkmal des Alten Reiches von der Insel Kythera mit dem Namen des Sonnenheiligtums des Königs Userkaf, in: *ZÄS* 53, 55–58
1933 *Urkunden des Alten Reichs*, Leipzig, J. C. Hinrichs'sche Buchhandlung

SHALOMI-HEN, R.
2006 *The Writing of Gods. The Evolution of Divine Classifiers in the Old Kingdom*, Wiesbaden, Harrassowitz Verlag

SHAW, I. M. E., BLOXAM, E. G.
1999 Survey and Excavation at the Ancient Pharaonic Gneiss Quarrying Site of Gebel el-Asr, *Sudan & Nubia* 3, 13–20

SILVERMAN, D. P.
1995 The Nature of Egyptian Kingship, in: O'Connor, D., Silverman, D. P. (eds.), *Ancient Egyptian Kingship*, (PdÄ 9) Leiden – New York – Köln, E. J. Brill, 49–92
2009 Non-royal burials in the Teti Pyramid Cemetery and the Early Twelfth dynasty, in: Silverman, D., Simpson, W. K., Wegner, J. (eds.), *Archaism and Innovation: Studies in the Culture and Society of Middle Kingdom Egypt*, New Heaven, Department of Near Eastern Languages and Civilizations, Yale University – Philadelphia, University of Pennsylvania Museum of Archaeology and Anthropology, 47–101

SIMPSON, W. K.
1978 *The Mastabas of Kawab, Khafkhufu I and II. Giza Mastabas*, (Giza Mastabas vol. 3) Boston, Department of Egyptian and Near Eastern Art, Museum of Fine Arts
1995 *Inscribed Material from the Pennsylvania–Yale Excavations at Abydos*, (Publications of the Pennsylvania – Yale Expedition to Egypt No. 6) New Haven, The Peabody Museum of

Natural History of Yale University – Philadelphia, The University of Pennsylvania Museum of Archaeology and Anthropology

SIMPSON, W. K., RITNER, R. K., TOBIN, V., WENTE, E. Jr.,
2005 *The Literature of Ancient Egypt. An Anthology of Stories, Instructions, Stelae, Autobiographies, and Poetry*, Cairo, The American University in Cairo Press

SOUROUZIAN, H.
1982 L'apparition du pylône, in: *BIFAO* 82, 143

SOWADA, K. N.
2009 *Egypt and the Eastern Mediterranean during the Old Kingdom. An Archaeological Perspective*, (OBO 237) Fribourg, Academic Press – Göttingen, Vandenhoeck & Ruprecht

SPALINGER, A. J.
1992 *Three Studies on Egyptian Feasts and Their Chronological Implications*, Baltimore MD, Halgo Inc.
1994-a 'Calendars: Real and Ideal,' in: Bryan, B., Lorton, D. (eds.), *Essays in Egyptology in Honor of Hans Goedicke*, San Antonio, 297–308
1994-b The first four feasts of the Old Kingdom Mastabas, in: Spalinger, A. J. (ed.), *Revolutions in Time: Studies in Ancient Egyptian Calendrics*, (VA Supplement 6) San Antonio Texas, Van Siclen Books, 50–60
1996 *The Private Feast Lists of Ancient Egypt*, (ÄA 57) Wiesbaden, Harrasowitz Verlag
2001 Callendars, in: Redford, D. B. (ed.), (OEAE vol. I) 224–227
2007 Osiris, Re, Cheops, in: *ZÄS* 134, 173–184
2013-a Egyptian and Greek time frames. The date of the Kronia Festival, in: Bárta, M., Küllmer, H. (eds.), *Diachronic Trends in Ancient Egyptian History. Studies dedicated to the memory of Eva Pardey*, Prague, Charles University in Prague, Faculty of Arts, 109–118
2013-b Further Thoughts on the Feast of *Wꜣgj*, in: *ÉT* 26, 616–624
2013-c The organization of the pharaonic army (Old to New Kingdom), in: Moreno García, J. C. (ed.), *Ancient Egyptian Administration*, Leiden – Boston, Brill, 393–478
--- Concepts of Kingship: The Golden Horus Name, in: Coppens, F., Janák, J., Vymazalová, H. (eds.), *VII. Tagung zur Königsideologie: Royal versus Divine Authority. Acquisition, Legitimization and Renewal of Power*, (Königtum, Staat und Gesellschaft früher Hochkulturen), Wiesbaden, Otto Harrassowitz, in press

SPENCER, A. J.
1974 Researches on the topography of north Saqqâra, in: *Or* 43, 1–11

STADELMANN, R.
1981-a Die *ḫntyw-š*, der Königsbezirk *š n pr-ꜥꜣ* und die Namen der Grabanlagen der Frühzeit, in: *Bulletin de Centenaire*, (Suppl. au *BIFAO*, t. 81) Le Caire, IFAO
1981-b La ville de pyramide à l'Ancien Empire, in: *RdE* 33, 67–77

1984-a Pyramidenstadt, in: LÄ V, 9–14
1984-b Sonnenheiligtum, in: LÄ V, 1094ff.
1985 *Die ägyptischen Pyramiden. Vom Ziegelbau zum Weltwunder*, Darmstadt, Wissenschaftliche Buchgesellschaft
1990 *Die grossen Pyramiden von Giza,* Graz, Akademische Druck- u. Verlagsanstalt
1991 Das Dreikammersystem der Königsgräber der Frühzeit und des Alten Reiches, in: *MDAIK* 47, 373–388
1994 König Teti und der Beginn der 6. Dynastie, in: Berger, C., Clerc, G., Grimal, N. (eds.), *Hommages à Jean Leclant. 1. Études pharaoniques*, (BdÉ 106/1) Le Caire, IFAO, 327–335
2000 Userkaf in Saqqara und Abusir. Untersuchungen zur Thronfolge in der 4. und 5. Dynastie, in: Bárta, M., Krejčí, J. (eds.), *Abusir and Saqqara in the Year 2000*, Prague, Academy of Sciences of the Czech Republic, Oriental Institute, 529–542
2011 The *heb-sed* Temple of Senefru at Dahshur, in: Bárta, M., Coppens, F., Krejčí, J. (eds.), *Abusir and Saqqara in the Year 2010*, Prague, Czech Institute of Egyptology, Faculty of Arts, Charles University in Prague, 736–746

STASSER, T.
2013 *La mère royale Seshseshet et les débuts de la VIe dynastie*, (Connaissance de l'Égypte Ancienne no. 14) Paris, Éditions Safran

STEINER, P.
2012 Symbolic Connotations of Pyramid Temples in the 5th and 6th Dynasties, in: Muhlestein, K. (ed.), *Evolving Egypt: Innovation, Appropriation, and Reinterpretation in Ancient Egypt*, (BAR International Series 2397) Oxford, Archaeopress, 25–36

STOCKFISCH, D.
2003 *Untersuchungen zum Totenkult des ägyptischen Königs im Alten Reich. Die Dekoration der königlichen Totenkultanlagen*, Bd. 1–2, Hamburg, Verlag Dr. Kovač

STROUHAL, E.
2002 Anthropological Evaluation of the Human Skeletal Remains from the Mastabas of Djedkare Isesi's Family, in: Verner, M., Callender, V. G., *Djedkare's Family Cemetery,* Prague, Czech Institute of Egyptology, Faculty of Arts, Charles University – Set out, 127–132

STROUHAL, E., VYHNÁNEK, L., GABALLAH, M. F., SAUNDERS, S., WOELFLI, W.
2001 Identification of royal skeletal remains from Egyptian pyramids, in: *Anthropologie* 38/1, 15–23

STRUDWICK, N.
1985 *The Administration of Egypt in the Old Kingdom. The Highest Titles and their Holders*, London, KPI Limited
2005 *Texts from the Pyramid Age*, Atlanta, Society of Biblical Literature

SWEENY, D.
1993 Egyptian masks in motion, in: *GM* 135, 101–104
2004 Forever Young? The Representation of Older and Ageing Women in Ancient Egyptian Art, in: *JARCE* 41, 67–84

SWELIM, N.
1988 The Dry Moat of the Netjerykhet Complex, in: (Baines, J., James, T. G. H., Leahy, A., Shore, A. F. (eds.), *Pyramid Studies and Other Essays Presented to I. E. S. Edwards*, London, The Egypt Exploration Society, 12–22

SWINTON, J.
2012 *The Management of estates and their Resources in the Egyptian Old Kingdom*, (BAR International Series 2392) Oxford, Archaeopress

TALLET, P.
2010 Prendre la mer à Ayn Soukhna au temps du roi Isési, in: *BSFE* No. 177–178 Juin – Octobre, 18–22
2012-a New Inscriptions from Ayn Soukhna 2002–2009, in: Tallet, P., Mahfouz, S. (eds.), *The Red Sea in Pharaonic Times. Recent Discoveries along the Red Sea Coast. Proceedings of the Colloquium held in Cairo / Ayn Soukhna 11th–12th January 2009*, Le Caire, IFAO, 105–115
2012-b *La zone minière pharaonique du Sinaï – I. catalogue complémentaire des inscriptions du Sinaï*, (MIFAO 130) Le Caire, IFAO
2014 Des papyrus du temps de Chéops au ouadi el-Jarf, in: *BSFÉ* no. 188, Février 2014, 25–49
--- Un aperçu de la région Memphite à la fin du règne de Cheops selon le «journal de Merer» (P. Jarf I–III), in: Dhenin, S., Somaglino, Cl. (eds.), *Toponymie et perception de l'espace en Egypte de l'Antiquité au Moyen Age*», Le Caire, IFAO (in press)

TAVARES, A.
2011 Village, town and barracks: a fourth dynasty settlement at Heit el-Ghurab, Giza, in: Strudwick, N., Strudwick, H. (eds.), *Old Kingdom, New Perspectives. Egyptian Art and Archaeology 2750–2150 BC*, Oxford, Oxbow Books, 270–277

TAYEB, H. A. el-
2014-a The burial chamber of Rashepses at Saqqara, in: *EA* 44, Spring 2014, 8–9
2014-b *The Tomb of Rashepses LS 16 at Saqqara*, PhD Dissertation Cairo University, Cairo

TEFNIN, R.
1988 *Statues et Statuettes de l'Ancien Égypte*, Brussels, Musées Royaux d'Art et d'Histoire

UPHILL, E. P.
1984 *The Temples of Per Ramesses*, Warminster, Aris & Phillips

VALLOGIA, M.
2004 *Les oasis d'Égypte dans l'Antiquité. Des origines au deuxième millénaire avant J.-C.*, Gollion, Infolio, 80–86
2011 *Abou Rawash. I. Le complexe funéraire royal de Rêdjedef*, Le Caire, IFAO 2011

VACHALA, B.
1979 Ein weiterer Beleg für die Königin Repewetnebu?, in: *ZÄS* 106, 176
1991 Zur Frage der Kriegsgefangenen in Ägypten. Überlegungen anhand der schriftlichen Quellen des Alten Reiches, in: Endesfelder, E. (ed.), *Probleme der frühen Geselschaftsentwicklung im alten Ägypten*, Berlin, Humboldt-Universität zu Berlin, Institut für Sudanarchäologie und Ägyptologie, 93–101

VERCOUTTER, J.
1985 Les «affamés» d'Ounas et le changement climatique de la fin de l'Ancien Empire, in: P. Posener-Kriéger (ed.), Vol. I, Le Caire, IFAO, 327–337

VERHOEVEN, U.
1986 Totenfeste, in: LÄ VI, 645–647

VERNER, M.
1977 *Abusir I. The Mastaba of Ptahshepses. Reliefs I/1*, Prague, Charles University
1978 Discovery of an Obelisk at Abusir, in: *RdE*, 28, 111–118
1980 Excavations at Abusir. Season 1978/1979 – Preliminary Report, in: *ZÄS* 107, 158–168
1982 Excavations at Abusir. Season 1980/1981 – Preliminary Report, in: *ZÄS* 109, 157–166
1982 Eine zweite Unvollendete Pyramide in Abusir, in: *ZÄS*, 109, 75–77
1987-a Remarques sur le temple solaire *ḥtp-rʿ* et la date de mastaba de Ti, in: *BIFAO* 87, 293–297
1987-b A Slaughterhouse from the Old Kingdom, in: *MDAIK* 42, 181–189
1992 *Abusir II. Baugraffiti der Ptahschepses Mastaba*, Praha, Universitas Carolina Pragensis
1995 *Abusir III. The Pyramid Complex of Khentkaus*, Praha, Universitas Carolina – Academia
1997 Further Thoughts on the Khentkaus Problem, in: *DE* 38, 109–117
1999 Khentkaus I, Khentkaus II and the title *mwt nśwt bity nśwt bity* (or: *nśwt bity, mwt nśwt bity*), in: *GM* 173, 215–218
2000 Who was Shepseskara, and when did he reign?, in: Bárta, M., Krejčí, J. (eds.), *Abusir and Saqqara in the Year 2000*, (*ArOr* Supplementa 9) Praha, Academy of Sciences of the Czech Republic, Oriental Institute, 582–585
2001-a *The Pyramids. The Mystery, Culture, and Science of Egypt's Great Monuments*, New York, Grove Press
2001-b Archaeological remarks on the 4th and 5th dynasty chronology, in: *ArOr* 69, 363–418
2002-a *Abusir. The Realm of Osiris*, Cairo – New York, AUC Press
2002-b Once more to Niuserre' dyad (München, AS 6974), in: Eldamaty, M., Trad, M. (eds.), *Egyptian Museum in Cairo. Centenary Volume*, vol. 2, Cairo, Supreme Council of Antiquities, 1195–1204

2003 *The Mysterious Sun Temples*, in: *KMT* 14/1, 44–57
2006-a An Unusual Burial Practice, in: Czerny, E. *et al.* (eds.), *Timeless Studies in honour of Mannfred Bietak* I, (OLA 149) Leuven – Paris – Dudley, MA, Uitgeverij Peeters en departement oosterese studies 2006, 399–401
2006-b The columns of Abusir, in: Bárta, M. (ed.), *The Old Kingdom Art and Archaeology. Proceedings of the conference held in Prague, May 31 – June 4, 2004*, Prague, Czech Institute of Egyptology, Faculty of Arts, Charles University in Prague, 333–355
2010 Eine neue Königsfamilie erringt die Macht, in: Brinkmann, V. (ed.), *Sahure. Tod und Leben eines grossen Pharao*, Frankfurt, Liebieghaus
2011-a The 'Khentkaus Problem' Reconsidered, in: Bárta, M., Coppens, F., Krejčí, J. (eds.), *Abusir and Saqqara in the Year 2010*, Prague, Czech Institute of Egyptology, Faculty of Arts, Charles University in Prague, 778–784
2011-b One seal and two sealings of the Fifth Dynasty and their historical implications, in: Bechtold, E., Gyulas, A., Hasznos, A. (eds.), *From Illahun to Djeme.* Papers Presented in Honour of Ulrich Luft, (BAR International Series 2311) Oxford, Archaeopress, 33–336
2012 Pyramid towns of Abusir, in: *SAK* 41, 2012, 407–410
2013 Missing royal boat graves at Abusir? in: Witkowski, M. G., Iwaszczuk, J., Makowski, M. (eds.), *Studies in honour of Karol Myśliwiec.* (*ÉT* 26) Varsovie, Wydawnictwo NERITON, 714–718
--- *Pr-twt* – The cult Place of Raneferef's Statues, in: Landgráfová, R., Mynářová, J. (eds.), *Rich in Years, Great in Victories: Studies in Honour of Tony Spalinger*, Prague – in press

VERNER, M., BRŮNA, V.
2011 Why was the Fifth Dynasty cemetery founded at Abusir?, in: Strudwick, N., Strudwick, H. (eds.), *Old Kingdom, New Perspectives. Egyptian Art and Archaeology 2750–2150 BC*, Oxford, Oxbow Books, 286–294

VERNER, M., CALLENDER, V. G.
2006 *Abusir VI. Djedkare's Family Cemetery*, Prague, Czech Institute of Egyptology, Faculty of Arts, Charles University in Preague – Set out

VERNER, M. *et al.*
2006 *Abusir IX. the Pyramid Complex of Raneferef. The Archaeology*, Prague, Czech Institute of Archaeology, Faculty of Arts, Charles University

VLČKOVÁ, P.
2005 Abusir South at the End of the Old Kingdom, in: K. Piquette, S. Love (eds.), *Current Research in Egyptology 2003. Proceedings of the fourth annual symposium. University College, London 2003*, Oxford, Oxbow Books
2006 *Abusir XV. Stone Vessels from the Mortuary Complex of Raneferef at Abusir*, Prague, Czech Institute of Egyptology, Faculty of Arts, Charles University in Prague

VOSS, S.
2004 *Untersuchungen zu den Sonnenheiligtümern der 5. Dynastie. Bedeutung und Funktion*

eines singulären Tempeltyps im Alten Reich, PhD Dissertation Universität Hamburg, Hamburg
2010 Das Sonnenheiligtum des Niuserre, in: V. Brinkmann (ed.), *Sahure. Tod und Leben eines Pharao*, Frankfurt am Main, 225–233

VYMAZALOVÁ, H.
2006 An extraordinary revenue account from the papyrus archive of Raneferef, in Daoud, K., Abd el-Fatah, S. (eds.), *The World of Ancient Egypt. Essays in Honor of Ahmed Abd El-Qader el-Sawi*, (Suppl. ASAE 35) Cairo, Supreme Council of Antiquities, 261–265.
2008 Some remarks on the *w3g*-festival in the papyrus archive of Raneferef, in: Vymazalová, H., Bárta, M., *Chronology and Archaeology in Ancient Egypt (The Third Millenium B.C.)*, Prague, Czech Institute of Egyptology, Faculty of Arts, Charles University in Prague, 137–143
2010 Abusir aus der Vogelperspektive, in: *Sokar* 20, 60–65
2015 The builders' inscriptions and masons' marks from the mastaba of Werkaure (AC 26), in: Krejčí, J., Arias, K., Vymazalová, H., Pokorná, A., Beneš, J., *Abusir XXIV. The Mastaba of Werkaure 1 (Old Kingdom strata)*, Prague, Czech Institute of Egyptology, Faculty of Arts, Charles University in Prague

VYMAZALOVÁ, H., COPPENS, F.
2008 König Menkauhor. Ein kaum bekannter Herrscher der 5. Dynastie, in: *Sokar* 17, 32–39
2011 Statues and Rituals for Khentkaus II. A Reconsideration of Some Papyrus Fragments from the Queen's Funerary Complex, in: Bárta, M., Coppens, F., Krejčí, J. (eds.). *Abusir and Saqqara in the Year 2010*, Prague, Charles University in Prague, Faculty of Arts, 785–799
2013-a The Clothing Ritual in the Royal Temples of Abusir – Image versus Reality, in: Kurth, D., Waitkus, W. (eds.). *IX. Ägyptologische Tempeltagung. Kultabbildungen und Kultrealität*, (Königtum, Staat und Gesellschaft früher Hochkulturen 3/4), Wiesbaden, Harrassowitz, 21–31
2013-b Two hieratic inscriptions from the tomb of Werkaure (Lepsius Pyramid no. XXIII in Abusir, in: Bárta, M., Küllmer, H. (eds.), *Diachromic Trends in Ancient Egyptian History*, Charles University in Prague, Faculty of Arts, 123–135

VYMAZALOVÁ, H., DULÍKOVÁ, V.
2012 Sheretnebty, a King's Daughter from Abusir South, in: *ArOr* 80, 339–356
2014 New evidence on princess Sheretnebty from Abusir South, in: *ArOr* 82, 1–9

VYSE, H.
1840–1842 *Operations carried out on the Pyramids of Gizeh in 1837: with an Account of a voyage into Upper Egypt. Vols. I–III*, London, James Fraser, Regent street

WALLE, B. van de
1978 *La chapelle funéraire de Neferirtenef*, Bruxelles, Musées Royaux d'Art et d'Histoire

WEEKS, K.
1971 Preliminary Report on the First Two Seasons at Hierakonpolis. Part II. The Early Dynastic Palace, in: *JARCE* 9, 29–33

WEIGALL, A.
1907 *A Report on the Antiquities of Lower Nubia (the First Cataract to the Sudan frontier)*, Oxford, University Press

WELC, F.
2014 Climate change in Egypt in the 3rd Millenium BC in regional and global context, in: Kuraszkiewicz, K. O., Popielska-Grzybowska, J. (eds.), *Old Kingdom Art and Archaeology. 6th Conference, Warsaw, 2-6 July 2014. Abstracts,* Warsaw, Institute of Archaeology, University of Warsaw *et al.*, 108

WELLS, R. A.
1990 The 5th dynasty sun temples at Abu Ghurab, in: Schoske, S. (ed.), Akten des Vierten Ägyptologenkongresses München 1987, (BSAK 4) Hamburg, Helmut Buske Verlag, 95–104
1992 The Mythology of Nut and the Birth of Ra, in: *SAK* 19, 305–322

WENIG, S.
1963 Ein Siegelzylinder mit dem Namen Pepi's I, in: *ZÄS* 88, 6–69

WENKE, R. J. *et al.*
1988 Kom el-Hisn: Excavation of an Old Kingdom Settlement in the Egyptian Delta, in: *JARCE* 25, 5–35

WESTENDORF, W.
1987 Zur Etymologie des Namens Osiris: *wꜣst-irt* „die das Auge trägt", in: Osing, J., Dreyer, G. (eds.), *Form und Mass. Beiträge zut Literatur, Sprache und Kunst des Alten Ägypten., Festschrift für Gerhard Fecht zum 65. Geburgstag am 6. Februar 1987*, (ÄAT 12) Wiesbaden. Otto Harrassowitz, 456–461

WILD, H.
1953–1966 *Le tombeau de Ti. II–III*, (MIFAO 45), Le Caire, IFAO

WILDUNG, D.
1969-a *Die Rolle ägyptischer Könige in Bewusstsein ihrer Nachwelt.* I, (MÄS 17) Berlin, Verlag Bruno Hessling
1969-b Zur Frühgeschichte des Amun-tempels in Karnak, in: *MDAIK* 25, 212–219
1984 Ni-user-re. Sonnenkönig – Sonnengott, (SAS 1) München, Staatliche Sammlung Ägyptischer Kunst

WILKINSON, T. A. H.
2000 *Royal annals of Ancient Egypt. The Palermo Stone and its associated fragments*, London and New York, Kegan Paul International

WINTER, E.
1957 Zur Deutung der Sonnenheiligtümer der 5. Dynastie, in: *WZKM* 54, 222–233

WIT, C. de
1951 *Le rôle et le sens du lion dans l'Égypte ancienne*, Luxor, Gaber Aly Hussein

WOHLGEMUTH, G.
1957 *Das Sokarfest*, unpublished PhD Dissertation Georg-August-Universität Göttingen, Göttingen

WOLINSKI, A.
1986 Ancient Egyptian Ceremonial Masks, in: *DE* 6, 47–53

WRIGHT, M.
1988 Contacts Between Egypt and Syria-Palestine During the Old Kingdom, in: *BA* 51, 143–161

YOUSSEF, M.
2011 New scenes of hunting a hippopotamus from the burial chambre of Unas, in: Bárta, M., Coppens, F., Krejčí, J. (eds.), *Abusir and Saqqara in the Year 2010*, Prague, Czech Institute of Egyptology, Faculty of Arts, Charles University in Prague, 820–822
2014 Szenen einer Nilpferdjagd in der Grabkammer des Unas, in: *Sokar* 29, 14–19

YOYOTTE, J.
1957 À propos de la parenté feminine du roi Téti (VIe dynastie), *BIFAO* 57, 91–98

ZIEGLER, Ch.
1997-a Sur quelques vases inscrits de l'Ancien Empire, in: Berger, C., Mathieu, B. (eds.), *Études sur l'Ancien Empire et la nécropole de Saqqâra dédiées à Jean-Philippe Lauer*, (OrMon 9) Montpellier III, 461–469
1997-b *Les statues égyptiennes de l'Ancien Empire*, Paris, Réunion des musées nationaux
1999 La vase au nom du roi Ounas, in: Ziegler, Ch. *et al.* (eds.), *L'art égyptien au temps des pyramides. Paris, Galeries nationales du Grand Palais 6 avril – 12 juillet 1999*, Paris, Réunion des musées nationaux

ABBREVIATIONS

ACE	Australian Center for Egyptology, Sydney
AH	Aegyptiaca Helvetica, Genève
Anthropologie	Anthropologie. International Journal of the Science of Man, Brno
ArOr	Archiv orientální, Praha
ASAE	Annales du Service des antiquités de l´Égypte, Le Caire
ÄA	Ägyptologische Abhandlungen, Wiesbaden
ÄAT	Ägypten und Altes Testament, Wiesbaden
ÄF	Ägyptologische Forschungen, Glückstadt – Hamburg – New York
Ä&L	Ägypten und Levante, Wien
AH	Aegyptiaca Helvetica, Basel – Genf
AV	Archäologische Veröffentlichungen, Deutsches archäologisches Institut, Abt. Kairo, Mainz am Rhein
ÄW	Ägyptisches Wörterbuch I, Wiesbaden (see Bibliography)
BA	Biblical Archaeologist, Vancouver
BACE	Bulletin of the Australian Center for Egyptology, Sydney
BÄBA	Beiträge zur ägyptischen Bauforaschung und Altertumskunde, Kairo – Wiesbaden
BASOR	Bulletin of the American Schools of Oriental Research, New Haven
Berytus	Archaeological Studies, American University of Beirut
BdÉ	Bibliothèque d´études, Institut français d´archéologie orientale, Le Caire
BIÉ	Bulletin de l'Institut d'Égypte, Le Caire
BIFAO	Bulletin de l´ Institut français d'archéologie orientale, Le Caire
BMHBA	Bulletin du Musée Hongrois desBeaux–Arts, Budapest
BOREAS	Uppsala Studies in Ancient Mediterranean and Near Eastern Civilizations, Uppsala
BWZKM	Beihefte zur Wiener Zeitschrift für die Kunde des Morgenlandes, Wien
BSAK	Beihefte der Studien zur altägyptischen Kultur, Hamburg
BSFÉ	Bulletin de la Societé française d'égyptologie, Paris
CAJ	Cambridge Archaeological Journal, Cambridge
CASAE	Cahiers. Supplément aux *ASAE*, Le Caire
CdE	Chronique d´Égypte, Bruxelles
CRIPEL	Cahiers de recherches de l'Institut de papyrologie et égyptologie, Lille
CUP FA CEI	Charles University in Prague, Faculty of Arts, Czech Institute of Egyptology
DE	Discussion in Egyptology, Oxford
EA	Egyptian Archaeology, London
EAO	Égypte Afrique & Orient, Paris
ENiM	Égypte Nilotique et Méditerranéenne, Montpellier

ESA	Egyptian Studies Association, London
ÉT	Études et Travaux, Varsovie
GM	Göttinger Miszellen, Göttingen
GOF	Göttinger Orientforschungen, Göttingen
HÄB	Hildesheimer ägyptologische Beiträge, Hildesheim
HPBM	Hieratic Papyri in the British Museum, London
JAS	Journal of Archaeological Science
JARCE	Journal of the American Research Center in Egypt, Boston
JNES	Journal of Near Eastern Studies, Chicago
JSSEA	The Journal of the Society for the Study of Egyptian Antiquities, Toronto
KÄT	Kleine Ägyptische Texte
Kêmi	Revue de philologie et d'archéologie égyptiennes et coptes, Paris
KMT	A Modern Journal of Ancient Egypt, New York
Kush	Journal of Sudan Antiquities Service, Khartoum
LÄ	Lexikon der Ägyptologie, Wiesbaden
LingAeg	Lingua Aegyptia, Göttingen
MAIBL	Mémoires de l'Academie des inscriptions et belles-lettres, Paris
MÄS	Münchener ägyptologische Studien, Berlin
MÄU	Münchener Ägyptologische Untersuchungen
MDAIK	Mitteilungen des Deutschen archäologischen Instituts, Abteilung Kairo, Kairo – Berlin – Wiesbaden – Mainz
MIFAO	Mémoires publiés par les membres de l'Institut français d'archéologie orientale du Caire, Le Caire
MonAeg	Monumenta Aegyptiaca, Fondation Reine Élisabeth, Bruxelles
MRE	Monographies Reine Élisabeth
NAWG	Nachrichten der Akademie der Wissenschaften in Göttingen. I. Philologisch-historische Klasse, Göttingen
OBO	Orbis biblicus et orientalis, Fribourg – Göttingen
OEAE	The Oxford Encyclopedia of Ancient Egypt, Oxford
OLA	Orientalia lovanienssia analecta, Leuven
Or	Orientalia, Roma
OrMon	Orientalia Monspeliensia, Montpellier
PdÄ	Probleme der Ägyptologie, Leiden – New York – Köln
PM	see *Bibliography* s. v. Porter, B. *etc.*
PSBA	Proceedings of the Society of Biblical Archaeology, London
RdÉ	Revue d´égyptologie, Paris
SAK	Studien zur altägyptischen Kultur, Hamburg
SAOC	Studies in Ancient Oriental Civilisations, Chicago
SDAIK	Sonderdruck des Deutschen archäologischen Instituts, Abteilung Kairo, Mainz am Rhein
SEAP	Studi di Egittologia e di Antichità Puniche, Pisa
Sudan & Nubia	Bulletin of the Sudan Archaeological Research SocietySudan and Nubia Bulletin, London

TAVO	Tübinger Atlas des Vorderen Orients, Wiesbaden
Urk I	see Sethe, K. ...
VA	Varia Aegyptiaca, San Antonio
Wb	see Erman, A., Grapow, H., ... *Wörterbuch der aegyptischen Sprache. I–V*, Leipzig, J. C. Hinrichs'sche Buchhandlung 1929–1931
VDI	Vestnik drevnei istorii, Moskva
WZKM	Wiener Zeitschrift für die Kunde des Morgenlandes, Wien
ZÄS	Zeitschrift für ägyptische Sprache und Altertumskunde, Leipzig

INDEX

Personal names

Toponyms and Buildings

Titles and Epithets (see also Egyptian Terms)

Varia

EGYPTIAN TERMS